DATE DUE

DEC 1 6 1992	
OCT 1 0 1993	
OCT 3 0 1993	
NOV 1 3 1993	
NOV 2 9 1993	
DEC 1 3 1993	
MAR 2 4 1995	

THE HUAROCHIRÍ MANUSCRIPT

y mayna runa cunapas tucoy ni llan as ban uan
suyac carcan chay mi ña chay man chaya mup hinca
aneda say cos cam amun nis pa as bañan yanca
y chaspa runa sauapas pacha pipas chay llacsatam
bo man yaicunu na poner llapi y na yelac carcan
paicuña Vra manta amue cunam as lla aychata
paicu nap puy ñon pa siminsaua churapue carca
cay tasta puedo cospam ñatac tucoy ynantin
runa cuna pam papi ñay cospa as ñis catoquitos
ña callaxircan cay cunam cacan. chancos tunoc
chay montam ña chan cup hinca pacbapos ñañospa
tamyamue cay chan cup mitampis ysquicaya nisca
chay yan cap suasinpi Sue saclechos of y mael chas
pis canan chaspacha nis conedic ⁿᵐᵃⁿᵗᵃˡˡ yaco sapa vr ma
rayata chos cunaitas cornan pay cona conchay y
naita sicuspaicanan Suatica alli pucoy mi canca
nispa nir cancu/mana tamya nampaesi chaquisca
cae chaysi aneda muebsy mi carca nespa nir caoca cu

Capitulo 12 y manam cay
potui a cacos chuzincunatucoy
y un ca cunaita atista ña
calla xir can

y nam aui cay chun campi capilt pi zi mar conedic
cay paria cacos chuzin cunapas tis can ~~conedic~~ simiota
y~~nas~~ naspa villar conedic tacmi axi ymanam tu
coy ynantin llaita cuna yuncasapa carcan chay
cunaita Canan mis cay. Sucpaico. chanedaruna
Suariruma. Vtco chuco tutay quire. sasin mani pa
chachuy ro nis conedic cunaita zimoson ymanam
paicuna puzic carcanes chay chay cunaeta cay
cuna nis con edic cunas ñaupa pacha tucoy hin

THE HUAROCHIRÍ MANUSCRIPT

A Testament of Ancient and Colonial Andean Religion

Translation from the Quechua by
FRANK SALOMON and GEORGE L. URIOSTE

Annotations and Introductory Essay by
FRANK SALOMON

Transcription by
GEORGE L. URIOSTE

University of Texas Press, Austin

This book has been supported by a grant from the National Endowment for the Humanities, an independent federal agency.

First edition, 1991

Requests for permission to reproduce material from this work should be sent to Permissions, University of Texas Press, Box 7819, Austin, TX 78713-7819.

♾ The paper used in this publication meets the minimum requirements of American National Standard for Information Sciences—Permanence of Paper for Printed Library Materials, ANSI Z39.48−1984.

ISBN 0-292-73052-7
ISBN 0-292-73053-5 pbk.

Library of Congress Cataloging-in-Publication Data

Manuscrito quechua de Huarochirí. English & Quechua.
    The Huarochirí manuscript : a testament of ancient and Colonial Andean religion / translation from the Quechua by Frank Salomon and George L. Urioste ; annotations and introductory essay by Frank Salomon ; transcription by George L. Urioste. — 1st ed.
        p.   cm.
    English and Quechua version of the Manuscrito quechua de Huarochirí, Colonial era narratives, compiled by Francisco de Avila ca. 1598, now held at the Biblioteca Nacional de Madrid as part of Mss. group 3,169.
    Includes bibliographical references and index.
    ISBN 0-292-73052-7. — ISBN 0-292-73053-5 (pbk.)
    1. Quechua Indians—Religion and mythology.
2. Incas—Religions and mythology.   3. Indians of South America—Peru—Huarochirí (Province)—Religion and mythology. 4. Quechua language—Texts.   I. Salomon, Frank.   II. Urioste, Jorge.   III. Avila, Francisco de, ca. 1573−1647.   IV. Title.
F3429.3.R3M3513   1991
299'.883—dc20   90-25510
                                                      CIP

To our kids
Abraham, Malka, Susanna

tucoy hinantin huc yuric canchic
we are all of one birth

Contents

THE HUAROCHIRÍ MANUSCRIPT

Acknowledgments

Among the colleagues who taught and helped us from the start were John V. Murra and Donald F. Solá. We thank them deeply. For discussions, communications, clarifications along the way, and the occasional productive disagreement, we owe our thanks to many scholars, including but not limited to Rodolfo Cerrón-Palomino, the late Antonio Cusihuamán, Roswith Hartmann, Bruce Mannheim, María Rostworowski de Diez Canseco, John H. Rowe, Karen Spalding, John J. Swetnam, Jan Szemiński, Gerald Taylor, Lorena Toledo, Terence Turner, Freda Y. Wolf, and R. Tom Zuidema. Blenda Femenias' able editing is greatly appreciated. To the late John Treacy, who compiled the map, we owe a special and lasting debt of gratitude. And we thank our students for many good questions.

We also thank our institutional benefactors: the National Endowment for the Humanities, the Instituto de Estudios Peruanos in Lima, and the University of Wisconsin's Institute for Research in the Humanities as well as its Cartographic Laboratory. The William F. Vilas Trust Estate afforded valuable support through its Associateship program. All shortcomings, of course, are our own.

THE HUAROCHIRÍ MANUSCRIPT

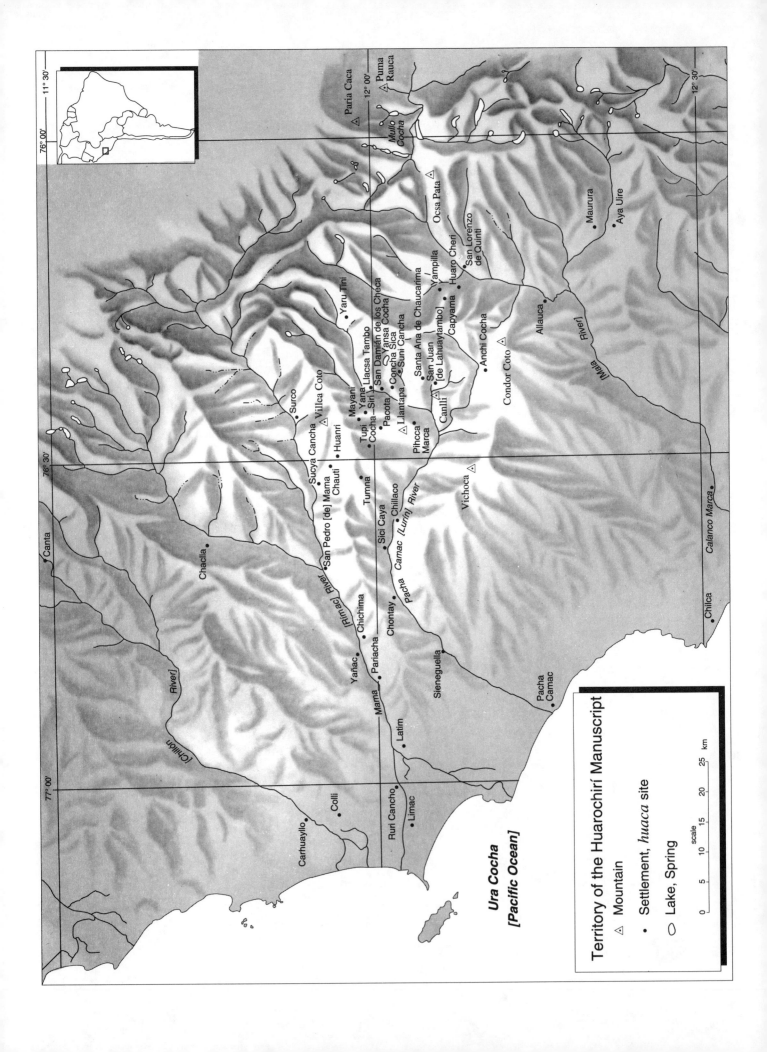

76° 00'

Paria Caca △

12° 00'

△ Puma Rauca

Mullo Cocha

Maururra •

• Aya Uire

Ocsa Pata △

• San Lorenzo de Quinti

Yaru Tini •

Vampilla • Huaro Cheri •

Santa Ana de Chaucarima

San Damián de los Checa • Yansa Cocha

Llacsa Tambo Concha Sica

Mayani • Yana Suni Cancha

Tupi Cocha Siri Pacota• San Juan [de Lahuayrambo]

Surco • Villca Coto △

Sucya Cancha Huanri • △ Llantapa Pihcca Canlli △ Capyama Anchi Cocha

Marca

Allauca •

Condor Coto △

Mala River

San Pedro [de] Mama Chauti • Tumna •

Chichima Sici Caya• Chillaco

Chaclla • Chontay• Pacha *Camac [Lurin] River* Vichoca △

• Canta

Yañac• Pariacha•

[Rimac] River

[Chillon River]

Carhuayllo •

• Colli

Ruri Cancho• • Limac

Latim• Sieneguella • Pacha Camac •

Calanco Marca

Chica •

Ura Cocha [Pacific Ocean]

Territory of the Huarochirí Manuscript

△ Mountain

• Settlement, *huaca* site

○ Lake, Spring

scale

0 5 10 15 20 25 km

77° 00'

76° 30'

12° 30'

Introductory Essay: The Huarochirí Manuscript
Frank Salomon

The manuscript as testament

The Huarochirí manuscript alone of all colonial sources records a prehispanic religious tradition of the Andes in an Andean language. It tells us of a remote age when cannibal deities preyed on otherwise immortal humans, of the mountain deity Paria Caca who emerged to expel the fire deities of antiquity, of the human groups that traced their victories from Paria Caca's five simultaneous avatars, of Paria Caca's brotherhood with the fivefold female power Chaupi Ñamca, and of the society ritually organized in their names around a grand complementarity of male and female superhumans. It unfolds the splendor of ceremonies that prehispanic priests devoted to a landscape alive with the diverse sacred beings called *huaca*s. It recalls memories of Inca rule and of how unknown invaders, the Spanish, brought new gods to displace the children of Paria Caca and of Chaupi Ñamca. Nothing else in all the sources from which we seek the Andean "vision of the vanquished" (Wachtel 1971) rivals it for immediacy, strangeness, and beauty.

But the voices we hear in its pages do not relay to us a verbatim record of what was said and believed before the Spanish invasion. It is true that when Father Francisco de Avila reworked part of the same or similar testimony to make his 1608 *Treatise on the False Gods . . .* (hereafter referred to as *Tratado*), he judged that the narrative "does not refer to the present but to history" (Arguedas and Duviols 1966: 198). Yet the way people recalled their ancient tradition and the occasion of their recalling it were themselves facets of a colonial situation the tellers had already endured throughout their whole lives. The telling could not but be influenced by the seventy preceding years of colonial turbulence, during which one potent innovation

was the art of writing itself. Andean peoples used no writing before the Spanish "Vira Cochas" arrived. So the process of capturing their culture as text in the alphabet of the padres and bureaucrats was inextricably bound up with forced conversion and persecution, even when the actual authors were themselves Andean and the actual narrators at least partly faithful to the old *huaca*s.

The manuscript is a complex composite testimony of these changes as well as a compendium of ancient memories. The research it contains was apparently sponsored by a clerical persecutor, Father Francisco de Avila, who seems to have used it as secret intelligence for his assault on American deities from 1608 onward. The text does contain opportune denunciations of "idols" (as the Spanish called the sacred beings of the Andes) and of those who steadfastly fed and served them in secret long after official conversion. Yet at least one of the actual makers of the text seems to have thought of the task as one of historical remembrance. The untitled preface to the manuscript looks to a future in which the ancient deities would be remembered with pride, promising a monument of Andean greatness to match Spanish chronicles:

> If the ancestors of the people called Indians had known writing in earlier times, then the lives they lived would not have faded from view until now.

> As the mighty past of the Spanish Vira Cochas is visible until now, so, too, would theirs be.

> But since things are as they are, and since nothing has been written until now,

> I set forth here the lives of the ancestors of the Huaro Cheri people, who all descend from one forefather;

What faith they held, how they live until now, those things and more.

Village by village it will all be written down: how they lived from their dawning age onward.

One gets a strong impression that the creator of these lines was engaged in reconceptualizing the Andean mythic tradition rather than destroying its memory.

The exact process of composition is unknown, but this passage differs from the wholeheartedly anti-Andean viewpoint that Avila expressed in other writings. It may contain the words of a native writer or editor to whom Avila gave some leeway in compiling the text. A measure of unselfconscious candor would have increased its intelligence value. Whether or not he was present at its composition, Avila did read and annotate at least part of it; his devastating subsequent attacks on the deities mentioned suggest that the stratagem of leaving the witnesses some freedom of expression succeeded. But the text's partly intra-Andean genesis also had a paradoxical long-term effect: because it was composed in relative independence from Spanish preconceptions about native religion, it has in the end provided a uniquely authentic monument of the very beliefs Avila meant to destroy.

Whoever composed the untitled preface thought of the manuscript as a totalizing book about inherited tradition, custom, and lifeways that would give Andean memory, like Spanish literate memory, immortal visibility. The usual genre term by which the text identifies the separately remembered and narrated traditions could hardly be more oral; it is *simi*, which the greatest Quechua lexicographer of the age glossed as "mouth, language, commandment, law, mouthful, news, the word and its answer" (Gonçález Holguín [1608] 1952: 326). Clearly the testimonies are products of a culture in which orality encompassed the weightiest functions of language. But the book is not conceived simply as a body of speech on paper. It partakes of the assumption that written language, and specifically book language, should subsume and subordinate orality. The conception of a totalizing book that underlies the manuscript seems to be influenced at one or more levels by the Hebrew or Old Testament Bible and to some extent by the New Testament. Of course, few Indians studied the Vulgate. But the Huarochirí area had been missionized with special intensity by Jesuits in 1570–1571, with the conscious intent of popularizing Christian lore in Quechua. In the late sixteenth century, both officially promulgated catechetical summaries and popular-ized summaries of Bible stories called *historias sagradas* were widely read by or read to laypeople. Literate Indians c. 1600 usually knew traditions from both Hebrew antiquity and the New Testament through publications of the Third Council of Lima. Those who had access to churchmen's libraries or discussions could learn much more.

Although the manifest content of the manuscript only rarely syncretizes biblical material with Andean, the text as a whole has an "astonishingly Biblical" overall architecture (Turner 1988: 249). Like the Bible, the manuscript begins with myths that contrast the human condition with an imagined alternative, a time when the relations between humans and deity were radically different (chaps. 1, 2). A flood myth (chap. 3) signals the end of this era. Like the Bible, the manuscript pictures antiquity as the story of hero-ancestors who share a common descent and a covenantlike relation to an ethnic deity (including an episode resembling Abraham's averted sacrifice of Isaac; chap. 8, secs. 99–103). Its collective subject is a set of groups, each of which considered itself the progeny of a focalized ancestor. As with the biblical tribes, these groups relate to each other, at least in ideology, approximately as a phratry. As in the biblical redactions, their disparate traditions of origin and separate cults have been welded *ex post facto* onto the unifying argument of kinship and imperfectly articulated with apical priestly cults. Their story, like that of the biblical tribes, is intensely concerned with control over specific resources in a sacralized landscape; many of its myths encode political struggles with surrounding peoples and even internecine struggles as mythic combats with superhuman intervention. Also like the Bible, the manuscript is greatly concerned with the relation between the local *sacra* and the leaders and priests of immense invading empires—first the Inca, later the Spanish. The manuscript shares the biblical tendency to accrete genre within genre. Texts about priesthood, sacrifice, ritual law, and prophecy jostle with vernacular myth, claims concerning land and water, and mythicized remembrance of historic events. Bits of oracular response, religious formulas, and perhaps songs have become embedded in the text, too. And finally, as in the Bible, particularly the Deuteronomic books and later prophets, one clearly senses the pressure of contemporary political defeat on religious testimony.

We do not know all the reasons for the resemblances. One possibility is that Father Avila imposed European opinions on the text itself or indirectly on others who processed it (for example, by preparing a questionnaire or by overseeing the editing). Much European opinion of the time held that pagan myths, Andean ones included, reflected ancient traces of "true" (that is, biblical) religious and historical knowledge, which Satan's deceptions had distorted in intervening centuries. The tendency to force non-Christian testimony into patterns congruent with "universal history" and a unified Bible-based chronology is conspicuous in many Peruvian chronicles, both indigenous and Spanish, and Avila's *Tratado* shows that he partook of it (Arguedas and Duviols 1966: 206–208). The person who arranged or edited the myths expressed frustration at the difficulty of arranging episodes into one scheme of chronology (e.g., chap. 14, sec. 189; chap. 15, sec. 199), a step required for correlation with Bible-centered history. This literal-minded historicist reading of myth, which seems misleading to modern readers, was then thought to be a correct way of restoring American data to their "true" place in a unified world scheme of salvation history.

But above and beyond this exogenous process, the myths themselves seem Bible-like in their style of mythifying. Like the biblical writers, and unlike some myth-tellers from more "tribal" Amazonian societies, the Huarochirí narrators tend to intertwine mythic (miraculous) processes with social causation, rather than locating them in a primordial age before the world began to be as it is. Perhaps the likeness is multilayered or overdetermined: it may result in part from intra-Andean facts distinguishable from the European influences that also affected it. Such forms of synthesis may arise endogenously in societies of a certain scale, setting, and organizational form. Terence Turner (1988) offers a complex argument that a generically rather than locally biblical type of mythology occurs in societies whose status is intermediate between autonomy and complete subsumption in larger states; certainly this was the condition of Huarochirí-area societies for many centuries before the European invasion.

There is a third possibility for explaining the biblical parallel. After seven decades of exposure to European culture, Andean people had consciously or unconsciously gone far in reconceptualizing their mythology as a systematic response to imposed belief. By 1600 this reconceptualization seems to have coalesced into a distinctive ideology. Andean literati of the first generation born after conquest—Felipe Guaman Poma de Ayala and Joan de Santa Cruz Pachacuti Yamqui Salcamaygua— were not simple nativists; they partook of a Renaissance consensus in arguing that Andean people had already passed through ages of antiquity strictly parallel to those of pre-Christian biblical antiquity. But they dissented from the Spanish in their evaluation of the Andean achievement as a part of it. Where writers like Avila, Cabello Valboa, or Antonio de Calancha saw in Andean myth only a deteriorated and diabolically confused memory of original connections with biblical humanity, and therefore a culture worthy of being forgotten, some native intellectuals believed their history and its memory to be not only parallel with that of the Spanish, but equal in value. The theories of these bicultural "native chroniclers" shored up waning hopes of Andean privilege under Christian rule and appear characteristic of Andean natives descended from noble families but deprived of colonial power. Although we do not know the identity of the person(s) who selected the oral material for inclusion and/or wrote the ethnographic and editorial material in the manuscript, the final redaction of the text does seem to partake of this mentality.

And what of those who actually told the myths to the book creators? What revisions of religious thought had occurred among less bicultural natives during these decades? It is important to remember that by the date when the manuscript was written the cults of the *huaca*s had coexisted with Christianity for a whole lifetime. If *huaca* priests had retained the loyalty of people officially bound to Christianity, it was in all likelihood because they had succeeded, under the adverse conditions of clandestinity and church hegemony, in presenting *huaca* religion as comparable in cogency with the church's teachings. It is possible that by 1600 local thinkers and perhaps priests had been engaged (consciously or not) in remobilizing and reconceptualizing the inheritance of *huaca* religion so as to construe it as *a religion*, a "faith" (as the preface to the manuscript says, using the Spanish word) whose overall claims and dimensions could bear comparison with those of the imposed church. It is not beyond possibility that the welding of the Andean deities into a unified kindred partook of post-1532 efforts. Individual *huaca* myths seem to accord the *huaca* cults many of the same attributes as Christian religion: for example, a covenantal concept of obligation, an image of superhuman action as law giving, a notion of history as the continuing interaction of deity and society, and a tendency to express "moral economy" norms in terms of prophetic action. As has been suggested, it is likely that any or all of these may be overdetermined facts, arising from preexisting, and now remobilized, prototypes in aboriginal culture as well as from European models. Perhaps there would have been an Andean story like the rescue of Isaac even if Spaniards had never invaded. Nonetheless, it would be unrealistic not to consider apologetic processes arising in *huaca* priests' efforts to match Catholic priests in the breadth of their claims while at the same time maintaining distinctness from Catholicism. The importance of such interactive processes in sustaining *huaca* religion is attested by Father Avila's remark that the *huaca* cults thrived most not in the areas where they had remained unmolested, but in the villages where Catholic priests had been most zealous (Arguedas and Duviols 1966: 205).

Despite the importance of all these factors, in the end nothing could be more wrong than to think of the manuscript as merely an Andean counter-Bible. For one thing, obviously, the mythic material overall is radically foreign to Europe; few books in the world give the Western reader such a powerful sense of encountering a cultural unknown. Another and more fundamental reason is that the structuring of myth—the formal architecture of event and process that gives each story internal regularity and resolution—owes everything to Andean patterns and resembles biblical ones little if at all. The dominant model in the stories is that of passage from mere difference (for example, the juxtaposition of antagonistic deities strange to each other) to complementary difference (for example, a revised juxtaposition in which the deities become male and female spouses or siblings embodying opposite ecological principles). This pattern occurs at the greatest and smallest levels of the mythology, in domains from the cults of apical deities Paria Caca and Chaupi Ñamca to the household relationship between in-laws. To imagine this pattern consistently applied to the battles of biblical Adonai is difficult. Comparison with non-Andean South American material (a task scarcely begun) may offer another path to the isolation of underlying prehispanic content. R. Tom Zuidema (1977: 44–47) argues that some Huarochirí myths share specific structures with a myth of the Brazilian Bororo, presumably because the two mythologies share roots much older than Spanish domination.

Andean religion and "Inca religion"

Much of what is published (especially in English) about prehispanic and colonial Andean religion treats the terms "Inca" and "Andean" as near synonyms. Vira Cocha, popularized as the invisible "creator god of the Incas" (Demarest 1981; Pease 1986; Rowe 1960; Szemiński 1985b; Urbano 1981) fascinated colonial Spaniards who thought they detected in him a possible intuition via "natural religion" (MacCormack 1985) of Christendom's supreme deity. This idea still absorbs modern scholars captivated by the sophistication of Tawantinsuyu, the Inca Empire. The Incas partly persuaded non-Inca Andean people, too. As we learn from chapters 18, 19, 20, 22, and 23, the Incas tried to reorganize local cults into a hierarchy capped by Inca numina, and partly succeeded. Indeed, their persuasions lasted longer than their sovereignty. By the mid-colonial era, when Inca rule had receded into the golden mists of ideological nostalgia, many Peruvian Indians themselves came to recall the deified Sun and his incarnation the Inca god-king as compelling symbols of native identity and native glory (Flores Galindo 1987).

But in order to interpret the Huarochirí manuscript one must appreciate that the equation between Inca religion and Andean religion is an ideological sleight. The invisible Vira Cocha relates to Andean religious life somewhat as the Prime Mover Unmoved does to Mediterranean saint cults. At the summit of priestly and imperial society, prayers like Pachacuti Yamqui's stirring Inca invocations ([1613] 1968: 287–288, 292, 294) to the unseen source of order and beauty may have voiced metaphysical questions that we define as preeminently religious. But the religious life of most of the people who made up Tawantinsuyu's innumerable subject "nations" had little to do with abstract or universalizing expressions. Worship usually focused on sacred beings peculiar to particular kin groups, villages, mountains, canals, and so forth. In fact, religious particularism, expressed in terms of place and descent, lies at the heart of much Andean myth. No doubt discourse of this sort can embody philosophical concerns, no less readily than overtly metaphysical expressions do. But the content is only available by a route that leads through the study of what particular places or mummies (etc.) meant.

This village-based, particularistic version of Andean religious thinking saturates the Huarochirí text. The world that the Huarochirí myth-tellers imagined was structured in terms of grass-roots geography and of genealogy—*their* pastures and valley lands, *their* mythicized family tree. The unity of the text, such as it is, is achieved by an attempt (perhaps on the part of the priests called *yancas*) to locate the historically diverse *huaca*s and their cults in Paria Caca's and Chaupi Ñamca's regional hierarchy and genealogy. Other traditions—the lordly priesthood of the Incas, the onset of Catholicism—are seen through the filter of such local and regional concerns. For long stretches the viewpoint belongs to one group, one collective ego: a group called the Checa, devotees of the ceremonial center Llacsa Tambo, resident (at least nominally) in and around the Spanish resettlement village of San Damián, who considered themselves children of Paria Caca while retaining origin myths apparently separate from his cult (chap. 24). Some of the ritual complexes and myths attached to local features—especially to springs, lakes, and canals—have survived with great vitality into modern times and have been studied by ethnographers (Gelles 1984; Ortiz Rescaniere 1977). For example, the modern descendants of the Concha, who live in an outlying hamlet of San Damián de Checa, still maintain today both the myth and the ritual attached to the lake that feeds their irrigation canals (see chap. 31).

The durability of these myths reflects the Huarochirí people's tenacious attachment to the local resources on which they depend. But it is possible after all to exaggerate the local quality of the myths. Paria Caca was not uniquely the deity of the peoples who speak here; he and his sanctuary were renowned throughout a wide swath of the central and southern Andes. It is likely that, when worshipers from Llacsa Tambo went on pilgrimage to him, they met worshipers from many other places and that their own practice had something in common with that of different kinds of "people called Indians." The same applies to the great coastal shrine Pacha Camac and to Cuni Raya, sometimes called Vira Cocha. Even when the names, episodes, and personalities seem peculiar to Huarochirí, the tellers' general religious concepts (e.g., classes of shrines, types of action attributed to deities and heroes, duties of humans to *huaca*s) are shared among a wider spectrum of Andean societies, including, for example, groups in the Arequipa and Cuzco areas. In these limited senses, while it is mistaken to take the Huarochirí myths as expressions of a pan-Andean religion, one may take them as representative of broader Andean cultural premises and tendencies that are manifest even in apical Inca cults. The sharing of underlying concepts makes possible ethnographic comparison with societies beyond the bounds of Huarochirí Province, both as seen in past times (for example, via the "extirpation of idolatry" trials that postdate the manuscript; see Duviols 1986) and as witnessed by modern ethnographers (see, for example, Valderrama and Escalante 1988, who have studied in distant Arequipa a complex resembling the water cults in chapter 31).

General outline of the Huarochirí manuscript

The Huarochirí manuscript appears not to be the product of polished editing, but neither is it a jumble. With the possible exception of the two unnumbered chapters here called supplements I and II, it seems to be a fair copy edited and in the process of further editing for coherence as a unified narrative. The unification is, however, in many respects incomplete and imperfect. The editor's original intent seems to have been to treat ancient matters earlier in the text and recent ones later, but sometimes when turning to a new source (e.g., at the beginnings of chaps. 13, 24, and 31) he is forced to return to a different origin story. Recollections of past ritual practice and interpolated bits of current ethnographic observation further complicate the text by introducing into many narrations, with specious smoothness, references to times other than the time of the main narrated story. Moreover, the manuscript is full of second thoughts (cross-outs and interlineations, marginalia), tangents, overlaps, cross-references, marginal queries (probably by Father Avila), and cryptic allusions. For all these reasons, to appreciate the coherence of a theme one often must pull together partial accounts from disparate chapters. For this purpose the index supplied by the translators may be useful.

Early times and peoples

The preface (untitled in the original) promises to tell the achievements and beliefs of "the people called Indians" from their "dawning age" up to the present, village by village.

The first chapter sketches the world as it was before the present human race appeared. People lived forever (after a five-day temporary death), at the price of sacrificing half their children to the fire-monster Huallallo Caruincho. At that time, too, the subtropical abundance of the lower valleys extended far up into the heights. This whole rich and cruel world order would be destroyed with the advent of Huarochirí's great deity Paria Caca.

Huallallo's dominion is grouped with other stories of remote antiquity: chapter 2 tells how the Trickster-demiurge Cuni Raya, who "almost matches" the figure of Vira Cocha, passed through the landscape and through the lives of the female deities he seduced. In a Christian-influenced interlude (chap. 15), Cuni Raya, as Vira Cocha, is credited, almost parenthetically, with originally creating nature in an empty universe. Chapter 3, telling the myth of the deluge, and chapter 4, telling of the

Sun's disappearance, end the section dedicated to remote antiquity.

The Paria Caca cycle and the myths of group identity

The mythic cycle that forms the unifying core of the text tells the apparition of Paria Caca (chap. 1, sec. 6; chap. 5, secs. 72–73), the fivefold deity who symbolized inclusive ethnic unity among the tellers' various residential and kinship groups. Like many great Andean deities, he is a mountain, a majestic double-peaked snowcap visible on the eastward horizon from the heights of Huarochirí. Many groups venerated him. We hear most about the Checa who gathered at Llacsa Tambo, but chapter 13 concentrates on a relatively distant cluster of villages, the Mama region in the lower Rímac valley. Chapter 30 is a myth of the Allauca, and chapter 31 copiously recounts the viewpoint of the Checa's neighbors, the Concha.

Paria Caca first appeared as five eggs that became five falcons that became five men, the founders of the human groups who appear as the main collective protagonists. These groups are sometimes spoken of in ways suggesting clanlike or sib-like qualities and together, within Paria Caca's cultic organization, are seen as a phratrylike collectivity of groups who "all descend from one forefather" (pref., sec. 2). But before calling them clans one should be careful to note that the text uses no term clearly translatable as 'clan' and that, although the manuscript uses the unilineal idiom for certain limited purposes, other principles of descent, marriage, and residence appear to play at least as important a role in defining groups.

Paria Caca was a stormy being of the heights. He made himself known to humans by favoring a poor man with power to defeat the rich (chap. 5), or, in another tradition, by saving a Huallallo worshiper from the obligation to sacrifice his child (chap. 8). He first appeared on a mountain in what was formerly the domain of the lowland aborigines called Yunca, which was dominated by the (possibly Huanca) deity Huallallo (chap. 5, secs. 38, 55). Once his bond with some of these people was formed, Paria Caca ascended to Huallallo's seat on the high cordillera. There he attacked and expelled the ancient cannibal deity in a world-shaking combat between storm water and volcanic fire (chap. 6, sec. 74; chap. 8; chap. 9, sec. 110; chap. 16, secs. 203–209; chap. 17, secs. 214–219). He carved out in this struggle the titanic landscape of snowcaps

and lakes that is his seat and his likeness. It became the sanctuary on the icy heights to which his pilgrims brought their llamas (chap. 9, secs. 119, 127, 138–139; chap. 24, secs. 309–310; chap. 28, sec. 364). Huallallo, exiled, was left to the care of a rival ethnic group called the "dog-eating Huanca" (chap. 9, secs. 110–111; chap. 16, sec. 209). The victorious Paria Caca in his multiple incarnations swept down from the windy heights through the various fertile valleys of the Pacific slope (chap. 8). As he went, he subjected the Yunca to his own people, expelling many of them, reorganizing their lands, creating a cultic order in which both victors and vanquished would participate, and winning the Yunca wealth (e.g., chaps. 9, 25).

What human movements does the Paria Caca mythology allegorize? In a series of highly original studies María Rostworowski de Diez Canseco (1978: 31–147) has interpreted the narratives as reflections of a large and gradual prehistoric movement in which pre-Incaic highlanders of the ethnic group called Yauyo worked their way downward and southwestward, from their early home on the high tundras at the Cañete River headwaters, through various warm irrigated valleys (including the Mala, Lurín, and Rímac valleys, which form the heartland of the mythology), toward the Pacific shore and its rich deltas. Using independent and ostensibly nonmythical bureaucratic records she has been able to document Yauyo populations all over the territory of the manuscript and has mapped their major territorial divisions as understood in the mid- to late sixteenth century (Rostworowski 1988: 56–57). One of these Yauyo populations (that of Chaclla) attested a folk history closely resembling stories in the manuscript (Rostworowski 1988: 54–57).

Linguistic indices are less clear but also suggest some association between Paria Caca's mythology and a Yauyo expansion. Traces of Aymara-like lexicon and phonology in the Huarochirí manuscript indicate that the informants knew or were influenced by the same ethnic language whose modern forms persist as residual "islands" in old Yauyo territory (Gentile Lafaille 1976: 14).

In Inca and early colonial times those natives who classed themselves as Yauyo regarded the focal area of the manuscript, especially what later became the parish of Santa María Jesús de Huarochirí, as the very core of Yauyo political space. The early colonial Yauyo do not seem to have had a king or center of political command, but Yauyo witnesses said that in conducting intranative diplomacy their ancestors had recognized the Ninavilca lords of Huarochirí village as paramount authorities for several generations. In 1558, Cristóval Malcachagua of Huarochirí gave unambiguous testimony that the Ninavilcas meant to rally "all the Yauyos" in defending Yauyo coca claims in the middle Chillón valley against Huamantangas and Spaniards (Rostworowski 1988: 94). "Yauyo" is the only term the manuscript uses in categorical contrast to the ethnic terms for foreign neighbors (the various Yunca groups, the Huaman Tanca, and the Huanca; supp. II, sec. 485). All this evidence seems a *prima facie* reason for treating the manuscript as substantially an artifact of Yauyo culture.

On first inspection Paria Caca does appear to be simply the chief deity of these Yauyo populations, ennobled by Inca patronage but still very much an ethnic symbol. Felipe Guaman Poma de Ayala thought of him so ([1615] 1980: 1:241). And when Maca Uisa himself, one of Paria Caca's "sons," asked the Inca to dance a priestly dance essential to the Paria Caca cult, he told the Inca to dance it "the way our children from the Yauyo do" (chap. 23, sec. 297).

Nonetheless, one must account for some striking slippages in the association between Paria Caca and Yauyo identity. The predominant tellers of the Huarochirí myths, the Checa, thought the ancient founders of their leading kindreds were not Yauyo but Yunca. They scorned the Yauyo kindreds in Checa as half-wild nomads and barely tolerated their presence in the pilgrimage to Paria Caca (chap. 24, secs. 305–309) until Paria Caca himself taught them to respect the newcomers. In neighboring Concha, "Yauyo country" was a byword for a remote and fruitless backwater (chap. 31, secs. 391, 408). Perhaps such scorn reflects the fact that by 1586 the self-identified Yauyo had shrunk to a tiny ethnic minority comprising only about 5% of the 7,000 tributary households in the huge province to which they gave their name (Dávila Brizeño [1586] 1965: 155).

How should one read these seeming contradictions? One clue is that although the Checa narrator applied the word "Yauyo" to immigrants whose exact place of origin in Yauyos Province was still remembered, and who were considered nomads only recently attached to Checa, he also credited higher-ranking kindreds in Checa with invader origins. The difference was that the higher-ranking kindreds had arrived of old and had inserted themselves in the agricultural social structure created by the ancient Yunca founders in the days of Huallallo Caruincho. A Concha teller gave much the same account of his group in chapter 31.

Apparently the Checa and Concha used the term "Yauyo" to refer to recent herder migrants, while regarding their own ancestry, which might well have been historically no less Yauyo, as quasi-autochthonous because it had been grafted by ritual and marriage onto the regimen that included "village-owning," valley-oriented agricultural *huaca*s. Perhaps they saw no paradox in scorning people of the very sort that Paria Caca favors in his myths—impoverished wanderers from the heights—because they regarded their own ancestors as more powerful "children of Paria Caca." The proof of their superiority was that these ancestors had won dominion over Yuncas and the right to aggregate Yunca *huaca*s into their religion while their compatriots still wandered the heights in monoethnic pastoral groups.

As a working hypothesis, one may imagine that Paria Caca's cult as recorded here—that is, in a state of bipolar coordination with Chaupi Ñamca's cult and with Yunca components generally—is the precipitate of, and a commentary on, a long and apparently still continuing series of migrations or incursions from the southerly highland fringes of the manuscript's territory. As in other world areas where pastoralists penetrated the edges and eventually the centers of agricultural societies (e.g., China under Mongol rule), the assimilated descendants of early invaders came to inhabit preexisting social and ritual forms and champion them against later invaders.

The crux of Checa and Concha religion appears to be a systematic priestly synthesis that exalts early invader groups by placing their origin myths, eloquent of a mostly pastoral highland way of life and a kinship-based social ideology (that is, the myths of Paria Caca's "children"), into a dyadic relation with ancient macroregional cults rooted in coastal agropastoral society (those of Chaupi Ñamca, Pacha Camac, etc.). It does so by interpreting the deity who was taken to represent the sum total of invader origins, namely, Paria Caca, as Chaupi Ñamca's brother and wife-giver to Pacha Camac. In this way Paria Caca was imbued like Pacha Camac and Chaupi Ñamca with a power and an identity transcending immediate ethnicity and locality.

The spokesmen of the system, perhaps Yanca priests belonging to Caca Sica *ayllu* or their followers, defined Checa cultural identity as descent from the creators of one local instance of such highland-valley fusion. To be an ancestrally entitled worshiper of *both* Chaupi Ñamca and Paria Caca, and of their local affiliated cults, was the crux of belonging. The term "Yauyo" in Checa and Concha accordingly connoted neither 'foreigner' nor 'compatriot' but 'parvenu': immigrants not yet fully inserted into the regional-scale cultic order and its local apparatus.

This view helps us understand a problem of belief, namely, why outsiders like Guaman Poma saw the Paria Caca religion as a Yauyo cult par excellence, while the people of Checa used the word "Yauyo" to label a group barely admitted to Paria Caca's pilgrimage. To characterize the historical connection between Yauyos and Yuncas objectively is much harder. Whether the early highland aggressors whom the tellers identified with the mummified heroes called "children of Paria Caca" were in fact exclusively Yauyo, or whether such groups can be dated and archaeologically linked to Yauyo populations at all, remains unknown. For these reasons in the introduction we shall simply call the mythic protagonists "invaders" except where there is a specific warrant for using the term "Yauyo."

Rostworowski identifies the Yunca or coastal groups at whose expense the children of Paria Caca purportedly expanded as the two large politically unified collectivities (*señorios*) closest to modern Lima. One, occupying the lower Rímac and Lurín valleys, was called Ychma locally and Pacha Camac in Inca usage; it housed the mighty shrine of Pacha Camac and enjoyed great religious prestige even after Yauyo and Inca depredations reduced its political reach. The other was the domain of the lord called Colli Capac, whose people the Huarochirí narrators called the Colli and whose seat the Spanish called Collique. It was based in the lower Chillón valley (Rostworowski 1988: 60–62). The Checa thought the Colli had founded the highland settlements their own ancestors conquered (chap. 24, sec. 341; chap. 25).

Chapters 11, 12, 17, 24, 25, and 26 contain what appear to be "charter" myths of specific invader groups that identified their founders as "children" of Paria Caca. If they have a unified thrust, it is that Paria Caca's fivefold self, ambiguously developed as a union of brother-*huacas* (chap. 8, secs. 99, 105; chap. 16, sec. 202) or of Paria Caca's human "children" (chap. 9, sec. 113), through many victories created a regional order embracing both victors and vanquished. By a combination of warfare and courtship at superhuman and human levels, Paria Caca turned his relation with the rich aborigines of the valleys, the Yunca, from one of strangeness and enmity into one of coordinated worship, in-law kinship, and interdependency (though certainly not without an abiding tension between groups). The Paria Caca heroes' victories over the Yunca, whom the myths picture as wealthy but im-

moral, fill several chapters. Chapter 31, the charter of the lineages of the Concha (neighbors to the Checa; see especially secs. 388–403) pictures the invaders as trying to assimilate to the aboriginal norms of their in-laws. Paria Caca's complementarity of form and function with the local female (possibly Yunca) *huaca* Chaupi Ñamca suggests that, overall, the mythology of Huarochirí construes a folk memory of conquest as an ideology of affinal interdependence.

How does this happen? The memorable fifth chapter is the *locus classicus* of a theme repeated many times in the manuscript: the poor ragamuffin who, because he is privy to a superhuman secret, carries within him a future power that his rich and splendid contemporaries cannot see. In chapter 5 it is the Baked Potato Gleaner, a byword for poverty, who makes Paria Caca's potential power real by a twofold action: he overturns the extant order's hierarchy (curing but simultaneously humbling a Yunca lord) and at the same time he becomes literally wedded to it (marrying the humbled lord's daughter). Empowered, he introduces Paria Caca's cult to a society transformed by combat and courtship.

The manuscript's ideological image of the invader-aborigine interaction as a passage from hostility to symbiosis may be seen as a one-sided rendering of, rather than a mere fiction about, the politics of coexistence between highlanders and coastal peoples. The dynamic it mythically expresses seems to have been driven by the highlanders' need for cultivable land, which they sought by downward invasion and establishment of "vertical" outliers in the mid-altitudes. Lowlanders in turn sought to capture more water sources by extending their canals upward and exerting political power over the lakes and streams of the heights (Torero 1974: 73–79). The 1558 lawsuit involving the Yauyo of Chaclla and the Yunca of Collique (among others) shows how in prehispanic times the downward penetration of Yauyo "vertical archipelagos" (Murra [1972] 1975a) led to conflicts so mutually costly that Yunca and highlanders reached a *modus vivendi* including cooperation on shared irrigation work and ritual reciprocity between leaders. The Huarochirí text glorifies some roughly comparable *modus vivendi* in mythic idiom. But the lawsuit also shows what the Huarochirí manuscript deemphasizes: that such arrangements were delicate and unstable, liable to lapse into prolonged violence when politically stressed. Even under Inca pacification, the Yauyo of Chaclla, their non-Yauyo Canta rivals, and the Colli Yunca incessantly tried to cheat and coerce each other. When the Spanish invasion unleashed the resulting tensions, the fights and suits that followed did much to drive several polities into helpless poverty (Rostworowski 1988: 83–291).

Chaupi Ñamca and the mythology of gender

Several passages detail the priesthoods, games, sacrifices, *huaca*-impersonating dances, and oracles that ritually organized the interlaced aboriginal-invader societies that the tellers saw as the product of their ancestors' victories. Although the relationships among groups and deities are complex and often far from obvious, one unifying motif is clear: the union between invaders and aborigines is ideologized in terms of a fraternal tie between the highest male deity of the invaders and the highest female deity of the aborigines. The link is taken to warrant marriage alliance between their respective human progenies. In this scheme female deities play an enormous role.

Chaupi Ñamca, supreme among female *huaca*s, was a land and river deity of the lower Rímac whose great temple at Mama symbolized her ancient standing as Pacha Camac's wife (Dávila Brizeño [1586] 1965: 163). Her name means 'center Ñamca' and she may, like her spouse, have had a following across various valleys; in 1562, Mama was the place chosen for a summit meeting of native lords from the whole region (Murra 1980: xviii). The devotees of Paria Caca have conceptualized her component cults as a fivefold sisterhood, so as to match the form of Paria Caca (chap. 10, sec. 147; chap. 13, secs. 175–183). In the synthesis that dominates the manuscript, Paria Caca and Chaupi Ñamca are made into siblings (chap. 13, sec. 172; Avila [1645] 1918: 64). These claims apparently mirror increased Yauyo penetration of domains in which her marriage to Pacha Camac had once formed a dominant cultic axis. Indeed, in one version the newcomers' claim goes beyond fraternal symmetry to imply superiority: Chaupi Ñamca's five selves are styled "daughters" of Paria Caca, whereas Paria Caca's selves are never said to be her children (chap. 8, sec. 101). The "children of Paria Caca" have also expressed their conviction of political superiority by making their father-*huaca* wife-giver in relation to Pacha Camac.

In establishing a sibling relation between male mountain-*huaca* and female valley-*huaca*, the Paria Caca priests may have followed an earlier prototype. A partially obscured tradition (chap. 8, secs. 106–107; chap. 10, sec. 143) allows us to glimpse Mana Ñamca or Mama Ñamca, a synonym or component of Chaupi Ñamca who was once a lowland female counterpart to the male highland *huaca* Huallallo Caruincho (and who, like him, was a fiery power expelled by Paria Caca).

Within the dominant synthesis, ritual order richly embodied the idea of male-female symmetry at the apex of *huaca* genealogy. Paria Caca's priesthoods and his great festival the Auquisna (chap. 9, secs. 117–140) find their explicit counterpart in Chaupi Ñamca's festival the Chaycasna (chap. 9, sec. 122; chap. 10, secs. 149–151), so that the ritual and mythical order opens out in a grand sexual complementarity on the pattern Invader : Paria Caca : Male :: Aborigine : Chaupi Ñamca : Female. The fraternal treatment of the male-female apical deities tends to express ideals of harmony or equilibrium between groups at a totalizing, whole-society level.

However, as one passes from the supreme powers to their *huaca* offspring and their human descendants, the dominant gender metaphor changes from brother-sister fraternity to marriage. A repetitive motif concerns invaders, sons of Paria Caca, who marry Yunca-descended women, implicitly daughters of Chaupi Ñamca (chap. 5; chap. 24, secs. 305–314). Thus the sons of Paria Caca become indebted wife-takers to Yunca groups and their *huaca*s.

This conviction of indebtedness parallels what was remembered as invader expropriation of the female and Yunca element in nature, namely, irrigable land. On the ecological plane the relationship between invader and aborigine is likened to the union of wild water from the heights (Yauyo-like, male) with the soil of the valleys (Yunca-like, female). The motif is discussed in the section below on the concept *pacha*. Because this union—irrigation—was in fact the greatest agrarian wealth of the western Andes, many myths can also be read as combined cosmic and political charters for local groups' rights to specific lands and canals. The abundance of landmark detail in the text, which we have tried in notes to key to modern cartography, reflects the function of myth as a memory bank of information about the tellers' generally invasion-based claims on resources.

The conjugal metaphor for invader-aboriginal relations carries a different symbolic load from the fraternal one. Whereas the siblinghood of the apical *huaca*s is a static, merely classificatory relation, marriage myths are myths of social dynamics. They express not only an ideal of productive and reproductive union, but also an image of the many tensions involved in creating such union. For example, Collquiri, a water-*huaca* from the heights (chap. 31, secs. 408–436), must fight with his prospective in-laws and submit to their humiliating discipline before his desire for their beautiful land-*huaca* daughter can turn from destructive lust (flooding) into productive marriage (irrigation). Indeed, all the myths related to marriage treat it as an image of social stress and change latent in union. In chapter 5 Paria Caca's protégé Huatya Curi, a foreign male who wants to marry a human incarnation of Chaupi Ñamca, garners the hatred of his brother-in-law and establishes himself in his new household only by fighting within it (secs. 49–70). On the political level, accepting a foreign spouse is always a gesture of submission that one accepts at peril to one's autonomy, and for this reason Paria Caca's son Maca Uisa turns down the Inca's honorific gift (chap. 23, sec. 300). Even the Inca himself forfeited his empire by accepting a bride from a secret power that turned out to be the Spanish (chap. 14). While one may read these texts as comments on marriage as such, they also give voice in kinship idiom to fundamental doubts about the political stability of conquest-based agropastoral society.

In sum, the gender mythology of Huarochirí, though centered on an idealized complementarity, is at the same time emphatically a conflict model of society. It envisions every complementarity, whether marital, ritual, ecological, or political, as shadowed by submerged conflicts that had to be repressed in order to institute it. The inseparability of complementarity from conflict is implied to be a motor force in the mutability (what we would call the historicity) of west Andean society.

The Incas as seen from Huarochirí

Chapters 18, 19, 20, 22, and 23 vividly illustrate how the Inca conquest looked to provincial natives and give important clues as to how Incas manipulated the local pantheon. The Inca himself was said to have acknowledged and even subsidized local *huaca*s—both those that local people thought of as ancient, like Paria Caca (chap. 18, sec. 220), and those newly emerging, like Llocllay Huancupa (chap. 20, sec. 243). This policy may be related to the fact that the Yauyos were reputed to be generally pro-Inca. Early evidence from the northernmost part of the Huarochirí orbit indicates that the Incas favored Yauyo efforts to penetrate the Yunca and gradually enlarged Yauyo enclaves based at Chaclla to the detriment of the anti-Inca Yunca of Collique and rival non-Yauyo highland groups (Rostworowski 1988: 148, 161, 178). Guaman Poma ([1615] 1980:

1:240–241) drew a picture of the Inca adoring an image of Pacha Camac in the shrine of Paria Caca.

The tellers of the manuscript likewise expressed their alliance with Incas in the idiom of ritual, adoring and helping finance some of the pan-Andean deities that Inca propaganda promoted. Among these figured Pacha Camac, the originally Yunca 'World Maker and World Shaker' whose shrine-citadel lay at the western edge of the mythic landscape (chap. 22, secs. 276–284; Patterson 1984[?]). So thoroughly had the Incas intercalated regional and local cults with royal religion that the Huarochirí people thought the Incas themselves owed some of their victories to help from Paria Caca's offspring (chap. 19, secs. 228–229; chap. 23).

The tendency to equate Cuni Raya, a coastal Trickster-demiurge embodying the transformation of landforms by water, with the invisible Vira Cocha fostered by Inca cult may also have been heightened by interaction with Incas. But for the Huarochirí narrators, this *huaca* stood over and against Inca power as against all other human power. Chapter 14 recounts an enigmatic Cuni Raya Vira Cocha myth alluding to the fall of the Incas. It apparently refers to the fact that the Incas had divided their domains in dynastic struggle just before the Spaniards arrived. The narrator tells how Cuni Raya Vira Cocha inveigled the Inca king with a beautiful bride and then, inducing him to "draw a line across the world" (chap. 14, sec. 196), made him fatally retreat from his sacred center at Cuzco. During the resultant outbreak of chaos, "people scrambled for political power, each saying to the others, 'Me first!' 'Me first!'" (chap. 14, sec. 197). While they wrangled uselessly in civil warfare the Spanish appeared at Cajamarca.

The Spanish invasion as seen from Huarochirí

Even more remarkable are the unique chapters that give us a glimpse of how natives, after a lifetime of colonial afflictions, looked back on the first confused moments of their contact with the Spanish. The first inkling of the epochal events arrives in the same way that the prophecy of Paria Caca's imminent victory had arrived long before (chap. 5), as a secret that Paria Caca vouchsafed to a despised ragamuffin from the heights. This time the prophet of the coming crisis is the "Mountain Man" Llacuas Quita Pariasca (chap. 18). The same chapter tells how one *huaca* priest survived the Spaniards' attempt to burn him alive and became a leader in preserving and sheltering the *huaca*s amid Spanish attacks. Many references (e.g., chap. 9, secs. 122, 125, 136, 137; chap. 10, secs. 144, 148, 149; chap. 13, sec. 175; supp. I, secs. 449, 469, 473) show that those who rescued the *huaca*s succeeded in hiding their cults (sometimes, a censorious voice warns, by camouflaging them in Catholic ritual) far into the colonial era. At least one of the contributors to the text regularly obliges Father Avila by warning that many Indians' conversion was a façade (chap. 9, secs. 133–134). Other chapters (20–21) reveal that even Father Avila's most obsequious ally, Don Cristóbal Choque Casa, in a certain sense still believed in—was even dominated by—the "evil ancient demons." These chapters tell with astonishing vividness and intimacy of Cristóbal's visionary combat with the *huaca* Llocllay Huancupa and of how Llocllay returned to battle Cristóbal once more in a dream. Cristóbal's dilemma—the need to validate his Christianity by conquering *huaca*s, combined with inability to conquer them convincingly without invoking the same mythic paradigm he proposed to replace—adds up to a uniquely moving image of the Andean convert's stressful and compromised position.

Specialized chapters

The manuscript contains some specialized chapters perhaps given in reply to questions about arts that Tridentine Catholicism forbade as diabolically inspired, heretical, or superstitious. Chapter 29, short but important, sketches Andean astronomy or astrology. It suggests that the tellers thought of certain "black" constellations and certain star clusters as the celestial prototypes of the earthly beings they resembled. Visionaries saw these constellations "descend" to earth and shower their protégés with specific vital force.

Chapters 27 and 28 treat the cult of the dead. Chapter 27, a droll explanation of why the dead no longer come back, echoes a motif from chapter 1, namely, that humans must accept irremediable death as the alternative to Malthusian disaster. Chapter 28 recounts funeral and commemorative custom, somewhat evasively in the crucial matter of how ancestors' bodies were treated. Perhaps the tellers hoped to avoid setting persecutors on the trail of their beloved and (ideally) everlasting ancestral mummies.

Two "supplements" (which may be rough drafts) lay down the ritual duties of couples who give birth to magical children—twins or babies with small birth defects. These unusually difficult sections af-

ford an idea of the complex ritual obligations embedded in in-law ties, with emphasis on the ritual exchange of immense amounts of coca and other wealth.

The Huarochirí region's people and their historic situation

These myths relate intimately to the real-life landscape and the historic conjuncture that generated them. For one thing, the deities themselves are land features and local climatic forces. For another, these priesthoods and celebrations themselves organized productive work, so that the religious regimen encodes practical as well as ideological information. Finally, every facet of religious organization—spatial, calendric, and hierarchical—reflects the pressure of colonial circumstance.

The westernmost range of the high Andes runs northwest-southeast, parallel to Peru's Pacific shore. The long slope from its icy crests down to the desert beaches forms a rugged watershed cut at intervals by many small rivers carrying meltoff from the heights to the ocean. The scene of the Huarochirí mythology is a segment of that slope. Most of the places mentioned in it are close to three valleys: the Rímac River valley, on whose lower banks the Spanish built Lima, but whose upper tributaries, the Chaclla and Mama rivers of the manuscript, were still mostly native territory in 1600; to the south, the Pachacámac River valley, today called the Lurín, on whose headwaters stood the colonial parish of San Damián; and still farther south the "River of Huarochirí," today the Mala, which gave its name to a colonial parish as well as to the province and to the manuscript. The people who made the manuscript also seem to have included in their range of meaningful geography one valley to the north of Lima, the Chillón, and two more to the south of Huarochirí, the valleys of the Omas and Lunaguaná (today Cañete) rivers.

Karen Spalding's *Huarochirí: An Andean Society under Inca and Spanish Rule* (1984) meticulously reconstructs the colonial society from which the manuscript emerged. Spalding (1984: 3) cautions us that colonial Huarochirí Province was no huddle of hamlets but a region the size of Massachusetts. Yet neither is the landscape whose meanings the myths unfold too huge for Andean travelers to have absorbed from personal experience. Taylor's map (1987b: 39) suggests that the widest span of the mythic landscape reaches about 85 air km (53 miles) from ocean to mountaintops, and about 120 air km (74.5 miles) from north to south. A separate reckoning by John Treacy (1984) estimates the main mythic scene as about 108 air km (67 miles) east to west and about 56 air km (35 miles) north to south. Of course, estimates using air kilometers hardly simulate the twisting paths pedestrians and llamas actually followed across the contorted mountain landscape. Even on foot, highland travel involves innumerable hairpin turns up and down the faces of river chasms. Yet, even allowing for steep climbs and zigzags, these distances would hardly have discouraged Andean travelers. Averaging Cotler's (1958: 113–114) and Spalding's (1984: 31) statements on walking speed over the Huarochirí terrain yields 2.4 km/hour as a usual rate for the area. If so, a person walking eight hours a day might have descended from the high shrines of Paria Caca to the Pacific shores in about four days. These are only order-of-magnitude estimates, but they suffice to remind us that the world pictured in the Huarochirí text is mostly a world of experienced rather than imagined landmarks and spatial relations.

Ecologically, the mythic scene spans a remarkable spectrum of "vertical tiers" (Murra [1972] 1975a; ONERN 1976). The uppermost points mentioned are icy peaks more than 5,000 m above sea level. The myths clearly take as their backdrops the "pluvial tundra" of Mullucocha (5,000–4,300 m above sea level) where Paria Caca annihilated a mountain. The heroes' downward course traversed the "very humid páramo" (4,500–3,900 m above sea level; páramo means high grassland) and the "humid woodland" (3,800–2,300 m above sea level). This is all high, seasonally rainy and snowy country with numerous lakes and probably included the llama-herding lands of the ancient peoples up to 4,600 m above sea level. The tellers of many myths identified with the splendor of the heights and with their product, camelid wealth on the hoof. One of the major ceremonies was a llama race to the sacred heights, with the first llama acclaimed and given a sacred name (chap. 9, secs. 120–122, 128).

Agriculture belonged to lower tiers, four cultivation zones compressed within narrow valleys: the "montane steppe" at San Damián, and three increasingly lower, dryer grades of "desert scrub" (matorral desértico). The colonial resettlement villages in which the manuscript seems to have been made stood in the upper part of this range, 3,000 to 3,500 m above sea level. The agricultural terraces immediately around them were and are irrigated, but on the "montane steppe" above them dry farming of high-altitude crops is also possible. There

people cultivated tubers, especially potatoes, and the Andean grain Chenopodium quinua, which one tradition mentions as a mythic plant that gave birth to people (chap. 24, sec. 302).

Irrigable crops grew best in places where canal water fertilized pockets of sun-warmed soil amid the rocky river canyons. Irrigated valley lands symbolized abundance, and access to warm land with water was seen as the limiting factor in winning wealth. The tellers of the myths especially associated maize with irrigation, for example, in the poignant figure of the young woman who stood in her field and cried as she watched her insufficiently watered maize shrivel up (chap. 6, sec. 83). Chapters 30 and 31 are vivid mythic renderings of the struggle between water-poor and water-rich groups.

Still further down-valley but short of the coastal plain, at altitudes around 1,000 m above sea level, irrigation takes place in small patches of warm riverbank land commonly called chaupi yunca ('mid-yunca' or 'semi-yunca'). These sheltered, garden-like river margins were coca lands in antiquity, prized for the abundance of the sacred leaf that Huarochirí natives ceremonially lavished on each other and on their superhuman patrons. The manuscript is especially detailed in explaining how coca cultivators fit into Paria Caca's cult regimen (e.g., chap. 8, sec. 109).

Where the fertile valleys meet the sea, a rich fishing industry combined with delta and riverbank agriculture to yield wealth that awed even the Incas. Prehispanic seaboard dwellers developed pisciculture intensively (Espinoza Soriano 1974). Although the myth-tellers thought of themselves as highland-descended, they, too, imagined salt water as part of the humanized and culturalized landscape. Fish-farming was so familiar that the teller of chapter 2 thought of ocean fish as runaways turned wild:

> At that time there wasn't a single fish in the ocean.
> Only Urpay Huachac used to breed them, at her home, in a small pond.
> It was these fish, all of them, that Cuni Raya angrily scattered into the ocean . . . (chap. 2, sec. 26)

At the time when the manuscript was written, much of the prehispanic technology and some of the prehispanic land tenures that once governed use of these productive zones still functioned. But the Yunca, Yauyo, and Inca claims were no longer the only factors. The social organization of land—administrative divisions of territory, settlement patterns, and legal land rights—had become an even more complex, multilayered scheme composed of native and colonial elements. Diego Dávila Brizeño's ([1586] 1965) report on the "Province of the Yauyos" and Karen Spalding's monograph (1984) afford valuable clues to the *de facto* world the myth-tellers inhabited.

The most modern part of the settlement pattern was the one Dávila Brizeño himself had helped impose—concentration into forced resettlement villages (*reducciones*). Each village gathered together numerous non-nucleated settlements scattered up and down the valleys to make a conveniently taxable package on the model of a planned Spanish village (see the section on the concept *llacta* below). These parishes inorganically merged fragments of various units earlier defined by the Inca and aboriginal political orders. One of the things that makes the Huarochirí manuscript hard to read is the fact that the tellers are constantly comparing the (to them) arbitrary *reducción* map against the (to them) intelligible distribution of groups and deities that their hidden ritual still commemorated. Thus their toponymy refers to both ancient and current mental maps.

Nonetheless, the Spanish administrative plan did still make use of some older orderings. A map made by Dávila Brizeño representing Spanish administrative geography of the 1580s in the context of native toponymy (Rostworowski 1988: unpaginated insert) shows the Yauyos Province bisected by what appears to be an Inca-style moiety dividing line: the southern half is called Anan ('upper') Yauyos and the northern Lorin ('lower') Yauyos. This feature the Spanish apparently retained or at least recognized. Colonial Huarochirí Province corresponded to Lorin Yauyos. And when it came to sharing out the right to rule and tax Andean people, the Spanish availed themselves of other Inca demographic and organizational schemes. The Spanish *repartimiento*, or political apportionment of tributary subjects, proceeded by assigning each established native lord to a Spanish *encomendero*. The patterning of colonial lordship thus legalized appears to echo Inca rules albeit with innovations and distortions. So the initial colonial system, while it functionally overturned many native norms, retained the gross anatomy of Inca political divisions, and some of these are detectable in the Huarochirí manuscript even after subsequent reorganizations.

The Incas saw each half of the region as composed of large blocs of people (perhaps ethnically defined), each comprised of several *huaranga*s or 'thousands' of tributary households. In what Dávila Brizeño called Lorin Yauyos, which housed the ancestors of the manuscript's authors, the Incas

recognized and the Spanish retained three major groupings:

LURIN YAUYOS

Huarochirí People

Huaranga Colcaruna
Huaranga Quinti
Huaranga Langasica
Huaranga Chaucarima
Huaranga Checa

Chaclla People

Huaranga Chaclla
Huaranga Carampoma
Huaranga Casta

Mamaq People

Huaranga Matucana
Huaranga Huanchor

ANAN YAUYOS
(Spalding 1984: 54)

Each "thousand" had a native lord, or *curaca*. An overlord or *curaca principal* was recognized by the Spanish, on purported Inca or aboriginal precedent, as lord of all *huaranga*s in the bloc. This was the highest office held by a non-Inca lord. By such a title the Ninavilca lords of Huarochirí (chap. 7, sec. 93; chap. 19, sec. 230) were recognized as having precedence among, if not power over, the *huaranga*s most prominent in the manuscript.

Finally, within these Inca-influenced political arrangements there remained elements of a still older order. The pre-Inca (or non-Inca) settlements that the informants called their *llacta*s, some already reduced to ghost towns, were still the points of mythic reference. At the microscopic level, a system of partly localized extended kinship reckoning, discussed below, remained the matrix for relations within and among households. To what degree the large, purportedly hereditary categories that dominate the overall scheme of the myths corresponded to any territorial reality or to any practical pattern of residence by 1600 is uncertain. But it is likely that the large, purportedly genealogical formations whose founders are the greatest heroes of the text, and the *ayllu*s or ancestor-focused kindreds, still counted, at least theoretically, as the corporate holders of important rights in productive assets (see below, especially on the concepts *yumay* and *ayllu*).

In the later sixteenth century the Huarochirí people were not numbered among the poor. They were heavily taxed, and Spaniards vied for chances to exploit them. Far from being an obscure hinter-

land, their region lay astride the best-known route
from the Spanish capital, Lima, to the Inca one,
Cuzco. But their relative wealth did not protect
them, and in some respects the inhabitants of
Huarochirí were an afflicted people. Epidemics
of the 1550s, 1580s, and 1590s, within the living
memory of myth-tellers, had mowed down a huge
share of a population with weak immunological de-
fenses. "If we accept Dávila Brizeño's estimate of
approximately 6,000 household heads in Huarochirí
in the 1540s, shortly after the entry of the Europe-
ans, then the province lost . . . almost 30 percent of
its adult male population in the quarter century between 1545 and 1571" (Spalding 1984: 173). The
rest of the century was a period of continuing se-
vere population decline in Huarochirí as in many
Andean regions (Spalding 1984: 176). Around 1560
and again in the 1580s, survivors of the epidemics
in some parts of the Andes (including southerly
Yauyos) had asked the *huaca*s to defend them, but
suffered bitter disappointment in the failure of nativist movements (Taki Onqoy, Moro Onqoy, and
others; Curatola 1978; Stern 1982: 51–71). When
Jesuit fathers conducted a conversion campaign in
Huarochirí in 1577, they reported finding many
people sick in their fields (Arguedas and Duviols
1966: 244). Missionaries routinely procured con-
versions by exploiting the desperation of the mor-
tally ill.

So by the probable date of the manuscript—
1608—the inhabitants of the Huarochirí region had
reason to wonder, like Quita Pariasca the Mountain
Man (chap. 18, sec. 221), whether the world itself
had turned bad. Several passages in the manuscript
are colored by anxiety about sickness and depopulation (chap. 19, sec. 233; chap. 25, sec. 345; chap. 26,

Some of the myth-tellers were probably old
enough to remember other calamities. When Spanish forces crushed the forty-year-old neo-Inca re-
doubt in Vilcabamba and then in 1572 executed
the last independent sovereign of Inca blood, Tú-
pac Amaru, Andean people everywhere went into
mourning. The administrative overhaul that followed increasingly reduced native chiefs to the
compromised status of tribute enforcers and cultural brokers. Some of the myth-tellers may have
been among those routed from their homes and
chased into strategic hamlets by Spanish function-
aries in the 1580s. The "people called Indians" also
had to comply with increasingly exhausting tribute regimens. Meanwhile, the authorities allowed
Spaniards to appropriate landholdings that the natives lacked enough population to defend and sometimes let clerics exploit parishioners outrageously.

sec. 357). Observing that the natives of the rocky
heights seemed to be holding their own even as the
aborigines of the coast were perishing (and indeed
became entirely extinct, through both depopulation
and assimilation), the tellers of chapter 9 (sec. 140)
wondered whether perhaps the rustic highlanders
did not owe their vitality to greater faithfulness to
the Andean religious tradition.

Into the world of the *huaca*s

Some of the basic terms in Huarochirí myths embody unfamiliar Andean assumptions or categories.
While glosses cannot capture their full senses, a
reader at least needs some idea of what is lost in
translation. The following paragraphs comment
minimally on the most important ones.

Pacha: *'earth, world, time, place'*

Huarochirí people called the world and time together *pacha*, an untranslatable word that simultaneously denotes a moment or interval in time and
a locus or extension in space—and does so, moreover, at any scale. In chapter 18 (sec. 221) the Mountain Man, foreseeing the arrival of those destroyers
who would turn out to be the Spanish, says, "Alas,
brothers, the *pacha* is not good." He could have
meant anything from 'this is not a good situation'
(or 'moment' or 'conjuncture') to an idea as grand as
'the world is no longer good' or 'the epoch is no
longer good'. The same word *pacha* is also the
name of earth in general and in modern folk religion means Earth as a personified female being.

Cosmological ideas are not spelled out in the
Huarochirí manuscript. Despite the use of solar
gnomons for calendric astronomy (chap. 9, sec. 108),
the Sun appears as a person in Checa lore only tan-
gentially (chap. 4; chap. 13, secs. 172, 188). Sun
worship figures as an Inca idea (chap. 22, secs. 276,
279) and as a motif in the genealogy of the *huaca*s
as the people of the lower Rímac valley imagined it
(chap. 13, sec. 172). The moon is not personified
anywhere. The Andean cosmos can be partly understood from these myths, but not because the myths
explicitly describe it. We deduce what we can by
noticing what the tellers take for granted. To some
degree the picture can be augmented with data
from other written sources and from recent ethnographic research that offers conceptual analogies.
(Earls and Silverblatt 1978 propose a synthetic
model.)

Two pervading generalities seem to order the

data. One is that earth has predominantly female associations and water predominantly male. The second, partially overriding the first, is that altitude and motion connote maleness, while depth and stability are associated with femaleness.

Earth's living mass was imagined rising up from the waters of the surrounding ocean. (Whether the waters circled earth like Saturn's rings or whether earth's base was immersed like a boat's hull is not clear.) Especially in local instances, particularly when visualized as the green irrigable valley lands, earth is usually female. But the land's highest points, the great peaks whose ice-crusted crowns overtower the habitable earth, are usually male. One of them is Paria Caca. Roughly, the solid part of the world might be imagined as a single world mountain made of all the Andean ranges, rising from femalelike valleys to malelike snowcapped heights.

Water—rainstorms and mudslides, snow and glacial runoff, tiny irrigation canals and mighty rivers, even that astral river we call the Milky Way—is the kinetic part of the world. Water moves over *pacha* in a circular path. It rides up from the ocean into the sky along the Milky Way "river." Chapter 29 (sec. 375) tells us that water rises because a celestial llama constellation carries water up from below by drinking before ascending. Then water washes down onto the heights of the earth as storm and rain, bathing and fecundating earth as it descends to the ocean. People worshiped the great snowcapped peaks "because that is where their water comes from" (Avila [1645] 1918: 83). Water is often male, especially storm water and downward-flowing water. Several myths liken the chasm-cutting power of rivers in spate, or the storm and flash flood that create disastrous mudslides, to warlike male violence:

> As soon as they brought him up a hill, Maca Uisa, child of Paria Caca, began to rain upon them, gently at first.
>
> The natives of that country said, "What could this mean?" and began to ready themselves.
>
> When they did so, Maca Uisa reduced all those villages to eroded chasms by flashing lightning and pouring down more rain, and washing them away in a mudslide. (chap. 23, secs. 295–296)

Although the Pacific Ocean plays a key part in organizing mythic space, it is not personalized in the manuscript. In modern Andean myth, the ocean (*Mama Cocha* 'mother lake') is usually female. The *huaca* most closely associated with the sea is Pacha Camac (chap. 22, secs. 276–284), but this great force is not clearly defined as a maritime deity.

The hydraulic embrace of moving water and enduring earth was imagined as sex. Their embrace yielded a biotic system (Dumézil and Duviols 1974–1976) in which life forms emerge from mixed earth and water. Hydraulic sex was sometimes imagined as a turbulent affair. The myth-tellers, who seem to have faced the harrowing vicissitudes of a water-poor irrigation economy with a good deal of humor, likened its hazards to the comical chaos of undisciplined desire. In four myths (chap. 6, secs. 82–90; chap. 12, sec. 170; chap. 30; and chap. 31, secs. 406–432) voluptuous earth-women offer their parched bodies to the virile water-*huaca*s who rush down from the heights. The earth-women's self-serving tricks and the water-men's lecherous ineptitude can turn their meetings into comic disasters. In chapter 31, when the lake-*huaca* Collquiri rushes downhill to his earth-lover Capyama, the bursting pressure of his virility squirts out of every channel and sprays destructive floods all over Capyama's people:

> . . . Capyama's elders shouted at Collquiri from their <crossed out:> [spring] village:
> "Son-in-law, everybody's mad at us! Don't send us so much water!"
> "Shut it off!"
> "Hey, Collquiri! Hold back on the water!" they yelled.
> With them shouting like that, Collquiri plugged the hole with a blanket and other stuff.
> But the more he plugged it the more the barrier crumbled and the more the water kept bursting through over and over again.
> Meanwhile the people from down below kept yelling at him nonstop:
> "PLUG IT UP!!" (chap. 31, secs. 425–426)

Pacha, the world as a given arrangement of time, space, and matter, is not supratemporal. It clearly admits change, even cataclysm. There have been times when *pacha* "wanted to come to an end," and the manuscript tells us how this can happen. Water might fail to ascend into the astral "river" and the world might drown as the ocean rose (chap. 3; chap. 29, sec. 375). Or Pacha Camac Pacha Cuyuchic, the 'World Maker and World Shaker' who sleeps under the ruined shrine that still bears his name, might turn over in his dreams and pulverize the world in an earthquake (chap. 22, sec. 284); the region is in fact subject to devastating earthquakes. Everything, including humanity, has been crushed and refashioned. The social order, too, is constructed and transformed in superhuman violence; the tellers imagine the original theophany that was their group birth as one of many cataclysms that simultaneously gave form to the land and to society.

In gross terms, then, the Huarochirí world opposes the qualities of still centricity—depth, solidity, dryness, stability, potential fecundity, womanliness—to those of a restlessly moving outer orbit—height, fluidity, wetness, movement, potential for insemination, virility. As the outer waters wash over the inner earth, these two fundamental lives mix in the circulation of water over soil. Lives that are both watery and earthy emerge: plants, animals, people. Born fat, wet, and juicy, all beings eventually—in the space of a dry season or a long life—separate out again into their original substances (Allen 1982). Moisture departs as vapor, leaving a weatherbeaten husk and the dry seeds of a future cycle. Nature and ritual combine to return the parts to their sources so the cycle can start anew. Humans like all others emerge fat and wet, but at the end of life their dried husk containing the potential for future life goes as a mummified ancestor (*mallqui*) back to earth. In chapters 27 and 28, a dry, seedlike being that emerges from the dead human husk—a fly—is the living residue of a dead generation. The function of ritual and sacrifice is to ensure a steady circulation of biological energy through *pacha* by conducting social exchange among its living parts.

Camay: *a concept of specific essence and force, 'to charge with being, to infuse with species power'*

The act by which *huaca*s bring other entities into being is not expressed with the plain word meaning 'to make' (*ruray*), nor with the verb *huallpay*, which González Holguín took to mean a divine act of creation ([1608] 1952: 174), but with a different verb: *camay*. *Camay* escapes the seemingly handy glosses 'to create' (because 'create' connotes an *ex nihilo* act, while *camay* connotes the energizing of extant matter) and 'to fashion' (because 'fashion' suggests only an initial shaping of inert matter, whereas *camay* is a continuous act that works upon a being as long as it exists). But what does *camay* mean? The astronomical or astrological chapter 29 gives a crucial clue: it labels a llama-shaped constellation the *camac* (agentive form, '*camay*-er') of llamas. On descending to earth this constellation infuses a powerful generative essence of llama vitality, which causes earthly llamas to flourish. All things have their vitalizing prototypes or *camac*, including human groups; the *camac* of a human group is usually its *huaca* of origin. Religious practice supplicates the *camac* ever to vitalize its *camasca*, that is, its tangible instance or manifestation. Taylor (1974–1976) has likened this idea to Platonic idealism, an insight that helps one understand the profoundly

plural and ongoing nature of Andean creation but also minimizes its earthiness. *Camac* in the manuscript seems to suggest a being abounding in energy as physical as electricity or body warmth, not an abstraction or mental archetype.

*Huaca*s could be *camac* to great or small categories of beings. The great coastal deity Pacha Camac bears in his very name—'*Camac* of space and time'—an all-embracing function as the vitalizer of worldwide realities, while local *huaca*s animate smaller entities. Likewise, ordinary beings could be *camasca* (participial form; 'infused with *camay*') to different degrees. An *ancha camasca* person is a 'very powerful' one. But one can clearly see that *camay* means specific form and force, not general potency. In chapter 14 (sec. 191) three men boast of their speed, saying:

> "I am a condor shaman!" some men answered.
> "I am a falcon shaman!" said others.
> "I am one who flies in the form of a swift!" replied still others.

What they said more literally is:

> "I am the *camasca* of the condor!"
> "I am the *camasca* of the falcon!"
> "I am one who flies as a swift!"

The point appears to be that these men are three shamans whose patrons, the archetypes of birds who symbolize speed, have infused in them the species powers of speed and range of the condor, the falcon, and the swift.

Huaca: *'superhuman person, shrine, holy and powerful object'*; huaca *priesthood*

The Huarochirí manuscript is in large measure a reading-out of its space. The horizon, not the cosmos—geography, not metaphysics—poses the questions to which its most vibrant deities give answers. Andean numina lodge in places or placed objects: mountains, springs, lakes, rock outcrops, ancient ruins, caves, and any number of humanly made objects in shrines: effigies, mummies, oracles, and so forth.

Like all the other persons English forces us to call "deities," Paria Caca is a *huaca*. The half-Andean historian Garcilaso Inca de la Vega tried in 1609 to convey the sense of this all-important term by telling us that:

> *huaca* . . . means "a sacred thing," such as . . . idols, rocks, great stones or trees which the enemy [i.e., Satan] entered to make the people believe he was a god.

They also give the name *huaca* to things they have offered to the Sun, such as figures of men, birds, and animals. . . . *Huaca* is applied to any temple, large or small, to the sepulchers set up in the fields, and to the corners in their houses where the Devil spoke to their priests. . . . The same name is given to all those things which for their beauty or excellence stand above other things of the same kind, such as a rose, an apple, or a pippin, or any other fruit that is better or more beautiful than the rest. . . . On the other hand they give the name *huaca* to ugly and monstrous things . . . the great serpents of the Antis . . . everything that is out of the usual course of nature, as a woman who gives birth to twins . . . double-yolked eggs are *huaca* . . .

They use the word *huaca* of the great range of the Sierra Nevada. . . . The same name is given to very high hills that stand above the rest as high towers stand above ordinary houses, and to steep mountain slopes . . . (Garcilaso Inca de la Vega [1609] 1966: 1:76–77; Livermore's translation)

A *huaca* was any material thing that manifested the superhuman: a mountain peak, a spring, a union of streams, a rock outcrop, an ancient ruin, a twinned cob of maize, a tree split by lightning. Even people could be *huaca*s. Modern ethnography tells us that one extraordinary ethnic group, the Uru of Bolivia, was collectively called *haqe huaca* 'a human *huaca*' by Aymara-speaking neighbors because the Aymara thought the Uru had survived from primordial times (Manelis de Klein 1973: 143). In the manuscript, too, people can become *huaca*s. Mummified ancestors of high rank (see below) could be *huaca*. The Inca rite of Capac Hucha (chap. 22, sec. 280) turned live humans—spotless children and youths—into new *huaca*s by burying them alive. The discovery of new *huaca*s never ceased. Avila recalled that when one native brought home a black silk button with gold thread, which he had found in a garbage heap in Lima, a "master" of *huaca* worship revealed to him that it should be enshrined as a household *huaca* ([1645] 1918: 74). Chapter 20 details the discovery and career of another new-found *huaca*.

People owed *huaca*s reverence and also plenty of goods: llama and guinea pig meat, brilliantly colored mineral powders, thorny oyster shell, clothing, coca leaf, maize dumplings, and maize beer. The Huarochirí manuscript lays down the priestly regimen for sacrifice and gives examples of the responses priests delivered on *huaca*s' behalf:

They [*huaca* priests] gave people advice, telling them all sorts of things:
"You are to bathe in the confluence of two streams."

"You must sacrifice one of your llamas."
People were more than happy to obey their dicta. (chap. 13, sec. 186)

The Huarochirí manuscript tells a good deal about priesthoods, but not much about rules regulating lay worshipers' individual or group affiliation to *huaca*s. People appear to have belonged to the cults of *huaca*s considered as apical ancestors of their patrilineages, of their *ayllu*s, and of the clanlike large groups identified with major founder-*huaca*s. Apparently, heredity was a primary determinant of local religious duty, because when people went on their own initiative to consult the *huaca* oracle of the five Ñamca sisters, the Ñamcas would ask if the petitioners had properly consulted their hereditary *huaca*s beforehand:

. . . these *huaca*s would ask those who went to them, "Have you come on the advice of your own Con Churi [hereditary household deity], your father, or your elders?"
To those who answered "No," the *huaca*s would reply, "Go back, return, consult your Con Churi first." (chap. 13, sec. 185)

Huaca shrines were powerful social and political corporations. When a *huaca* gained legitimacy, we learn from the "biography" of the *huaca* Llocllay Huancupa (chap. 20), worshipers built it a temple precinct and offered costly service. Politically sponsored *huaca*s had endowments of both herds and fields that common people were required to serve:

The Incas worshiped these two *huaca*s [the Sun and Pacha Camac] most, beyond all the others, exalting them supremely and adorning them with their silver and gold, putting many hundreds of retainers at their service, and placing llama herds for their endowments in all the villages.
The llamas of Pacha Camac sent from the Checa people stayed at Sucya Villca. (chap. 22, sec. 277)

*Huaca*s also had human servitors and even spouses. Avila in 1645 reminisced about having met a good-looking eighteen-year-old girl, crippled and walking on two staffs, who had "been dedicated as a woman of an idol" (the *huaca* Maca Uisa). Maca Uisa lived with her in the form of a sacred blue stone, "no bigger than the palm of a hand," which she kept in a basket with tiny but luxurious garments to dress it ([1645] 1918: 69–70). He also mentions that a "*saçerdotisa* [priestess] very celebrated among the Indians" was known as a "woman of Pariacaca's" ([1645] 1918: 65). Both examples use the Spanish term *muger*, meaning 'woman' literally and 'concubine' or 'secondary wife' more freely, rather than the legal Spanish term for 'wife'. Because the Spanish terminology of marriage implies a sacrament, Father Avila might have scrupled to use it in connection with *huaca* marriage no matter how natives regarded the matter; so we cannot tell whether these unions counted as full marriages in the native system.

Some *huaca* priests clearly enjoyed class privileges. For example, common people did all the agricultural work on fields belonging to the *yanca* priests who had hereditary authority over a lake and its irrigation water (chap. 31, sec. 435) and they gave priests huge amounts of meat (chap. 24, sec. 335). Water priests are credited in the manuscript with almost dictatorial power over some of the processes by which society reproduced itself, including vital decisions about people's rights and duties in basic subsistence agriculture:

> Because he was the *yanca* for this purpose, all the arrangements of the season were made in compliance with his commands.
> When it came to irrigation he'd be the only one to give orders about it, saying, "It'll take place now" or "It'll be so many days." And all the Concha obeyed him to the last word. (chap. 31, sec. 434)

Early in his extirpation campaign, Father Avila imprisoned an important priest of Chaupi Ñamca in Mama village named Hernando Paucar (who may be a source of the distinctive subregional mythology contained in chapter 13) and wrung from him a confession about the privileged life of *huaca* priests. It should be read with caution, since it comes to us via a paraphrase composed four decades after the event:

> . . . it is true that I've been a priest [*saçerdote*] of Chaupiñamocc since I was a youngster, and I inherited [the priesthood] from my father, and in all these villages of this parish and others, they've respected me a great deal, and I used to come visit them twice every year, and if I was late they used to send someone to call on me, and they would send me horses, and people to serve me on the road, and whenever I entered a village they would erect arches, and they would come out dancing, with the women beating their drums, and they would give me lodging, and fed me, and served me, and they gave me so much that I didn't know what to do with it all. At my rear they made something like a cabin of boughs, and they would cover it and close it off with cloaks, and the floor used to be covered with fresh straw, and I would enter into it alone, by day or by night as I preferred. There they

would come to consult me, and I responded, and sacrificed guinea pigs, pouring out maize beer, and I used to perform other ceremonies in view of those who attended, and some used to say that they wanted to hear a response given by Chaupiñamocc, and I used to make her speak by placing there a little idol that represented her, and sometimes I would talk in a very high voice and other times very low. . . . And for this everyone respected me, as much as they do you [Father Avila], and much more. On the third or fourth day they would bring together maize, potatoes, and a lot of food for me, and they would dispatch it to my wife in my village. In this village I'd be lodged in one fellow's house the first time, a different fellow's the next . . . (Avila [1645] 1918: 68–69)

Through oracles and through their privileges in ratifying rites of passage, the *huacas*' priestly representatives closely governed the ongoing business of society. Another sort of priesthood, the nonhereditary *huacsa* office, rotated among members of appropriate kin groups. *Yanca*s seem to function as calendric and technical authorities, oracles and mediators, while the *huacsa*s' main duty was to impersonate the great *huaca*s in festivals and reenact their myths. Some of the narratives may be verbal "scripts" of *huacsa* performances.

In comparison to the priesthoods, the manuscript has little to say about the power of nonpriestly leaders such as the political "native lords" called *curaca*s or the native magistrates (*alcaldes*) appointed by Spanish colonial officials. It mentions several postconquest *curaca*s by name, often commenting on their attitudes toward *huaca*s or as a device for setting a chronological context. Several passages imply that the *curaca* was expected to take a prominent part in *huaca* ceremonies (chap. 13, secs. 173–174, 176), and that he could exert leadership over a community's decision to adopt or neglect particular *huaca*s (chap. 19, sec. 231; chap. 20, secs. 244–245).

*Huaca*s had vibrantly individual personalities. Paria Caca, whether in his incarnation as the hailstorm of the icy heights or as the five-in-one hero who beat the Yunca down toward the sea, seems haughty, brilliant, and cold, a driving deity. Llocllay Huancupa (chaps. 20 and 21) lurks in the dark like an inarticulate beast, roaring dully over his immolated meal. Chuqui Suso, the sexy agricultural *huaca* (chap. 6, secs. 82, 88–90), and her sister who seduced the Paria Cacas into irrigating her (chap. 12, sec. 170), as well as the great maternal *huaca* Chaupi Ñamca, were associated with sensuality and playful ease:

"Chaupi Ñamca enjoys it no end when she sees our <crossed out:> [cocks] private parts!" they said as they danced naked.

　After they danced this dance a very fertile season would follow. (chap. 10, sec. 151)

They used to stay there all night long, staying awake till dawn, drinking and getting drunk. They got real happy performing the dance called Aylliua, and danced that night drinking and getting drunk until dawn.

　After that they went out to the fields and simply did nothing at all. They just got drunk, drinking and boozing away and saying, "It's our mother's festival!" (chap. 13, sec. 174)

Clearly *huaca*s are living beings, persons in fact. Avila and other Christian seventeenth-century observers seem to think of the *huaca*s as real beings, material in form but animated by demonic spirit. When Avila applied the terms "god" and "goddess" to *huaca*s (for example, Cuni Raya's beloved Caui Llaca; Arguedas and Duviols 1966: 202–203), he seemed to be thinking of them as linked to natural forms, anthropomorphic and tangible, something like the deities of Greco-Roman mythology and the "demons" of medieval Europe whose lore he apparently knew in some detail (Arguedas and Duviols 1966: 207, note 3). In this partly Greco-Roman sense, the word "deity" might fit the *huaca*s. But one must be careful; the dualism of substance enfolded in the Christian usage of the words "god" and "divine" seems superfluous for understanding Andean worship. The world imagined by the Checa does not seem to have been made of two kinds of stuff—matter and spirit—like that of Christians; *huaca*s are made of energized matter, like everything else, and they act within nature, not over and outside it as Western supernaturals do.

　The tellers give *pacha* shape by mapping onto it a society of *huaca*s that mimics idealized human social structure, mainly genealogical and affinal. Earth forms, superhumanity, and society match each other in a structure of correspondences. Great snowcaps are great creators. Their myths are often shared among large populations (perhaps tens or hundreds of thousands before the Spanish conquest) united by language and other markers of public identity; often they are the groups called "nations" by some Spanish authors and "ethnic groups" by modern students of Inca polity. Paria Caca, whose body was a double-peaked snowcap high in the rugged western range, was known to Guaman Poma ([1615] 1980: 241) as one of the greatest deities. The pilgrimage to his shrine (Bonavia et al. 1984) united

thousands of people in a trek over the last lap, a race up the "steps of Paria Caca" still visible today. The pilgrims visited the lake where Paria Caca quenched the Huanca deity Huallallo's fires, sacrificed llamas at Paria Caca's dwelling, and, according to Dávila Brizeño ([1586] 1965: 161), "climb[ed] the peak of the snowcap to offer their sacrifices."

　The Huarochirí narrators explained their various ancestor *huaca*s as heroic offspring of this great regional *huaca*. In the Huarochirí manuscript Paria Caca is said to consist of five beings who are, in various contexts, equal or ranked component selves of a fivefold being. In the overall textual architecture, which seeks to weld *huaca*s of diverse origin into a single ideological kindred, the five heroes were felt to have established what were apparently large fraternal sections of society. The main teller of the Paria Caca mythology thinks of the landscape as divided into domains of influence corresponding to the various large highland-derived groups, each defined by putative descent from a persona or child of Paria Caca. These domains are not said to be contiguous territories. They emerge in the form of mythic trajectories: the paths of heroes, along which the heroes achieved society-defining deeds and left areas of dominion over specific lands and people in the scattered or "archipelago" form known from secular and bureaucratic sources.

Yuriy/yumay: *concepts of human birth and descent*

Colonial Andeans imagined human descent groups as continuations of the genealogy of *huaca*s. Intermediate-sized, named ascriptive groups like the Checa "thousand" (whose viewpoint often dominates the text) were fitted into a unified regional ideology by defining their founders as the progeny of Paria Caca's component heroes. Paria Caca's followers thus construed the "original" organization as sib- or clanlike. The spacial foci of superhuman and human genealogy seem to have been symbolized by shrines called *pacarina*s or 'dawning places' that represented founders' and heroes' appearances on earth. *Pacarina* myths are by their very nature peculiar to each group; since the Huarochirí mythology as a whole sometimes seeks to coordinate the mythic legacies of several "originally" separate groups, it is not surprising that *pacarina*s are the theme on which Paria Caca mythology is least consistent. One example is the *pacarina* where a people-producing *quinua* plant grew (chap. 24, sec. 302); the person who composed the chapters seems uncertain how to reconcile this myth (which Taylor [1987b: 163] takes as a component predating the subsumption of origins in Paria Caca) with other accounts of emergence.

Andeans traced the descent lines of actual humans from revered ancestors, whom they credited with living on as guardians of fertility and order as long as their mummified bodies endured. We know from "idolatry" trials and the testimony of chroniclers that the cult of mummies (*mallquis*) formed the link between the mythology of *huacas* and the purportedly known genealogy of named groups of the living. One witness on trial for "idolatry" explained: "This *mallqui* [the mummy Guaman Cama] was a nephew of the idols Caruatarqui Urau, and Ticlla Urau, and the progenitor of this *ayllo* Chacas, and he was a son of Libiac ['Lightning'], and he nurtured people, multiplied them, guarded their fields and gave them money and wealth" (Huertas 1981: 104–105). Mummified ancestors lived in caves or special houses (chap. 11, sec. 155). Their progeny dressed them richly, periodically "embraced" and feted them, served them with food and sacrifices, and petitioned their approval of major transactions (Guaman Poma [1615] 1980: 1:262–271; Polo de Ondegardo [1571] 1916: 116–119). Garcilaso ([1609] 1966: 1:76–77) mentioned that mummies of special importance were *huacas* and in Huarochirí it seems to be mummified leaders of successful invasions who achieved this role. The two Huarochirí chapters about the fate of the dead (chaps. 27 and 28) are evasive about mummification but difficult to understand unless one assumes that people preserved human remains in some way. A few Huarochirí passages seem to refer to mummy *huacas*:

> The one [*huaca*] called Ñan Sapa was a human being.
> Later on, the Inca took away the *huaca* himself.
> But they made another one to be his proxy.
> This is the one that we know Señor Doctor Francisco de Avila carried away.
> They say Ñan Sapa, when he was human, wore the *quisay rinri* in his ears and bore the *canah yauri* scepter in his hands. (chap. 24, secs. 319–320)

In connecting ancestors to living humans, unilineal principles play an explicit role. The myths employ a concept of patrilineage (*yumay* 'sperm') used in relation to a concept of sibling or birth group (*yuriy* 'birth'). The preface tells us that the peoples whose story is to be told here constitute a group by virtue of sharing a father: "I set forth here the lives of the ancestors of the Huaro Cheri people, who all

descend from one forefather" (pref., sec. 2). The vocative *yaya* 'father' as a form of address is used to express deference to any male authority, human or superhuman.

The most prominent collective ego of the myths, the Checa, thought of their group as defined by mythic descent from one of the component Paria Caca persons; it is not stated to be patrilineal, but the Yauyo subgroup called Morales as a whole is treated as male relative to the Yunca, and the persons whose acts define it are males. Within such clanlike categories, there appear to have been more clearly genealogical patrilineages uniting people with specific rights and duties. Portions of society characterized as patrilineages (*yumay* 'sperm') are mentioned as the holders of hereditary water rights and priesthoods (chap. 7, sec. 91; chap. 31, sec. 445).

When comparisons among sectors of a collectivity are made, whether at a vague clanlike or a more genealogical lineagelike level, they are usually made in terms of birth order within an original sibling set (*yuriy*). Genealogical myths from all over the world "justify existing stratifications by denying them (we are all brothers) while at the same time providing detailed guidance to inequality by distinguishing between 'elder' and 'younger' branches. They also record alliances by tying allied groups into common genealogies" (Vansina 1985: 103). The concept *yuriy* 'sibling group' carries exactly this contradiction. In all cases, siblinghood seems to imply rank even more saliently than it implies solidarity. "The Quinti thoroughly despised the Checa because the Checa were born last" (chap. 11, sec. 153). The notion of unranked kin solidarity is treated as an abstraction or mystique at the highest level of mythic generality: Paria Caca, the union of all Huarochirí-area invader groups, came into being as five unnumbered eggs. The set of eggs could be considered a sibling set, but one without birth order because not yet born. No such transcendent paradox occurs among humans. The transition from power *in ovo* to power in action is also the transition to rank order.

As in many Andean contexts (for example, the political organization of colonial Andean communities), the firstborn or leading member of a set (e.g., noble heads of a village's component *ayllus*) functions within the set as first among equals, but outside the set as the totalizing representative of it. (The political authority of *curacas* over *ayllus*, for example, seems to have worked on this principle.) So, too, among *huacas*. Paria Caca can be considered the first among five brothers (chap. 8, sec. 99), yet at the same time as the overarching deity of which the five are only parts. In this latter function Paria Caca is often spoken of as the father rather than the brother of the heroes. Chaupi Ñamca has the same structure (chap. 10, sec. 147).

So thoroughly does the ideology of genealogical inequality govern ritual order that the birth of human siblings whose rank order closely approached equality—that is, twins—was seen as a major anomaly warranting the immense expiatory efforts that occupy supplement I.

Naturally there is some tension between rank ascribed by descent and rank achieved through warfare. The "children of Paria Caca" fought for the military supremacy of their ethnic group, but also for precedence among themselves, and this produces anomalies; chapter 17 expresses the Checa claim to have risen above their Quinti rivals by their achievements. Sometimes a group's junior standing seems to reflect its lesser achieved power. The Concha, a local group described as an *ayllu* (see below), were said to have originally been a *yuriy* of five brothers and a sister; the resulting five groups' unequal land resources are explained as the result of the first three brothers' having conquered energetically while the last two lagged or got lost:

> . . . these two [Hualla and Calla] fell somewhat behind.
>   So, lagging behind, they missed the trail and headed instead toward the Yauyo country, thinking, "Maybe our brothers went over there."
>   A long time afterward, only after the other three brothers had finished dividing up the fields and other goods among themselves, they did come back. (chap. 31, sec. 391)

Patrilineal grouping and birth-order ranking do not exhaust the kinship content of the ideology expressed in the manuscript. Some episodes suggest that descent through females also played a large part in the tellers' idealized vision of social organization. No named principle used in myths of group origin offers a matrilineal counterpart to *yumay*. Yet, in rituals, there is a strong tendency to treat the engendering of females as a separate type of parentage from the begetting of males. In the fertility-giving ritual game of spearing giant dummies called *yomca* and *huasca*,

> Once they'd prepared everything, they named one of the effigy bundles Yomca and set it as a target symbolizing males.
>   The other, the one called Huasca, they set as a target symbolizing females.
>   After they set them up, the men would put on their best clothing and feather ruffs called *tamta*, and they'd begin to let fly at the targets. (chap. 24, sec. 328)

Then they threw spears at the Huasca effigy for females, saying,
> "She'll give me daughters and all kinds of food!"
and then at the Yomca effigy, saying,
> "He'll give me sons, agave fiber goods, and all kinds of animals!" (chap. 24, sec. 334)

Separate female *huacas* were credited with being great producers of female offspring: "Chaupi Ñamca was a great maker of people, that is, of women; and Paria Caca of men" (chap. 13, sec. 172). *Mama* 'mother' was a term of honorific address strictly parallel to *yaya* 'father'. Certain priestesses held rank apparently equal to that of priests (chap. 13, sec. 178; chap. 31, sec. 417; see also Avila [1645] 1918: 65). Overall, the implicit suggestion seems to be that male and female fertility run through separate channels, which cross over each other in a braidlike pattern as each generation reproduces itself sexually. The female channel of fertility was fortified by a priestly religious structure, as was the male. The Huarochirí data seem compatible with—but do not declare the existence of—inheritance of some religious identity or obligation through parallel descent (Lambert [1977] 1980: 37; Silverblatt 1987: 20–39).

Ayllu: *corporate landholding collectivity self-defined as ancestor-focused kindred*

The tellers of the myths habitually described their society as built of collectivities called *ayllus*. In many passages the *ayllu* figures as the basic unit of ritual action:

> . . . in the old days, people used to go to consult Paria Caca at night, taking along llamas or other things.
>   They used to go taking turns, *ayllu* by *ayllu*. (chap. 24, sec. 309)

A person's immediate religious responsibility was to his or her *ayllu's* senior members. When Lanti Chumpi discovered what she guessed might be a new *huaca* (perhaps a buried figurine or unusual stone), her first thought was to take the find to them (chap. 20, sec. 237). We know that each *ayllu* made its own claim to religious authority because each told its own version of certain myths (chap. 13, sec. 187).

But what was the makeup of the *ayllu*? The classic sources look unhelpful at first glance. The great lexicographer Diego Gonçález Holguín ([1608] 1952: 39–40) gives a definition of *ayllu* so broad as to include virtually all kinds of descent, kinship, and even territorial solidarity. Avila thought an *ayllu* was something like the Spanish kin group defined by a shared surname (Arguedas and Duviols 1966: 257), which would suggest patrilineal bias.

Internal evidence from the manuscript, however, suggests something other than a corporate unilineal principle. Chapter 7 (sec. 91) says, "There is within this *ayllu* a patrilineage [*yumay*] which bears the name Chauincho." From this we infer, first, that *ayllu* is a separate concept from patrilineage, and second, that an *ayllu* could contain more than one patrilineage. *Ayllu* is therefore not the minimal or the only unit of descent ideology. However, the fact that the passage just cited goes on to speak of the Chauincho patrilineage as an *ayllu* (with a crossing-out eloquent of hesitation on someone's part) suggests that the term *ayllu* could subsume the concept of lineage. This makes it difficult to distinguish the two in certain instances.

We also know, because chapter 13 (sec. 187) implies as much, that a given territorial settlement (*llacta*; see below), which we usually gloss 'village', could have multiple *ayllu*s: "in each village, and even *ayllu* by *ayllu*, people give different versions . . ." People understood the internal dynamics of their local communities as a play of more or less rival *ayllu*s.

The tellers saw rights to land and other immovable assets as lodged in the *ayllu*s: "As soon as Tutay Quiri's children had expelled those Yunca, they began to distribute among themselves, according to their own *ayllu*s, the fields, the houses, and the *ayllu* designations" (chap. 24, sec. 316). This passage then tells us that even the invaders felt bound to redefine their own organization on the pattern of preexisting local *ayllu*s, which suggests they had a high degree of corporate definition and legitimacy as well as important functions. Since it goes on to say the Yasapa *ayllu* people were silversmiths, one may further speculate that some *ayllu*s practiced, or at least were traditionally associated with, occupational specialties.

So it is relatively safe to think of the *ayllu* as a named, landholding collectivity, self-defined in kinship terms, including lineages but not globally defined as unilineal, and frequently forming part of a multi-*ayllu* settlement. But what exactly were the kinship criteria of inclusion? This question, an ancient mare's nest in Andean research, yields partly to Karen Spalding's exploration (1984: 28–30, 48–52; see also Castelli, Koth, and Mould de Pease 1981). Gonçález Holguín shows us that the most general sense of *ayllu* and its derived words is "that of grouping elements or persons together on the basis of similarity or species, or dividing up a larger

group on the basis of the same criteria" (Spalding 1984: 29). "Similarity or species" could mean taxa such as animal or plant species, but, when applied to people, *ayllu* usually meant "descendants of a common ancestor." "The term was commonly defined as any group—family, lineage, or generation—whose members were related to one another through their descent from a common ancestor" (Spalding 1984: 28–29), that is, an ancestor-focused bilateral kindred. Zuidema (1973: 16–21) has developed the argument toward a detailed model of ancestor classification and cultic organization.

Spalding's definition has useful corollaries. First, it reminds us that, like such spatial terms as *pacha*, *ayllu* is the name of a concept of relatedness and not of an entity with specific dimensions. It has no inherent limits of scale; in principle, it applies to all levels from sibling groups to huge kindreds, clanlike groups, or even whole ethnic groups defined by reference to common origin and territory. An *ayllu* can readily be understood as consisting of multiple patrilineages (or, in principle, matrilineages) insofar as any given member can trace descent from the "founder" or apex via a given child of the "founder" (and so forth, in potentially segmenting ramifications). Platt ([1978] 1986: 230–231) has clearly demonstrated a varied-scale usage among modern Bolivian highlanders, who reckon upward from the "minimal *ayllu*"—small clusters of patrilocal rural neighborhoods—up through "minor," "major," and finally "maximal" *ayllu*s that ascend to include the entire ethnic group. The various levels of *ayllu* organization may each have specific terminologies, typically referring to their political functions. For example, in Platt's area, the "minimal" *ayllu* was called *cabildo* (civic council) in its political functioning, and Spalding (1984: 51) adduces a Spanish witness who understood the Inca decimal term *pachaca* ('hundred') to mean an *ayllu* of a hundred households or over, suitable by its size for treatment as an administrative entity in its own right. In the Huarochirí manuscript, the usage of *ayllu* terminology becomes less confusing if one recognizes that an *ayllu* may be part of a larger *ayllu*. In this sense, the "children of Paria Caca," the large (perhaps ethnic) group that forms the mythology's collective subject, a group of people "who all descend from one forefather" (pref., sec. 2), is a "maximal *ayllu*."

Second, as Spalding also emphasizes, for practical purposes it was not precise genealogy that finally decided who belonged to an *ayllu*, but rather social conduct—including political alliance—befitting a genealogically connected person. As with many concepts in the domain of kinship, *ayllu* may be understood partly as an ideology built up to explain patterns of behavior rooted in the residence rules, which in turn often reflect the demands of a given geographical, technological, and demographic reality. Access to *ayllu*-held assets (and claims to collective *ayllu* ownership continued far into the colonial era) was given in return for exchanged labor and exchanged ritual participation on a kinship model. One can see in the myths of Concha *ayllu* (chap. 31, sec. 391) that genealogical connection alone was insufficient to bestow land on the two Concha lineages that had become politically disconnected. But adoption combined with political or marital alliance was seen as sufficient to create *ayllu* entitlements even when there was no genealogical tie (chap. 31, sec. 403). *Ayllu* was a political fact, and cultic practice lodged in it regulated practical matters of economy and power.

Llacta: *'village' as cultic and territorial unit*

By the time the Huarochirí manuscript was written, colonial coercion had overhauled the relationships between people and territory. If the prehispanic Huarochirí region resembled those known elsewhere in the Peruvian Andes, each of its major settlements probably controlled "archipelagos" of mostly non-nucleated residence spread over the various productive tiers of the mountain slope and the coast. But by 1608 the parishes where Avila was working—for example, San Damián de Checa, focal point of the manuscript—no longer entirely followed this model. Villages like San Damián had been carved out in a scheme of forced resettlement (*reducción*) that Viceroy Francisco de Toledo had begun almost forty years earlier. When administrators herded Andean peasants into resettlement villages (Gade and Escobar 1982; Spalding 1984: 214–216) they fused together multiple Andean settlements—the ones called *llacta* in prehispanic usage—into a larger, more accessible, more governable and exploitable "Indian town" on a Spanish plan with plazas, churches, and streets laid out on a grid. Most of the places with Spanish (saint) names in the manuscript belong to this Toledan reordering of territory.

Why, then, did people keep orienting their religion around a map that no longer strictly fit the productive space of politics and economy? After the initial coercions of resettlement, from the 1580s on, older relations to the landscape partly reasserted themselves both in practice and in ideology. In practice, productive efficiency and the chance to

hide from tribute collectors enticed people back upward into the non-nucleated pastoral hamlets of the heights and downward into relatively hidden farming settlements in river canyons (Málaga 1974). Nor, in imagination, did the establishment of a Christian sacred geography centered on parish churches empty the landscape of non-Christian meaning. The Huarochirí storytellers c. 1600 saw all around them their parents' ruined "old settlements" (*pueblos viejos*, a common term in papers of the period) and their ancestors' stone "houses of the dead." The pre-resettlement scheme of territoriality, a mental map of social groups attached to place-deities and localized ancestors, still formed a complete and intelligible shadow-geography projected onto the landscape that colonial organizations had already reshaped *de facto*. Immense *huaca*-studded spaces of canyons and high tundra, fields and trails, embodied an Andean world view at least as cogently as the small, dense space inside the new churches figured Christianity. Since outdoor space was also the space of work and livelihood, the very cycles of herding and farming continuously retaught what Sunday sermons sought to erase.

The commonest term for the anciently defined settlement, *llacta*, is not the simple equivalent of 'town' or 'village', which denote a portion of territory or the legal corporation that governs it. A *llacta* in its old sense might be defined as a triple entity: the union of a localized *huaca* (often an ancestor-deity), with its territory and with the group of people whom the *huaca* favored. The word *llacta* could thus be used to mean the deity that was master of a settlement. In chapter 24 (sec. 325), where the original text says that the "*llacta*s" divided up the llama herds among themselves, a marginal note clarifies that this means the "idols," that is, the *huaca*s that defined the *llacta*s, and our translation uses the latter sense.

The word *llactayuc* (glossed 'aborigine', 'native', or 'founder') therefore means something more complex than 'original resident'. It implies both being possessor of a local *huaca*'s sanctum and being possessed by it. When the heroes of the myths conquered lands and peoples, they also acquired local ritual obligations and even, it seems, grafted themselves into the genealogical categories reckoned from the *huaca*: "As we said in another chapter, this land was once all full of Yunca. As soon as Tutay Quiri's children had expelled those Yunca, they began to distribute among themselves, according to their own *ayllu*s, the fields, the houses, and even the *ayllu* designations" (chap. 24, sec. 316).

The chain of human movements and transformations by which the Checa people explained their social organization emphasizes at every stage a pattern of *huaca*s among whose territories human groups move and fight. *Huaca*s might travel on the way to establishing their dwellings but once victorious they had—they *were*—their locales, and it was the deity-locale that gave wealth and identity to human groups. The Checa explained all changes, both prehispanic and recent, with reference to the geography and the relative fortunes of *huaca*s. To the tellers, the explanation of society and its genesis was written out in the landscape—even where Spaniards had wrecked every visible monument or substituted crosses for *huaca*s.

Even now *llacta* is essentially the name of a relationship, not of a type of settlement. Like *ayllu*, the term implies no particular scale. In modern Quechua one calls any unit from one's hamlet to one's country "my *llacta*." Since the word gives no suggestion of size, either demographic or spatial, the manuscript usually leaves us guessing as to whether a given *llacta* is a hamlet, village, town, city, region, or country. The answer will come, if at all, from archaeological work as yet undone. Most of the actions in the myths seem from context to concern agricultural villages, and in most cases we have glossed *llacta* as 'village'. But 'town', 'city', 'region', and 'country' are hardly out of the question. When one visits the immense ruined city of Cajamarquilla, within the space of the manuscript but predating it, one wonders if the mythic scene could not have been far more urban than generally imagined.

The original text

The Huarochirí manuscript is ff. 64r–114r of manuscript number 3169 of the Biblioteca Nacional, Madrid. The original lacks title, date, and author. It is the fourth item among six manuscripts about Andean religion, from Francisco de Avila's own collection, all bound together. Among these writings are whole texts and abstracts from some of the most important sources on the subject, such as the *Relación de las fábulas y ritos de los Incas* ([1575?] 1959) of Cristóbal de Molina "cuzqueño" and the original of Joan de Santa Cruz Pachacuti Yamqui Salcamaygua's partly Quechua *Relación de antigüedades deste reyno del Perú* ([1613] 1968) as well as works by Juan Polo de Ondegardo and Garcilaso Inca de la Vega. It also contains the manuscript of Francisco de Avila's *Tratado*, a translation, or more accurately a paraphrase with digressive commen-

tary, of the same material contained in chapters 1–7 of the Huarochirí manuscript.

The Huarochirí manuscript is written in an ordinary competent scribal handwriting. The chapter divisions and titles used here are from the original. But the original does not have a consistent system of paragraph divisions or sentence divisions: some sentence boundaries are ambiguous. Various pen strokes resembling parentheses, commas, and other small symbols occur in the text, but they do not seem to add up to a consistent system of punctuation. (Scribal papers of the period normally lack consistent punctuation.) The text is in a variety of Quechua with the exception of the Spanish chapter headings of chapters 1–6, some borrowed Spanish words, and some marginal queries and annotations, probably by Father Avila. Irregular pagination and handwriting size indicate that the manuscript may have been compiled in noncontinuous bursts of effort. The text comes "from the hand and pen of Thomás," according to a marginal note over halfway through the text (chap. 23, sec. 291), but we do not know anything about "Thomás" save that he seems (from his Quechua-influenced errors in Spanish) not to have been a native—or a particularly accomplished—Spanish speaker. Whether he was only an amanuensis or was also the compiler of the testimonies is unknown. Thomás' practiced handwriting suggests he may have been an *escribano de naturales* (bilingual scribe), village council scribe, or other native functionary of the colonial regime.

The date of the Huarochirí manuscript is debatable. Avila's *Tratado* partially paraphrases the manuscript, or a draft of it, and bears the date 1608, so the manuscript seems *prima facie* to predate the end of 1608. But by how much? In chapter 9 (sec. 133) a narrator tells us it is *cay pisi huatallarac*, which at first glance seems to mean 'scarcely a year', since Father Avila came onto the San Damián scene. Were that reading unambiguous, we could agree that the date must be 1598 because, as Duviols ascertained, Avila arrived in Huarochirí in 1597 (Arguedas and Duviols 1966: 235). But *cay pisi huatallarac* could also mean 'just a few years', admitting a later date. And as Antonio Acosta's important researches (1987a, 1987b), summarized in the next section, suggest, there are strong reasons to consider dates considerably later than 1598.

The possible genesis of the text in the local conjuncture

The common attribution of the manuscript to Father Francisco de Avila is erroneous, but he certainly was a key figure in the local conjuncture that forced the manuscript into being. The following paragraphs summarize recent research by the Spanish historian Antonio Acosta, whose archival inquiry (1987b: 551–616) brings the local crisis into clearer focus and suggests a more plausible genesis for the text than the self-serving version available from Avila's own testimony.

The pioneer of seventeenth-century anti-*huaca* persecution was born in Cuzco probably in 1573, the abandoned, perhaps illegitimate baby of an unknown couple. The Spanish couple who found him at their doorstep gave him the Spanish name Francisco de Avila Cabrera. Avila later, but dubiously, claimed he knew his ancestry to be noble; others claimed he was half-Indian, and to his misfortune this became the common opinion. Acosta (1987b: 557–558) finds reason to question it. If Avila thought himself mestizo, it would have been against his interest to say so given the racial impediment to ordination during his youth, so his silence on the point cannot be decisive. One witness in 1610 called him mestizo, without proof, and a 1641 witness thought he looked Indian (Acosta 1987b: 556–557, note; Spalding 1984: 253–254). But these accusations of mixed birth came after Avila had risen to prominence and could well have been falsehoods intended to sabotage his career. Such doubts leave room to question the common supposition that his vengeful attitude to Indian religion grew from the pain of mixed (therefore impure and stigmatized) birth or from resultant abandonment.

Avila showed talent in a Cuzco Jesuit school and went to Lima to study at San Marcos University in 1592. In 1596 he was ordained and in 1597 posted as curate to San Damián de Checa, one of the *reducción* parishes near Huarochirí. It was a plum appointment. Avila's Jesuit connections probably had much to do with his career there, for the Jesuits over twenty years earlier had pioneered what they recognized as an unusually rich mission field—one where Andean religion had already shown strong resistance to some forty years of intermittent Catholic intervention. One passage (chap. 20, secs. 244–247) sketches the fluctuating, but never extinguished, fortunes of the *huaca* priesthood through three generations of colonial leadership.

Even within normal limits of law, a curate like Avila had access to ample native labor. But, in addition, by the date of Avila's arrival it had become usual though illegal for priests serving Indian parishes to parlay their ecclesiastical holiday levies and salaries, combined with legal leverage over native nobles, into business enterprises large enough to rival the incomes of rural Peru's opulent semi-feudal civil elite (Lavallé 1982). In time, it seems, this sort of practice led Avila into controversy. When he was a new curate, in 1598, an inspection praised his pastoral work. But a sign of conflict appeared in a 1600 "secret inspection and hearing" that turned up accusations of commercial abuses. Although he was officially cleared, the inspection reveals that like many rural clerics he had begun to make local enemies.

Four later inspections left Avila's record superficially restored. In 1607 Avila gathered testimonies on his "life and morals" to buttress his continuing appeal for a higher post. At the last minute, however, he met a fateful opposition: a faction of his native parishioners mounted an ecclesiastical lawsuit against him. Both colonial chieftains and commoners accused him, and their accusations were more numerous than in ordinary cases of this sort (frequent, to be sure, in the period). They accused him of absences from his parish (perhaps, Acosta suggests, he went to Lima in connection with his studies toward the doctorate; 1987b: 574), of charging excessive fees, and of exacting illegal labor levies. Like many other curates, he was said to collect huge amounts of native crops and sell them for private profit. Maybe natives tolerated this because priests of the Andean *huaca*s, too, had enjoyed huge gifts of produce (Acosta 1987b: 576). But Avila may have gone too far in helping himself to his parishioners' labor, which he used to support his partly illegal business enterprises in gunpowder, charcoal, and textile manufacture and to build himself a house in Lima using beams he made his parishioners remove from the roofs of their pre-resettlement village. In a period of declining native population, curates' rising and increasingly arrogant expectations of cheap or unpaid labor acutely angered some natives. It was apparently Avila's project to open a new textile factory at native expense that finally provoked chiefs of the "thousand" of Chaucarima to litigate against him.

The Indians went beyond economic grievances to introduce a doubt about Avila's religious and moral regularity, alleging sexual abuses of various native women (some married) and the fathering of an illegitimate son. He even forced Indian women, "under physical threats, to suckle at their breasts the same puppies which . . . when grown, chased and killed the Indians' chickens" (Acosta 1987b: 574). He beat up villagers, including his sacristan, for not serving his desires zealously enough. Once at a christening he hurled the oil at his sacristan's chest. Accusers said he encouraged Indians to give their venerated ancestors silver (see chap. 21, sec. 262) and then himself collected some of it (Acosta 1987b: 572).

.

If true, this suggests that in the early days of his curacy Avila had no urgent scruples about a *modus vivendi* with "idolatrous" religion. Apparently coexistence entailed the curate's acquiring traditional privileges of *huaca* priests—access to women, labor donations, crop gifts—and, in return, tolerating (or even profiting from) worship of *huaca*s on Catholic holidays (see chap. 7; chap. 9, sec. 125).

Avila spent some time in a church prison while charges were pending. But his emissaries pressed the natives to recant their accusations, and some did. The record of the trial contains a neat sheaf of the recantations, witness by witness, each with a cover sheet bearing Avila's elegant handwriting. One of Avila's allies in collecting these was the same Cristóbal Choque Casa whose visionary combats chapters 20 and 21 glorify, at that time an obscure son of native nobles. He prepared one of the recantations in Quechua (Taylor 1985: 180). In Acosta's judgment (1987b: 596), "It is believable that the narrative [i.e., the Huarochirí manuscript] could have been compiled at Avila's order in 1608, when his lawsuit with his Indians was in full swing, maybe on his emergence from prison and as a part of his reaction against the Indians who had accused him." Avila probably secured the testimony through one or more native cat's-paws who either interviewed anti-*huaca* natives or else secured the testimony of *huaca* believers by lulling them into unawareness of their testimonies' future utility. Cristóbal Choque Casa probably played a key role. It is hard to guess what parts fear, self-interest, and sincere conversion (Cristóbal's or others') played in the extraction of testimonies. Certainly intimidation played a part; for example, Avila made a point of interrogating Indians made vulnerable by frightening illnesses (Acosta 1987b: 600–601, 603). Although in later years Avila never mentioned the manuscript's existence, he probably did use it in hunting down *huaca*s.

When the court responsible for the Indians' suit took depositions in San Damián, a decision only minimally damaging to Avila appeared likely. But instead of letting procedure take its course, he seized the offensive by asking the Ecclesiastical Chapter of Lima to authorize an inquiry into "idolatries" under canon law. Avila, according to his own much later testimony written in 1645 (1918), then led the ecclesiastical judges to the *huaca*s Llacsay Huancupa (perhaps equivalent to Llocllay Huancupa, chaps. 20 and 21), Qqellccas Ccassu (probably *quill-cas caxo* or 'Engraved Rod', chap. 24, sec. 320), and Maca Uisa (chaps. 18, 19, 23). In later testimonies Avila claimed his campaign had arisen only from disinterested zeal, but Acosta's research makes it

believable that the campaign was undertaken in revenge against the natives who had accused him of venality and immorality.

According to the 1645 testimony (Arguedas and Duviols 1966: 220), it was Cristóbal Choque Casa's revelation that the feast of the Assumption in Huarochirí for 1608 would be used to cover a rite of Paria Caca that provoked Avila to undertake massive anti-*huaca* campaigns. It is likely, of course, that in reality nothing new was being revealed. The only new element was Avila's urgent need for favorable publicity. Avila intensified his sleuthing in 1608 and procured public confessions of "idolatry" in a parish meeting that stirred and mobilized his pro-Christian allies. He asked the Jesuits for assistance in confessing a deluge of penitents and was sent two helpers. They pioneered the routine of breaking images, burning mummies, extracting public confessions, and punishing believers that was to become the periodic scourge of Lima archdiocese Indians until at least the 1660s. Avila was able to collect a great deal of stolen religious gear and forced testimony. By September 1609 he was amply ready to dictate his answer to the native accusations, laying the groundwork for a false autobiography that painted the accusations as a reaction to his anti-*huaca* zeal.

It was also during this crisis that Father Avila prepared the *Tratado*, that unfinished pamphlet retelling and commenting on the same myths that make up chapters 1 through 7 of the Huarochirí manuscript. The relation between the redaction of the Huarochirí manuscript and Avila's work on the 1608 *Tratado* has been debated between Hartmann (1981) and Taylor (1982, 1987b: 17–18). The former thinks it probable that Avila based his treatise on the manuscript, while the latter thinks that the two are separate workings of a prior source probably consisting of interview notes. In either case, it is likely that Avila intended the *Tratado* as a readable exposé designed to win Spanish support for his career. At the time of the *Tratado*'s composition Avila needed public support because the archbishop of Lima, Toribio Mogrovejo, had set policy against the aggressive persecutions that Avila favored.

But, luckily for him, an opponent of gradualist policy toward "backsliding" Indians and a bitter foe of *huaca* religion, Bartolomé Lobo Guerrero, succeeded to the Archbishopric of Lima in October 1609. According to Taylor (1987b: 18), Avila left continued compilation of anti-*huaca* intelligence to an Indian associate. Although he did read and annotate part of the product, the Huarochirí manuscript, he never fully edited it.

A bare ten days after Lobo Guerrero's accession,

Avila seized the moment to make his case behind the archbishop's closed Lima doors. Shortly afterward he staged a public propaganda spectacular. Avila had carted a load of *huacas* and mummies "800 years old" into Lima, perhaps the ones he tracked down thanks to the testimonies recorded in the manuscript. Amid immense pomp and publicity he directed a giant auto-da-fé in Lima's great cathedral square on December 20, 1609. Thousands of natives were forced to attend. A spectacle of music, Quechua sermons, and whipping of believers culminated in public sentencing. Among the victims was Hernando Paucar, the same ex-priest of Chaupi Ñamca and early denouncer of *huacas* whose confessions had opportunely helped Avila. Paucar was tied to a post, lashed two hundred strokes, and condemned to confinement among Jesuits in faraway Chile. Avila then burned the *huacas* and the ancestral mummies, to the inconsolable grief of those who felt themselves orphaned.

Four days later an ecclesiastical judge absolved Avila of all the accusations pending. Moreover, he was granted the title of *"visitador* [traveling judge] of idolatries."

These events marked the opening salvo of the "extirpation of idolatry" campaigns, in which Avila and his Jesuit allies developed standardized methods to destroy the partly clandestine forms of Andean religion that had grown out of the long confrontation with Christianity (Duviols 1972). Within a year of becoming *visitador*, he executed repressive campaigns in the main parishes that the Huarochirí manuscript mentions and collected, as he claimed, some 5,000 "idols." In 1611 he went with a Jesuit crew to climb the heights via Yampilla just outside Huarochirí (chap. 31, sec. 409). The climbers trekked for several days up what may have been the ancient pilgrimage route. After the ascent they followed a stairway hewn into the rock (Bonavia et al. 1984), up to what Avila believed to be the shrine of Paria Caca himself. They demolished everything they could. Then the extirpators "put in its place a cross and in the afternoon they returned to San Lorenzo de Quinti, where [local people] received him with illuminations, and the Indians said in their own language, 'Paria Caca has died'" (Duviols 1966: 224).

Avila continued to campaign widely and became an influential figure in the Jesuit-centered anti-indigenous movement that intermittently lashed the archbishopric for most of the seventeenth century. While legally separate from the Inquisition, and in some respects different from it, the "extirpations" were to inflict on Andean society some of the same sufferings, and the same clandestinity,

that the Inquisition visited on Iberian heterodoxy. Avila's track of destruction crossed the wanderings of the great native chronicler Felipe Guaman Poma de Ayala ([1615] 1980: 3:1017, 1022–1023), who met some of his victims and, notwithstanding his own dislike of *huaca* religion, cursed Avila for his greed and mercilessness: "Oh what a fine doctor, where is your soul? What serpent is eating you?"

But if many of "the people called Indians" had reason to hate Avila, many of the Spanish, and not just his Jesuit allies, had cause to rejoice at his success. One reason was that *huaca* hunting appealed to clerics' and laymen's greed for treasure. Spanish law allowed confiscation of pagan deities' wealth, and the persecutory movement that Avila promoted opened a rich vein. Guaman Poma was among those who suspected that Avila's motives included the theft of precious objects belonging to *huaca* cults ([1615] 1980: 3:1022–1023). The anti-Andean campaigns also offered career opportunities to Peru's numerous churchmen at a time when the church was hugely overstaffed relative to its parish infrastructure.

Avila built a long and prosperous career on these campaigns and was to win renown for his anti-*huaca* scholarship as well as for his militancy in missionizing. In 1611, at Archbishop Lobo Guerrero's request, he wrote a report on "idolatrous" domestic rituals and local deities. After a series of attacks on deities mentioned in the Huarochirí manuscript and in other places, in 1615 he wrote at the request of the new viceroy, Príncipe de Esquilache, a project on the means to achieve "real conversion." The next year he conducted a gigantic tour of repression affecting some 35,000 persons. He wrote extensively on ways to influence and intimidate *huaca* worshipers, emphasizing both intimate persuasion and institutional ways to confine those sorts of Indians (notably the sons of native nobles) thought prone to lead or protect clandestine worship.

In 1618 he won a mid-ranking post in the Archbishopric of La Plata (seated in Chuquisaca, now Sucre, Bolivia) and held the job for fourteen years. Why the church hierarchs decided to employ him in a place so far from his political base is unknown; nor is much known about his career there. In 1632 he returned to the Cathedral of Lima to serve the newly appointed archbishop, Hernando Arias de Ugarte, an old acquaintance, as a canon of the Lima Cathedral. He came to be known as a durable eminence of the church, popular among Spaniards for his charitable donations. Almost at the end of his life, he petitioned to enter the Jesuit order, but his alleged mestizo background was used to thwart him. When in 1641 Archbishop Pedro Villagómez saw fit to remobilize the old persecutor as instructor for what was to become the second great wave of "extirpation," Avila seized the occasion to build his own monument as the "discoverer" of crypto-Andean heterodoxy. The self-portrait he painted in the 1645 preface to his *Tratado de los Evangelios* (Treatise on the Gospels) enduringly and, as Acosta shows, misleadingly influenced his historic image. The treatise reached the press in 1648, the year after his death. Its two volumes of Quechua and Spanish sermons, a little-known monument of literary Quechua's Baroque florescence, memorialize Avila's vision of a Counter-Reformation culture in Quechua.

Some twenty-three years after the making of the manuscript, Don Cristóbal still figured in a Concha lawsuit as a minor native official (Taylor 1983: 266, note; the date of Choque Casa's signature is 1631, not c. 1660 as Taylor holds). Certain of the *curaca*s mentioned in the manuscript appear in tribute records and lawsuits both before and after the manuscript. In general the careers of Cristóbal Choque Casa and the other Indian makers of the Huarochirí manuscript remain obscure.

Among provincial religious sources the Huarochirí text has no peer, but it has many companions. Detailed testimonies about peasant and provincial belief appear, for example, in the "extirpation of idolatry" trials of which the Huarochirí crisis (chaps. 20–21) was a forerunner (Acosta 1987a; Duviols 1972, 1986; Millones 1967; Silverblatt 1987). Some of the Catholic priests who organized "extirpation" themselves wrote monographs on the Andean provincial religions and how to persecute them (Albornoz [1583?] 1984; Arriaga [1621] 1968; Avila [1608] 1966). Many missionary treatises and reports from the field reveal local cults and the memories of older practice in vivid detail (for example, Calancha [1638] 1974–1982; Hernández Príncipe [1613] 1919, [1622] 1923). After the waning of the "extirpation" campaigns, the record becomes thinner but still workable through, for example, trials of shamans implicated in political assassinations via magic (Dammert Bellido 1974, 1984; Millones 1984; Salomon 1983).

There may be room for doubt about some extirpators' personal sincerity, but little doubt that they played on widely believed ideological propositions. Local social conflicts like those of Huarochirí c. 1598 conspired with endemic conflicts arising from challenges to the Spanish state's commercial and religious hegemony to infuse in Jesuits and other anti-Andean militants a grim seriousness. Fear of "heresy" (meaning Protestantism and the northern European powers beginning to rival Spain) and enduring hatred against Iberia's Muslim and Jewish cultures, long since driven into clandestinity, helped clerics persuade the state that the fight against Andean religion contributed to a decisive world-historical struggle. The papers born of this effort offer ethnographic evidence, but because of their heavy ideological freight must be read with caution.

Given these facts, one might expect to find the particulars of Andean religion, and eventually the very fact of Andean worship, distorted in the direction of familiar European fantasies of anti-Christianity: satanism, the black mass, and so forth. Such distortions did happen, especially at later dates and more urban locations than those of the Huarochirí manuscript (Silverblatt 1987: 159–196). Likewise, one might expect that missionaries would picture Peruvian *huaca*s in the image of more familiar "gentile" deities or "idols"—for example, the *dei* of Greco-Roman antiquity. This also did occur (MacCormack 1985).

But to a surprising degree the testimonies of the victims retain freshness and unfamiliarity that give *prima facie* evidence of an origin other than Iberian demonology or the classical legacy as enshrined in seminary curricula. Perhaps because many of them were provincials lacking the know-how to package and process their culture in terms familiar to Spanish speakers, the myth-tellers in the Huarochirí manuscript created an image still largely framed by conceptual categories proper to local thought. The Huarochirí stories retain for us a certain irreducible strangeness, resistant to translation because, unlike the preprocessed Inca lore available in chronicles, they were seized by Spain but not made for it.

Previous editions of the Huarochirí manuscript

The following are the extant complete editions of the text. No attempt is made to cover excerpts, retranslations, or popularizations. (For critical discussion, see Hartmann 1975, 1981; Taylor 1982.)

Adelaar, Willem F. H. 1988. *Het boek van Huarochirí: Mythen en riten van het oude Peru zoals opgetekend in de zestiende eeuw voor Francisco de Avila, bestrijder van afgoderij.* Amsterdam: Meulenhoff. Dutch translation (no Quechua) with introduction and glossary.

Arguedas, José María (trans.) and Pierre Duviols (ed.). 1966. *Dioses y hombres de Huarochirí: Narración quechua recogida por Francisco de Avila [¿1598?].*

Lima: Instituto Francés de Estudios Andinos/Instituto de Estudios Peruanos. [Republished 1975] México: Siglo XXI.

First full and published Spanish translation. Includes Quechua. Although less accurate than Taylor's translation of 1987, Arguedas' translation is esteemed for literary merit. Duviols' biobibliographical essay on Avila, questioned by Acosta, remains important for its pioneering historic inquiry and for its primary source appendices. These include Avila's *Tratado* and other papers relevant to Avila, such as extracts of important Huarochirí reports by mostly Jesuit observers. Mexican republication is incomplete.

Galante, Hipólito (ed. and trans.). 1942. *Francisco de Avila de priscorum Huaruchiriensium origine et institutis . . .* Madrid: Instituto Gonzalo Fernández de Oviedo.

Contains the thirty-one chapters but not the appendices. Introduction in Latin, facsimile, transcription, critical notes, glossary of hispanisms, Latin translation, Spanish retranslation by Ricardo Espinosa M.

Mejía Xesspe, Toribio [unpublished translation]

Toribio Mejía Xesspe, a bilingual scholar who worked closely with Julio C. Tello in the pioneering days of Peruvian prehistoric archaeology, left in his posthumous estate an as yet unpublished version of the thirty-one chapters of the Huarochirí manuscript. Prepared in 1941–1943, it includes a rephonologization, a Spanish translation attempting morpheme-by-morpheme correspondence, an incomplete "literal translation," and an incomplete "free translation" with pictorial sketches (Szemiński 1989).

Szemiński, Jan (ed. and trans.). 1985. *Bogowie i ludzie z Huarochirí*. Cracow/Warsaw: Wydawnictwo Literackie.

Polish translation with brief introduction and general glossary. The title means 'Gods and Men from Huarochirí'.

Taylor, Gerald (ed. and trans.). 1980. *Rites et traditions de Huarochirí: Manuscrit quechua du début du 17e siècle*. Série Ethnolinguistique Amérindienne. Paris: Editions l'Harmattan.

Bilingual edition containing introduction, transcription with variorum notes, and French translation with interpretative notes providing original solutions to some dialectological and lexical problems. Interpretative glossary, bibliography, and supplementary notes follow.

Taylor, Gerald (ed. and trans.), with Antonio Acosta. 1987. *Ritos y tradiciones de Huarochirí del siglo XVII*. Historia Andina, no. 12. Lima: Instituto de Estudios Peruanos/Instituto Francés de Estudios Andinos.

Bilingual edition containing interpretative introduction, transcription, "phonological reconstitution," Spanish translation, bibliography, several indices (to Quechua words in the translation, hispanisms in original, names of places and groups, names of *huacas* and heroes, names of rites, and names of historical personages). Copious critical, variorum, and interpretative notes closely address dialectological, geographical, and lexical problems. The preferred study edition.

Trimborn, Hermann (ed. and trans.). 1939. *Francisco de Avila: Dämonen und Zauber im Inkareich*. Quellen und Forschungen zur Geschichte der Geographie und Völkerkunde, vol. 4. Leipzig: K. F. Koehler Verlag. [Republished with additional introduction and notes as] Hermann Trimborn and Antje Kelm (eds. and trans.). 1967. *Francisco de Avila*. Quellenwerke zur Alten Geschichte Amerikas Aufgezeichnet in den Sprachen der Eingeborenen, vol. 8. Berlin: Ibero-Amerikanisches Institut/Mann Verlag.

The earlier (1939) edition was the first publication of the original Quechua. Research for the 1939 edition was interrupted by the Spanish civil war; later bombing destroyed most copies. Contains preface, bibliography, introduction, transcription, German translation with notes, glossary, exegesis (1967), index of proper nouns. Hartmann (1975, 1981) judges that superior accuracy justifies the republication.

Urioste, George (ed. and trans.). 1983. *Hijos de Pariya Qaqa: La tradición oral de Waru Chiri (mitología, ritual, y costumbres)*. 2 vols. Foreign and Comparative Studies, Latin American Series, no. 6. Syracuse: Maxwell School of Citizenship and Public Affairs, Syracuse University.

Bilingual Quechua-Spanish edition: introduction, transcription with variorum notes and marginal material, translation with variorum and interpretative notes, indices (to proper nouns, Quechua words in the translation), bibliography.

An unreliable English version of Avila's *Tratado* by Clements R. Markham (Avila [1608] 1875) was the first modern edition of the Huarochirí mythology.

The character of the present translation

This book is a fresh working not based on any previous translation (including Urioste's 1983 Quechua-Spanish edition). Our study started from a newly made transcription from microfilm (reproduced here), collaboratively rendered into English by the co-authors. It is meant as a reader's edition rather than a study text. Scholars in need of a study edition should turn to Gerald Taylor's Quechua-Spanish version (1987b), which offers abundant apparatus as well as fuller contextual references. The 1966 Arguedas and Duviols edition also contains indispensable primary sources and bibliographic detail. The present version refers to other translations by way of mentioning some significant discrepancies, difficulties, or contextual findings but does not provide full coverage of alternative renderings.

We hope to address nonspecialists and have striven not only for accuracy but also for immediacy. We have intentionally left enough unresolved

strangeness on the surface to keep a reader aware
that this text is untranslatable in all the usual
senses, and perhaps a little more untranslatable
than most.

Aside from the hazards intrinsic to all translations, Huarochirí readers face some specific ones.

Language substrates and non-Quechua languages

Oddly enough, it is not known exactly what relationship obtained between the Quechua of the
manuscript and the language in which Huarochirí
religious life was conducted. Many dialectological
and linguistic questions about the manuscript remain pending.

Even the origin of the Quechua dialect used in
the text itself is less than obvious. Its general affiliation is clear: it is one of the many and far-flung
kinds of Quechua grouped as Quechua A or Quechua II. At least one member of this group spread
widely through Andean America long before the Incas, and the Incas promoted a Quechua II dialect
(probably not identical to Cuzco Quechua) as their
administrative tongue. Perhaps working from this
precedent, the Spanish invaders styled a widespread
Quechua II (or perhaps several overlapping Quechua
II dialects) the "general language" (Cerrón-Palomino 1985: 552–553; Taylor 1985: 158–160). In ecclesiastical councils especially, Spaniards promoted
it for colonial use through efforts such as standardizing orthography and providing norms for translation and nontranslation of religious concepts.

"General" Quechua functioned c. 1600 as a lingua franca shared by many linguistically diverse
peoples including Spaniards, among them clergymen who used it to simplify missionary work in
a dialect landscape already reverting to pre-Inca
diversity. Colonial native chiefs and others who
traded on relationships with the Spanish also relied
on it. On the whole, this church-influenced "general" Quechua is the language of the manuscript.
The person who actually did the writing appears to
have learned the art of Quechua writing for ecclesiastical purposes. But precisely because it was a
partly artificial lingua franca—many speakers' second or third language and few if any speakers' first
language—specific examples of "general" Quechua
would normally be affected by underlying patterns
of local speech. Linguists disagree on whether the
text's peculiarities indicate an attempt to render
speech similar to Cuzco Quechua (Urioste 1973: 4)
or similar to the Quechua of modern Ayacucho
(Hartmann 1981: 189). Mannheim (1991: 195) notes
phonological reasons for questioning whether the

manuscript records any member of the group of
south highland dialects to which both Cuzco and
Ayacucho belong.

The question actually goes far beyond Quechua
dialectology. There is room for doubt about whether
any Quechua was the language of religious practice
or of the original testimony. In Huarochirí the particular version of Quechua that functioned as a
"general language" for such churchmen as Father
Avila still, at the probable date of the manuscript,
thinly overlay at least one non-Quechua Andean
tongue. Twenty-two years before the manuscript,
Diego Dávila Brizeño ([1586] 1965: 155) noted that
the common folk did not all know Quechua. A
1577 Jesuit report tells us that missionaries needed
to have Quechua sermons repeated in a local language "because the women there don't know the
general language" (Arguedas and Duviols 1966:
245). Almost two centuries after the Huarochirí
manuscript, another visitor observed that local use
of the "general language" sounded peculiar and
"mixed" (Taylor 1983: 270, 273). It is therefore
highly likely that the religious life of the generation
Avila persecuted had been conducted at least partly
in a language other than Quechua.

So the text probably stands at some distance
from habitual and traditional usages in religious
speech. We do not have any specific proof that the
texts were translated from a local tongue into Quechua, but the possibility cannot be discarded. At a
minimum it seems likely that processing of local
discourse by a person fluent in "general" Quechua
played a role in creating the text.

The following are languages that appear to influence and in some cases to underlie the Quechua text.

Quechua other than the "general" dialect

"Thomás" the scribe (or persons dictating to him)
probably knew at least one dialect of Quechua
other than the one the church promoted as "general." It may have been influenced by an Aymara-
like tongue (see below). It is also a possibility,
though a difficult one to demonstrate, that local
Quechua was influenced by a coastal speech proper
to the Yunca people whom Huarochirí folk considered aboriginal; their language, too, may have been
a Quechua different from the "general." Finally,
some usages in the Quechua of "Thomás" (e.g.,
chacuas 'old lady'; chap. 21, sec. 261) are attested
in Quechuas of the Quechua I or Quechua B group
native to the central Peruvian highlands. Quechua I
languages differ widely from the Quechua of the
text, but other colonial examples of mutual influ-

ence are known. In some cases the writer has hesitated between words of the Quechua II or A group, as, for example, in the repeated crossings-out of *punchao* 'sun' and substitutions of another word for 'sun': *ynti*. The discrepancy may have to do with Inca versus non-Inca religious vocabulary.

Language(s) of the Jaqi (Aymara) family

The terms "Jaqi" and "Aru" denote a group of languages today represented most notably by Aymara, an important language spoken from the Lake Titicaca basin southward into Bolivia. Jaqi tongues share some lexicon with Quechua but are entirely separate languages. Although Quechuas have displaced Jaqi tongues from a large part of their formerly enormous range, certain Jaqi languages (Kawki and Jaqaru) were and to some degree still are spoken in two areas close to the Huarochirí terrain (Briggs 1985: 546). Both areas are in Yauyos Province, from which Huarochirí people were thought to have immigrated (chap. 23, sec. 297; chap. 24, secs. 305–309; chap. 31, secs. 391, 408, 443). Taylor has argued that some of the testimony may have been given in a Jaqi tongue, because Aymarisms are common in the ritual terminology (e.g., the names of the two greatest celebrations described, *Auquisna* and *Chaycasna*). He also notes that certain "Aymara-type" phonetic alternations (*ñamca/ñamoc*, etc.; Taylor 1985: 162) commonly occur in words connected with Huarochirí religion, suggesting Jaqi interference. These Jaqi-like phenomena offer the strongest clue for identifying the ethnic language of the myth-tellers. It is probable that at a minimum the text has been modified from a more Jaqi-influenced speech toward "general" Quechua.

Non-Quechua, non-Jaqi native lexicon?

A few common nouns and many names of persons and places do not seem to derive by any evident route from Quechua, Jaqi, or Spanish. There may be an additional influence from an unknown ethnic tongue, perhaps predating the supraethnic Jaqi and Quechua diffusions. Huallallo Caruincho's name, the *hugi* monster he created, and the untranslated common nouns *callcallo* (chap. 31, secs. 413, 415) and *llaullaya* (chap. 21, sec. 271) may be examples. If so, the persistence of such words in both Quechua and Jaqi cultic vocabulary may eventually yield a clue to the antiquity of Huarochirí religious categories.

Spanish

Father Avila reported that most Huarochirí people knew at least some Spanish (Arguedas and Duviols 1966: 255). However, as Urioste notes, not all of the many Spanish words that found their way into the manuscript are there for obvious reasons. Some words do lack Quechua equivalents and are therefore hardly surprising: *cauallo* 'horse', *yglecia* 'church'. Others overlap Quechua terms but "cover a different semantic space" (Urioste 1982: 106). For example, *animalcona* ('animals'; Spanish with a Quechua plural marker) combines categories of wild and domestic beasts that, in Quechua, are named with separate words. But a few do have close Quechua counterparts and are not used out of any obvious necessity: *doze año* 'twelve years' (in Quechua a plural numeral obviates the need for a pluralizing suffix on the head of the phrase, hence the singular form *año*), *gato montés* 'wildcat', and so forth, which have close and obvious Quechua equivalents. It is not known why the writer chose them.

Although the text was probably made as a tool for excising Andean belief from the religion of converts, it sometimes uses Christendom's lexicon to name Andean religious categories. All the seven occurrences of *saçerdote* and *saçerdotisa* (Spanish for 'priest'/'priestess'; chap. 13, secs. 178, 183; chap. 18, sec. 224; chap. 20, sec. 252; chap. 21, sec. 273; supp. I, secs. 462, 466) refer to priests of *huacas*. *Saçerdotisa* suggests an analogy from the Renaissance lore of Greco-Roman antiquity, but some usages are more markedly Christian: the preface (sec. 2) categorizes the regional belief system as a *fe* 'faith', implying that as a whole it is an entity comparable in scale and kind with the True Faith. Given the tellers' and writers' free use of specialized Andean religious terminology, they probably did not include these words for the convenience of Spanish readers. It is more likely that there already existed some habitual code of correspondences perhaps arising unconsciously from the habit of expressing Andean ideas in a fashion responsive to Christian hegemony.

Sometimes the influence of Spanish norms operates in a hidden fashion by affecting choice between Quechua words. This is especially notable in sexual lexicon, where the pro-Christian speaker substitutes shame-oriented and therefore Spanish-like phrases for plainspoken Quechua ones. For example, in chapter 10 (sec. 151), the word *ollonchicta* 'our cocks' has been crossed out in favor of *pincayninchicta* 'our private parts' or, more literally, 'our shame'.

The problem of redaction

An editing process has given the manuscript a veneer of organizational unity. But no one has yet subjected it to text criticism detailed enough to uncover the "seams" where testimonies have been stitched together or to determine how many voices enter in. For the time being, this can only be recognized as an unknown requiring future study. It appears likely that the myth-tellers and retellers are multiple, probably from a minimum of three different places. Whether a separate translator beside the scribe and/or editor intervened is unknown. We neither know whether the interviewer used a written questionnaire (a common Spanish practice) nor whether the edited text as we find it was organized by a native researcher, by the scribe Thomás himself, or by someone employing native informants (Avila?).

It is highly likely that chapters 1–31 are rewritten and edited text, because they are fair copy (standardized at thirty-six lines per page) already augmented with contextual material, especially at beginnings and ends of chapters (Urioste 1973: 7–10). These chapters, however, appear to be an intermediate draft because editorial work continues in the form of interlinear and marginal comments and corrections (some seemingly in Avila's hand). Supplements I and II differ in grammar from the body of the manuscript, are written in a less polished handwriting, and come after a word meaning 'the end'. They may be surviving fragments of less-processed testimony. Or they may be a set of rough notes prepared by the editor/redactor on the basis of personal knowledge, apart from the compiled testimonies.

The problem of validation

One property of the text that may yield clues about the editing process if closely studied is the problem of validation. Quechua, like many American languages, requires the speaker to attach suffixes that clarify his or her relationship to the data conveyed. When conveying data learned from personal experience, the speaker uses the witness validator *-mi* (alternatively *-m*, *-n*), which implies that the content of the sentence or (sometimes) larger speech unit is something learned through direct sense experience. When passing on data learned secondhand—for example, an account heard from somebody else—the speaker will switch to the reportive (sometimes called "hearsay") validator *-si* (alternatively *-s*). We suspect that predominant reportive validation may reflect the intervention of a *re*-teller, perhaps a translator; but when speaking of legendary events, original informants might well have used it, too. When speculating without evidence, or when uncertain, the speaker employs the conjectural validator *-cha*.

There are two types of passage in the manuscript in which witness validation predominates. One is the contextual remarks and interpolated comments that appear to be supplied by someone other than the myth-telling informants, probably the editor/redactor. Sentences with *-mi* often introduce or end a chapter, stating with witness validation the relation of a *huaca* or ritual to a narrative or geographic context. Witness validation is normal in chapter titles. The preface has predominant *-mi*. Also, at least one contributor often uses *-mi* witness validation to report apparently contemporary local circumstances, as opposed to mythic or ancient events. For example, a mythic place name will be identified with a modern landmark using *-mi*. Accusations that local people are secretly carrying on some of the rites that the myths explain carry *-mi*: for example, *ynatacmi musiasca tucoy ynantin llactacunapipas rurancu* 'those who are privy to these customs do the same in all the villages' (chap. 9, sec. 133). The other passages in which *-mi* witness validation predominates are the two supplements, which appear to be rough notes. Perhaps their witness validation is related to their focus on contemporary ceremonies (and not ancient rites or myths of the past), which the writer or informant might have seen. Or perhaps, if they are transcriptions of unprocessed testimony, the validation is the original informant's own.

In the remainder of the text (the great majority of it), which consists of mythic narratives and descriptions of rites and rules of the past, reportive *-si* validation predominates. It is the usual validation of narrative passages: *cay chaupi ñamca sutiocsi huc runa anchi cochapi apo tamta ñamca sutiocpac churin carcan* 'the one called Chaupi Ñamca was the daughter of a man in Anchi Cocha, a lord named Tamta Ñamca' (chap. 10, sec. 142). Because it contains *-si*, this sentence could be rephrased 'Chaupi Ñamca was, they say, the daughter of . . .' Such locutions might be expected of any person telling a myth with a slight authorial distance. But *-si* could also come from a translator or reporter paraphrasing or repeating, without necessarily endorsing, an informant's words. A rendition using that assumption would be 'Chaupi Ñamca was, (s)he says, the daughter of . . .' These rephrasings are overtranslations insofar as the original does not contain the verb 'say' or imply anything one way or the other about who does the saying.

The exceptions to predominant *-si* reportive validation in narrative passages occur mostly in dialogue, where the characters speak what is putatively their own experience, and also in utterances that are not dialogue but performative speech (i.e., speech that actually changes the world rather than telling something about it): *camca vinaymi causanque tucoy hinantin sallcacunamanta huañuptinca huanacuctapas viconactapas yma ayca cactapas camllam micunque chaymanta camta pillapas huañochi sonque chayca paipas huañuncatacmi ñispas ñircan* 'You'll live a long life. You alone will eat any dead animal from the wild mountain slopes, both guanacos and vicuñas, of any kind and in any number. And if anybody should kill you, he'll die himself, too' (chap. 2, sec. 19).

There are passages and even whole chapters (e.g., chap. 9) in which it appears that the editor/redactor validates substantive content (as opposed to expository asides) with -*mi*, as if telling what he had seen with his own eyes. These passages tend to be descriptions of ritual, typically set in explicitly colonial context. A good example is the explanation of how Chaupi Ñamca's ritual dances were scheduled into a purportedly Catholic calendar (chap. 10, secs. 148–151). The authorial voice claims witness knowledge of incriminating facts, but coyly slips into reportive where naked dancing is concerned.

There are also passages in which significant mythic material is witness-validated. The crucial passage in chapter 9 (secs. 112–116) where Paria Caca lays down the fundamental rule of his cult is one. This validation may relate to the convictions expressed in the preface, which credits the narrative tradition with evidential worth comparable to that of Spanish writing. It is difficult, however, finally to decide whether such validation indicates belief in the factuality of the Paria Caca myth (on a witness's part or on the editor/redactor's part?) or only signals that some passages, the parts in the editor/redactor's own words, contain a true rendering of a story that may or may not finally be true.

Validation presents frustrating problems for translation, because nothing in English has rhetorical force similar to it. Added phrases like 'It's a fact that' (-*mi*), 'It's said that' (-*si*), or 'It could be that' (-*cha*) do convey validators' informational function, but at such expense to narrative quality as to falsify the text (by making it sound hesitant and colorless) more than they clarify it. We have availed ourselves of the regularities already noted in order to establish norms that minimize encumbrances on the text, while also alerting readers to each significant validation shift. (Some particulars of validation completely escape translation or are difficult to interpret, such as the many instances of a witness-validated discourse marker introducing a reportively validated sentence.) The redactor/editor's

stage-managing contributions routinely have witness validation, so the reader may assume its presence in sentences that are obviously editorial, even if they lack explicitly translated validation, unless an overtranslated phrase such as 'it's said that', 'they say', or 'reportedly' suggests otherwise. Such passages occur at the beginnings and ends of chapters. Mid-chapter editorial asides such as 'we told this story in the fifth chapter' (chap. 10, sec. 142) also routinely carry witness validation. In the chapter titles, too, readers should assume -*mi* witness validation. At mid-chapter validation shifts, notes signal how far the new validation extends. The two supplements are exceptions to these rules. In them the reader can assume witness validation throughout unless reportive validation is explicitly indicated.

Following such curtain-raising editorial formulas as 'the story goes like this' validation regularly shifts to reportive. 'In ancient times' and similar formulas also herald reportive passages. Generally, in the narrative passages of chapters 1–31, except in direct quotations, -*si* reportive validation may be assumed unless a phrase such as 'it's a fact that', 'in fact', or 'as we know' suggests otherwise. In direct quotations and performative utterances within the narratives, -*mi* can normally be assumed and is not specially marked. Readers interested in explicitly translated validation should look at Taylor's 1987b Spanish version, which translates validation more fully than we do (though still less than universally).

Translation of style

Validation is not the only respect in which the manuscript varies somewhat in tone and "feel" from passage to passage. Despite the likelihood that coerced elicitation, editing, and translation (or at least "correction" away from a local dialect of Quechua) put us at considerable distance from the myths' oral embodiment, and despite the probability that some of the testimony's oral qualities have been blurred as a result, nonetheless there do seem to be identifiable variations of oral-derived styles within the manuscript. We have tried to suggest them in the translation, giving the more bookish and editorial sentences a slightly different sound from utterances that probably replicate storytelling, ritual speech, and maybe even verse or song.

Framing sentences

An editorial voice intervenes particularly at the beginnings and ends of chapters as a stage manager of testimonies: 'we have already told', 'now we shall tell', and so forth. In the translation we have sought to make this "framing" verbiage easily recognizable by its semiformal and faintly pompous diction. Perhaps the person who composed the framing sentences is the same one who occasionally obtrudes with politically opportune comments:

> . . . no matter how people behave, neither the *alcalde* nor anybody else would ever try to stop them by asking, "Why do you do these things?"
> On the contrary, they dance and drink right along with them until they get drunk. And as for the Catholic priest, they fool him, saying, "Padre, I'm back from cleaning the canal, so I'm going to dance, I'm going to drink."
> As far as that goes, all the people do the same thing.
> True, some don't do it anymore because they have a good padre.
> But others go on living like this in secret up to the present. (chap. 7, sec. 95)

One possible source of such language is Cristóbal Choque Casa, Avila's political ally, who glorifies his own struggle against the *huaca*s in chapters 20 and 21. The same voice or pen may well be the source of the many passages that tell about non-Christian rites surviving clandestinely at the time of writing.

Narrative passages

The bulk of the chapters consists of myths and descriptions of past ritual practice. Often the "framer" alerts us to the shift to mythic discourse and the recalling of past practices with a formula such as *chay simire caymi* 'that story goes like this'. On the whole what follows is vivid and powerful narration, with *-si* reportive or "hearsay" validation predominating.

It is hardly accidental that translators differ on how "oral" or how "bookish" the manuscript is. Adelaar called his Dutch translation (1988) *Het boek van Huarochirí*. Our introduction also emphasizes the likelihood that its redaction was influenced by a European concept of the book and that the redactor thought of myth as material for the making of history books. On the other hand, Urioste gave his 1983 Spanish version a subtitle meaning 'The oral tradition of Huarochirí', and Taylor says that the manuscript "preserves the spontaneous composition of its oral informants" (1987b: 9). Arguedas, sensitive to both qualities, described it as "the voice of antiquity transmitted . . . through the mouths of common people," yet also called it "a little regional bible" (Arguedas and Duviols 1966: 9–10).

Taken separately, both the oral and the bookish emphases can easily turn into distortions that obscure the text's peculiar qualities. We see the intersection of orality and literacy as essential. Rather than filtering out bookish traits the better to approximate oral sources, we seek to capture a form of literacy in the act of engulfing one or more oral genres. This approach has the advantage of faithfulness to the manuscript's historic function. But it entails technical problems.

Something would be lost by simply leaving the translated text in solid blocks of page-filling prose like those of the scribal page. It would be a sacrifice of authenticity not to make at least some use of Dennis Tedlock's ([1971] 1983) and Dell Hymes' ([1977] 1981) demonstrations of how internal evidence helps the translator restore qualities of spoken performance to transcriptions that bury performance rules in prose conventions, because some qualities of oral genre do shine through the editorial veils.

It might even be feasible to produce a fully ethnopoetic rendering of at least some Huarochirí texts (that is, one whose goal is to restore oral organization, with versification, by detecting written correlates of pauses, turns, etc.). We have not followed this method entirely, because, for reasons already mentioned, we doubt our ability to create a hypothetical likeness of the performances from which the manuscript was compiled (or, more likely, recompiled from earlier notes). Also, to make explicit the features that warrant line and stanza breaks (etc.) requires putting into the English text many particles that impede fluent reading of narrative content. Finally, it may be that some of the pauses marked with *chaymanta* 'and next' and the like do not reflect local norms of oral performance but rather are effects of making the speaker (translator?) wait for the scribe to catch up.

Though inhibited by these caveats, we have sought to indicate, partially and tentatively, some performance qualities of the Huarochirí material detectable within the bookish frame that is also part of its substance. Like most Native American narrative texts, the Huarochirí manuscript is spotted with innumerable "empty" words or discourse markers, especially at the beginnings of sentences, that add no literal content to the flow of action. Common ones include, for example, *chaymanta* 'and next' or 'after that', *chaysi* 'so' (with reportive validation), and *chaymi* 'so' (with witness validation). Translating these words directly gives an effect the very opposite of oral. It makes the text sound hesitant and finicky, disrupted. But they are, of course, not "empty" in spoken performance; they serve to separate utterances in a patterned way, imparting a quality of measure and helping the listener keep pace. We believe they served this function in the oral performances that the manuscript partly mimics and have tried to convey as much. Some words that we read this way are sentence-initial *cay* 'this'/*chay* 'that'; *ychaca* 'however'; *yna*, *ynaspa*, and other derivatives of *yna* 'thus'; *ña* and *ñatac* 'already', 'then', 'so', 'again'; *huc . . . huc* and *huaquin . . . huaquin* 'some . . . others'. Certain other touches, such as emphasized changes of topic or words indicating change of time or setting, also are taken as signaling a new "turn." Many sentences begin with clauses whose informational contribution is minimal (*chay yna captinsi* 'while it was like that') but which similarly seem to serve a function of measure or pace, introducing a new burst of the storyteller's speech.

Our objective is a compromise, an attempt to make a likeness of the manuscript that suggests its "feel" as a manuscript: that is, a prose presentation following norms of book organization, which for long stretches subsumes oral performances without strictly transcribing them. Stopping short of an attempt to reconstruct the oral performances that the writers heard, but also stopping short of an undivided prose that would silence their clearly audible echo, we have chosen to render the above-mentioned discourse markers and other devices of measure into prose divisions that somewhat suggest the quality of turn or strophe, namely, short indented paragraphs. (The section numbers alongside them are only meant as aids to correlating with the transcription.)

Another "oral" characteristic of the Huarochirí manuscript is heavy reliance on direct quotation and dialogue. Quechua *ñispa . . . ñin* 'saying . . . (s)he said' delimits quotations, but instead of translating the formula we have simply used 'said' and quotation marks (unlike Taylor 1987b, who often favors indirect quotation). Because the Quechua verb *ñiy* can mean 'to think' or 'to intend' as well as 'to say', some direct quotations are rendered as quotations of thought: *ñocaracpas ñaupac umanman chayaiman ñispa* 'thinking, "I mean to get to the summit first!" ' (chap. 9, sec. 120).

In order to clarify the dialogue structure of many passages, we have placed each turn of quoted speech in a separate indented paragraph, even when the original quotes more than one speaker within a single sentence. Most Huarochirí dialogue (and narration) sounds lifelike and colloquial, and to convey this quality we freely use English contractions ('isn't',

etc.). In some cases, a quotation contains several sentences that sound like simultaneous comments on the same point, and in these cases we have interpreted the effect as a chorus of comments:

> Then they derided Quita Pariasca with spiteful words:
> "That smelly mountain man, what could he know?"
> "Our father Paria Caca has subjects as far away as the limits of the land called Chinchay Suyo. Could such a power ever fall desolate?"
> "What does a guy like that know?" (chap. 18, sec. 223)

Question marks in the translation securely reflect Quechua grammar, but exclamation points are supplied. Parentheses are also supplied.

Versified speech in semantic couplets

A few passages clearly employ the Andean oral device called "semantic coupling" or "thought rhyme" (Mannheim 1985), and we have rendered them as couplets. They appear inset in the translation. The semantic couplet is a pair of sentences that express closely related ideas phrased in related (sometimes syntactically parallel) fashion. Semantic coupling is common in modern Andean folk poetry and song, as in many of the world's oral traditions. Huarochirí examples include:

> We go in Tutay Quiri's steps,
> We go in the path of his power. (chap. 11, sec. 158)

> Tell me, I beg: what have I done to make them ill?
> For what fault of mine do I live in suffering? (chap. 13, sec. 179)

Semantic coupling typically occurs in invocations to, or sayings of, sacred beings—*huacas* themselves, legendary ancestors, priests and oracles delivering responses, or Christian deities. Cristóbal Choque Casa's moving prayer to the Virgin Mary (chap. 20, secs. 254–255) consists largely of couplets. It might be an example of those "devout and elegant" religious songs that Jesuits in Huarochirí heard "idolatry" defendants sing in their cells at night c. 1620 (Arguedas and Duviols 1966: 259–260). Much earlier witnesses, the Jesuits who conducted the path-breaking mission of 1571, found out that such songs were reworkings of prehispanic hymns: "The same [hymns of praise] which in former times they used to give to the sun and to their king, they have converted into praise of Jesus Christ by taking material from what they heard preached" (Arguedas and Duviols 1966: 243). Some couplets are brief ritual formulas rather than hymns and a few might be humbler bits of folk song or familiar sayings.

Margot Beyersdorff (1986: 219) comments that in the Huarochirí manuscript "intercalated fragments of sacred verse . . . follow the same norms of versification as the 'prayers' of [Cristóbal de] Molina ["cuzqueño"] and [Felipe Guaman] Puma de Ayala, and can be included in the genre *wayllina*." She does not identify the fragments. Beyersdorff infers from Molina that *wayllina* denominated a specific verse form unique to sacred speech. Husson (1985: 330–331), on the contrary, emphasizes Guaman Poma's couplets' affinities to popular and profane song.

Other translation conventions

In addition to translation problems arising from idiosyncrasies of the Huarochirí text, the translation reflects some decisions that face anyone working from Quechua. Readers who want to avoid spurious accuracy in using the translation should take note of them.

This book does not aspire to morpheme-by-morpheme translation, for several reasons. Rendering an agglutinative language morpheme-by-morpheme (to the degree that it is possible at all) yields verbose, obscure formulations. The following example of a translation process uses the slash (/) to signal morpheme boundaries and suggests the sort of problems that occur within a single random and typical clause. The original is *ña chori/n/cuna/pas collo/pti/n/rac/si* . . . Analyzed using Urioste's (1973) terminology, this clause consists of three roots (italicized), each with additional morphemes: *already child* / (3d person) / (plural) / (additive) *perish* / (contrastive adverbial) / (third person) / (continuative) / (reportive validator) . . . This could be rendered, forcing a morpheme-by-morpheme translation, as: *already child* / his / (plural) / even *perish* / (verb with different subject to follow) / they / first / it's said . . . To make intelligible English one must drop a morpheme (-*pti*) that has and needs no English analogue and make choices whether to translate -*pas*, -*raq*, and -*si* explicitly. We chose not to translate most -*si* reportive validators, and the remaining content can be made clear by implication in a simple English form: 'When his children had already perished . . .' (chap. 19, sec. 233; the referent of 'his' is supplied in the body of the translation).

Our translation generally preserves sentence boundaries, but in some cases the original sentences contain chains of subordinate clauses so long that a single-sentence translation (without Quechua's devices for clarifying switches of subject) comes out congested. In these cases sentences have been divided. Sometimes the order of clauses has been altered. The order of sentences has not been altered. Where sentence boundaries are significantly uncertain, notes indicate the alternate readings. Where the grammatical subject of a sentence is unstated but unambiguous in the original, an explicit subject has been supplied in English. In cases of ambiguity, we tried for English translations with a similar ambiguity. Where this was not achieved, notes indicate the nature of the ambiguity.

Aside from unique cases, there are generally common sources of ambiguity (as the English reader sees it) in regard to gender, number, and time. Quechua does not have grammatical male-female gender and in some cases the sex of a named person is unclear (for example, the master weaver mentioned in chap. 1, sec. 8). Also, because singular forms may be used to mean plural, Quechua nouns are sometimes indefinite as to singular and plural. Finally, the tense in Quechua that most resembles English present sometimes refers to a (usually recent) past, making certain sentences ambiguous as to whether they describe current reality. Such cases are noted where they cause significant doubt about the meaning of a passage.

A given root, especially a verb root, is not always translated by the same English word because the root with its varied suffixes often gives a net sense that varies from the root sense by a distance that only a different English word can render. In the following example the common verb root *yalli-* ('to exceed, surpass') yields English 'to compete' when coupled with the suffix -*naco-* (denoting reciprocal action) but English 'to win' when not modified: *pomacta aparispa yallinacoson* 'Let's compete in putting on puma skins' (chap. 5, sec. 64); *pomancunacta aparispa yallita munarcan* '[he] wanted to win by wearing the puma skins he had' (chap. 5, sec. 64). However, in passages where repetition appears to be an element of rhetoric or measure, as, for example, with the four-times repeated *canancama* 'until now' in the preface, the translation mimics the repetition.

The numbers given in the margin are added by the translators. Numbered sections are there only to help readers compare the original and the transcription and to facilitate index references and cross-references. They do not define a unit intrinsic to the method of composition.

The translation does not show the small pen strokes and marks (symbols?) scattered in the original manuscript. The punctuation is added. In addition to sentence-, quotation-, and clause-delimiting punctuation, we have added:

( ) Parentheses to signal apparently parenthetical remarks in the original text.

> (This spring flowed from a large mountain that rises above San Lorenzo village.
> This mountain is called Suna Caca today.)
> At that time, they say, it was just a big lake. (chap. 6, sec. 81)

[ ] Square brackets to signal marginal or crossed-out material on manuscript pages.

< > Angle brackets to identify translators' words referring to marginal or crossed-out material.

> <**margin**, in Quechua:> [Paria Caca crossed over to the village of the Cupara.] (chap. 6, sec. 80)

We have translated crossed-out material (words or phrases) that adds substantively to the text, but not crossings-out that only change a spelling or crossed-out single morphemes or letters. All these details are reproduced in Taylor's (1987b) study edition.

Note conventions

Unless otherwise noted, English versions of quotes from non-English sources in notes and in this introduction are by Salomon. Sources cited in notes appear in the general bibliography. Notes provide context sufficient only for novice readers and do not contain full comparisons with other translations or exhaustive references to literature.

Transcription conventions

The transcription strives for the nearest simulation of the original page's qualities compatible with easy comparison to the translation.

The page breaks, signaled with *foja* or folio notations *R* for recto and *V* for verso, are those of the original.

In the transcription the following conventions are used:

Uppercase letters stand for large letters in the original. The original does not use uppercase (rare in scribal papers) but does use large lowercase letters in headings.

[ ] Square brackets contain the section numbers for keying passages to corresponding parts of the translation.

< > Angle brackets identify crossed-out material in the original.

( ) Parentheses identify the expansion of abbreviations. For example, the original's *ca-piº* is rendered *capi(tul)o*.

Toponymic and onomastic spelling conventions

It is important to note that in the translation (not the transcription) we have standardized the names of persons, places, and *huaca*s so that each has (as nearly as possible) only one name in English context, regardless of the often considerable variations in the original. (Exceptions are cross-referenced in the index.) When the original spelling varies, it is standardized in the translation according to the following rules:

First: If a proper noun appears only once in the manuscript, or if all occurrences are spelled the same way, we have retained the original spelling.

Second: If a proper noun has multiple spellings in the manuscript, we have chosen one of these and maintained it throughout the translation and index. The criteria for choosing the form are:
1. For words ending alternately in *o* or *u*, we selected the *u* ending.
2. Wherever *i*, *e*, and *y* vary, *i* was selected.
3. Wherever *s*, *ss*, *x*, and *ç* vary, *s* was preferred. The manuscript's apparent sound system does not preclude reading *x* as a palatalized fricative different from *s*, nor does it conclusively prove this to be correct.
4. Wherever *n* and *m* alternate in final position, *n* was selected.
5. Wherever *ai* and *ay* alternate, *ay* was selected.
6. Wherever *hua*, *gua*, and *ua* alternate, *hua* was selected.
7. Wherever *quia* and *quio* alternate with *cya* and *cyo*, the latter spellings were selected.

Some place names as standardized are different from their nearest modern equivalents (identified in notes at the toponym's first occurrence). For example, the modern place is written *Huarochirí* but the manuscript uses *guaro cheri* and *huaro cheri*. We use the latter in the translation. Such standardizations from the text, not modern toponyms, appear on the map.

In Spanish names (Thomás, Luzía, etc.) we have

conserved the manuscript's spelling and added the acute accents corresponding to their modern forms.

A caution: standardizing is intended to minimize the novice reader's problem in keeping track of the *dramatis personae* and to make the index simpler. But it sacrifices data important to the analysis of the original text's sound system, to its dialectology, and to source criticism. Students who need such data are urged to use the transcription.

In the transcription and translation, we have followed a common Quechua structure of proper names by treating them as two-word phrases (Paria Caca, Huatya Curi, etc.). Large onomastic corpuses such as the 1588 *revisita* of Sisicaya clearly show that Huarochirí names are binomial, whether or not a space separates the elements (Archivo General de la Nación, Buenos Aires, ms. 13-17-5-1). Applying this norm involves some interpretation because word boundaries in the original are sometimes inconsistent or unclear. By normal Quechua syntax rules, the first word would express an attribute applying to the second; some names can be interpreted using this rule (e.g., Sullca Yllapa 'Last-born Lightning'; chap. 8, sec. 108; chap. 16, sec. 202). Indeed, Huarochirí onomastics remains problematic in general; uncertainty about whether all the names are binomial is only one of many ob-stacles preventing general translation of proper nouns. A few name meanings are nonetheless clear enough and important enough to warrant bringing them into the translation (e.g., Pacha Camac Pacha Cuyuchic 'World Maker and World Shaker').

Index and glossary

The index gives numbered section (not page) references to both proper nouns and topics and themes, classifying many specific items under rubrics common to anthropology (e.g., for material on sibling relationships, look under "kinship"; for the symbolic value of red, see "color"). The references are to the translation, not to the Quechua original. An instance of a proper name supplied in the translation will be indexed even if only a pronoun or an unambiguous implied reference is present in the original. Personal names are alphabetized according to the first term of the native name. For example, *Diego Chauca Huaman* is alphabetized under *Chauca*. The glossary of untranslated words lists all the terms that appear italicized in the translation, giving simple glosses and numbered section references to all their occurrences. Material in notes is not indexed.

THE HUAROCHIRÍ MANUSCRIPT

[Preface]¹

If the ancestors of the people called Indians² had known writing³ in earlier times,⁴ then the lives they lived would not have faded from view⁵ until now.⁶

As the mighty past of the Spanish Vira Cochas⁷ is visible⁸ until now, so, too, would theirs be.

But since things are as they are, and since nothing has been written until now,

2   I set forth here the lives of the ancestors of the Huaro Cheri people, who all descend from one forefather:⁹

---

1. The whole preface has witness validation, suggesting that it expresses the native editor/redactor's own convictions. Quechua grammatical validation is discussed in the introduction, in the section on the character of the present translation (see especially the section on the problem of validation). The opening lines have a sharp rhetorical structure. They start with a matched pair of contrafactual sentences (-*man* . . . -*man*), continue with a matched comparison (*hina* . . . *hina*), and link the two pairs by a pointed contrast between their respective conclusions (. . . *manam . . . hinacho canman/ . . . hinatacmi canman*, which might be rendered 'it wouldn't be so/ . . . it would be exactly so').

2. *runa yn(di)o ñiscap* 'of the people called Indians': suggests a shade of authorial distance from the term "Indian," perhaps because it lumps together the many distinct peoples whose differences and relations form the axis of the text. The phrase recurs at the very end of the text (supp. II, sec. 485).

3. *quillcacta* 'writing': more literally, 'writer(s)'; derives from a verb whose prehispanic sense appears to have been 'to paint' or 'to ornament' (Gonçález Holguín [1608] 1952: 301).

4. *ñaupa pacha* 'earlier [or former] times': although other translators give 'ancient', this passage could also refer to an earlier moment of the colonial era.

5. *chincaycuc hinacho canman* 'would not have faded from view': more literally, 'would not be like something getting lost'; that is, if Andean tradition partook more of literacy, colonial conditions would not have led to its recent erosion.

6. The four repetitions of *canancama* 'until now' give a feeling of arrested motion, released at last in the final sentence of section 2. Similarly, the sentence verbs of section 1 form a series of three contrafactuals (with conditional suffix -*man*) that yields in section 2 to three finite verbs, in past, present, and future tenses, respectively. The tone shifts from speculation toward concreteness and dynamism. One feels the engines of narration gripping, moving forward.

7. The original contains only *vira cochappas* 'the Vira Cochas', a colonial and modern Quechua usage that employs the name of a principal deity (salient in chapters 2 and 14) to refer to the Spanish. The Spanish erupt onto the Andean scene under this name in chapter 18 (sec. 223). Modern Cuzco Quechua still uses the expression. We have supplied 'the Spanish' to avoid confusion between the deity and the nationality.

8. The verb *ricurin* 'be visible' seemingly emphasizes the *visibility* of the new Spanish mnemotechnology, writing, as opposed to the *audibility* of the endangered oral tradition.

9. *huc yayayuc . . . machoncunap* 'ancestors . . . from one forefather': more literally, 'of the old ones . . . possessors of one father'. The manuscript repeatedly expresses diachrony in terms of patrilineal ancestry. The point in this passage is that, despite their diversity, the social units that are protagonists of the following chapters unite at the apex in a single male progenitor, namely, Paria Caca.

What faith[10] they held,[11] how they live up until now,[12] those things and more;

Village by village it will be written down:[13] how they lived from their dawning age onward.

---

10. *yma ffeenioccha* 'what faith' uses a Spanish term, *fe* 'faith', to denominate non-Christian religious practice. In Christian context this categorizes the *huaca* cults as members of the same class of phenomena as the "true" faith (and therefore subject to graver penalty than mere "superstition"). Quechua had no term similar to *fe*. But the suffix *-yoc*, usually translated 'possessor of', is usually used in the manuscript to signify a non-Christian worshiper's bond to the *huaca*. It signifies not so much belief as a social connection in which the worshiper owes service and the deity protection.

11. The original *ffeenioccha* has a conjectural validator *-cha*: overliterally, 'what faith they may have held'. One common usage of *-cha* is to convey the degree of doubt appropriate to guesses about what is in another person's mind (secs. 133, 247, 279). Here *-cha* suggests that the author regards knowledge of the ancient religion (based on the reportively validated data that make up most of the manuscript) as a conjectural construct, in effect an ethnographically derived model intended to explain "idolatrous" practices of the present.

12. In addition to the reconstructed faith of the past, the maker of the manuscript will also set down ethnographic observations on current mores. Most of this material appears with witness validation in subsequent parts.

13. In fact, the manuscript does not proceed village by village. It expresses primarily the viewpoint of one group, the Checa of San Damián village, and secondarily those of perhaps three other groups (the inhabitants of Mama in chap. 13, the Allauca in chap. 30, and the Concha of Concha Sica in chap. 31) filtered through some Checa interference. In spatial terms its mythology centers on the Checa ceremonial center, Llacsa Tambo, near the colonial village of San Damián.

CHAPTER I

How the Idols of Old Were,
and How They Warred among Themselves,
and How the Natives Existed at That Time[14]

In very ancient times,[15] there were *huacas*[16] named Yana Ñamca and Tuta Ñamca.[17]

Later on another *huaca* named Huallallo Caruincho defeated them.

After he defeated them, he ordered the people to bear two children and no more.[18]

He would eat one of them himself.

The parents would raise the other, whichever one was loved best.[19]

4 Although people did die in those times, they came back to life on the fifth day exactly.[20]

And as for their foodstuffs, they ripened exactly five days after being planted.

These villages and all the others like them were full of Yunca.[21]

<**margin**, in Quechua:> [full of Yunca]

5 When a great number of people had filled the land, they lived really miserably,[22] scratching and

---

14. Like all of the first six chapters, this one bears a Spanish title in the original: *Como fue anteguamente los ydolos y como guerreo entre ellos y como auia en aquel tiempo los naturales.* In the original the Spanish titles appear to be insertions *ex post facto.* Their awkwardness often derives from specific Quechua interferences: for example (in this case), discrepancies between Quechua and Spanish rules about pluralization and number agreement (*fue . . . los ydolos,* etc.). Quechua's trivocalic sound system influences *anteguamente* via hypercorrection. The composer of the titles has also chosen an unidiomatic translation for *tiay* 'to dwell, to exist'. Such facts make it more than likely that Spanish was not his or her first language.

15. This formula regularly introduces a passage with reportive validation.

16. As detailed in the introduction, *huaca* is a broad term designating all physical objects taken to embody superhuman and sacred persons. Many mountains, springs, river junctions, mummies, and manmade objects as well were *huaca.*

17. The untranslated term *Ñamca* seems to designate a class of *huaca*s associated with coastal peoples and the remote past. It also appears as a component of names of persons favored by *huaca*s. In Quechua *Yana* means 'black' and *Tuta* 'night', so these might well be the powers extant before the present, solar world began.

18. *yscayllacta huachacunampac camarcan* could also mean 'he ordered people to give birth only by twos'. But when Francisco de Avila, who presumably knew the context, composed his *Tratado* using the same or a similar source, he chose this meaning ([1608] 1966: 200).

19. *huctas mayquintapas cuyascanta* 'whichever one was loved best' is ambiguous as to whether it means the one that the parents loved best or that Huallallo Caruincho loved best (because the *-n* third person possessive marker on *cuyascan* could refer either to the parents or to Huallallo).

20. Chapter 27 elaborates on this.

21. *yunca,* a common term in the manuscript, has a triple sense. It refers to the warm valley regions of the Pacific littoral; to the ecology, landscape, and biota typical of such regions; and (capitalized in translation) to the peoples who dwelled there. The Checa and other highlanders thought of Yunca people as aboriginal, in opposition to the invading peoples with whom at least some of the narrators identified.

22. The motif of an overfertile ancient humanity in Malthusian crisis reappears in chapter 27; it is analyzed by Fernando Fuenzalida (1979). The idea seems to be that by excessive human sacrifice to Huallallo they won excessive vitality. The argument implies that immortality is incompatible with human life: even if fertility were curbed to the extreme of allowing each immortal couple only one live (immortal) child, an overpopulation fatal to well-being would eventually ensue. Death is indispensable.

digging the rock faces and ledges to make terraced fields.

These fields, some small, others large, are still visible today on all the rocky heights.

And all the birds of that age were perfectly beautiful, parrots and toucans[23] all yellow and red.

6   Later, at the time when another *huaca* named Paria Caca[24] appeared, these beings and all their works were cast out to the hot Anti lands[25] by Paria Caca's actions.

Further on we'll speak of Paria Caca's emergence and of his victories.

7   Also, as we know,[26] there was another *huaca* named Cuni Raya.[27]

Regarding him, we're not sure whether he existed before Paria Caca or maybe after him.

<**margin**, in Spanish:> [Find out whether he[28] says that it isn't known if he was before or after Caruincho or Paria Caca.]

However, Cuni Raya's essential nature[29] almost

---

23. *caquipas*: 'toucan' is a guesswork translation. Although the color suggests 'macaw', other references (chap. 9, sec. 131; chap. 24, secs. 331, 333) show that different words refer to macaws. Chapter 16 (sec. 207) says *caqui* is a parrotlike bird. Taylor (1987b: 47) points out an Ayacucho usage of *caqui* meaning a large parrot and an Aymara reference saying that *caqui* has long red, blue, and yellow feathers. Mejía Xesspe (Szemiński 1989: 6) chose *periquito* 'parakeet'.

24. This is the first mention of the dominant deity in the manuscript. Paria Caca is surely a sacred mountain, but which one? Bonavia et al. (1984: 5–7) offer a detailed identification: "Pariacaca Mountain has a distinctive shape, two twin snowcapped peaks with a saddle-shaped depression separating them. The low point between them is 75° 59' 24" longitude west and 11° 59' 20" latitude south (Department of Junín, Province of Jauja, District of Canchayllo, Peru)." Bonavia and his co-authors point out that because Paria Caca was close to the royal road from Lima to Cuzco, it was well known by sixteenth-century authors, including Dávila Brizeño (who drew it as a twin peak on his map; Rostworowski 1988: unpaginated insert) and Avila. Avila's own 1611 description of Paria Caca (Arguedas and Duviols 1966: 257) is compatible with Bonavia's identification. Modern villagers in Huarochirí readily identify a twin-peaked snowcap on the eastern horizon as Paria Caca.

The literal sense of Paria Caca's name is unclear. *Caca* means 'cliff' or 'crag' in ancient and modern Quechua. Arriaga's *The Extirpation of Idolatry in Perú* ([1621] 1968: 45; Keating's translation) suggests that Paria might be 'vermilion': "*Paria* are powders of a vermilion color, brought from the mines of Huancavelica and made from the metal from which mercury is derived, though its appearance is more like that of lead oxide."

Several common modern verbs with the root *pariy* express the idea of heat radiating from a solid object; there may be a connection with chapter 8 (sec. 103), where Paria Caca creates his shrine by quenching a huge fire.

But Urioste's suggestion (personal communication) that *Paria* is cognate to modern Cochabamba Quechua *pari* meaning 'split' (as in, for example, a harelip) is also tempting because of the mountain's cleft appearance.

25. *antiman*: more literally, 'toward the Anti'. The Incas termed the eastern slopes of the Andes and the

western fringes of Amazonia *Anti Suyu*. *Andes* in Spanish usage c. 1600 usually meant the same region. These lands stand in most Andean mythology for savagery and the precultural life, a setting in which Huallallo might have been thought to belong. But it may also be that the Huarochirí narrators used *anti* in a more general way to mean warm lowlands, including the seaward valleys of the west Andean slope. When Francisco de Avila paraphrased a source similar or perhaps identical to this one, he said that the natives call hot lands "*yunca* or *andes*" and wrote of evil aborigines in "these Andes" (*estos andes*) whom Paria Caca expelled to "other Andes" (*otros andes*; *Tratado* [1608] 1966: 200; see also 216). The two *andes* areas are perhaps the Pacific lowlands and Amazonia, respectively. Because the term may be generic (a type of land) and not toponymic, we have avoided glossing *anti* as 'Amazonia'.

26. 'As we know' added to indicate witness validation, which continues to the end of the chapter.

27. The predominantly coastal *huaca* Cuni Raya has been identified as a water deity, creator of irrigation (Rostworowski 1977). The Incas thought the ability to create rivers and springs was the unique sign of his power (Betanzos [1551] 1987: 264). Chapters 2, 14, and 31 (secs. 409ff.) belong to Cuni Raya's mythology.

28. The marginal note is ambiguous in original. The subject of 'says' could be 'he' or 'she' or 'it' (i.e., a manuscript).

29. *cascanracmi . . . cascanman* 'his essential nature . . . Vira Cocha's': *cascan* is a past participial form of the Quechua verb meaning 'to be' and might more literally be rendered 'what he was'. For this reason we have used 'essential', also derived from a verb meaning 'to be'. *Cascan* is, however, less abstract in tone than 'essence'; hence 'nature'. Taylor's renders *cascan* as 'his cult' (*su culto*; 1987b: 28, 51), taking the point to be 'what he was in human practice'. But there are reasons for thinking *cascan* refers to 'what he was in himself'. In both colonial and modern Quechua this form often implies action previous to the speaker's cognition and/or surprise at discovering it (Cusihuamán 1976: 170–171; Urioste 1973: 96). We might read *cascan* as 'what he was all along (without our knowing it)'. This motif emerges more clearly in chapter 14 (sec. 190 and note 374), where Vira Cocha inveigles the Inca by promising to reveal *ñoca cascayta*, 'my *casca*'—'what I was all along'.

matches Vira Cocha's.[30] For when people worshiped this *huaca*, they would invoke him, saying,

"Cuni Raya Vira Cocha,

You who animate mankind,
Who charge the world with being,[31]

All things are yours!
Yours the fields and yours the people."

8   And so, long ago, when beginning anything difficult, the ancients, even though they couldn't see Vira Cocha, used to throw coca leaves to the ground,[32] talk to him, and worship him before all others, saying,

"Help me remember how,
Help me work it out,
Cuni Raya Vira Cocha!"

And the master weaver[33] would worship and call on him whenever it was hard for him[34] to weave.

For that reason, we'll write first about this *huaca* and about his life, and later on[35] about Paria Caca.

---

30. Because of his alleged importance as a supreme deity, comparable to the Christian God, Vira Cocha has become the subject of a large and frequently misleading literature. Many Andean sources about him are handily compiled in *Wiracocha y Ayar* (Urbano 1981: 1–31).

Here, however, this deity's role has little to do with the Christian concept of God and a lot in common with the pan–New World concept of a Trickster, whose buffoonery is at the same time a force making and remaking the world. In suggesting that Cuni Raya's nature "almost matches" Vira Cocha's, the teller seems to be taking note of a popular tendency, exemplified by the invocation that follows, to equate a Trickster-like deity associated with the hydraulic transformation of landforms (Cuni Raya) with a south highland, Inca-promoted deity (Vira Cocha). Chapter 14 emphasizes the latter component.

Szemiński and Mejía Xesspe before him have suggested that *cunirayap cascanracmi ñahca viracochap cascanman tincon* might mean the two deities' existences 'almost coincide' chronologically rather than qualitatively. This makes sense if one reads the statement as a reply to the chronological question just raised, rather than a comment on what follows. If one takes *viracocha* in this passage to refer to the Spanish, still other readings result (Szemiński 1989: 8–9).

31. *runa camac pacha camac* 'who animate mankind, who charge the world with being': the two lofty epithets employ the key verb *camay*, discussed in the introduction under "Into the world of the *huaca*s." *Camay* has no clear equivalent in Spanish or English and is translated in the present work as 'to charge' or 'charge with being', 'to make', 'to give form and force', or 'to animate'.

32. That is, to sacrifice or perhaps to take an augury.

33. *compi camayuc* 'master weaver': both *compi* 'luxury-grade textile' and *camayuc* 'specialist' are Inca-style bureaucratic terms. *Camayuc* means more literally 'possessor of a specific force or energy [*camay*]', in this case the specific virtue of weaving.

34. Or 'for her'.

35. The manuscript contains cross-references that refer backward to earlier chapters by number, but the forward-pointing cross-references only use vague terms like 'later'. This suggests that the text, while it may be a fair copy, has not undergone a final editing.

CHAPTER 2

How Cuni Raya Vira Cocha Acted in His Own Age. The Life of Cuni Raya Vira Cocha.[36] How Caui Llaca Gave Birth to His Child, and What Followed

<margin, crossed out, in Spanish:> [Note that it isn't known whether this was before or after Caruincho.]

A long, long time ago,[37] Cuni Raya Vira Cocha used to go around posing as a miserably poor and friendless[38] man, with his cloak and tunic all ripped and tattered. Some people who didn't recognize him for who he was yelled, "You poor lousy[39] wretch!"

Yet it was this man who fashioned all the villages. Just by speaking he made[40] the fields, and finished the terraces with walls of fine masonry. As for the irrigation canals, he channeled them out from their sources just by tossing down the flower of a reed called *pupuna*.[41]

After that, he went around performing all kinds of wonders, putting some of the local *huacas*[42] to shame[43] with his cleverness.

10 Once there was a female *huaca* named Caui Llaca.

Caui Llaca had always remained a virgin.

Since she was very beautiful, every one of the *huacas* and *villcas*[44] longed for her. "I've got to sleep with her!" they thought.

But she never consented.

11 Once this woman, who had never allowed any male to fondle[45] her, was weaving beneath a *lúcuma*[46] tree.

---

36. 'The life of Cuni Raya Vira Cocha' is in Quechua and seems not to be part of the inserted Spanish title.

37. A formula introducing a passage with reportive validation.

38. *huaccha* 'poor and friendless': literally, 'orphan'. Throughout the manuscript and in modern Quechua, *huaccha* means 'poor' not so much in the sense of lacking property, as in the sense of lacking social ties that enable one to be productive. It is also translated here as 'wretch', 'powerless', or 'a nobody'.

39. Lice have a peculiar double meaning; Marie-France Souffez (1986), relying partly on findings by Christopher Donnan and María Rostworowski, notes that in Mochica imagery of shamanism the lice growing on a shaman's body emblematize the many people her or his power can sustain. Latent wealth hidden in apparent squalor is a common attribute of Huarochirí protagonists.

40. 'Made' supplied.

41. In the *Tratado* (Arguedas and Duviols 1966: 201) Avila identifies the object as "a hollow reed of the sort we call 'Castillian reed'." The *pupuna* is described in a marginal note to supplement I (sec. 454) as a pole with a noose for catching parrots.

42. *llacta huacacunactapas*: the phrase contrasts Cuni,

a wandering nonlocal deity, with rooted local deities. Cults and toponyms with names reminiscent of Cuni's (Kon, Concón, etc.), appear to have been farflung over the coast (Rostworowski 1977).

43. *allcuchaspa*: literally, 'making dogs of them'. 'Dog' is consistently a term of abuse in the manuscript.

44. The exact sense of *villca* in the manuscript is uncertain but perhaps related to a contemporaneous Aymara word meaning both 'sun' and 'shrine' (Bertonio [1612] 1956: 386). Internal evidence (chap. 31, sec. 417) suggests that in the Huarochirí context it means a person who has entered into the society of *huacas* by achievement or marriage. In the *Tratado* (Arguedas and Duviols 1966: 209), the word *villca* is translated 'a very important *cacique*' (*cacique muy principal*; see also Zuidema 1973: 19). In Huánchor village in 1621, the founding hero Huánchor was mummified and housed underneath a *huaca* called Huanchorvilca (Arguedas and Duviols 1966: 264). Overall, the implication seems to be that a *villca* is a human being who partakes of a *huaca*'s status.

45. *chancaycochicuspa* 'fondle': Gonçález Holguín ([1608] 1952: 94) glosses related verbs as meaning 'to stroke or touch lightly'. Similar verbs in modern Quechua usually sound sexually piquant.

46. "*Lucuma bifera*, an evergreen tree, eight to ten meters high, has spreading branches with entire, elliptic-ovate leaves. The globose to ovate fruits, seven to ten cm. in diameter, are green in color and have a bright orange to yellow, dry, mealy pulp. . . . This species is a native of Peru

Cuni Raya, in his cleverness,[47] turned himself into a bird and climbed into the *lúcuma*.

He put his semen into a fruit that had ripened there and dropped it next to the woman.

12 The woman swallowed it down delightedly.

Thus she got pregnant even though she remained untouched by man.

In her ninth month, virgin though she was, she gave birth just as other women give birth.

And so, too, for one year she nursed her child at her breast, wondering, "Whose child could this be?"

13 In the fullness of the year, when the youngster was crawling around on all fours, she summoned all the *huaca*s and *villca*s to find out who was the child's father.

When the *huaca*s heard the message, they were overjoyed, and they all came dressed in their best clothes, each saying to himself, "It's me!" "It's me she'll love!"

14 This gathering took place at Anchi Cocha,[48] where the woman lived.

<**margin**, in Spanish:> [The gathering was in Anchi Cocha.]

When all the *huaca*s and *villca*s had taken their seats there, that woman addressed them:

"Behold, gentlemen and lords. Acknowledge this child. Which of you made me pregnant?"[49] One by one she asked each of them:

"Was it you?"

"Was it you?"

But nobody answered, "The child is mine."

15 The one called Cuni Raya Vira Cocha had taken his seat at the edge of the gathering. Since he looked like a friendless beggar sitting there, and since so many handsome men were present, she spurned him and didn't question him. She thought, "How could my baby possibly be the child of that beggar?"

Since no one had said, "The child is mine," she first warned the *huaca*s, "If the baby is yours, it'll crawl up to you," and then addressed the child:

"Go, identify your father yourself!"

16 The child began at one end of the group and crawled along on all fours without climbing up on anyone, until reaching the other end, where its father sat.

On reaching him the baby instantly brightened up and climbed onto its father's knee.

When its mother saw this, she got all indignant: "Atatay, what a disgrace! How could I have given birth to the child of a beggar like that?" she said. And taking along only her child, she headed straight for the ocean.

17 And then, while all the local *huaca*s stood in awe, Cuni Raya Vira Cocha put on his golden garment. He started to chase her at once, thinking to himself, "She'll be overcome by sudden desire for me."

"Sister Caui Llaca!" he called after her. "Here, look at me! Now I'm really beautiful!" he said, and he stood there making his garment glitter.[50]

18 Caui Llaca didn't even turn her face back to him.

"Because I've given birth to the child of such a ruffian, such a mangy beggar,[51] I'll just disappear into the ocean," she said. She headed straight out into the deep sea near Pacha Camac,[52] out there

---

and is cultivated for its edible fruit. . . . Specimens of whole and halved fruits of this species . . . are among the most common plant remains found in archaeological sites on the Peruvian coast. . . . *Lucumas* were an important part of the diet of the ancient Peruvians, and halved fruits are frequently found in *petacas* [pouches, hampers] with remains of other food plants. . . . The fruit is also a familiar motif in pre-Columbian art" (Towle 1961: 76–77).

47. *amauta cayninpi* 'in his cleverness': *amauta* is the term Garcilaso Inca popularized as the Inca title of learned men or counselors, but in connection with Cuni Raya it connotes an earthy or practical kind of cleverness.

48. Avila characterized Anchi Cocha as "a terribly cold and bad place halfway between Huarochirí and Chorillo" (Arguedas and Duviols 1966: 201). Today, Anchicocha is the name of a bleak settlement, plateau, and peak 17 km southwest of Huarochirí, 3,700 m above sea level (IGM 1954). But in chapter 5 Anchi Cocha is the luxurious tropical home of a Yunca lord. *Anchini* (González Holguín [1608] 1952: 27) meant 'to live amid delights, to spend splendidly on food, drink, clothing and gifts'. Perhaps the sense is that Anchi Cocha, a Lake of Earthly Delights in the pre-invasion age when all the land was warm and belonged to Yunca people, has (like other places mentioned in chap. 8) been transfigured by the power of later *huaca*s from the cold heights.

49. *yumahuarcanquichic* 'made me pregnant': The root is *yumay* 'sperm'. The literal sense is 'inseminated me'.

50. If Cuni Raya is indeed a water deity, as Rostworowski (1977) persuasively argues, his glittering garment may be a metaphor for water sparkling in sunlight.

51. *cachcaçapap* 'of . . . such a mangy beggar': Avila glosses *cachca* as *sarna* (i.e., scabies or mange) in his *Tratado* ([1608] 1966: 202).

52. Pacha Camac, whose name means something like 'animator of space and time', was a coastal deity whose colossal shrine complex south of Lima (still visible at the

where even now two stones that clearly look like people stand.[53]

And when she arrived at what is today her dwelling, she turned to stone.

19   Yet Cuni Raya Vira Cocha thought, "She'll see me anyway, she'll come to look at me!" He followed her at a distance, shouting and calling out to her over and over.

First, he met up with a condor.[54]

"Brother, where did you run into that woman?" he asked him.

"Right near here. Soon you'll find her," replied the condor.

Cuni Raya Vira Cocha[55] spoke to him and said,[56]

"You'll live a long life. You alone will eat any dead animal from the wild mountain slopes, both guanacos[57] and vicuñas,[58] of any kind and in any number. And if anybody should kill you, he'll die himself, too."

20   Farther on, he met up with a skunk.[59]

---

mouth of the Lurín valley, next to the modern village of Pachacámac) attracted worship from remote prehistory and from regions far up the Pacific littoral. His cult is prominent in chapters 20, 22, and 23; see Patterson (1984[?]).

53.   The two guano-whitened offshore islands visible from the Inca pyramid at Pachacámac. This landmark and Caui Llaca's lithification complete the trajectory of a story that follows the course of the Lurín River from its high headwaters (Anchicocha) to the Pacific. Cuni Raya's fertilizing action on Caui Llaca seems a mythic image of the river's life-giving effect on its valley.

54.   "Andean condor, *Vultur gryphus* (*Cóndor*). Twice the size of a vulture. Black, head bare and yellowish-red, white collar, wing coverts whitish. Male with a flesh caruncle on the bill. Juvenile dusky brown without the collar and white wing patches. Seen flying high it differs from the turkey vulture only in its size and the diagnostic fingering of the feathers of the wingtips. Feeds principally on dead animals. Nests in the Andes; comes down regularly to the sea beaches and coastal hills with fog vegetation" (Koepcke 1970: 38).

55.   'Cuni Raya Vira Cocha' supplied.

56.   Cuni Raya's speeches to the animals have witness validation, which is consistently used in performative (world-changing rather than world-describing) speech.

57.   *Lama guanicoe*, a large wild camelid ranging from the Andes into lower semiarid lands (Cabrera and Yepes 1940: 257).

58.   *Lama vicugna*, a small wild camelid of the heights, prized for its excellent wool (Gade 1977: 113).

59.   "Zorrino chileno, *Conepatus chinga* . . . its Quichua name used in Peru is *añas*" (Cabrera and Yepes 1940: 153).

"Sister, where did you meet that woman?" he asked.

"You'll never find her now. She's gone way far away," replied the skunk.

When she said this, he cursed her very hatefully, saying,

"As for you, because of what you've just told me, you'll never go around in the daytime. You'll only walk at night, stinking disgustingly. People will be revolted by you."

21   Next he met up with a puma.[60]

"She just passed this way. She's still nearby. You'll soon reach her," the puma told him.

Cuni Raya Vira Cocha[61] spoke to him, saying,

"You'll be well beloved. You'll eat llamas, especially the llamas of people who bear guilt. Although people may kill you, they'll wear you on their heads during a great festival and set you to dancing.[62] And then when they bring you out annually they'll sacrifice a llama first and then set you to dancing."

22   Then he met up with a fox.[63]

"She's already gone way far away. You'll never find her now," that fox told him.

When the fox said this, he replied,

"As for you, even when you skulk around keeping your distance, people will thoroughly despise you and say, 'That fox is a sneak thief.' When they kill you, they'll just carelessly throw you away and your skin, too."

<A **marginal** addition in Quechua begins here:>

23   Likewise he met up with a falcon.[64]

---

60.   *Puma concolor* (Cabrera and Yepes 1940: 167–172).

61.   'Cuni Raya Vira Cocha' supplied.

62.   *taquechisonque* 'they'll . . . set you to dancing': more literally, 'they will make you dance'; here as elsewhere in the manuscript, this means celebrants carry or wear the sacred preserved skin as they perform. In his *Tratado* Avila explained that the dancer placed the animal's preserved head over his own and let the attached skin fall over his body like a cape (Arguedas and Duviols 1966: 203).

63.   Probably the Peruvian fox, *Pseudalopex inca* (Cabrera and Yepes 1940: 125).

64.   The region of the myth has seven species of hawks, harriers, and kites, and three of falcon. *Huaman* may refer to a species that, like some other birds prominent in the mythology (the condor and the swift), nests on the Andean heights but sometimes flies to the coast and thereby parallels the axis of movement in these myths. "Aplomado falcon, *Falco femoralis pichinchae* (*Halcón perdi-*

"She's just passed this way. You'll soon find her," said the falcon.

He replied,

"You're greatly blessed. When you eat, you'll eat the hummingbird first, then all the other birds. When people kill you, the man who has slain you will have you mourned with the sacrifice of a llama. And when they dance, they'll put you on their heads so you can sit there shining with beauty."

24 And then he met up with some parakeets.[65]

"She's already gone way far away. You'll never find her now," the parakeets told him.

"As for you, you'll travel around shrieking raucously," replied Cuni Raya Vira Cocha.[66] "Although you may say, 'I'll spoil your crops!' when people hear your screaming they'll chase you away at once. You'll live in great misery amidst the hatred of humans."

<The **marginal** addition ends here.>

And so he traveled on. Whenever he met anyone who gave him good news, he conferred on him a good fortune. But he went along viciously cursing those who gave him bad news.

---

guero). Larger than the Kestrel, with a longer tail. Lead-colored above, superciliary line cinnamon; below buffy cinnamon, tail and flanks blackish with horizontal white stripes. Generally seen in our region above 2000 m., but occasionally it comes down to the coastal area. Feeds largely on birds to the size of a tinamou" (Koepcke 1970: 42). The hummingbird allotted to the falcon as food below might represent any or all of the six Lima Department hummingbird species (Koepcke 1970: 79–80).

65. *horitocunahuan* 'with some parakeets': *horito* in chapter 16 (sec. 207) is equated to the poorly identified bird *caqui* (toucan?), but in chapter 1 (sec. 5) it is distinguished from it. Here it clearly refers to a crop pest. The likeliest identification is

Mountain parakeet, *Bolborhynchus a. aurifrons* (*Psilopsiagon a. aurifrons*) (*Perico cordillerano*). The only native wild parakeet of our coastal region. Small, with a very long tail; F. and J. completely green; M. with the forehead, face, and underparts yellowish. Common on the steppes and shrubby places of the coast and Andean slopes; also gathers in cultivated fields, tree plantations, gardens, and parks of Lima. During the winter it is abundant on the coastal hills and in wooded and shrubby places with fog vegetation, especially at Lachay.

It could also be Andean parakeet, *Bolborhynchus andinicolus* (*B. orbygnesius*) (*Perico Andino*), found only above 1500 m., or (less probably, because of its rarity) the Scarlet-fronted parakeet, *Aratinga wagleri frontata* (*Cotorra de Wagler*; Koepcke 1970: 74).

66. 'Cuni Raya Vira Cocha' supplied.

25 When he reached the seashore, <crossed out in original MS:> [he went straight over it. Today people say, "He was headed for Castile," but in the old days people said, "He went to another land."][67] he turned back toward Pacha Camac.

He arrived at the place where Pacha Camac's two daughters lived, guarded by a snake.

Just before this, the two girls' mother had gone into the deep sea to visit Caui Llaca. Her name was Urpay Huachac.

While Urpay Huachac was away, Cuni Raya Vira Cocha seduced[68] one girl, her older daughter.

When he sought to sleep with the other sister, she turned into a dove[69] and darted away.

That's why her mother's name means 'Gives Birth to Doves'.

26 At that time there wasn't a single fish in the ocean.

Only Urpay Huachac used to breed them, at her home, in a small pond.[70]

It was these fish, all of them, that Cuni Raya angrily scattered into the ocean, saying, "For what did she go off and visit Caui Llaca the woman of the ocean depths?"

Ever since then, fish have filled the sea.

27 Then Cuni Raya Vira Cocha fled along the seashore.

When Urpay Huachac's daughters told her how he'd seduced them, she got furious and chased him.

As she followed him, calling him again and again, he waited for her and said, "Yes?"

"Cuni, I'm just going to remove your lice," she said, and she picked them off.

28 While she picked his lice, she caused a huge abyss

---

67. *huc pachamansi* could also be read 'another world'. The crossed-out version matches Vira Cocha myths circulated in the highlands and better known among Spaniards (Urbano 1981: 1–31).

68. Or perhaps raped her; *puñochircan*, more literally, 'he made her sleep', could mean either. We chose 'seduce' because it is Gonçález Holguín's preferred gloss ([1608] 1952: 296) and because deception, not violence, is Cuni Raya's consistent mode of action.

69. Of nine species of doves known in the region, three are common near the seashore: the white-winged dove (*Zenaida asiatica meloda*), the eared dove (*Zenaidura auriculata hypoleuca*), and the croaking ground dove (*Columbina cruziana*) (Koepcke 1970: 69–71).

70. Probably an allusion to pisciculture, perhaps in excavated tanks (Espinoza Soriano 1974: 19; Rostworowski 1981: 30–31).

to open up next to him, thinking to herself, "I'll knock Cuni Raya down into it."

But Cuni Raya in his cleverness realized this; just by saying, "Sister, I've got to go off for a moment to relieve myself,"[71] he made his getaway to these villages.

He traveled around this area for a long, long time, tricking lots of local *huaca*s and people, too. <**marginal note**, in Spanish, crossed out:> [n.b. This *huaca*'s end will be told below.]

---

71. The verb in the original, from the root *ysmay*, is merely plainspoken. But the plain translation 'to shit' sounds jarringly obscene.

CHAPTER 3

What Happened to the Indians in Ancient Times When the Ocean Overflowed

29

Now we'll return to what is said of very early people. The story goes like this.[72]

In ancient times, this world wanted to come to an end.[73]

A llama buck, aware[74] that the ocean was about to overflow, was behaving like somebody who's deep in sadness. Even though its <crossed out:> [father] owner let it rest in a patch of excellent pasture, it cried and said, "In, in," and wouldn't eat.

30 The llama's <crossed out:> [father] owner got really angry, and he threw the cob from some maize he had just eaten at the llama.

"Eat, dog! This is some fine grass I'm letting you rest in!" he said.

Then that llama began speaking like a human being.

"You simpleton, whatever could you be thinking about? Soon, in five days, the ocean will overflow. It's a certainty. And the whole world will come to an end," it said.

31 The man got good and scared. "What's going to happen to us? Where can we go to save ourselves?" he said.

The llama replied, "Let's go to Villca Coto mountain.[75]

<margin, in Spanish:> [This is a mountain that is between Huanri[76] and Surco.][77]

There we'll be saved. Take along five days' food for yourself."

So the man went out from there in a great hurry, and himself carried both the llama buck and its load.

32 When they arrived at Villca Coto mountain, all sorts of animals had already filled it up: pumas, foxes, guanacos, condors, all kinds of animals in great numbers.

And as soon as that man had arrived there, the ocean overflowed.

They stayed there huddling tightly together.

33 The waters covered all those mountains and it was only Villca Coto mountain, or rather its very peak, that was not covered by the water.

Water soaked the fox's tail.

That's how it turned black.

Five days later, the waters descended and began to dry up.

34 The drying waters caused the ocean to retreat all the way down again and exterminate all the people.

---

72. Text shifts at this point from witness to reportive validation.

73. *cay pachas puchocayta munarcan* 'this world wanted to come to an end': *puchocay* means the ending of something that has an intrinsic conclusion (as, for example, the finishing of a task), not a truncation or accidental end (González Holguín [1608] 1952: 293).

74. The prescience of llamas: see chapter 18 (secs. 221–222), on llama divination, where the animal's body is credited with containing signs of the future.

75. A mountain today called by this name exists 12

km northwest of San Damián, between modern Huanre and Surco (Treacy 1984: 18). Villca Coto may be the same *huaca* mentioned in chapter 23 (sec. 301), the most beautiful one at the Inca court in Cuzco.

76. Modern Huanre is 5 km south of San Bartolomé (IGM 1970–1971).

77. The modern (former *reducción*) town of San Gerónimo de Surco is 17 km north-northwest of San Damián at 2,300 m above sea level, sheltered in the Rímac valley (IGM 1970–1971).

Afterward, that man began to multiply once more.

That's the reason there are people until today.

Regarding this story, we Christians believe it refers to the time of the Flood.[78]

But they believe it was Villca Coto mountain that saved them.

---

78. This sentence has *-mi* eyewitness validation.

CHAPTER 4

How the Sun Disappeared for Five Days. In What Follows We Shall Tell a Story about the Death of the Sun

In ancient times[79] the sun died.[80]
Because of his death it was night for five days.
Rocks banged against each other.

Mortars and grinding stones began to eat people.
Buck llamas started to drive men.[81]
Here's what we Christians think about it:[82] We think these stories tell of the darkness following the death of our Lord Jesus Christ.[83]
Maybe that's what it was.

---

79. This formula introduces a passage with reportive validation.

80. Like various New World mythologies, Andean myths both ancient and modern include a motif of successive deaths and replacements of suns. Juan Ossio believes this chapter and Guaman Poma's scheme of "ages" are related to Montesinos' mid-seventeenth-century account of an Andean myth about successive suns equated to millennia (Ossio 1973: 188). Many modern Andeans interpret precolumbian structures as the houses of people who lived before the current sun arose.

81. The myth of the revolt of the objects, of which this appears to be a summary, also appears in a fuller

Mayan version that, like this one, follows on a flood incident (Tedlock 1985: 84–86). Hocquenghem (1987: 142–143) and Jeffrey Quilter (personal communication) point out analogues in Mochica ceramic imagery from the Peruvian north coast.

82. This sentence has witness validation.

83. Luke 23: 44–45: "It was now about the sixth hour and darkness came over the whole land until the ninth hour, for the sun stopped shining."

CHAPTER 5

How in Ancient Times Paria Caca Appeared on a Mountain Named Condor Coto in the Form of [84] Five Eggs, and What Followed. Here Will Begin the Account of Paria Caca's Emergence [85]

In the four preceding chapters we have already recounted the lives lived in ancient times.

Nevertheless, we don't know the origins of the people of those days, nor where it was they emerged [86] from.

37 These people, the ones who lived in that era, used to spend their lives warring on each other and conquering each other. For their leaders, they recognized only the strong and the rich. [87]

We speak of them as the Purum Runa, 'people of desolation'. [88]

38 It was at this time that the one called Paria Caca was born in the form of five eggs on Condor Coto mountain. [89]

A certain man, and a poor friendless one at that, was the first to see and know the fact of his birth; he was called Huatya Curi, but was also known as Paria Caca's son.

Now we'll speak of this discovery of his, and of the many wonders [90] he performed. [91]

---

84. 'In the Form of' supplied.

85. The last part of the title here is in Quechua and does not form part of the Spanish insertion.

86. *pacarimuscancunactam* 'the origins' and *pacarimurcan* 'they emerged' both derive from a single root meaning literally 'to dawn' (González Holguín [1608] 1952: 266–267; see also preface, sec. 2). An Andean group's 'dawning' or emergence from inside earth to outer daylight is its origin myth and primordial title to a place on the landscape that engendered it.

87. *rico* 'rich': the Spanish word is sometimes used in this chapter (secs. 46, 60) as the opposite of *huaccha* 'friendless, poor'. *Rico* seemingly implies wealth in possessions (chap. 19, sec. 235) rather than the rich social and superhuman connectedness suggested by Quechua *capac* (opposite of *huaccha* in sec. 49). Its use here may reflect the ascendancy of economic concepts connected with the Spanish market system.

88. The age here mythologized seems to be the Late Intermediate period of the archaeologists, that is, the centuries preceding Inca unification and characterized by a multitude of warring polities. *Purum* (González Holguín [1608] 1952: 297) covers a spectrum of meanings from the agricultural ('sterile lands, lands abandoned from cultiva-

tion') to the political ('unconquered people, enemies'). 'Desolation' is chosen to evoke the linkage between warfare and infertility.

The "Indian chronicler" Felipe Guaman Poma de Ayala also gave the name "Purun Runa" to an ancient age of warfare ([1615] 1980: 1: 47–50).

89. Condor Coto may be the peak called Condorcoto today, only 14 km southwest of Huarochirí, that is, nowhere near Paria Caca mountain but close to Anchi Cocha (IGM 1970–1971). The fact that Paria Caca's emergence takes place within what was seen as old Yunca country may suggest that the myth-tellers saw themselves as a foreign minority group enclaved and formerly oppressed in Yunca country.

Condor Coto would mean 'Condor mountain' in Aymara (Bertonio [1612] 1956: 53) or Quechua (González Holguín [1608] 1952: 70).

90. *ahca misterio* 'many wonders': in Spanish, a *misterio*, according to Cobarruvias ([1611] n.d.: 807) meant any sacred thing that was to be kept hidden from profane view. Basic Christian doctrines were called *misterios* in the Quechua sermon books from which the clergy were required to teach natives (*Tercero catecismo* [1585] 1985: 363–458). The usage of *misterio* implicitly compares the secret meaning of Paria Caca's action, revealed to Huatya Curi, to the meanings of Christian revelation.

91. End of an introductory passage with witness vali-

39   They say[92] that fellow called Huatya Curi sub-
sisted at the time just by baking potatoes in earth
pits,[93] eating the way a poor man does,[94] and people
named him the "Baked Potato Gleaner."

At that time there was another man named
Tamta Ñamca,[95] a very rich and powerful lord.
<**margin**, in Spanish:> [n.b. Tamta Ñamca]

Both his own house and all his other houses[96]
looked like *cassa* and *cancho* feather-weavings,
for they were thatched with wings of birds.[97] His
llamas were yellow llamas, red and blue llamas; he
owned llamas of every hue.
<**margin**:> [Tamta Ñamca]

40   Seeing that this man lived so well, people who
came from all the villages paid him homage and
worshiped him.

For his part, he pretended to be very wise and
spent his life deceiving a whole lot of people with
the little that he really knew.

---

dation. The editor/redactor is not always explicitly skep-
tical of the content of traditional narration.

92. 'They say' supplied to indicate shift to reportive
validation.

93. *huatya*, potatoes baked in an earth pit, were and
are characteristic food of high-altitude peasants who
cook outdoor meals while harvesting tubers on the high
slopes.

94. 'The way a poor man does': Avila in his *Tratado*
(Arguedas and Duviols 1966: 208–209) adds a comment
that eating *huatya* (earth-baked potatoes) was a mark
of poverty. Avila may, however, have missed part of the
name's meaning, namely, the part connected with its second element *Curi*. It may come from "*ccorini* to gather
and collect small or scattered things." A derived verb
means 'to glean through the harvested fields or pick up
spilled or abandoned things' (Gonçález Holguín [1608]
1952: 69). A person reduced to picking through other
people's abandoned barbecue pits is dispossessed in the
highest degree, lacking even subsistence rights and in
this sense eats 'the way a poor man does'.

95. This man's name contains the word *tamta* 'feather
ruff' (Arriaga [1621] 1968: 50; Keating's translation).
Featherwork is the symbol of his wealth and glory; his
house is thatched with feathers. Andean featherwork
found in tombs is made from tropical birds and probably
symbolizes the biotic plenty of warm *yunca* lands.

96. That is, the houses for his wives, servitors, and so
forth.

97. The image seems to be that of a house thatched
with the brilliantly colored feather-weavings sometimes
found in prehispanic elite burials. Avila says in his *Tratado* that the roof was of yellow and red feathers (Arguedas and Duviols 1966: 209).

Then this man called Tamta Ñamca, who pretended to be so wise, even to be a god,[98] contracted
a really horrible disease.

41   His illness went on for a great many years, and in
time people talked. "How can a man who knows so
much, who's so powerful, be so sick?" they said.

Just like the Spaniards who, on such occasions,
summon experts and doctors, Tamta Ñamca, hop-
ing to recover, summoned all sorts of shamans and
wise men.[99]
<**margin**, in Spanish:> [The wise men gathered.]
But no one at all could diagnose that disease
of his.

42   Just then Huatya Curi was coming from the vicinity of Ura Cocha,[100] and he went to sleep on the
mountain by which we descend to Sieneguella.[101]

(Today this mountain is called Latab Zaco.)

While he was sleeping, a fox who'd come from
down below and one who'd come from up above[102]
met face to face[103] there. One fox asked the other,
"Brother, how are things in Upper Villca?"

43   "What's good is good. But a lord in Anchi Cocha,

---

98. *dios*: the Spanish word 'god', perhaps used in a
Greco-Roman rather than Christian sense.

99. *amautacunacta doctorcunacta . . . yachaccunacta
sauiocunacta* 'experts and doctors . . . shamans and wise
men': the teller draws an implicit contrast between two
pairs of terms, each consisting of a Quechua and a Spanish word: *amauta : doctor :: yachac : sauio*. The suggestion seems to be that a doctor, a bureaucratically licensed
expert, can be compared with an *amauta*, and a *sauio* or
wise man with a *yachac*. *Yachac* (literally, 'knower') today means a shaman.

100. *ura cochañicmanta* 'from the vicinity of Ura Cocha' is more literally 'from someplace around [the?] lower
lake'. The 'lower lake' is probably the Pacific Ocean
(called *mama cocha* 'Mother Lake' today). This term recurs in chapter 8 (sec. 103) and chapter 22 (sec. 278).

101. Modern Cieneguilla is in the low end of the Lurín valley 62 km west of Huarochirí (IGM 1970–1971),
close to the ocean and to Lima.

102. In his *Tratado* ([1608] 1966: 209) Avila explains
that this means one fox came down from Anchi Cocha
and the other up from the Pacific.

103. *chaypi pactalla tincuspas* 'face to face' under-
states the Quechua's emphasis on symmetry. A fuller
though ungainly gloss would be 'symmetrically opposing
each other there in an exact fit'. The verb *tincuy* carries a
complex set of associations with the idea of opposed
parts forming a complementary totality (Platt [1978]
1986).

a *villca* as a matter of fact, one who claims to know a whole lot, to be a god himself, is terribly ill. All the wise men who found their way to him are wondering, 'Why's he so ill?' No one can identify his sickness. But his disease is this: while his wife was toasting maize, a grain of *muro*[104] maize popped from the griddle and got into her private part.[105]

44   "She picked it out and served it to a man to eat. Because of having served it, she became a sinner in relation to the man who ate it." (Nowadays they reckon that act tantamount to being an adulteress.)[106]

"As a result of this fault," he told the fox who'd come from down below, "a snake[107] has made its dwelling on top of that magnificent house and is eating them up. What's more, a toad, a two-headed one, lives under their grinding stone. And nobody is aware of these devouring animals."

45   Then he asked, "And how are people doing in Lower Villca, brother?"

The other fox answered similarly, saying, "There's a woman, the offspring of a great lord and a *villca*, who almost died because of a penis."[108]

(But the story leading up to the woman's recovery is very long.[109] Later on we'll write about it. For now, we'll return to the first story.)

---

104. *muro*: could mean 'particolored, spotted' (the generic meaning of *muro*) but may also be a local form of the term *muruchu* 'maize of the coastal flatlands, very hard' (Gonçález Holguín [1608] 1952: 252).

105. *pincayninmanmi*: literally, 'into her shame'. Shame-oriented terms from Quechua lexicon but reflecting Christian mentality are common in most but not all the sexually colored passages and are sometimes written in over scratched-out plainspoken Quechua terms.

106. The speaker adds this remark as if aware that his listeners would find the classification of the mistake as adultery puzzling. Perhaps the word *huachuc* 'adulterer' formerly covered a gamut of sexual transgressions besides adultery proper. Avila deviates from this version in saying the woman actually committed adultery with the man (Arguedas and Duviols 1966: 209).

107. *huc machachuay* 'a snake': in sec. 50 the snakes are clearly said to be two, but the discrepancy may only be apparent since the phrase with *huc* could mean 'some snakes'.

108. This alludes to a myth that would be the symmetrical counterpart (*tinkuy*; see chap. 5, sec. 43) of the first fox's story: a false nobleman ill from a vagina; a true noblewoman ill from a penis. Taylor (1987b: 92) detects an interlineation translatable as 'daughter of that great lord' (i.e., of Tamta Ñamca). If so, the woman made ill by a penis might be Chaupi Ñamca.

109. Chapter 10 (sec. 146) may be a truncated version

46   As the foxes were telling each other these tidings, the man called Huatya Curi heard that the great lord who pretended to be a god was ill.

This great man had two daughters.

He had joined the elder daughter to a fellow *ayllu* member[110] who was very rich.

<margin, in Quechua:> [He married her.][111]

The poor man called Huatya Curi came to that lord while he was still ill.

47   When he arrived, he went around asking surreptitiously, "Isn't someone sick in this town?"

"It's my father who's sick," replied the younger daughter.

Huatya Curi answered, "Let's get together. For your sake I'll cure your father."

<crossed out:>(We don't know this young woman's name.)[112]

<margin, in Quechua:> [But later on they called her Chaupi Ñamca.][113]

The young woman didn't agree right away.

48   She told her father, "Father, there's a poor man here. He came and said to me, 'I'll cure your father.'"

All the wise men who were sitting there burst into laughter when they heard these words, and said, "If we ourselves can't cure him, how can this nobody make him well?"

But that lord wanted a cure so badly that he called for Huatya Curi. "Let him come, never mind what sort of man he is," he said.

49   When the great lord summoned him, Huatya Curi entered and said, "Father, if you want to get well, I'll make you well. But you have to give me your daughter."

Overjoyed, Tamta Ñamca replied, "Very well then!"

But when his older daughter's husband heard this proposition he flew into a rage. "How dare he join her, the sister-in-law of such a powerful[114] man as me, to a nobody like that?"

---

of this myth. This aside has the witness validation typical of the editor or redactor's comments.

110. *ayllonhuantac* 'to a fellow *ayllu* member': *ayllu* endogamy is common in Andean societies.

111. *casarachircan* 'he married her': the verb root is a Spanish one, clarifying the perhaps unfamiliar sense of *tinquichircan* 'he joined [her]' in body of text.

112. This aside has witness validation.

113. I.e., in chapter 10 (sec. 142).

114. 'Powerful' is a weak rendering of *camac*, agentive

50   Later on we'll tell about this angry man's struggle with Huatya Curi.

But for now we'll return to the cure the poor man called Huatya Curi effected.

Huatya Curi began his cure by saying, "Father, your wife is an adulteress. Because she's an adulteress, a sinner, she's made you ill. As for what's eating you,[115] it's the two snakes that dwell on top of this magnificent house of yours. And there's a toad, too, a two-headed one, that lives under your grinding stone.

51   "Now we'll kill them all. Then you'll get well. After you recover, you must worship my father above all things. He'll be born tomorrow or the day after. And as for you, you're not such a powerful man. If you were really powerful, you wouldn't be sick."

The rich man was astonished when Huatya Curi said this.

52   And when Huatya Curi said, "Now I'll take apart this gorgeous house of his," he became distraught.

And his wife started yelling, "This nobody, this crook, is slandering me! I'm no adulteress!"

53   Nonetheless the sick man wanted his health back very badly, and he let his house be dismantled.

Then Huatya Curi removed the two snakes and killed them. Next he clearly explained the facts to the rich man's wife: just how a grain of *muro* maize had popped out and gotten in her private part, and how she, after picking it out, had served it to a man.

After that, the woman confessed everything. "It's all true," she said.

54   Next he had the grinding stone lifted.

A toad, a two-headed one, came out from under it and fled to Anchi Cocha ravine.

It exists in a spring there to this day.
<**margin**, in Spanish:> [Ask the name of this spring and where it is.]

When people come to that spring, it either makes them disappear or else drives them crazy.

55   Once Huatya Curi finished all these deeds <crossed out in original:> [her[116] father] the ailing man got well.

After Tamta Ñamca's recovery, on the day that had been foretold, Huatya Curi went for the first time to Condor Coto mountain.

It was there that the one called Paria Caca dwelled in the form of five eggs.[117]

All around him a wind rose up and began to blow.

In earlier times no wind had been observed.

56   Just before he went there on the appointed day, the man who'd recovered his health gave him his unmarried daughter.

While the two of them were traveling in the vicinity of that mountain they sinned together.[118]

57   As soon as that elder brother-in-law heard they'd sinned together he set out to compete against Huatya Curi.

"I'll bring deep shame on that beggarman," he muttered.

And so one day that man challenged him, saying, "Brother, let's have it out in a contest, whatever kind. How dare a nobody like you marry the sister-in-law of a powerful man like me?"

That poor man agreed, and went to inform his father Paria Caca,
<**margin**, in Spanish:> [That is, <he went> to one of the above-mentioned eggs that this man had for a father.]
and said, "This is how he spoke to me."

"Very well then. Whatever he tells you, come to me right away," his father replied.

58   The contest between them was like this.

---

form of the key verb *camay* discussed in the introduction and note 31 in chapter 1 (sec. 7). A *camac* man would be one who can impart his own power to others and impose his will.

115. *camta micucri* 'as for what's eating you': the illness may be leishmaniasis, an infectious disease often pictured in Mochica ceramics, which eats away at the soft tissues of the nose and lip.

116. *yayanca* 'her [or his] father' is the crossed-out word; it might refer to the father of Huatya Curi's young woman or of her sister (i.e., to Tamta Ñamca).

117. *runto* 'egg': can also mean 'hailstone' (Gonçález Holguín [1608] 1952: 321), a relevant association because Paria Caca regularly acts in the form of a storm.

118. *hochallicorcan* 'they sinned together': *hochalliy*, like *pincay* 'private part' (literally, 'shame'), is a shame-oriented term of Quechua lexicon and Christian mentality. The verb root employed seems to have meant a ceremonial debt or obligation (it is still used in this sense), but Christian missionaries chose it as the translation for 'sin'.

One day the challenger said, "Let's have a drinking and dancing contest."

So that poor man Huatya Curi went to inform his father.

His father Paria Caca advised him, "Go to that mountain over there. There you'll pretend to be a guanaco and lie down as if dead. Early in the morning a fox with his skunk wife will come there to see me.

59   "They'll bring their maize beer in a small long-necked jar[119] and they'll also bring along their drum. When they spot you, a dead guanaco, they'll set their things on the ground, and as soon as the fox puts down his panpipes, they'll start to eat you. Then turn back into a man, scream so loud it hurts their ears, and run away. When they scamper off forgetting their possessions, you'll take them and go to the contest."

60   The poor man did as he was told.

The rich man was the first to dance in the contest.

His wives, who numbered almost two hundred, danced along with him, and after they were done the poor man entered by himself, with only his wife, just the two of them.

As they entered through the doorway, as they danced to the skunk's drum he'd brought along, the earth of that whole region quaked.[120]

With this, he beat them all.

61   Next, they began drinking.

Huatya Curi went with just his wife to sit at the head of the group,[121] exactly as guests do until today.

And all of those people who were sitting there served him drink after drink without giving him a break.

Even though he drank every bit of it he sat there with no problem.

62   Then it was his turn. He began to serve the maize beer he'd brought in that little long-necked jar, and everybody ridiculed him. "How could he possibly fill so many people from such a tiny jar?" they said.

But when he began to serve, starting from the head of the gathering, they dropped down drunk in no time, one after another.

63   The next day, since Huatya Curi had won, the other man wanted a different contest.

This contest was all about outdoing each other in splendid costumes decorated with the exquisite feather-weavings called *cassa* and *cancho*.[122]

So Huatya Curi again went to his father.

His father gave him a snow garment.

<margin:> [or *riti*][123]

In that garment he dazzled[124] all the people's eyes and won the contest.

64   Then the challenger said, "Let's compete in putting on puma skins."

That man wanted to win by wearing the puma skins he had.[125]

The poor man, following his father's advice, went to a spring early in the morning and brought back a red puma skin.

He danced. And while he was dancing in that red puma, a rainbow appeared in the sky, like the rainbow that appears in the sky today.

65   Next the rich man wanted to compete at house-building.

Since that man had access to many people, he almost finished a large house in a single day.

The poor man just laid down the foundations and then strolled around all day long with his wife.

That night all kinds of birds, snakes, and other animals of the land walled the house.

---

119. *huchoylla porongo* 'small long-necked jar' sounds like the aryballoid form jars made in various sizes for carrying maize beer. They have been found in virtually all Inca-influenced archaeological sites.

120. Avila spells out the point in his *Tratado*: not just the people but "the whole earth danced to the beat of its sound" (Arguedas and Duviols 1966: 211).

121. The seating of ceremonial guests in rank order, recurrent in many parts of the text, can be seen today in various parts of the Andes. Sponsors of the ceremony sit on stools at the head places, while guests sit in descending order of prestige and strangers or mendicants at the opposite extreme.

122. That is, the same feather-weavings that adorned Tamta Ñamca's roof (chap. 5, sec. 39).

123. *riti*: another Quechua word for snow.

124. *rupachispa* 'dazzled': the word is derived from a root meaning 'to burn' and may mean that his snow garment dazzled them with snowblindness. It is different from *tutayachic* 'which . . . dazzles' (chap. 20, sec. 250). The latter literally means 'benights'.

125. See note 62. In chapter 10 (sec. 150) we learn that owners of llama herds symbolized their prosperity by wearing puma skins; like pumas, they lived off llamas. Since the challenger is said to be rich, he presumably had many herds and therefore many puma skins. Zuidema (1985: 225) suggests that wearing puma skins in ceremony signified sovereignty over a body politic.

The next day, seeing it already finished, the challenger was awestruck.

66 Likewise Huatya Curi won at roofing the house. All the guanacos and vicuñas brought his thatching straw.

As for the other man, while his materials were being transported on llamas, Huatya Curi availed himself[126] of a bobcat's[127] help. He lay in ambush for them by a cliff, stampeded them, and destroyed them by making them fall over it.

By this trick[128] he won again.

67 After winning all these contests, the poor man spoke just as his father had advised: "Brother, we've competed so many times now, always agreeing to your rules. Now you agree to my rules."

"Very well then," the rich man agreed.

Huatya Curi said, "Now, with blue tunics! And let our breechclouts be of white cotton! That's how we'll dance!"

"Very well then," the rich man agreed.

68 The rich man, since he'd danced first from the beginning <crossed out in original:> [danced], went ahead and danced first.

As he was dancing, Huatya Curi charged down on him from outside screaming. That man panicked, turned into a brocket deer,[129] and ran away.

And his wife followed him, saying, "I'll die with my own old man!"[130]

69 Then that poor man flew into a rage: "Go, idiot! You two have victimized me so much, I'll kill you!" he said, and he chased after them.

Chasing them, he caught the wife on the road to Anchi Cocha and stood her upside down on her head. "People coming from up above and those coming from down below will gape at your private parts as they pass by," he said.

And right then and there she turned to stone[131] instantly.

70 This stone, just like a woman's legs with thighs and a vagina,[132] stands there until today.

Even now people put coca on top of it when they undertake something.

<**margin**, in Spanish:> [Ask why they put this coca.]

But the man who'd turned into a brocket deer climbed up a mountain and disappeared.

71 (Now, in ancient times, brocket deer used to eat human beings.[133]

Later on, when brocket deer were very numerous, they danced, ritually chanting, "How shall we eat people?"

Then one of their little fawns made a mistake and said, "How shall people eat us?"

When the brocket deer heard this they scattered. From then on brocket deer became food for humans.)

72 After Huatya Curi finished all these deeds, Paria Caca flew forth from the five eggs in the shape of five falcons.

<**margin**, in Quechua:> [The birth of Paria Caca.]

These five falcons turned into humans and they began to roam around.

And at that time, hearing all about the things people had done, about how that man called Tamta Ñamca had said, "I am a god," and about how the man had himself worshiped, Paria Caca went into a rage over all these sins of theirs. Rising up as rain, he flushed them all away to the ocean, together

---

126. *mincaspa* 'availed himself': more literally, he 'contracted' the bobcat's help (Gonçález Holguín [1608] 1952: 240). While his brother-in-law had access to the labor of many people and domesticated animals (llamas), Huatya Curi has access, thanks to Paria Caca's help, to creatures of the wild (skunk, fox, guanaco, bobcat, etc.).

127. *oscullo* 'bobcat': a cat of the genus *Oncifelis*, possibly *Oncifelis geoffroyi* or *Oncifelis salinarum* (Cabrera and Yepes 1940: 161).

128. 'Trick' supplied.

129. *lloychu* 'brocket deer': *Mazama simplicicornis*. A small species widespread in the southern half of South America, up to 65 cm tall, found especially in "savannas with trees and forest edges on the flatlands, as well as on the heights" (Renard-Casevitz: 1979: 24–25).

130. *cosallayhuantac* 'with my own old man': to convey the affectionate tone that *-lla* imparts to *cosa* 'husband'.

131. Mythic figures commonly lithify (i.e., become local *huacas* consisting of geological features) when they complete their role in the mythic drama.

132. *racayoc* 'with a vagina': unlike many sexual words in the manuscript, this is a plain Andean one without Christian-style euphemism.

133. Interpolated myth-within-a-myth: how brocket deer became human food. The myth echoes a theme of chapters 1 and 27: the way overpopulation caused hunger in ancient times. The brocket deer, like ancient people, overreproduced until getting food became a problem. The conditions of their life had to be reversed. They became subject to individual death so that they could have collective life. The same happens to humans in chapter 27.

with all their houses and their llamas, sparing not
a single one.

73   At that time, too, there was something called the
Pullao, which bridged like an arch Llantapa mountain[134] and another mountain called Vichoca.[135]

---

134. Llantapa mountain today is 14 km southwest
of Llacsa Tambo (if the latter is modern Llaquistambo)
(IGM 1970–1971).

135. Modern Guichuca peak, 4,000 m above sea level,
14 km southwest of Llantapa (IGM 1970–1971). This co-

That thing called the Pullao was a gigantic tree.
Monkeys, toucans, and birds of all colors used to
live on it.
These animals, too, all of their kind, he swept to
the sea.
After he finished these feats, Paria Caca ascended
to the place that's known today as Upper Paria Caca.
In the next chapter we'll speak about his ascen-
sion.[136]

---

lossal bridge over the Lurín river canyon must have been
the mythic portal of the middle and lower *yunca* lands.

136. This sentence has witness validation.

CHAPTER 6

How Paria Caca Was Born as Five Falcons and Then Turned into Persons, and How, Already Victorious over All the Yunca of Anchi Cocha, He Began to Walk toward Paria Caca Mountain, and What Happened along the Way

Once Paria Caca had become human and was full grown, he began to search for his enemy.

His enemy's name was Huallallo Caruincho, the Man Eater, the Man Drinker.[137]

Later on we'll describe him together with his battles.[138]

In fact we already did talk in the first chapter about Huallallo Caruincho's life, how he ate people, and all his deeds.

<margin, in Spanish:> [the first chapter]

75 Now we'll tell about the things he did in Huaro Cheri and all around there.

The story goes like this.

When Paria Caca was already a full-grown person, he went to Huallallo Caruincho's dwelling, to the place called Upper Paria Caca.

76 In the valley that lies below Huaro Cheri there once was a village named Huauqui Usa, a village of the Yunca.

On that occasion the villagers[139] were celebrating an important festival. They drank, and drank hard.

While they were drinking, Paria Caca arrived at the village. He sat down at the end of the banquet as he arrived, just like a friendless stranger.

77 Not a single one of the villagers offered him a drink while he sat there. He was there all day long. Finally a woman, who was also a native of that village, exclaimed,

"Oh, no! How come no one is offering this poor fellow a drink?"

She brought over some maize beer in a large white gourd and gave it to him.

78 "Sister," Paria Caca said to that woman, "it's a lucky thing for you that you offered me this beer. Five days from now, you'll see something awful happen in this village. So take care not to be in the village that day. Back off far away. Otherwise I might kill both you and your children by mistake. These people have made me damn mad!"

And he added, "As for these people, don't let them hear even a single word about it. If you let them hear anything, I might kill you, too."

79 Five days later the woman, together with her children and her brothers, did go away from that village.

But the people of the village went right on drinking without a care.

Then Paria Caca climbed the mountain that overlooks Huaro Cheri.

(That mountain is called Matao Coto now.

Farther down there's another mountain called Puypu Huana, the one we descend on our way from here to Huaro Cheri. These are the names of those mountains.)[140]

80 On the mountain Paria Caca started a torrential rainstorm.

---

137. The chapter opens with two sentences in reportive validation.

138. This and the following three sentences form an explanatory aside with witness validation.

139. *llactayoc runacunaca* 'villagers', more literally, 'the village-owning people' (i.e., the aborigines who lived in union with the place and its deities before Paria Caca and his devotees overran them).

140. The whole parenthesis has witness validation.

Rising up as yellow hail and red hail,[141] he washed all those people away to the ocean and didn't spare a single one.

At that moment, the waters gushed down in a mudslide[142] and shaped the high slopes and the valleys of Huaro Cheri.

When Paria Caca finished all these things, he didn't explain them to the rest of the aboriginal Yunca people, who'd <crossed out:> [quite clearly] seen it all happen without knowing or understanding what it meant, but instead headed to the fields of the Cupara, which are across the river.
<**margin**, in Quechua:> [Paria Caca crossed over to the village of the Cupara.]

81   The native people of Cupara village survived just by channeling some water from a spring to their fields, and they were suffering greatly for lack of water at that time.

(This spring flowed from a tall mountain that rises above San Lorenzo village.[143]

This mountain is called Suna Caca today.)

At that time, they say,[144] it was just a big lake.

They used to irrigate their fields by channeling the water downhill to fill some small reservoirs.

82   In those days there was a native woman of that village named Chuqui Suso, a really beautiful woman.

This woman was weeping while she irrigated her maize plants because they were drying out so badly, and because her water supply was so very scarce.

When Paria Caca saw this, he obstructed the mouth of her little pond[145] with his cloak.

83   The woman started to cry even more bitterly when she saw him do that.

"Sister, why are you crying so hard?" Paria Caca asked her.

"Sir, this little maize field of mine is drying up on me for lack of water!" she replied.

"Don't worry about it," Paria Caca said to her. "I'll make water flow from this pond of yours, plenty of water. But first, let me sleep with you."

84   "Get the water flowing first," she retorted. "When my field is watered, then by all means let's sleep together."

"Fine!" said Paria Caca, and released an ample amount of water.

Overjoyed, the woman thoroughly watered all her fields.

After she finished irrigating, Paria Caca said, "Let's sleep together."

"Not right now," she replied. "Let's sleep together tomorrow or the day after."

Paria Caca, who desired the woman ardently, thought, "I wish I could sleep with her right now!" and promised her all kinds of things.

"I'll fix this field of yours up with a water source direct from the river,"[146] he said.

85   "Do that first, and then we'll sleep together," the woman replied.

"All right," Paria Caca said. He widened an irrigation canal that had belonged to the Yunca people, a little ditch that descended long ago from the ravine called Coco Challa to the small hill overlooking San Lorenzo. He extended this canal down as far as the fields of Lower Cupara.[147]

86   Pumas, foxes, snakes, and all kinds of birds cleaned and fixed that canal.

Pumas, jaguars, and all kinds of animals[148] vied with each other to improve it, saying, "Who'll be the leader when we lay out the watercourse?"[149]

---

141. In the *Tratado* Avila mentions that Huarochirí people interpreted a local geological formation, seemingly a steep alluvial fan of yellowish-white stones, as the remnant of Paria Caca's hail (Arguedas and Duviols 1966: 215).

142. *yaco lloclla purispas* 'waters gushed down in a mudslide': a typical west Andean disaster then and now. Repeatedly in the manuscript the rainy power of the heights destroys the dry Yunca people by washing them out. The topography of western Peru, cut by many water-eroded canyons, was read as the record of such mythic cataclysms.

143. Modern San Lorenzo de Quinti, 2 km east of Huarochirí at 2,550 m above sea level (IGM 1970–1971). This and the following sentence form an aside with witness validation.

144. 'They say' supplied to indicate resumption of reportive validation.

145. *cochap siminta* 'the mouth of her . . . pond': a literal translation, probably meaning the sluice through

which water passed from the reservoir to the irrigation canal.

146. *mayomanta yacuyuctam* 'with a water source direct from the river' (i.e., not reliant on the spring or the reservoir system).

147. The teller is at pains to relate the extant pattern of canals with *huaca*s and thereby express the teller's group's claims to water rights. In this myth a non-Yunca group (Checa?) seems to be holding that the neighboring Cupara (seemingly of Yunca origin) owe their water to the invaders and not to the ancient Yunca builders.

148. 'Animals' supplied.

149. This sentence has witness validation; since it

"Me first! Me first!" exclaimed this one and that one.

The fox won, saying, "I'm the chief, the *curaca*,[150] so I'll lead the way first."

And so he, the fox, went on ahead.

87 While the fox was leading the way, <**margin**, in Quechua:> [leading the way,] after he'd laid the watercourse out halfway up the mountain over San Lorenzo, a tinamou[151] suddenly darted up, whistling "Pisc pisc!"

Startled, the fox yelped "Huac!" and fell down the slope.

Then those animals got indignant and had the snake direct the way.

If the fox hadn't fallen, that canal of theirs would've run at a higher level.

But now it runs somewhat lower.

The spot from which the fox fell is clearly visible to this day. In fact the water flows down the course the fox's fall opened.[152]

---

overlaps the preceding reportive sentence in content, one suspects an imperfect joining of two sources.

150. *curaca* means "the lord or ruler (*señor*) of the community (*pueblo*)" (Gonçález Holguín [1608] 1952: 57); it derives from a root denoting priority in rank (especially birth order), not sovereignty. Under Spanish colonial influence, *curaca* roles were modified toward Spanish ideas of nobility and estate-based privilege.

151. *yutu* 'tinamou': *yutu* is the bird Peruvians call *perdiz* 'partridge' in Spanish. Its shape and behavior resemble those of a partridge, but it is in fact a tinamou. Three species inhabit Lima Province. Of these, the likeliest (because it inhabits the middle altitudes that are the scene of this myth) is: "*Andean Tinamou, Nothoprocta pentlandii oustaleti (Perdiz serrana)*. A tinamou the size of a small chicken; upper parts brownish, finely marked with cinnamon and black, with longitudinal buffy white streaks; underparts buffy, breast gray with small light spots. Lives in the steppes of the Andean slopes up to an altitude of 3500 m., also on the coastal hills. A terrestrial bird, it flushes with noisy wingbeats . . ." (Koepcke 1970: 16).

152. This interpolated myth is an etiological story ex-

88 When in fact[153] he'd finished all this, Paria Caca said to Chuqui Suso, "Let's sleep together!"

"Let's climb to a high ledge. There we'll sleep together," she <crossed out:> [enticed him] answered him.

(Today, this ledge is called Yana Caca.)[154]

There the two of them did sleep together.

Once she'd slept with him, that woman said, "Let's just the two of us go off someplace."

"Let's go!" he replied and led her to the mouth of the canal called Coco Challa.

89 When they got there the woman named Chuqui Suso said, "Right in this canal of mine, that's where I'll stay!" And she froze stock still, and turned to stone.

Paria Caca left her there and went on climbing upward.

We'll tell about that next.[155]

90 Someone congealed into stone does in fact stand today at the mouth of the canal named Coco Challa. It's the woman called Chuqui Suso. <**margin**, in Quechua:> [Cuni Raya's dwelling is near Chuqui Suso.]

Cuni Raya, also frozen to stone, dwells today above this place in a different canal, at the spot that was named Vincompa at that time.

It was there that Cuni Raya came to his end.[156]

But we'll tell about the various things he did in some later chapters.

---

plaining a conspicuous quirk of Quinti village's water system: why does a certain canal deviate downward from a higher and seemingly optimal course?

153. 'In fact' supplied to indicate that this sentence has witness validation.

154. This parenthesis has witness validation.

155. This sentence and the remainder of the chapter have witness validation, hence 'in fact' supplied in the next sentence.

156. The speaker insists with peculiar emphasis on the spot where Cuni Raya's course ended, perhaps because this version clashes with the better-known myth of his disappearance over the sea. This latter version is itself acknowledged, but crossed out, in chapter 2 (sec. 25).

CHAPTER 7

How Those Cupara People Revere the One Called Chuqui Suso Even to This Day

All the Cupara people, as we know,[157] make up a single *ayllu* called Cupara.

These people now live in San Lorenzo, where they remain forcibly relocated[158] right up to now.

There is within this *ayllu* a patrilineage[159] that bears the name Chauincho.

Chuqui Suso was <crossed out:> [a woman[160] of] a member of the Chauincho *ayllu*.

In the old days, in the month of May when the canal had to be cleaned (as is done today, too),[161] all these people went to the woman Chuqui Suso's dwelling; they went with their maize beer, *ticti*,[162] guinea pigs,[163] and llamas to worship that demon woman.[164]

In worshiping her, they built a *quishuar*[165] enclosure and stayed inside it for five days without ever letting people walk outside.

It's said that[166] when they finished that, and accomplished everything else including their canal-cleaning, the people came home dancing and sing-

---

157. 'As we know' supplied to indicate witness validation, which continues to predominate, with three interruptions, throughout the chapter. Because this chapter consists primarily of what appears to be a witness testimony by the editor/redactor, the three *-si* reportive passages are signaled in translation.

158. *reduzisca* 'forcibly relocated' (i.e., in San Lorenzo de Quinti). The Cupara are one of the *ayllu*s that colonial authorities had relocated (probably in the 1580s) in Spanish-style parishes (*reducciones*). Among places mentioned in the manuscript, San Pedro Mama, San Francisco de Chaclla, San Damián de Checa, San Francisco de Siçicaya, and Santa María Jesús de Huarochirí were also Toledan *reducciones* rather than prehispanic *llacta*s (Spalding 1984: flyleaf).

159. As noted in the introduction, the term *yumay* (literally, 'sperm') signifies a patrilineal group or corporation. See also chapter 31 (sec. 445).

160. Or 'a wife'.

161. In modern Andean villages the canal-cleaning festival, *yarq'a hasp'iy*, continues to be a ritual climax. A full account from the Huarochirí region is given by Paul Gelles (1984: 115–130 and *passim*).

162. *ticti*: a food-offering for *huaca*s made from the thick maize residue left as a by-product of maize beer brewing.

163. The guinea pig, *Cavia porcellus* (also called *Cavia cobayo*), is native to the Andes and is raised in most rural Andean kitchens for festive or sacrificial food.

164. *supay huarmicta* 'demon woman': clergymen consistently used *supay* to translate the Christian concept 'demon', and in the manuscript *supay* sometimes seems to be used in this sense. But the word may retain a nuance of its older Andean sense, which is the shade or light, volatile part of a living being (Duviols 1978).

165. *quishuar*: a small tree whose wood was prominently used in ritual context. "*Buddleia sp. Quishuar* and its variants. . . . The plants of this genus are shrubs or occasionally herbs, with opposite lanceolate leaves and four-lobed white, violet to purple flowers borne in heads, panicles, or spikes . . . grown in the temperate regions as ornamentals and for their wood, which is used in tool-making and cabinet work . . . the wood of *Buddleia incana* had symbolic meaning and was used ceremonially by the Incas . . . a pre-Columbian temple at Cuzco [was] known as Quishuar-Cancha, in which was kept a gold idol the size of a ten-year-old boy, . . . idols burned at the festivals of R'aimi [*sic*] were also made of the wood of *Buddleia longifolia*. A number of small branches . . . were found in a grave of the Classic Maranga Period at Vista Alegre . . ." (Towle 1961: 75–76).

166. 'It's said that' supplied to indicate reportive validation, which continues through the end of section 92.

ing. They'd lead one woman along in their midst, reverencing her as they did the *huaca*[167] and saying,

"This is Chuqui Suso!"

93 As this woman arrived at their village, we'd see[168] some people awaiting her, laying out maize beer and other things and greeting her:

"This is Chuqui Suso!"

On that occasion they say[169] people celebrated a major festival, dancing and drinking all night long.

In fact that's why, when the late lord[170] Don Sebastián[171] was still alive, during Corpus Christi and the other major Christian holy days, a woman used to proclaim,

"I am Chuqui Suso!"

and give maize beer from a large gold or silver jar with a large gourd[172] to everyone in rank order, saying,

"This is our mother's beer!"

Then she would also hand out toasted maize from a large hollow gourd.

94 When they'd finished cleaning the canal, they reportedly[173] used to invite a tremendous lot of people and give them maize, beans, and other things.

Since they always used to give things away like that, people from Huaro Cheri and from all the other communities used to go there. "They've cleaned Chuqui Suso's canal. Come on, let's go have a look!" they'd say.

95 In fact[174] today people who are in the know[175] about these practices still do the same thing and perform the same rites when they clean the canals. Even now, no matter how people behave, neither the *alcalde*[176] nor anybody else would ever try to stop them by asking, "Why do you do these things?"

On the contrary, they dance and drink right along with them until they get drunk. And as for the Catholic priest, they fool him, saying, "Padre, I'm back from cleaning the canal, so I'm going to dance, I'm going to drink."

As far as that goes, all the people do the same thing.

True, some don't do it anymore because they have a good padre.[177]

But others go on living like this in secret up to the present.

---

167. 'The *huaca*' supplied. Original has *payta yna* 'as her'.

168. 'We'd see' supplied to convey the witness validation of this sentence.

169. 'They say' supplied to indicate reportive validation of this sentence.

170. *apo* 'lord': while Spanish speakers commonly knew this honorific, it did not belong to the legal jargon of colonial authority (which typically used the titles *curaca* or *cacique*). It is more suggestive of traditional legitimacy and connotes both religious and political authority.

171. Possibly the same Sebastián mentioned in chapter 19 (sec. 230) as an earlier *curaca*. Both passages could refer to Sebastián Quispe Ninavilca. He was the son of the man who had ruled Huarochirí before the Spanish conquest under the name Ninavilca and continued to rule after it as Don Antonio. Sebastián enjoyed Spanish favor, helped Dávila Brizeño organize forced resettlement of natives, and supported the Jesuit missions of the 1570s. He was rewarded in the 1580s with an office as a high native magistrate (Spalding 1984: 222). Here we are told (perhaps with malice) that despite such activities he also favored the *huaca*s.

172. *poto* 'gourd': conjectural translation. In some regions of the Andes today, women serve maize beer ritually by doling out liquid from a large pail with a smaller gourd cup.

173. 'Reportedly' supplied to indicate reportive validation, which continues throughout section 94.

174. 'In fact' supplied to indicate resumption of witness validation, which continues through the end of the chapter.

175. *musiasca* 'in the know' (also translated 'privy to'): this locution is used in several parts of the manuscript to designate those involved in Andean worship. Taylor (1987b: 143) gives a different reading: 'confounded (by the demon)', based on the fact that this verb often denoted foreknowledge such as that gained by magical means.

176. *alcalde*: *alcaldías* were Spanish magistracies, of which certain ranks were assigned to natives for purposes of indirect rule. Higher-ranking native *alcaldes mayores* had province-level administrative duties (Espinoza Soriano 1960). But the ones alluded to here, in chapter 13 (sec. 173) and in supplement II (sec. 481), are probably village-level *alcaldes* of the sort appointed under Toledan ordinances of resettlement (Spalding 1984: 216–217). The Toledan viceroyalty intentionally gave them powers overlapping those of the *curaca* or native lord, encouraging them to prohibit traditional rites (like this one) that the native lord might be tempted to permit.

177. This politically prudent afterthought may reflect awareness that Father Avila would scrutinize the text.

CHAPTER 8

How Paria Caca Ascended. How One Man Came Back with His Child by Following Paria Caca's Commands, and, Finally, How He Struggled with Huallallo Caruincho

96

We've already told about Huallallo Caruincho's life.

But we didn't speak about his dwelling place, the place he made his shrine and community.[178]

In ancient times, they say,[179] Huallallo Caruincho dwelled in the area of Upper Paria Caca.

We don't know for certain that dwelling's original name. We do know[180] that it's called Mullo Cocha lake[181] today because, when Paria Caca defeated Huallallo, who was a burning fire, he turned the place into a lake to extinguish him.

97 It was on the location of Mullo Cocha lake that they say[182] Huallallo's dwelling place stood.

At that time the whole region was completely Yunca.[183] When he lived there huge snakes, toucans, and all sorts of animals filled the land.

In fact things were just as we described in the first chapter,[184]

<**margin**, in Spanish:> [1ˢᵗ chapter]

when we told how he ate people.

98 They say that[185] when Paria Caca set out to defeat Huallallo Caruincho, the five persons who composed him[186] whirled hunting *bolas*[187] at Ocsa Pata.[188]

<**margin**, in Spanish:> [Ocsa Pata is next to Paria Caca.]

While they swung their *bolas*, that region got intensely cold, and hail fell upon the ground where he played.

---

178. The first two sentences have witness validation.

179. 'They say' supplied to indicate reportive validation.

180. 'We do know' supplied to indicate witness validation, which continues throughout section 96.

181. The lake whose modern name is Mullucocha is 30 km by air east-northeast of Huarochirí in the barren heights, at 4,300 m above sea level (IGM 1970–1971). Mullo Cocha means 'Lake of Thorny Oyster Shell'. Sections 99–104 show why. Because the lake's name is well known in this form, we have deviated from the practice of presenting terms like *cocha* 'lake' or *urcu* 'mountain' in translation only.

182. 'They say' supplied to indicate reportive validation, which continues through the next sentence.

183. *yuncasapa* 'completely Yunca' or 'full of Yunca': from the following sentence, which tells us that subtropical animals of the coast then inhabited the extreme heights, we learn that this means ecologically as well as culturally *yunca*.

184. 'In fact' supplied to indicate witness validation of this sentence. The reference is to chapter 1 (sec. 4).

185. 'They say that' supplied to indicate reportive validation.

186. *pihcantin*: 'five' plus the suffix -*ntin*, which denotes the combination of intrinsically related or fitted parts: 'the five of him together'. The best-known instance of -*ntin* is the Inca name for the Inca Empire, *Tauantin Suyo*, meaning 'the Fourfold Domain' (see chap. 17, secs. 213, 215; chap. 22, sec. 280; chap. 23, sec. 288).

187. *riuicorcan* 'whirled . . . *bolas*': the *riwi* is a native South American hunting weapon made by tying round stones together and hurling them at the legs of prey so that the thongs entangle and fell it.

188. The toponym *ocsa pata* means 'grassy ledge' and evokes the windswept panorama of the high grasslands. It may signify a place on modern Cerro Ocsa. "Ocsa Mountain might be the modern Ocsha Mountain, which is found to the southwest of Lake Piticocha, which is also found in the area of the deeds [i.e., of Paria Caca], although somewhat farther away" (Bonavia et al. 1984: 12). Modern maps (IGM 1970–1971) show a plateau and a ravine called Ocsha 10 km southwest of Mullucocha.

99 At that moment a man[189] came along weeping <**margin**, in Spanish:> [Tell the part about the snake.]
and carrying one of his children.[190] He was also bringing his thorny oyster shell,[191] coca, and balls of *ticti*, meaning to give them to Huallallo in a drink offering.

"Son, where are you going crying like that?" one of the Paria Cacas asked him.
<**margin**, in Spanish:> [Find out the names of these 5 brothers.
The names of these five brothers are

Paria Caca
Churapa
Puncho
Paria Carco

We don't know the name of one of these five.][192]

"Father," he replied, "I'm taking this dear little kid of mine as food to serve Huallallo."

"Son," replied the Paria Caca, "don't take your little one there. Carry him back to your village. Give me that thorny oyster shell of yours, your coca, and your *ticti*, and then take your kid right back.

100 "In five days you must come back here to see me do combat with Huallallo Caruincho," Paria Caca said. "If I overwhelm him with floods of water, you must call out to me,
'Our father's beating him!'
But if he overpowers me with a blaze of fire, you must call out to me,

'The fighting's over!' "
The man got scared when Paria Caca said this, and said, "Father, won't that Huallallo Caruincho be enraged at me?"

101 "Let him get angry! He won't be able to do a thing to you. And what's more I will bring people into being, males under the care of Ami and Llata,[193] <**margin**, in Spanish:>

[Sons

Curaca or Ancacha the 1st
Chauca the 2d
Llunco the 3d
Sullca the 4th
Llata the 5th
Ami the 6th

Daughters

Paltacha or Cochucha the 1st
Cobapacha the 2d
Ampuche the 3d
Sullcacha the 4th
Ecancha the 5th
Anacha Añasi the 6th]

and females under that of Añasi; one as the male and one as the female, that's how I will have them live,"[194] replied Paria Caca. And while he was speak-

---

189. Here there is an imperfectly legible Quechua marginal note that Taylor (1987b: 146) renders 'This man was Quinti'. If correct, the interpretation is important because it shows that the Quinti, a group associated with the lineages of Paria Caca, were alleged to have ancestors who worshiped a Yunca deity.

190. *huc churinta* 'one of his children': see chapter 1 (sec. 1), about how Huallallo ate one of every two babies born. The weeping man was going to make his sacrifice.

191. *mullo*, the shell of the thorny oyster, *Spondylus princeps*, or powders and beads made from it, was among the commonest offerings to Andean deities and a major cargo in prehispanic deepwater seafaring (see Marcos 1980; Murra 1975b; Paulsen 1974).

192. In section 101 there is a birth-order list that may give general words meaning 'firstborn', 'secondborn', etc., rather than the personal names of Paria Caca's incarnations or offspring. In chapter 9 (sec. 113) and chapter 12 (sec. 166) there appear separate lists of the apparently human sons of Paria Caca.

193. *Ami* and *Llata*: these poorly understood persons reappear in chapter 11 (sec. 157). The phrasing *amiyoc . . . llatayoc . . . añasiyoc* 'possessors of Ami . . . possessors of Llata . . . possessors of Añasi' suggests that these persons are prototypes of a group that held Ami, Llata, and Añasi as their *huaca*s and protectors. While this detail has not been resolved, the gist can be partly clarified.

This foretelling allusion, addressed to a prototypical man of the group whose origin chapter 11 relates, seems to mean, 'You are afraid now because you are powerless, but I later will supply a kind of people to be subordinate to you. The man will have *Ami* and *Llata* as his *huaca*s and the woman will have *Añasi*'. The prophecy comes true in chapter 11, where the lastborn persona of Paria Caca relieves the equally lastborn Checa of their powerlessness by forcing some of the Yunca aborigines to subordinate themselves as the "little Amis and Llatas" of the Checa.

Ami means sick from overeating; *llata*, 'naked' (González Holguín [1608] 1952: 24, 212). *Añasi* may relate to *añas* 'skunk'. If they are Quechua, which is uncertain, the names seem to suggest lowly attributes of babies: nakedness, nausea, smelliness. Babyhood may symbolize junior genealogical rank.

194. *hucta cari hucta huarmicta ynam camasac* 'one

ing, his breath came out of his mouth like bluish smoke.

<**margin**, in Spanish:> [It was a clear blue.]

When the man saw this, he got scared and handed over everything he'd brought.

The five men ate the thorny oyster shell, making it crunch with a "Cap cap" sound, and all the other offerings.

Then the man went back, carrying his child.

102   Five days later, he did return just as Paria Caca had told him to, thinking, "I'll go and witness it!"

<**margin**, in Quechua:> [Paria Caca's victory]

And five days after his prophecy, Paria Caca did begin fighting Huallallo Caruincho.

The story is like this.

Paria Caca, since he was five persons, began to rain down from five directions.

That rain was yellow and red rain.

Then, flashing as lightning, he blazed out from five directions.

103   From early in the morning to the setting of the sun,[195] Huallallo Caruincho flamed up in the form of a giant fire reaching almost to the heavens, never letting himself be extinguished.

And[196] the waters, the rains of Paria Caca, rushed down toward Ura Cocha, the lower lake.[197]

Since it wouldn't have fit in,[198] one of Paria Caca's five selves, the one called Llacsa Churapa, knocked down a mountain and dammed the waters from below.

104   Once he impounded these waters they formed a lake.

(Nowadays this lake is called Mullo Cocha.)[199]

As the waters filled the lake they almost submerged that burning fire.

And Paria Caca kept flashing lightning bolts at him, never letting him rest.

Finally Huallallo Caruincho fled toward the low country, the Antis.[200]

105   Another of Paria Caca's offspring

<**margin**, in Spanish:> [Find out if these are brothers since it's said that they came out of the eggs, or if they're the Paria Caca's children.—They were brothers.]

chased after him.

He stays at the pass down to the lowlands, the Antis, until today, "Lest Huallallo Caruincho return," as he says.

His name was <crossed out:> [Sullca Yllapa] Paria Carco.[201]

106   During Paria Caca's victory, a certain woman named Mana Ñamca[202] appeared, a demon who'd accompanied Huallallo Caruincho.[203]

This woman lived below Mama,[204] somewhere down there.

It was to conquer her that Paria Caca came to her.

Mana Ñamca also burned in the form of a fire.

---

as the male and one as the female, that's how I will have them live': may mean that the Ami/Llata and Añasi groups, respectively, have male and female identity with regard to each other.

195. *ña hora pachacama* 'to the setting of the sun': an alternative translation would be 'to lower Pacha Camac'. Both possibilities are problematic, but 'Pacha Camac' more so since it is normally spelled with final *c* in the manuscript.

196. There is a crossed-out phrase, *paria cacap huquinca*, of uncertain meaning.

197. *hura cochañicman*: 'lower lake' or alternatively 'Pacific Ocean'; accepting the 'Pacha Camac' reading would warrant the latter.

198. *manatac yaycuptin* 'since it wouldn't have fit in': a problematic passage. It may mean that in order to prevent the ocean from overspilling its shores (see chap. 3; chap. 29, sec. 375), Llacsa Churapa built a reservoir for Paria Caca's water. 'Paria Caca's five selves' supplied.

199. Dávila Brizeño ([1586] 1965: 161) thought this story represented a combat between a volcano (*sierra del fuego*) and a snowcap, with Mullo Cocha the caldera left by the volcano's collapse. (It does not appear geologically to be a caldera.) This parenthesis has witness validation.

200. Taylor (1987b: 154) at this point refers to a Quechua marginal note that means, 'He didn't just flee instantly. We'll tell about it later on'.

201. This sentence has witness validation.

202. Mana Ñamca figures again in chapter 10 (sec. 143), where she is equated to Chaupi Ñamca, who in turn is equated to the daughter of Tamta Ñamca (chap. 5, sec. 47). This cluster of three female names seems associated with Yunca aborigines and with the remote past.

203. *caruinchouan cac supay* 'a demon who'd accompanied Huallallo Caruincho': more literally, 'who was with Caruincho'. This could mean Mana Ñamca was with him as sibling, or spouse, or ally. A marginal note to a later passage (chap. 10, sec. 143) interprets her as Chaupi Ñamca, perhaps meaning Mana Ñamca was a synonym or component of Chaupi Ñamca once matched to Huallallo as Chaupi Ñamca herself was later fraternally matched to Paria Caca.

204. Probably San Pedro de Mama (modern Ricardo Palma), 52 km northwest of Huarochirí, close to Lima in the lower Rímac valley (IGM 1970–1971).

Making an entry down through Tumna,[205] Paria Caca attacked her.

She shot[206] from below and hit the foot of one of Paria Caca's offspring, the one named Chuqui Huampo.[207]

<margin, in Spanish:> [Find out what condition this one is in.]

Nonetheless, it was Paria Caca who won and expelled her into the ocean.[208]

107 After he defeated them, he went back to his child Chuqui Huampo, who sat there lame with a broken foot.

"I can't go back. I'll keep watch over that woman Mana Ñamca from right here, just in case she comes back," Chuqui Huampo said to him.

His father said, "Very well then," and made provisions to supply him with all his food.

108 He gave his command: "All the inhabitants of these two valleys must give coca to you first, before any of them may chew it. Only after you have chewed it shall the people chew coca from their

harvest. Also, the people are to slaughter a llama in your honor, one that is still childless, one that has never given birth. And you shall always eat its ear-tips[209] and other such things first, before the rest may be eaten."

<margin, in Spanish:> [This place where <crossed out:> [Sullca Yllapa] Chuqui Huampo is is below Tumna between Sisi Caya and Sucya. I have to see it and find out what it's called.][210]

109 People respected these sacred edicts, and in accordance with them all the coca producers from

Saci Caya,[211]
Chontay,[212]
Chichima,[213]
Mama,
Huayo Calla,
and Sucya Cancha[214]

would bring coca to Chuqui Huampo first before all others.

They carry on the custom secretly to this day.

---

205. Modern Tumna is 15 km west-northwest of San Damián de Checa at 2,902 m above sea level, a long way downvalley from Mullo Cocha. It occupies the heights over the Rímac's left bank.

206. *chucamurcan* 'she shot': the verb more literally means 'she hurled' and is elsewhere used in connection with lance-throwing. Perhaps the idea here is that she hurled fire (Taylor 1987b: 157), but the injury she inflicted is a broken (*paquisca*) rather than burned foot, so some more solid weapon seems indicated. To avoid the problem we choose a less specific verb.

207. Taylor (1987b: 156) gives a Quechua marginal note meaning, 'He'll be the one with the disabled leg'.

208. *cochañicman*: 'ocean' or possibly 'lake'.

209. *rinrin chillpiscacta* 'ear tips': today herders slit small notches in the ears of llamas at *señalasqa* festivals,

as signs of ownership (Aranguren Paz 1975: 117). Perhaps a fragment of ear would then be the sacrifice mentioned.

210. Taylor (1987b: 158) interprets an imperfectly legible Quechua marginal note at this point as saying, 'We will speak of Capcahuanca later'. Capac Huanca is mentioned in chapter 25 (sec. 346).

211. Modern Sisicaya is about halfway up the Lurín valley from Pachacámac to San Damián (IGM 1970–1971). See chapter 11 (sec. 156).

212. Modern Chontay is in the Lurín valley slightly downriver from Sisicaya (IGM 1970–1971).

213. Modern Santa Inés de Chichima is near Chaclacayo in the lower Rímac valley (IGM 1970–1971).

214. On basis of Sucya Villca identification (see chap. 20, sec. 242), possibly San Bartolomé, 40 km northwest of Huarochirí in the lower Rímac valley between Mama and Surco (IGM 1970–1971).

CHAPTER 9

110

How Paria Caca, Having Accomplished All This, Began to Ordain His Own Cult

Now indeed we've finished telling all these victories of his.

But we haven't spoken about how Huallallo Caruincho later lived under Paria Caca's sentence.[215]

After Paria Caca's victory, and after Huallallo had fled to the lowlands, the Antis,
<margin, in Spanish:> [Find out how this Caruincho exists in the Andes now.]

Paria Caca passed sentence on Huallallo: "Because he fed on people, let him now eat dogs; and let the Huanca[216] people worship him."

111 When the Huanca worshiped him,[217] they'd propitiate him with dogs. And since he, their god, fed on dogs, they also ate them.

As a matter of fact, we speak of them as "dog-eating Huanca" to this day.[218]

112 Just as we indicated in the first chapter and in subsequent ones, where we said that all those villages were full of Yunca,
<margin, in Spanish:> [Chapter 1]
all the inhabitants of Huaro Cheri Province and of the provinces of Chaclla[219] and Mama and of all the other villages were once full of Yunca.

Paria Caca,[220] as we know,[221] drove these Yunca and all such Yunca groups down to the lowlands. "It will be my children who'll live in this region," he ordained.

113 All those who took part in conquering these groups are individually called Paria Caca's children.
<margin, in Quechua:> [Paria Caca's children]
"Each one of them is his child," people say.

Others deny it. In accord with their belief these say, "They were born from the seed of a wild plant."[222]

The victors' names are these, starting from the oldest one:

---

215. End of an introductory passage with witness validation.

216. The Huanca were a large ethnic group inhabiting the upper Mantaro valley in the central Peruvian highlands. The Huarochirí myth-tellers' belief that their *huaca* Huallallo once tyrannized west Andean peoples seems to indicate a further belief that Paria Caca and his people reversed an earlier Huanca penetration of the seaward valleys. There is an implied claim to have liberated the Yunca from the "dog-eating Huanca" and from the burden of human sacrifice. Recent works on the Huanca include D'Altroy (1987) and Espinoza Soriano (1971).

217. Julio C. Tello (1923: 510–549) observed what he thought to be a modern tradition maintaining Huallallo's mythology and cult.

218. The "Indian chronicler" Felipe Guaman Poma de Ayala also expresses disdain for the "dog-eating Guancas" and their dog-eating deity Huallallo ([1615] 1980: 1:241, 271). 'As a matter of fact' supplied to indicate witness validation of this sentence.

219. Modern San Antonio de Chaclla is 63 km northwest of Huarochirí (IGM 1970–1971). Spalding's map (1984: endpaper) shows San Francisco de Chaclla, a resettlement village of the 1580s, at a similar location. Taylor (1987b: 39) equates Chaclla with modern Santa Eulalia, adjacent to Mama.

220. 'Paria Caca' supplied.

221. 'As we know' supplied to indicate witness validation, which continues through the end of section 116. Taylor (1987b: 163) takes the *quinua* origin story to be typical of invading groups that had individually grafted their focal ancestors onto the descent of the pre-invasion *huaca*, Paria Caca, and thereby provided themselves with an alternative and discrepant origin story.

222. Allusion to an alternative myth of origin, developed in chapter 24 (secs. 302–303) and chapter 31 (sec. 389).

Choc Payco,
Chancha Runa,
Huari Runa,
Utco Chuco,
and Tutay Quiri with his brother Sasin Mari.

All these conquered the Yunca peoples.

114 According to them, one other child of Paria Caca likewise emerged from the earth.

His name was Pacha Chuyru.

We forgot this one's conquests in all the preceding chapters.

We'll set forth these matters in a later part.[223]

<**margin**, in Quechua:> [Further on we shall set forth Pacha Chuyru's victory.]

These whom we have mentioned defeated and drove out all the Yunca peoples.

115 These Yunca groups, all the Yunca, once they forgot their former god, began to worship Paria Caca.

The tradition about the Yunca is like this.

In this community of Checa[224] lived the ones called Colli,[225] building their settlements[226] all over the communal territory. To relate all the Yunca settlements in the whole area would be very laborious.

So in what follows we shall choose only a few of them for our consideration, compiling all their customs, because all the Yunca shared one single way of life.

116 Paria Caca then established his dwelling on the heights, on the same territory where he had conquered, and began to lay down the rules[227] for his worship.

His law was one and the same law in all the villages.

The law we speak of was this: "We are all of one birth."[228]

<**margin**, in Spanish:> [This is taken to mean of one family.]

117 They say[229] he gave a command to one particular person in each village: "Once every year you are to hold a paschal celebration reenacting my life."

He said, "As for their titles, the title of these people will be *huacasa* or *huacsa*.

"The *huacsa* will dance three times each year, bringing coca in enormous leather bags."

---

223. But the manuscript does not in fact contain the promised account.

224. San Damián de Checa, a village formed by forced resettlement (*reducción*) during the 1580s, appears to be the residence of one or more of the text's informants. Modern San Damián is 22 km northwest of Huarochirí at 3,235 m above sea level (IGM 1970–1971).

225. Here and at other points the myths of the Checa tell of expelling Yunca and at the same time of Yunca groups' becoming integrated with the Checa (Rostworowski 1978: 31–44). The kindred organized around Paria Caca and Chaupi Namca expresses the purported resulting unity. This theme becomes particularly explicit in chapter 24.

226. *tiascancunacta* 'their settlements': the possessive marker is ambiguous; could mean settlements of the Colli or Checa.

227. *hunancharcan* 'lay down the rules': this word as well as 'law' (*hunanchasca*) in the following sentences is derived from a verb that González Holguín ([1608] 1952: 355) glosses 'to make signals, to understand, to consider, to design or plan out'.

228. *huc yuric canchic* 'We are all of one birth' (i.e., sibling group).

The word *yuric*, which we take to mean 'birth group' does not mean the same as *yumay* 'patrilineage', or *ayllu* 'localized kindred'. González Holguín ([1608] 1952: 372) gives "yurini to be born, to come into being, for something to come forth with something or someone as its author . . . yurini . . . for a man or animal to be born." *Yuric* is an agentive form. See the section on *yuriy/yumay* in the introduction.

The point of Paria Caca's great judgment, the cornerstone of the ideological order expounded in subsequent chapters, is that:

(1) The dominant patrilineages of the region will be the descent groups self-identified as protégés of Paria Caca's selves and children.

(2) Yunca descent groups (of what sort remains unclear), once liberated from Huallallo, will be incorporated in the role of wives and wife-givers, and their major *huaca*s as 'sisters' or 'wives' of male *huaca*s from the Paria Caca kindred. They will be considered globally the progeny of Paria Caca's "sister" Chaupi Ñamca.

(3) Insofar as all the people of the region are "born" of unions between descendants of a brother and a sister, all are siblings at the apical level of kinship and religious reckoning.

Taylor and Urioste read the passage differently. Taylor in an early working took it to mean that "each of our communities is composed of a certain number of families" (1980: 77). He later translated it as "we all belong to different lineages" (1987b: 167). Urioste (1983: 63) reads it as alluding to a single lineage. Arguedas and Duviols (1966: 65) give "all of us, who are as one single son."

229. 'They say' supplied to indicate return to reportive validation.

118   To first become a *huacsa*, people in fact[230] perform a certain ritual.

It's like this: a man of the Caca Sica *ayllu* functions as officiant for these ceremonies. From early times these officiants were only one or two people, and, as for their title, it was *yanca*.[231]

<**margin**, in Spanish:> [The master is called *yanca*.]

The same title is used in all the villages.

This man observes the course of the sun

<**margin**, in Spanish:> [That is, the shadow that the wall casts in the sun.]

from a wall constructed with perfect alignment.

When the rays of the sun touch this calibrated wall, he <crossed out:> [proclaimed] to the people, "Now we must go"; or if they don't, he'd say, "Tomorrow is the time."[232]

119   Following this command, people go to Paria Caca in order to worship.

In the old times they used to go to Paria Caca mountain itself.

But now they go from Checa to a mountain called Ynca Caya

<**margin**, in Spanish:> [The snowcap of Paria Caca is visible from this mountain.]

to worship from there.

(This mountain rises over the ruined buildings of Purum Huasi and abuts on another mountain called Huallquiri.

It's on this mountain that all sorts of people, men and women alike, go to worship.)[233]

120   People run a race on their way to this mountain, in accordance with the *yanca*'s instructions, driving their llama bucks. The strongest ones even shoulder small llamas.[234] They scramble upward, each thinking, "I mean to get to the summit first!"

<**margin**, in Spanish:> [Which is where <Paria Caca> can be seen from.]

121   The first llama to arrive at the mountain top was much loved by Paria Caca.

In the old days Paria Caca himself used to give a name to this llama buck, proclaiming, "Let its name be thus!"

<**margin**, in Spanish:> [different names each time, of one sort or another, such as Yauri or Yllaca]

And as for the first little llama to arrive, the *yanca* would display it and praise it before all eyes, announcing, "The bearer of this llama is very fortunate. Paria Caca loves him."

122   This time of worship, as we know,[235] is called the Auquisna.

<**margin**, in Spanish:> [Auquisna 'for our father' or 'creator'][236]

Similarly the worship of Chaupi Ñamca is called the Chaycasna.

<**margin**, in Spanish:> [Chaycasna 'for our mother'][237]

But we'll explain the Chaycasna later.

Nowadays the Auquisna season <crossed out:> [falls] comes in the month of June or close to it. It either occurs close to <crossed out:> [Corpus Christi] the great pasch[238] or actually coincides with it.

All the *huacsa*s, who might be ten or even twenty, dance on this occasion.

This dance is not something their ancestors appropriated.[239]

---

230. 'In fact' supplied to convey witness validation, which continues through the next four sentences.

231. That is, the *yanca*, as priest entitled by heredity to supervise the rituals, establishes the new *huacsa*'s relation with the *huaca* he (or she?) is to embody.

232. That is, he observed a gnomon to determine the correct date. R. T. Zuidema has studied the use of gnomons in Incaic Cuzco (1981: 319–322). The past tense verb *villarca* 'he proclaimed' is inconsistent in tense with the adjacent verbs. Taylor's transcription (1987b: 170) gives *villancu*, in present tense and third person plural, which is more consistent.

233. This parenthesis has witness validation.

234. *ancha sinche runacuna huchoylla llamanhuanpas* 'the strongest ones even shoulder small llamas': 'shoulder' is supplied to make the more literal sense— 'the strongest people with small llamas'—intelligible.

235. 'As we know' supplied to indicate witness validation, which continues through the end of section 122.

236. In a Jaqi language, maybe Aymara.

237. In a Jaqi language, maybe Aymara.

238. Because Corpus roughly coincides with the dry-season climax of the Andean ritual calendar, it has consistently become in Andean eyes the "great" festival of Catholicism and an occasion for performing nominally forbidden Andean rites. But a 1609 Jesuit report studied in Taylor's article "Cultos y fiestas de la comunidad de San Damián" (1987a) gives April as the Auquisna season. In accord with this report we interpret the teller's editing out Corpus and substituting *aton pascua* 'the great pasch' as meaning that he thought Auquisna close to Easter, which usually falls in April.

239. *cay taquicoytas manatac yayancunap chapascan* 'This dance is not something their ancestors appropriated': problematic translation. González Holguín ([1608] 1952: 96) gives "thing appropriated" for *chapasca*. Perhaps this means that *huacsa*s' right to dance, unlike other dancing privileges, was not among the rights seized

<margin, in Spanish>: [Find out about this sort of song and write it down for me on paper in the Quechua language, from what they say.]

123 The *huacsa*s reportedly[240] perform this dance with absolutely no interruption.

If someone who stops dancing ever happens to die, people comment about him, "He died because of the fault he committed."

For that reason, they make little children or any other kind of people carry on the dance.[241] The people from Surco especially prefer to call on the Huayllas to dance in their stead.

124 If a Huayllas man is married to a native Surco village woman and performs these rituals, the members of that community don't take away his fields or anything else of his, even though he's an outsider. On the contrary, they respect him and help him.

What's more, when Huayllas people who live in Surco come to Sucya Cancha to trade coca, regardless of their standing they bargain, saying, "Give me a little extra, ma'am; I'm a *huacsa*."[242]

125 Nowadays, as we know,[243] people perform this pasch by making it coincide with any of the major Christian paschal rites, and the people from Surco still excel over all the other communities.

On account of this dance, the Catholic priests in their villages exact collections[244] of chickens, maize, and all sorts of other things. The people hand these things over more than cheerfully.

126 The *huacsa*s dance likewise during Chaupi Ñamca's paschal festival.

This paschal festival sometimes comes close to Corpus Christi, and sometimes actually coincides with it.

In another chapter
<margin, in Quechua:> [We'll set forth Chaupi Ñamca's life in a different chapter later on.]
we'll record Chaupi Ñamca's life, where she lived, and how people worshiped her.[245] But now let's return to Paria Caca's story and to all the things people did during the season of his paschal festival.

127 The story that explains these events is like this.

On the eve of the day when they were to arrive at Paria Caca for worship, people whose kin, whether men or women, had died in the course of that year would wail all night long,[246] saying, "Tomorrow we'll go and see our dead by Paria Caca's side!"[247]

128 They said regarding their deceased of the year, "Tomorrow is the day when we'll deliver them there."[248]

They offered the dead food and even fed them that night, and spread out the ingredients for their rituals.[249] They said,

"Now I deliver them to Paria Caca forever. They will never come back any more!"

And they worshiped with the sacrifice of a small llama, or, if they had no llamas, they'd bring coca in large skin bags.

129 As we know,[250] they'd examine this llama's in-

---

by invading ancestors from aborigines. Taylor follows another line, reading (1980: 79) *yayancuna* as "their *encomenderos*" (i.e., colonial Spanish tribute lords). The same translator gives "without their owners' being aware" in a later working (1987b: 175). Arguedas (Arguedas and Duviols 1966: 65) has "without vigilance by the [Catholic] priests."

240. 'Reportedly' supplied to indicate return to reportive validation.

241. Apparently, in order to keep the dance going when a dancer is exhausted.

242. This sentence has witness validation.

243. 'As we know' supplied to indicate witness validation, which continues through the narrative formula at the beginning of section 127.

244. *aguelando* 'collections': probably a variant of Spanish *agüinaldo*, meaning a holiday contribution or gift (traditionally, at Christmas or Epiphany). In colonial Peru the practice was expanded illegally into a form of tribute *de facto*.

245. The teller (or editor?) is at pains to remind the reader that the Chaupi Ñamca cult (chap. 10) and Paria Caca cult are inherently complementary, separated only for expository reasons.

246. A 1609 Jesuit report discussed by Taylor (1987a) explains that, on this occasion, the mourners would take their mummified dead to a certain cave, Chutinhuaque, dressed in gala clothes and carried on llama back. Mourners kept vigil weeping in the cave until the morning sacrifices.

247. This probably alludes to the custom of visiting the mummified ancestors; see chapter 28.

248. This may allude to the delivery of recently made mummies to their permanent shrine sites.

249. *ruranancunactapas* 'the ingredients for their rituals': *-na* suffix denotes potential and not preterite action. *Rurana* means 'to make or do', so the word means more literally 'their things to be done'.

250. 'As we know' supplied to indicate witness validation, which continues to the end of section 129.

nards. If the signs were favorable, the *yanca* would prophesy, "Everything is well." If not, he'd say, "It's bad. You've incurred a fault. Your dead relative has angered Paria Caca. Ask forgiveness for this transgression, lest that fault be charged to you as well."

130   After completing these rituals, the *yanca*s carried off the heads and loins of those llamas for themselves, no matter how many thousands there might be, declaring, "This is our fee!"

131   The *huacsa*s, who'd dance on three occasions in any given year, would finish their term on that day.[251] In order to enter a new cycle, when the old dance round was about to come to an end, all the people came to the center in Llacsa Tambo,[252] and the Concha were in the plaza, too,[253] carrying a macaw-wing display or the sort of thing known as *puypu*.[254]

They'd lay these items in the center, on the rock called Llacsa Tambo.

After they deposited these things, they stayed there all night long, in the place where a cross now stands, wondering, "Will I be well this year?"

132   The next day they went to all the villages, including Macacho hill, Chaucalla, and Quimquilla, and remained there until five days were up.

At the end of the fifth day, all the *huacsa*s who'd collected coca in bags would dance.

At daybreak on the same day, in Llacsa Tambo, they used to worship the demon with their llamas or other possessions.

133   Those who are privy to these customs do the same in all the villages.

Nowadays, it's true, some have forgotten these practices.

But since it's just a few years[255] since they've had Doctor Francisco de Avila, a good counselor and teacher, it may be that in their hearts they don't really believe. If they had another priest they might return to the old ways.

134   Some people, although they've become Christians, have done so only out of fear. "I'm afraid the priest or somebody else might find out how bad I've been," they think.[256]

Although they say the Rosary, they still carry some pretty *illa* amulet[257] everywhere; although they themselves might not worship these native divinities, they contract some old people to worship in their stead. Lots of people live this way.
<**margin**, in Spanish, crossed out:> [n.b.]

135   As we said earlier, the Concha, too, worship during Paria Caca's season from that other mountain called Huaycho. Their *huacsa*s do just the same as the Checa's own do, that is, they dance.

Likewise, the Suni Cancha also worship in the same manner during Paria Caca's season from that mountain called
<**margin**, in Spanish:> [n.b.]
<   >.[258]

136   The residents of Santa Ana,[259] those who live in

---

251. This sentence has witness validation, which continues up to 'they dance' in section 135.

252. This is the first passage about Llacsa Tambo, the ceremonial center of the Checa and reference point for much of the text. Llacsa Tambo was probably at or near modern Llaquistambo, a hamlet with numerous prehispanic structures 3 km northeast of San Damián (IGM 1970–1971). Its name (if Quechua) is partly intelligible. Arriaga ([1621] 1968: 45) gives the gloss: "*Llacsa* is a green color in the form of either powder or stone, like copper oxide." *Tambo* means a way-station. Alternatively, the name may allude to a verb *llacsay*, which Goncález Holguín ([1608] 1952: 207) translates as 'to freeze the blood' with fear.

253. *conchacunapas pampampi* 'and the Concha were in the plaza, too': the point of this slightly awkward insertion seems to be that the Concha, although a separate village (functioning as the Checa's opposite in the *reducción* village), were seated in the Checa's ceremony.

254. *puypu* is explained in chapter 24 (sec. 333) as synonymous with *huacamaypac ricran* 'a macaw's wing'.

255. *cay pisi huatallarac* 'just a few years': an ambiguity in this phrase adds to the difficulty of dating the manuscript. If read 'scarcely one year' it would support the 1598 date that Arguedas and Duviols favored (1966: 235). But it could just as well mean 'these few years', allowing a later date and with it the chronologies c. 1608 that Urioste and Taylor both favor (Acosta 1987b: 596; Taylor 1987b: 15–16; see the section on the possible genesis of the text in the introduction).

256. *ñispas*: the common verb *ñiy* or *niy* can mean either 'say' or 'think, intend'.

257. *Illa*s are small sacred objects, often figurines, that are felt to contain the fecundating essence of the good they represent. Archaeological examples are common. Ethnographic examples are discussed by Jorge Flores Ochoa (1977).

258. A space for the mountain's name was never filled in. Modern Sunicancha stands across a canyon from Conchasica, both close to San Damián.

259. Modern Santa Ana de Chaucarima is 18 km west-northwest of Huarochirí at 3,492 m above sea level (IGM 1970–1971).

San Juan,[260] and all the ones called Chauca Ricma, during Paria Caca's season, reportedly[261] worship from the mountain called Acu Sica, the one we descend on our way to the Apar Huayqui River.[262]

In fact[263] they'd never let anything stop them from performing[264] these rituals.

Some people make this festival coincide with the great pasch, Easter; others set it close to Pentecost <crossed out:> [and Corpus].

When it comes to celebrating it, the people in this village would be delighted if the priest were absent from town or went to Limac.[265]

This is a completely true account.

137   Regarding all these places on mountains for worship of Paria Caca, it was only later on, when the Spaniards had emerged and came to look into it, that they were established.

138   But, in the old times, they say[266] all these people used to go to Paria Caca mountain itself. All the Yunca people[267] from

Colli,
Carhuayllo,[268]
Ruri Cancho,[269]

Latim,[270]
Huancho Huaylla,[271]
Pariacha,[272]
Yañac,[273]
Chichima,[274]
Mama,[275]

and all the other Yunca from that river valley;

Also the Saci Caya,[276] who, together with the Pacha Camac come from another river valley,[277] and the Caringa and Chilca,[278] and those people who live along the river that flows down from Huaro Cheri,[279] namely, the Caranco[280] and other Yunca groups who inhabit that river region, used to arrive at Mount Paria Caca itself, coming with their *ticti*, their coca, and other ritual gear.

139   When those who'd come to worship returned from Paria Caca, people in their villages, aware of their impending arrival, used to await them in a gathering to ask, "How is our father Paria Caca?"

"Is he still well?"

"Isn't he angry?"

Then they'd dance full of happiness until the end of the fifth day, or however many days was their custom.

140   Regarding this worship, it may be that the Yunca don't practice it anymore, or that not all the Yunca do. But they do perform it away from their own places.

When they don't do it people speculate, saying,

---

260. San Juan de Lahuaytambo, seat of the 'Thousand' of Chaucarima (Taylor 1987b: 187). See note 457.

261. 'Reportedly' supplied to indicate reportive validation.

262. Apar Huayqui River: possibly the Mala or its tributary the Canchahuara, associated with a mountain named Ayarhuaque at its source (IGM 1970–1971).

263. 'In fact' supplied to indicate witness validation, which continues through the end of section 137.

264. *ruraypacca manam ancochanmancho* 'they'd never let anything stop them from performing': more literally, 'they'd not rest from doing it'. The phrase might allude to the people's tenacity in retaining pre-Christian rites, or might alternatively be taken to mean they are rigorous about the rule requiring continual dancing (chap. 9, sec. 123).

265. The name of the city of Lima is uniformly Limac in the manuscript.

266. 'They say' supplied to indicate shift to reportive validation.

267. The following locales making up this category are listed in groups. The first list covers the Rímac valley from the Pacific shore eastward into the highlands. Lurín and Mala valley villages follow.

268. Modern Carabayllo is north of the Chillón River within greater Lima (IGM 1970–1971).

269. Lurigancho, today an outlying neighborhood of Lima.

270. Ate, today an outlying neighborhood of Lima.

271. Huanchihuaylla, a neighborhood of Ate according to Taylor (1987b: 191).

272. Modern Pariachi is 67 km west of Huarochirí at 1,160 m above sea level (IGM 1970–1971). Taylor (1987b: 191) mentions an estate called Pariache.

273. Possibly Ñaña, a village in the lower Rímac valley slightly outside Lima.

274. Santa Rosa de Chichima (Taylor 1987b: 191) or the more prominent colonial village of Santa Inés de Chichima, both in the lower Rímac valley.

275. San Pedro de Mama, the modern town of Ricardo Palma.

276. Probably Sisicaya in the Lurín valley.

277. That is, the Lurín.

278. Probably the same groups mentioned in chapter 12 (sec. 171), inhabitants of the lower Mala. Modern Chilca is a coastal town slightly north of the mouth of the Mala River.

279. That is, the Mala River.

280. Caranco may have been at or near modern Calango, on the lower Mala River, 305 m above sea level. See also chapter 12 (secs. 170–171) and chapter 23 (sec. 285).

"It's because of that fault of theirs that the Yunca are becoming extinct."

And the Yunca, speaking for themselves, say, "The highlanders[281] are getting along all right. It's because they carry on our old way of life that their people flourish so."[282]

---

281. *sallcacuna* 'the highlanders': no English word ('mountaineer', 'hillbilly', 'mountain man') catches the exact flavor of *sallcacuna*. *Sallca* means the *puna*, the seasonally rainy but generally dry and (at night) cold lands that cover huge expanses around 4,000 m above sea level. The word evokes the roughness of llama herders' lives up on these treeless slopes.

282. This discussion probably concerns people's ideas, c. 1600, about the fact that the post-invasion epidemics had devastated the coastal native peoples much more than the highlanders (see Cook 1981: 253–254; Denevan 1976: 41).

CHAPTER 10

Who Chaupi Ñamca Was, Where She Dwells, and How She Arranged Her Cult

Now we've finished telling Paria Caca's life.

And now we'll tell who those children of his (the ones we mentioned in the ninth chapter) were, and then tell the things that each one did individually as well as how they collectively beat the Yunca out of these villages.

<marginal note in Quechua:> [After this we'll set forth the victories of Paria Caca's children.]

Next we'll write about who Chaupi Ñamca was.[283]

142   They say[284] that the one called Chaupi Ñamca was the daughter of a man in Anchi Cocha, a lord named Tamta Ñamca, and that she was the wife of the poor man named Huatya Curi.

In fact[285] we told this story in the fifth chapter.

143   This woman had five sisters.

The first woman, Chaupi Ñamca, went to dwell in Lower Mama in accord with Paria Caca's instructions.

The woman known as Mana Ñamca[286]

<margin, in Spanish:> [Her name is Chaupi Ñamca or Mama Ñamca.]

went around saying, "I am a maker of people."[287]

Some people say about Chaupi Ñamca, "She was Paria Caca's sister."

And she herself used to say, "Paria Caca is my brother."

144   Chaupi Ñamca was frozen into a stone with five arms.[288] In worshiping her, people would race each other to reach her, just as they did when they went racing to worship Paria Caca, racing along driving their llamas and other things.

They'd lead to her the very same llamas that went to Paria Caca.

Later on, when the Spaniards appeared on the scene, people hid Chaupi Ñamca, the five-armed stone, underground in Mama, near the Catholic priest's stable.

She's there to this day, inside the earth.

145   All the people called Chaupi Ñamca "Mother" when they spoke to her.

---

283. End of an introductory passage with witness validation.

284. 'They say' supplied to indicate shift to reportive validation.

285. 'In fact' supplied to indicate witness validation of this sentence.

286. The next passages tell us that Mana Ñamca, who was earlier described as accompanying the defeated Huanca(?) deity Huallallo Caruincho (chap. 8, sec. 106), is now equated with Chaupi Ñamca. Chaupi Ñamca, Pacha Camac's wife (Dávila Brizeño [1586] 1965: 163), is pictured as Paria Caca's sister and female counterpart. Thus the apex of divine kinship is structured as a fraternal union between an ancient Yunca pantheon and a newly

appeared male of the highlands, establishing a society that is 'one family' (chap. 9, sec. 116). This motif is expressed in human terms in chapter 5 (sec. 48), where Huatya Curi marries a Yunca woman who is also equated to Chaupi Ñamca.

287. More than one *huaca* has the epithet *runa camac*, here rendered loosely as 'maker of people' (Cuni Raya Vira Cocha in chap. 1, sec. 7; Chaupi Ñamca in chap. 13, sec. 172; Mira Huato and Llacsa Huato in chap. 13, sec. 179; Llocllay Huancupa in chap. 21, sec. 268). The premise is that different human groups receive their life-energy and specific powers from different *huaca*s. The fuller meanings of *camac* are explored in the introduction.

288. Or 'wings'.

(That's why San Pedro is also called Mama now.)[289]

In the old days this woman used to travel around in human form and used to sin with[290] the other *huaca*s.

But she never used to praise any male by saying, "He's good!"

146   There was a certain male on the mountain that overlooks Mama, a *huaca* named Rucana Coto.[291]

Men who had small cocks would implore Rucana Coto, thinking to themselves, "It'll get big."

One time he and his big cock satisfied Chaupi Ñamca deliciously.

Therefore she said, "Only this man, alone among all the other *huaca*s, is a real man. I'll stay with this one forever." So she turned into stone and stayed forever in Mama.

147   Now we'll tell about the sisters of Chaupi Ñamca whom we mentioned.[292]

Chaupi Ñamca was the oldest of them all.
Her next sister was Llacsa Huato.
Her next-born sibling was Mira Huato.
The next one was called Urpay Huachac.
We don't know about the other one.[293]
In all they were five.

When people sought Chaupi Ñamca's advice on any matter, she'd respond, saying, "I'll go and talk it over with my sisters first."[294]

148   We know[295] people schedule Chaupi Ñamca's

rites during the month of June, in such a way that they almost coincide with Corpus Christi.

When the *yanca*
<margin, in Quechua:> [*yanca*]
had made calculations from his solar observatory, people said, "They'll take place in so many days."

149   We already spoke in chapter nine about the *huacsa*s' annual dances.

However, regarding this dancing, we didn't clarify what kinds of dances they performed on the three occasions in a given year.

They celebrated Paria Caca's paschal festival on the first day of the period called Auquisna.

Next, they likewise danced during Chaupi Ñamca's time.

Finally, in the month of November, just about coinciding with the festival of San Andrés,[296] they'd perform still another dance called Chanco.

Further on we'll describe this dance fully.[297]

150   But now we'll return to Chaupi Ñamca's paschal festival.

During her paschal festival the *huacsa*s would dance for five days carrying coca bags.

Other people, if they had llamas, would dance wearing puma skins; those who had no llamas danced just as they were.

About those who wore puma skins people said, "They're the prosperous ones."

This dance is called Huantay Cocha.

They also performed another dance named Ayñu.

151   They performed still another one called Casa Yaco.

They say that[298] when they danced the Casa Yaco, Chaupi Ñamca rejoiced immensely, because in their dancing, they performed naked, some wearing only their jewelry, hiding their private parts with just a cotton breechclout.

"Chaupi Ñamca enjoys it no end when she sees our <crossed out:> [cocks] private parts!" they said as they danced naked.

After they danced this dance a very fertile season would follow.[299]

These are the rituals they performed during her paschal festival.[300]

289. The reference is to the resettlement village of San Pedro. This sentence has witness validation.

290. *vchallicuc carcan* 'sinned with': a Christian-style euphemism. Chaupi Ñamca's mighty sexual appetite is not seen as sinful in the context of the myth that immediately follows, or in that of the sexy Casa Yaco dance (sec. 151) that honored her. A pervasive though never explicit metaphor seems to liken the ardent genitalia of the female *huaca*s with the warm fertile valleys, much as the water-giving heights of the mountains are likened to males who fertilize them.

291. *Rucana Coto* 'Finger-shaped mountain' (Quechua and Aymara).

292. This sentence has witness validation.

293. Taylor (1987b: 198) signals a marginal note in Quechua, meaning, 'The other one was called Lluncuhuachac'.

294. This suggests that the five *huaca*s' priests or priestesses deliberated collectively.

295. 'We know' supplied to indicate witness validation, which continues through the first sentence of section 151.

296. St. Andrew's Day is November 30.

297. The Chanco is the subject of chapter 11.

298. 'They say that' supplied to indicate shift to reportive validation.

299. This is probably the sort of festival Catholic priests had in mind when they complained that Andean rites included "carnal excesses."

300. Concluding sentence with witness validation.

CHAPTER 11

How People Danced the Chanco Dance. In Speaking of These Matters, We Shall Also Tell Who Tutay Quiri, the Child of Paria Caca, Was. The Story Is Like This

In the ninth chapter, we referred to Paria Caca's children by name.

But we didn't say anything about their individual lives.

Here and in what follows we'll tell about them together with the victories of one from among them: Tutay Quiri.[301]

We mentioned that the ceremonial dancing in his season was the Chanco.

153   Tutay Quiri was Paria Caca's son. This is a fact.[302]

In early times, they say,[303] the Checa were Quinti, the younger brothers of the Quinti.

The Quinti thoroughly despised the Checa because the Checa were born last.[304]

154   One day, Tutay Quiri spoke to them, saying,

"Don't be sad, children, no matter what they say. Let them scorn you; in spite of it you, the Checa, will in future times have the title of *villca*. And as for those who belittle you, people will speak scornfully to them, saying,

'Little Quintis, little bugs!' "

155   A few days later, after the brothers had talked it over among themselves, Tutay Quiri set out from Llacsa Tambo[305] to conquer the Yunca.

When they heard this news the Yunca were scared stiff and immediately began to flee to the village known as Lower Colli.[306]
<margin, in Spanish:> [Colli without a forceful pronunciation][307]

(The Colli are neighbors of the Carhuayllo.

It's a fact that[308] to this day their dead are laid in the same house of the dead, in the old highland village.)[309]

---

301. A report dated 1611 tells how Fabián de Ayala destroyed the mummies of a sacred cave in Santiago de Tumna. Among the "ancient captains and valiant soldiers," he found "one called Tarayquiri [*sic*], who, although he died over 600 years ago, remains so intact in body, that it is amazing" (Arguedas and Duviols 1966: 252). This suggests that some of the *huacas* called children of Paria Caca were ancestor mummies.

302. End of an introductory passage with witness validation.

303. 'They say' supplied to indicate reportive validation.

304. Apparently segments of the patrilineages called *yumay* at any given level of inclusiveness were ranked according to the birth order of their respective apical ancestors. This is one of several narratives concerning how Tutay Quiri relieved the Checa of their lowly status as 'juniors' to the Quinti.

305. *llacsa tambomanta yuncacunacta* could also mean 'the Yunca from Llacsa Tambo'.

306. Concerning the Yunca of Colli (i.e., Collique, near Lima), see chapter 9 (secs. 115, 138).

307. 'Forceful pronunciation': because in Quechua the vowel *o* only occurs adjacent to postvelar consonants, the reader might take the written *o* in *Colli* to imply that the value of *c* is postvelar ('forceful'). The note warns the reader that this is not so. Perhaps the word *Colli* is of non-Quechua derivation.

308. 'It's a fact that' added to indicate that this whole parenthesis has witness validation.

309. *aya vasipe* 'in the . . . house of the dead': a 1609 Jesuit report said the houses where mummified ancestors dwelled were "little towers, always square, (each) with a

156 Tutay Quiri descended down Sici Caya[310] ravine and also down the ravine of the Mama river,[311] moving in the form of yellow rain and red rain.

The people, some of them,[312] waited for him in their own lands and villages in order to pay him homage.

He didn't humiliate these worshipers.

On the contrary, he said to them, "Stay here; you shall come to recognize my father. Living henceforth, address the Checa as 'brothers' and say, 'We're their brothers, the youngest ones.' "

157 And in fact[313] to this day, just as he said, people who live in San Pedro Mama address the Checa, saying, "I'm your little Ami, your little Llata."

So, both the *allauca*[314] moiety and the *vichoc* moiety lived as brothers of the Checa.[315]

158 Every year, in the month of November, the Checa (that is, all the males) would go out from this village on a giant surround hunt, saying,

"We go in Tutay Quiri's steps,
We go in the path of his power."

159 On that occasion they used to ask for rain. People said, "Now, in the Chanco season, the heavens will rain."

And following Tutay Quiri's track, all the *huacsa*s and the non-*huacsa*s alike left from here to conduct the hunt; they used to go and spend the night in a place called Mayani,[316] up above Tupi Cocha.[317]

160 On that day, they would trap some guanacos, brocket deer, or other animals. Regardless of who did the actual catching, if the successful hunter happened to have a *huacsa* in his own *ayllu*, he'd give the animal to him first, so that he might perform the Ayñu dance displaying its tail. Those who didn't capture anything would likewise dance but performed only the Chanco.

161 On the next day, they used to leave Mayani for Tumna.

People, men and women alike, would gather together and wait for them in the place called Huasuc Tambo, saying, "Here comes Tutay Quiri!"

This Huasuc Tambo is where a few rocks stand in the center of the plaza of Tumna itself.

In the old days, they say, people used to go there and worship on that spot.[318]

---

door to the east" (Arguedas and Duviols 1966: 247). Ruins of this form, looted but full of human bones, are visible in the San Damián and Huarochirí areas. In this passage the narrator points out that Tutay Quiri's action explains why Yunca people who live on the outskirts of Lima have ancestors enshrined in the remote mountains.

310. This is very likely to be the same toponym as Saci Caya (chap. 8, sec. 109; chap. 9, sec. 138; chap. 13, sec. 176), equivalent to modern Sisicaya. The ravine is the entrenched course of the Lurín River.

311. That is, he moved down both the Lurín (Pacha Camac) and Rímac (Mama) valleys, which form two separate courses toward the Pacific.

312. *runacunapas huaquenca* 'the people, some of them': presumably meaning a remnant of Yunca stayed there and submitted to Tutay Quiri. Chapter 24 extensively explains these people's role. By incorporating them as his worshipers, Tutay Quiri supplied the Checa, the former *sullca* (junior) group relative to the Quinti, with a group that is junior to the Checa. This sentence and the first of section 157 fulfill a prophecy of Paria Caca in chapter 8 (sec. 101).

313. 'And in fact' supplied to indicate witness validation. This begins a witness-validated passage, continuing with one interruption to the end of section 164.

314. *Allauca*, the name of a certain village, can also mean 'right-bank moiety'. Hernández Príncipe uses the term in this sense and it is mentioned in the Cajatambo idolatry trials studied by Duviols (1986: 494). The reason for supposing it functions here as a moiety title is the juxtaposition with *vichoc*, which may be related to *ichoc*, 'left-bank', the customary moiety complement. Occasionally present in Huarochirí (Gentile Lafaille 1976: 27, 89, 98), *allauca/ichoc* oppositions are common in the northern part of Lima Department and in Ancash. The name of the location today called Alloca and called Allauca in the manuscript, 16 km south of Huarochirí in the Mala–San Lorenzo valley, 1,750 m above sea level

(IGM 1970–1971; see chap. 30), probably is not a moiety term. Allauca *ayllu*s seem to exist in various settlements, and in the Huarochirí manuscript, too, *allauca* groups are often mentioned without moiety counterparts (chap. 20, sec. 240; chap. 22, sec. 282; chap. 24, secs. 304, 316–317, 323, 325, 332, 336; chap. 26, sec. 356; chap. 30, sec. 379, 385). In those cases the term seems to be an *ayllu* or *llacta*, not moiety, title.

315. This vaguely suggests, but does not explain, that these conquered Yunca became peacefully integrated as a pair of moieties jointly treated as fraternal to the Checa.

316. Mayani is the modern name of a high plateau 8 km west of Llaquistambo (Llacsa Tambo?) at 4,200 m above sea level.

317. Modern Tupicocha village is 10 km west-north-west of San Damián at 3,605 m above sea level (IGM 1970–1971).

318. This sentence and the following one are validated with reportive -*si*, which is indicated with supplied 'they say', but the narration then returns to witness validation.

There, too, the Chauti[319] and the Huanri would likewise go to worship with their maize beer.

162 We know that[320] on the next day, if they caught anything, no matter how few or many animals, the *huacsa*s who'd captured them gladly proclaimed, "Now we'll have *maca*[321] tubers!" and returned rejoicing to spend the night, this time in Pacota.[322]

163 On the following day, they used to arrive back at Llacsa Tambo.

When the hunters were about to return, everyone who'd remained in the village, the old men and old women, and other people as well, would gather all together to await them with maize beer.

As they were arriving there, the waiting people would say, "They're coming in exhausted!" and pour maize beer all over the place,[323] over the people and onto the ground.

They'd pour it out right at the very entrance gate of Llacsa Tambo.

164 The hunters who'd come up from the lowlands would in turn place chunks of meat on the mouths of their hosts' jugs.[324]

After finishing this, the whole crowd sat on the open ground and they began the dance called Ayñu.

These events are called the Chanco.

When they danced the Chanco, the sky would say, "Now!" and the rain would pour down.

165 They say that[325] at the house of the *yanca* called Ysqui Caya, there was a bush or something of the sort, and from that bush flowed abundant water during the Chanco festival.

If people saw this happen, they said, "This year will give a good harvest."

If a drought were coming the bush would be dry.

In that case, people used to say, "There'll be terrible suffering."

---

319. A place named Chaute today exists 5 km south of San Bartolomé at 2,600 m above sea level (IGM 1970–1971).

320. 'We know that' supplied to indicate return to witness validation.

321. *maca: Lepidium,* of which various species are mentioned in botanical sources; a plant of the freezing heights, whose green parts are used medicinally. "The root is edible and is customarily cultivated in some parts of the high plateau; it is medicinal too" (Soukup 1970: 186). "*Maka* (K). *Lepidium meyenii* Desv. A species cultivated in some regions of the high plateau (3900 m.) . . . tubers: fresh, boiled, and mashed . . . are eaten by sterile women who want to become fertile" (Girault 1984: 218–219). In this context, too, it is apparently a symbol of fertility.

322. Modern Pacota is 7 km west-southwest of Llaquistambo (Llacsa Tambo?; IGM 1970–1971).

323. *yanca* 'all over the place': assuming this is the common adverb *yanca* whose range of meanings includes

'freely', 'carelessly', 'without serious intent' (Gonçález Holguín [1608] 1952: 364). If it is the homonym meaning a class of priests, the sentence can also be read to mean that the priest did the pouring.

324. The hunters had finished a circuit from the heights of Mayani down to lower-lying Tumna and now back to their ceremonial center. The ceremony seems to symbolize the plenitude of varied Andean subsistence (Murra 1975a: 243–254). As well as uniting ecological levels it juxtaposes wild food—hunted meat—with beer, the cultivated and processed nourishment par excellence. The interrelationship of hunters and farmers is also highly elaborated in the dialectic of *huari* and *llacuaz,* a complex common in the Lima area, which envisions societies as antagonistic symbioses between two culturally different sorts of people (see Duviols 1973).

325. 'They say that' supplied to indicate shift to reportive *-si* validation, which continues to the end of the chapter.

CHAPTER 12

How Paria Caca's Children Undertook the Conquest of All the Yunca People

In the tenth chapter [*sic*], we already told the story about the victories of Paria Caca's children.

Likewise we mentioned that all those villages were once full of Yunca.

Now we'll speak about them[326] as earlier mentioned:

Choc Payco
Chancha Runa
Huari Runa
Utco Chuco
Tutay Quiri
Sasin Mari
Pacha Chuyru[327]—

how they used to behave, and things like that.[328]

167   In ancient times these people we just mentioned, since they were all brothers to each other, traveled into battle together as one.

Because he was the oldest of them all, the one called Choc Payco traveled in high honor on a litter.

But Tutay Quiri was the strongest, excelling beyond the others.

Because of his strength, he was the one who first conquered the two river valleys mentioned above[329] by setting his golden staff on a black mountain at the border of Pariacha[330] called Unca Tupi.

168   Planting his staff as a curse on the Yunca, and saying, as if in disrespect for them, "The Yunca will extend to this district,"[331] he set it in place.

(That mountain where he set his staff is now called Unca Tupi Capari Caya.)[332]

169   His other brothers went ahead, climbing up on the old road by which we go from Tupi Cocha (that is, the one called the Quisqui Tambo road; the other is called Tumnacha). When they heard somebody say, "Tutay Quiri has already finished conquering everything," they turned back, from the spot from which we can see to the outskirts of Limac.[333]

---

326. 'Them': Paria Caca's offspring, not the Yunca.
327. Compare with the similar but not identical list in chapter 9 (sec. 113).
328. End of an introductory passage with witness validation.
329. See chapter 8 (sec. 108) and chapter 9 (sec. 138).
330. Pariachi is 67 km west of Huarochirí at 1,160 m above sea level, far down the Rímac valley (IGM 1970–1971). So this is probably not the same Capari Caya mentioned in chapter 31 (sec. 398).

331. Tutay Quiri's point being that, after the seaward advance of the children of Paria Caca, the new and smaller limit of Yunca country would be Unca Tupi. This passage is difficult. Taylor (1987b: 219) gives "[Tutay Quiri] said, 'if anyone, as if to curse the Yuncas, knocks down this staff and shows disrespect, the Yuncas will conquer this territory.'"
332. This parenthesis has witness validation.
333. Modern Tupicocha is 10 km west-northwest of San Damián at 3,605 m above sea level (IGM 1970–1971). Santiago de Tumna is 15 km west-northwest of San Damián at 2,902 m above sea level, and Tumnacha ('little Tumna') might be close to it. The syntax is confusing, and it is not certain whether the place-names Tumnacha and Quisqui Tambo refer to the routes or to the places from which the discouraged heroes turned back. The apparent meaning of this passage is that when the other brothers learned how far Tutay Quiri had advanced in the Rímac valley, they decided instead to advance down the Mala valley. The next lines seem to excuse the lesser advance achieved in the Mala lands, down toward "Caranco," by saying that although Tutay Quiri also led that campaign, he let a mid-altitude agricultural *huaca* similar to Chuqui Suso seduce him and detain the

They feared Tutay Quiri a lot because he was really powerful.

170 So they descended through the Huaro Cheri district toward the vicinity of Lower Caranco.³³⁴

Once more it was Tutay Quiri who led the way on the descent.

One of Chuqui Suso's sisters waited for him in her field thinking to beguile him by showing off her <crossed out:> [vagina] private parts³³⁵ and her breasts.

---

whole movement well short of "Caranco" and the coastal Chilca area.

334. See chapter 9 (sec. 138) and chapter 23 (sec. 285).

335. <*racanta*> *pincaynintapas* '<crossed out:> [vagina] private parts': a plainspoken Quechua word has been replaced with a Quechua euphemism meaning more literally 'her shame'.

336. This concluding sentence and the marginal note

"Rest a while, sir; have a little sip of this maize beer and a taste of this *ticti*," she said.

171 At that moment, in that way, he fell behind.

When they saw him do that, his other brothers likewise stayed behind, carrying the conquest only as far as the place called Pacha Marca in Lower Allauca.

If this woman hadn't beguiled them, the Huaro Cheri and Quinti fields would now reach as far as Lower Caranco and Chilca.

Further on we'll write about their individual feats and everything they did.³³⁶
<margin, in Quechua:> [Further on we'll write about their individual feats.]

---

have witness validation. At this point Taylor (1987b: 220) transcribes a marginal note in Spanish meaning, 'Here we cease writing the lives of each of Pariacaca's children and what happened and we start on Chaupiñamca'.

CHAPTER 13

Mama [337]

When the people of Mama are questioned today about the *huaca* Chaupi Ñamca, they tell a different story.

The story told by them is like this. [338]

They say that in very early times, there was a *huaca* called Hanan Maclla. [339]

Her husband was the Sun.

Their children were Paria Caca and Chaupi Ñamca.

Chaupi Ñamca was a great maker of people, that is, of women; and Paria Caca of men. [340]

173   Accordingly they, the Mama people, in order to celebrate her festival on the eve of Corpus Christi, used to bathe Chaupi Ñamca in a little maize beer.

Additionally, some of them laid out all sorts of offerings for her, and worshiped her with guinea pigs or other such things; and all the people gathered together, both men and women, their *curaca* and their *alcalde*.

174   They used to stay there all night long, staying awake till dawn, drinking and getting drunk. They got real happy performing the dance called Aylliua, and danced that night drinking and getting drunk until dawn. <Crossed out in original:> [On the next day, Corpus Christi, saying, "It's our mother's festival!" their *curaca*, in full regalia, [341] and all the rest of the people] [342]

After that they went out to the fields and simply did nothing at all. They just got drunk, drinking and boozing away and saying, "It's our mother's festival!"

175   If somebody says, "How did you worship before the Spanish Vira Cochas appeared?" we know how [343] they reply:

"People used to drink for five days in the month of June wearing their most splendid clothes. Later, for fear of the Spaniards, they worshiped on Corpus eve."

Chaupi Ñamca's sister (the second one, Chaupi Ñamca being the oldest) was named Casa Llacsa.

---

337. At this point the manuscript leaps to another area, centered on a lower and more seaward village than San Damián de Checa. Mama, modern Ricardo Palma, lies in the lower Rímac valley, where desert hills hem in a narrow irrigable belt. It appears to belong to the old Yunca heartland, and this may help explain the discrepancies between its cults and those of the Checa and Concha. Mama's prominence in the manuscript may be connected to the fact that a *curaca* from Mama, Hernando Paucar, was among Avila's most important early informants and victims (Avila [1645] 1918: 68–69), and also to the fact that Huarochirí-area highlanders sought to integrate some of its warm fields into their economy.

338. End of an introductory passage with witness validation.

339. *hanan maclla* 'high' or 'upper Maclla' suggests a celestial deity, as does her marriage to the sun.

340. Gender parallelism in religious institutions, as suggested by these phrases, is considered a major theme of pre-Incaic organization by Irene Silverblatt (1987: 20–39).

341. This phrase is an uncertain rendering of *callañayoc* 'in possession of *callaña*', based on the dubious assumption that this is the same word as *collana* occurring in chapter 14 (sec. 194) and chapter 31 (sec. 409), where it refers to majestic garments or appearances. But if used in its wider sense, the phrase might mean 'with the leading people'.

342. Sentence fragment thus in original.

343. 'We know how' supplied to indicate witness validation, present in this sentence but not in the ensuing two sentences.

People also bathed her that evening, as well as her other sisters Urpay Huachac[344] and Vichi Maclla.[345]

176 "Chaupi Ñamca was said to be made up of five persons,"[346] the Checa say.[347]

Of these the eldest was Chaupi Ñamca, also called Cotacha or Paltacha.

Her second sister was named Llacsa Huato, the one we call Copacha.

They say[348] Llacsa Huato dwells in Chillaco.

(Not long ago, when Don Diego Chauca Huaman, the *curaca* of Saci Caya, was still alive, and until Don Martín's arrival,[349] people from Chillaco together with some other people supposedly used to celebrate her festival.

About this festival, we aren't sure in what month it took place.)[350]

177 Next, there was the one called Mira Huato, whom we call Ampuche or Ampuxi.[351]

Concerning this Mira Huato, we aren't sure where she lived. But people say, "She lives with her sister Llacsa Huato."

178 They say[352] if people from this region, or Huaro Cheri people, or any other sort of people had a son or a daughter, a brother, a father, or any other relative who was ill, they'd go to these *huacas*' shrine to consult them.

(Their priestess as of sixty years ago is still remembered; she was named Chumpi Ticlla. And not so long ago, when Don Diego[353] was still alive, a woman named Luzía, a very elderly woman, was their priestess, a tough[354] old lady. <crossed out:> [And maybe she's still alive.])

179 When people invoked these two *huacas*, they used to pray, saying,

"Oh Llacsa Huato, Mira Huato, it is you who make people;
It is you indeed who know my sin, better even than Chaupi Ñamca.
Tell me, I beg: what have I done to make them ill?[355]
For what fault of mine do I live in suffering?"

180 This being the case, people concluded, "No doubt they dwell as two sisters together."[356]

People came to honor these *huacas* all the more for the fact that Chaupi Ñamca wasn't straight; she'd tell people any sort of stuff. Actually, she was a liar.

So people used to visit them, saying, "Let's go and listen to our mothers Llacsa Huato and Mira

---

344. Urpay Huachac also appears in chapter 2 (sec. 25) as the mother of the girl *huaca* whom Cuni Raya Vira Cocha seduces.

345. Likely to be a complement to or relative of (or another name for?) Hanan Maclla (sec. 172). *Vichay* means 'uphill, upslope' (Gonçález Holguín [1608] 1952: 351).

346. Compare the ensuing list with the similar one in chapter 8 (sec. 101).

347. The sentence is witness-validated with *-mi* but the material in quotation marks is reportive, with *-si* ('said to be' supplied).

348. 'They say' supplied to indicate that this and the next sentence are reportive with *-si* in a context where witness validation predominates.

349. A 1588 *revisita* (tribute quota inspection; Archivo General de la Nación, Buenos Aires ms., 13-17-5-1) shows that Don Diego Chauca Huaman still held the office twenty years before the making of the manuscript. This helps date the period that the manscript's authors considered the heyday of pro-*huaca* colonial lords. "Don Martín" is probably his son, Martín Chauca Huaman, born in 1575 (Guaman Poma [1615] 1980: 3: 1024). The aspiration of an anti-*huaca* scion to the office of a father who had protected *huacas* is a motif of chapter 20 (secs. 247–249). 'Supposedly' supplied to indicate reportive *-si* validation.

350. This sentence has witness validation.

351. One of the forms given in the original, *Ampuxi*, would probably have sounded like 'Ampushi' in English orthography if, as Cerrón Palomino holds, Spanish *x* retained the *sh* value at the time of writing (1976b: 207). But the data are not conclusive according to Urioste. This sentence and the following have witness validation.

352. 'They say that' supplied to indicate reportive validation, which continues through the end of section 181.

353. That is, the same Don Diego Chauca Huaman mentioned in section 176.

354. *tacyasca* 'tough': derived from a verb whose main meanings are 'to be firm, constant'. But since the speaker is unsure if the priestess is still alive, it is also possible that he is thinking of a less-than-robust person. A derivative of *tacyay* denotes a different kind of inflexibility: it means 'to stiffen from illness' (Gonçález Holguín [1608] 1952: 335–336).

355. *ymamantam huncuchicuni* 'what have I done to make them ill?': might also be read 'to make myself ill'.

356. *yscaynin ñañantinhuantaccha* 'no doubt . . . as two sisters together': the suffix *-huan* 'with' is redundant for this reading, because *-ntin* alone signifies the union of parts. This fact leads Taylor (1987b: 231) to interpret the sentence as meaning that something else—the desired cure—is 'with' the sisters.

Huato. Whatever they advise about our faults, we'll carry it out exactly."

181   However, we know that even though people did worship them, they didn't celebrate their feast each year as they do[357] Chaupi Ñamca's festival.

And although they did honor them, they in fact went mainly to have their presence noticed,[358] saying, "I'll go" or "I'd rather not" according to their whim.

182   Next we'll talk about the *huaca* named Lluncho Huachac, the one we call Sullcacha or Sullca Paya.

She was the fourth sister.

This *huaca* reportedly[359] lived in the Canta[360] area. But we don't really know. Maybe the Canta people worship her, or even those farther on past Canta.

183   Finally, the one we call Añasi or Aña Paya lived in the ocean.

(In fact some people say, "She's the one who was Caui Llaca."[361]

Others say, "This is a different *huaca*. She lives on the seashore.")

Aña Paya[362] lives inside a cliff.

So she doesn't have a priest.

When people sought the advice of the *huaca* Urpay Huachac, they'd think it over carefully beforehand. For in speaking with her, they spoke face to face because the *huaca* had no *huacsa* priest.

When they came back from visiting her, they said, "I've gone and spoken with her," and they used to fast for a whole year, abstaining from sinning with their wives.[363]

184   All of these *huaca*s we've mentioned were named Ñamca, each one of them individually and also the sisters as a group.

When people who were worried about anything approached any one of them, in explaining their trouble to her they'd address her, saying, "Oh five Ñamcas!"

185   This is all we know about Chaupi Ñamca, Llacsa Huato, Mira Huato, Lluncho Huachac, and Urpay Huachac.[364]

In the old days, they say,[365] these *huaca*s would ask those who went to them, "Have you come on the advice of your own Con Churi,[366] your father, or your elders?"

---

357. Tense in original can be read as present, perhaps emphasizing continued colonial vitality of the Chaupi Ñamca cult. The fact that this sentence is witness-validated ('we know that' supplied) suggests either present or a not-too-remote past. Witness validation continues through the second sentence of section 182.

358. *musiachicuyllapacmi* 'to have their presence noticed': Taylor (1987b: 232) has *munachicuyllapacmi* 'when they felt like it', noting *musia-* as alternative reading. Witness validation is glossed 'in fact'.

359. 'Reportedly' supplied to indicate reportive validation, which continues through the first sentence of section 183.

360. Canta, an important colonial town, was in the upper Chillón valley at 2,837 m above sea level (IGM 1970–1971).

361. See chapter 2 (sec. 10). The point in question is whether Añasi was the same as Caui Llaca, who entered the sea and became lithified as an island, or a separate *huaca* who 'lives on the seashore'. This sentence and the next have witness validation ('in fact' supplied).

362. 'Aña Paya' supplied.

363. *mana huarminhuan huchallicuspa* 'abstaining from sinning with their wives': since sex under these conditions would only be sinful by the tenets of *huaca* worship, this instance of *huchalliy* may not be euphemistic or specifically colonial. This also applies to section 186.

364. This sentence has witness validation. The fact that this sentence contains an ending formula, while the chapter continues, suggests a transition to a different testimony at this point.

365. 'They say' supplied to indicate reportive validation.

366. What is Con Churi? See supplement I (sec. 462). Avila explains in the *Prefación* to his bilingual sermon book:

In all the said villages there were greater and lesser idols, and there is not an Indian family, even if but a single person remains of it, which lacks its particular *penate* god in the house, in such manner that, if they came from one, eight, or ten persons, these have an idol left to them by the person who preceded them. The most important person of each family guards this and he is the person who has the right of succession to the goods and the rest, in such a way, that to guard this idol is like having right of *patronazgo* [hereditary patronage] among us, passing with the inheritance, and when, by law of blood kinship, there is no one to whom it may be transmitted, the one who possesses it usually entrusts it to the person who seems to him most appropriate by reason of affinity, or his best friend, and when he has no one to leave it to, he takes it with him, if he can, to where his progenitor is buried, which would usually be in a cave, because he was

To those who answered "No," the *huaca*s would reply, "Go back, return, consult your Con Churi first." And so people went back.

186 Only after this was done first would they answer their concerns:

"You have angered that person."

"You have crossed this one."

"You are an adulteress."

"You have sinned with a woman on the feast of Paria Caca."

They gave people advice, telling them all sorts of things:

"You are to bathe in the confluence of two streams."

"You must sacrifice one of your llamas."

---

a prehispanic mummy, and there he leaves the said idol, and if he cannot take it there, he buries it in his house. This sort of idol has the general name of *cun churi* or *chanca*. (Arguedas and Duviols 1966: 255)

People were more than happy to obey their dicta. Some of them recovered completely, while others died no matter how fully they'd complied.

187 Now we've heard what Chaupi Ñamca and her other sisters were like.

But the fact is that[367] in each village, and even *ayllu* by *ayllu*, people give different versions, and different names, too. People from Mama say one thing and the Checa say another.

188 Some call Chaupi Ñamca Paria Caca's sister. Others say, "She was Tamta Ñamca's daughter." (We spoke earlier about Tamta Ñamca in the fifth chapter.)

Still others say, "She was the Sun's daughter." So it's impossible to decide.

---

367. 'The fact is that' supplied to indicate that sections 187–188 have witness validation.

<margin, in Spanish:> [n.b.]
In the first chapter we made some remarks about whether Cuni Raya's existence came before or after Paria Caca's.[368]

They say[369] Cuni Raya Vira Cocha did exist from very ancient times. Paria Caca and all the other *huaca*s used to revere him exceedingly.

In fact,[370] some people even say, "Paria Caca is Cuni Raya's son."

Next we'll speak about one of Cuni Raya Vira Cocha's feats.[371]

190   Just before the appearance of the Spaniards, it's said,[372] Cuni Raya headed toward Cuzco.

There he conversed with the Inca Huayna Capac:[373] "Come, son, let's go to Titi Caca. There I will reveal to you who I am,"[374] he said.

191   And there he told him, "Inca, mobilize your people, so that we may send magicians and all sorts of shamans to Ura Ticsi, the world's lower foundations."[375] As soon as he said this, the Inca promptly gave the order.

"I am a condor shaman!"[376] some men answered.

---

368. This sentence is written in large letters in the original, like the chapter titles. Its witness validation could make it a title, but it seems to function as an introductory remark.

369. 'They say' supplied to indicate reportive validation.

370. 'In fact' supplied to indicate that this sentence and the next have witness validation, except for the material in quotation marks, which has reportive ('called').

371. *puchucascanta* 'feats' is derived from a verb that implies reaching of an intrinsic completion: the completion of a task, payment of a debt, end of a cycle, and so forth (see chap. 3, sec. 29, where it refers to the ending of the world). So there is a suggestion that the events to come represent the unfolding of Cuni Raya Vira Cocha's purpose or will.

372. 'It's said' supplied to indicate reportive validation, which continues through the end of section 197.

373. Huayna Capac, the last leader of the Inca Empire before it was riven by dynastic warfare and then the Spanish invasion, ruled over an immense state at the height of its power. In various ways, most of the Quechua-speaking writers c. 1600 saw him as touched by premonitions of the impending calamity. A myth told by the "Indian chronicler" Joan de Santa Cruz Pachacuti Yamqui, seemingly related to this one, tells how a mortal illness in the form of butterflies or moths in a box felled him on the eve of Spanish invasion ([1613] 1968: 311).

374. *ñocap cascayta* 'who I am': more literally, 'my past-being (direct object)'. The perfective *-sca* suggests *ex post facto* knowledge: that is, 'what I was all along without your knowing it'. This appears to allude to chapter 1 (sec. 7), and to purported Inca prayers, which often address Vira Cocha with petitions for knowledge of where and who he is. Pachacuti Yamqui affords an example ([1613] 1968: 287–288). A recent translation from a rectified text gives the sense as:

Oh Viracocha, . . .

Where are you?
May I not see you?
Are you above, are you below,
Is your throne nearby?
Please show yourself to me . . .

We your servants
With our eyes of light and shadow turned toward you,
We wish to see you . . . (Itier 1988: 571–572)

(For a different rendering, see Szemiński 1985b: 249.)

375. *hura ticsiman*: Gonçález Holguín glosses *ticçi* ([1608] 1952: 340) as "origin, beginning, fundament, foundation, cause." Its sense here is not obvious. The 'lower foundations' may mean the underside of the world. Taylor (1980: 111) interprets it, with equal plausibility, as "lowlands."

376. *ñocam condorpac camasca canim* 'I am a condor

"I am a falcon shaman!" said others.

"I am one who flies[377] in the form of a swift!"[378] replied still others.

192   He[379] instructed them, "Go to the world's lower foundations. Then tell my father, 'Your son sent me here. Send me back bearing one of his sisters.'"[380]

The man who was the swift's shaman, together with the other shamans, set out intending to return within five days.

193   The swift's shaman was the first to arrive there.

When he arrived and delivered his message, he was given something in a small chest and warned, "You mustn't open this. Lord Huayna Capac himself must be the first to open it."

While the man was bringing it, when he'd almost delivered it to Cuzco, he thought, "No! I'll take a look inside. What could it be?" And he opened it.

194   Inside it there appeared a very stately and beautiful lady. Her hair was like curly gold and she wore a majestic[381] costume, and in her whole aspect she looked very tiny.

The moment he saw her, the lady disappeared.

195   And so, deeply abashed, he arrived at the place called Titi Caca in Cuzco.

Huayna Capac said, "If it weren't for your being the swift's shaman, I'd have you executed right this instant! Get out! Go back by yourself!"

The swift's shaman returned and brought the woman back. When he was bringing her back along the road, dying for something to eat and drink, he had only to speak and a set table would instantly be there. It was just the same when he needed to sleep.

196   He delivered her exactly on the fifth day.

When he handed her over to them, Cuni Raya and the Inca received her overjoyed.

But before opening the chest, Cuni Raya said, "Inca! Let's draw a line across this world.[382] I'll go into this space and you go into this other space with my sister."

"You and I mustn't see each other anymore!" he said as he divided the world.

And he began to open the box. At the moment he opened it, the world lit up with lightning.

---

shaman': more literally, 'I am the *camasca* of the condor', and so forth. The sense of *camasca* may be understood as the inverse of *camaque* (chap. 29, sec. 372): the latter means a power giving form and force to a specific class of beings, and the former the beings so favored. In context, the sense appears to be that the shaman acquires the species powers of his superhuman familiar.

377. The implication is that these shamans engage in magical flight, a common motif of South American shamanism.

378. The Lima area has three swift species. Of these, the likeliest is the Andean swift, because it is a sierran species that sometimes flies down to the coast like the shaman in the story. All swifts are fast fliers. "*Andean swift, Aeronautes andecolus (Vencejo andino)*. Distinguished from the preceding species [i.e., the Chimney Swift, *Chaetura pelagica*] by its longer wings, forked tail, and lighter color; with the collar, belly and rump white. Abundant in the sierra and Andean slopes, coming down from time to time on the coast" (Koepcke 1970: 78).

379. While the grammatical subject of this sentence is ambiguous (Inca? or Cuni Raya Vira Cocha?), the fact that the 'sister' mentioned is later clarified as being the latter's suggests that the subject is more likely to be Cuni Raya Vira Cocha.

380. *huc panantas* 'one of his sisters': the original is ambiguous as to whether this means Cuni's or Inca's sister, but this is cleared up later (sec. 196) when Cuni Raya Vira Cocha calls her 'my sister'.

381. The little lady's clothes were *collana*, a term used in social organization to label high-ranking descent groups of Cuzco and elsewhere (Zuidema 1964: 100–103). It implies majesty and political eminence. But 'lady' translates a Spanish word in the manuscript: *señora*. This word, like her blondness, suggests that she is an image foreshadowing the Spanish. In Inca-era politics, acceptance of a gift bride signified political subjection to the giver. So the story may be a mythic comment on the loss of Inca sovereignty. Contrast with chapter 23 (sec. 300), where Maca Uisa conserves his autonomy by refusing gift brides.

382. *cay pachacta sequison* 'Let's draw a line across this world': *ceqque* has the practical sense 'line, boundary, limit' (Gonçález Holguín [1608] 1952: 81) but was often used to mean a schematic line in ideal space. Rowe (1985) and Zuidema (1964) analyze what is known of the "lines" along which the Inca capital's *huaca*s were arranged.

The line that Cuni Raya Vira Cocha impels the Inca to draw may allude to the moiety line of Cuzco, but more likely alludes to the alleged division of the Inca Empire into two at Huayna Capac's death. Betanzos ([1551] 1987: 210) relays an Inca tradition equating the former with the latter. This division is mentioned by many chroniclers as the cause of the Inca civil war, and indirectly of Pizarro's easy victory over Cuzco.

The translation of this passage depends greatly on interpretation of *pacha*. The most concrete reading would make it 'ground, earth', in which case the passage seems to concern something as local and earthly as a line drawn in the dirt. But it can just as well mean 'time and space', or 'world', which gives the passage a feeling of the vastest mythic scale.

197   The Inca Huayna Capac said, "I'll never again return from here. I'll stay right here with my prin-
cess, with my queen." To one man, a kinsman
of his, he said, "You go in my stead.[383] Return to
Cuzco and say, 'I'm Huayna Capac!' "

At that very moment, then and there, the Inca
disappeared forever with that lady of his, and Cuni
Raya did the same.

Later on, after Huayna Capac had died, people
scrambled for political power, each saying to the
others,

"Me first!"

"Me first!"

It was while they were carrying on this way that
the Spanish Vira Cochas[384] appeared in Caxa Marca.

---

383. *ñocap rantij* 'in my stead' alludes to the well-
attested Inca institution of naming a 'second person' to
act in lieu of the Inca.

384. *vira cochacunapas*: in this passage and certain

198   Even up to the present we know[385] many stories
about Cuni Raya Vira Cocha's life.

We haven't yet finished writing down the other
things he did while he was roaming through this
area.

We'll treat these matters later on.[386]

---

later ones, as well as in the preface (sec. 1), 'Spanish' has
been supplied to avoid confusion with the same name as
applied to the deity. The use of this term to denominate
the Spanish and privileged Spanish speakers survives in
rural Cuzco Quechua to the present.

385. Original contains both *yachanchic* 'we know'
and *-mi* witness validator. Witness validation continues
to the end of the chapter.

386. Taylor (1987b: 250) shows a Spanish marginal
note meaning, 'what chapter back?'

CHAPTER 15

Next We Shall Write about What Was Mentioned in the Second Chapter, Namely, Whether Cuni Raya Existed before or after Caruincho

Cuni Raya Vira Cocha is said to have[387] existed from very ancient times. Before he was, there was nothing at all in this world. It was he who first gave shape and force to the mountains, the forests, the rivers, and all sorts of animals, and to the fields for humankind's subsistence as well.

It's for this reason that people in fact[388] say of Cuni Raya, "He's called Paria Caca's father."[389]

"It was he who made and empowered Paria Caca."

"If Paria Caca weren't his son, he probably would have humbled him," all the people say.

And it's said that[390] he did thoroughly humble some villages with his cleverness, playing all sorts of tricks on them.

We'll include these matters[391] later.[392]

---

387. 'Is said to have' supplied to indicate reportive validation.

388. 'In fact' supplied to indicate that the verb 'say' here and in the first sentence of section 200 has witness validation. The material in quotes has reportive validation ('called' supplied).

389. This short chapter implicitly addresses the question of whether Vira Cocha partakes (as early missionaries speculated, and later native writers affirmed) of the "true God" as seen through pagan intuition. If so, he

would be prior to all *huacas*, especially the archaic one par excellence, Huallallo Caruincho. The evidence that this chapter cites, however, is not actually relevant to that question. The chapter alludes only to testimony that Cuni Raya Vira Cocha preceded Paria Caca.

390. 'It's said that' supplied to indicate reportive validation.

391. Cuni Raya returns (not as Vira Cocha) in chapter 31 (sec. 409).

392. This sentence has witness validation.

CHAPTER 16

Here We Shall Write on Whether Paria Caca, Born from Five Eggs, Was Composed of Brothers or Whether Paria Caca Was Their Father, Things of This Kind

201 In chapter eight we already speculated on such matters as whether Paria Caca, when he was born from five eggs, was made up of brothers, or whether the others were Paria Caca's sons.

Now we'll write about them individually and by name.

202 As we suggested in the fourteenth chapter when we said they were sons of Cuni Raya, the Paria Cacas born from five eggs were brothers to each other.

These are their names, starting from the first:

Paria Caca
then Churapa
then Puncho
then Paria Carco

We don't know the other one.

We leave a blank space here in order to write it once we ascertain it.

Sullca Yllapa.

<margin, in Quechua:> [n.b. His name was Sullca Yllapa.][393]

203 They say[394] Paria Carco dwells to this day at a pass into the Anti lowlands, saying, "Huallallo may return!"

In fact, we already pointed this out.[395]

---

393. The introductory passage that ends here is witness-validated with -mi, but the marginal note is reportive with -si.

394. 'They say' supplied to indicate reportive validation.

395. 'In fact' supplied to indicate witness validation. The reference is to chapter 8 (sec. 105).

But this Huallallo Caruincho isn't supposed to have[396] just escaped all at once.

When Churapa, one of the Paria Cacas, penetrated the place we called Mullo Cocha[397] and turned it into a lake, Huallallo flew away like a bird.

204 Then he entered a mountain, a mountain called Caqui Yoca.[398]

This <crossed out:> [cliff] mountain was a gigantic rocky escarpment.

Huallallo Caruincho got inside the cliff and hid there.

Paria Caca, in the form of lightning, blasted it again and again; he and his five brothers shot lightning bolts so violently they almost demolished that

---

396. 'Supposed to have' supplied to indicate reportive validation, which continues through the first sentence of section 209.

397. Mullo Cocha is the place where Paria Caca dislodged Huallallo (chap. 8, secs. 96–97, 104; chap. 16, sec. 203); it lies along the probable pilgrimage route to Paria Caca's great shrine on the icy heights. With its many mentions of geological formations in the environs of Mullo Cocha and the mythic events they embody, this chapter and chapter 17 (secs. 210–212) give the impression of being a pilgrim's reminiscence or guide to the sights of the Paria Caca pilgrimage route. The geological landmarks are taken as a series of three tropical monsters loosed by Huallallo and killed by Paria Caca.

398. This name and that of the canyon Caqui Yoca Huayqui (sec. 207) allude to the bird *caqui* (toucan?) that acts later in the myth (sec. 207; see note 401). Taylor (1987b: 259) suggests that both derive via "Aru deformation" from *caquiyoc* 'having a *caqui*', perhaps in reference to the shape of a geological formation.

rocky mountain, and from there they once again forced Huallallo Caruincho to flee.

205 Then Huallallo Caruincho turned loose a huge snake called the Amaru,[399] a two-headed snake, thinking, "This'll bring misfortune on Paria Caca!"

When he saw it, Paria Caca furiously stabbed it in the middle of its back with his golden staff.

At that very moment, the snake froze stiff. It turned into stone.

206 This petrified snake, the Amaru, remains clearly visible to this day on the road named Upper Caqui Yoca.

People from Cuzco, and everyone else who knows about it, strike it with a rock and carry along the fallen chips as medicine, thinking, "Now I won't catch any disease."

207 As soon as Huallallo Caruincho fled from the cliff of Caqui Yoca, he entered a canyon called Caqui Yoca Huayqui.

Then, clambering up a mountain called Puma Rauca,[400] Huallallo thought, "From here I'll fence Paria Caca in so he can't pass through." He set

against him a certain kind of parrot called a *caqui* or toucan[401] and made it brandish its wing points.[402]

But Paria Caca effortlessly broke one of its wings, turned the toucan into stone, and climbed right over it.

Once Paria Caca stepped over it Huallallo Caruincho had no power left, so he fled toward the Anti lowlands.

208 But Paria Caca, with all the rest of his brothers, chased after him.

After Huallallo entered the Anti lowlands, Paria Caca left one of his brothers, the one named Paria Carco, at the pass into the tropical Antis. "Watch out lest he return!" he said.

209 Paria Carco
<**margin**, in Quechua:> [Paria Carco] remains there today in the form of a heavily snow-capped peak.

Who worships Huallallo is something we don't know.[403]

But in the ninth chapter[404] we already mentioned that Paria Caca declared, "Since he once ate people, let him now eat dogs. And let the Huanca people feed them to him."

---

399. *amarocta* 'Amaru' (direct object): Amaru is the great mythic water serpent, virtually omnipresent in Andean myths, and usually symbolic of disorder erupting in the transition to a new order. It may have been visualized as resembling the boa constrictor (*Constrictor constrictor*) or anaconda (*Eunectes murinus*). This particular Amaru, Cristóbal de Albornoz ([1583?] 1984: 201) tells us, was a vein or stratum of white marble. The belief that certain white minerals are prophylactic medicine is widespread in the modern Andes.

400. "Pumarauca mountain, where Huallallo Carhuincho took refuge, still exists . . . and is located exactly in the zone adjacent [to Paria Caca] when one leaves from the great ravine of the Steps [i.e., the 'Steps of Paria Caca', an ancient roadway], en route to Jauja, which is also the direction toward the jungle" (Bonavia et al. 1984: 13). Modern maps (IGM 1970–1971) show a Pumarauca Mountain 2 km north of Mullucocha, with its peak 4,950 m above sea level.

401. *huc orito caque ñiscacta* 'a certain kind of parrot called a *caqui* or toucan' (direct object): as noted in chapter 1 (sec. 5), the exact meaning of *caqui* is uncertain and 'toucan' is a guess. We leave the word *caqui* visible in the translation here to reveal the salience of this bird's name throughout the passage. Whatever its species, the *caqui* is a tropical bird that in reality would never be seen on the icy heights, which symbolizes the vanished power of the Yunca deity Huallallo.

402. *chuquirichispa* 'made it brandish': appears to derive from the verb that Gonçález Holguín ([1608] 1952: 122) gives as "*Chuquini . . .* to spear or strike spear blows." The image here seems to be that of a bird with its wing feathers fanned out and bristling like lances. The episode seemingly comments on a jagged mountain wall taken to resemble a broken wing.

403. This sentence and the remainder of the chapter have witness validation.

404. Sections 110–111.

CHAPTER 17

Now we'll explain how Paria Caca returned after he left his brother Paria Carco at the pass into the Anti lowlands.[405]

The story is like this.

We've already spoken about some of the words that Paria Caca said, and also about what he instituted to establish his own cult.

But there's one story we forgot.

211   After he finished the conquest, they say,[406] he returned with his other brothers to Paria Caca mountain.

There's another snowcapped peak there, unclimbable, the mountain called Huama Yaco.[407]

(In fact, some people say about this mountain, "That's the one, Paria Caca."

Later, too, after the Spanish Vira Cochas appeared on the scene, when people saw that mountain's snowy peak from the place we call Ynca Caya, they said, "That's Paria Caca.")[408]

212   But they say Paria Caca himself lived a little farther down, inside a cliff.[409]

Paria Caca and his brothers entered this crag and made it their home,[410] saying, "Here I shall dwell. From this place you must worship me."

We mentioned the other mountain, the one called Huama Yaco, by way of saying that it was a heavily snowcapped peak, and that it was atop this mountain that the Paria Cacas rested on their way back from the Anti lowlands.

213   From there, a great long time ago, even before the Incas were born, Paria Caca convoked all the people of Tauantin Suyo.[411]

Once all these people had gathered, Paria Caca founded the *huacsa* institution for his own worship.

Later on, when the Incas appeared on the scene and heard about this, they also acted as his *huacsa*s and held him in great honor.

We call the fashion in which they gathered at that time Tauantin Suyo.[412]

214   At that time, Huallallo Caruincho, never forget-

405. All of section 210 has witness validation. It seems to contain not one but two introductory passages, the first framing the second. It may be that the first is by the redactor/editor, and the second is the informant's own introduction; the fifth sentence of section 219 may be the informant's closing formula. Chapters 17, 18, and 19 lack titles.

406. 'They say' supplied to indicate reportive validation, which predominates through the fourth sentence of section 219.

407. Perhaps identifiable with the modern peak Huamalla Lapu (IGM 1954), a mountain 48 km east-southeast of Huarochirí, 5,290 m above sea level. But its location may be too distant to fit the context.

408. This whole parenthesis has witness validation.

409. Duccio Bonavia has identified a rock shelter close to Mullo Cocha, painted with llama petroglyphs, which might have been where Paria Caca dwelled 'inside a cliff' (personal communication). The fact that this sentence is validated reportively suggests that the teller may not have experienced the actual pilgrimage to this site.

410. In modern Andean myth, *apu*s or mountain deities are often spoken of as dwelling "inside" mountain peaks.

411. *Tauantin Suyo* 'fourfold domain' was the Inca name of the Inca Empire. Perhaps this passage claims for Paria Caca priority over the Incas in creating an all-Andean collectivity; but it is also possible that to the teller *tauantin suyo* had a less political sense analogous to English 'the four corners of the earth'.

412. If we take *ninchic* to be out of normal word order, between dashes so to speak, the sentence could read 'In that age when—as we said—the people of Tauantin Suyu . . .' (Taylor 1987b: 271).

ful of his treacherous purpose, caused an animal called *hugi*[413] to appear on the same mountain where he lived.[414] "This'll bring grief to Paria Caca!" he thought.

The moment it appeared, the *hugi* escaped into the countryside.

215 Had that *hugi* lived, it would have taken Paria Caca's life or something.

For that reason, Paria Caca commanded the people of Tauantin Suyo, "Go capture that animal called *hugi!*"

Once he gave this command,

All the people chased after it,
and yet it never fell prey.

Paria Caca flashed and stormed,
and yet it never died.[415]

216 But way far away, a man of the Checa, of the Caca Sica *ayllu*, did capture it.

Then a Quinti man spoke to him: "Brother, you've actually caught it! You're a lucky man! Just go right home displaying its tail as a sign of victory. As for the carcass, I'll take it away."

"All right," the man replied.

217 After this exchange, the Quinti man went back by a different route, and told Paria Caca, "Father, I'm the one who caught it."

Paria Caca rejoiced exultantly and praised him.

(That Quinti man's name was Choc Payco.)[416]

Later on, when the other man delivered the tail, Paria Caca upbraided Choc Payco in scathing language:

"For lying to me,
go fight with the Quinti;

They'll call you a stinker,
and your offspring, too."

218 But about the Caca Sica *ayllu* and about Huar Cancha and Llichic Cancha, Paria Caca himself said,

"Because you are the one who captured it,
you have become *yanca*.[417]

I will listen to you alone,
and to everything you may tell me.

If other people have something to tell me,
they must let you hear it first."[418]

Paria Caca bestowed a name on him, too, saying, "He shall be a Ñamca, Ñamca Pariya."

219 From that time on, they, too, were *yanca*s. As for the Concha, their *yanca*'s name, too, was one bestowed by Paria Caca himself. It was Huatusi.

And similarly in all the villages the *yanca* were given names by Paria Caca.

Of what we'd forgotten about Paria Caca's life, this is as much as we remember now.[419]

---

413. Unidentified, and an anomalous word in the graphophonemic system of the manuscript: the combination *gi* appears elsewhere only in borrowings (*regina* [chap. 20, sec. 256], *virgin* [chap. 20, sec. 258]). This is the third and last of the monsters Huallallo Caruincho loosed against Paria Caca.

414. The place where the *hugi* appeared is unknown, but a toponym Puente Piedra Huqui ('Huqui Stone Bridge') is recorded 6 km northwest of San Lorenzo de Quinti (Guillén Araoz 1953: 230). Since stone usually represents the end of a *huaca*'s trajectory, this may be the distant point where the *hugi* was caught (sec. 216).

415. *tucoy ynantin runacona catirircan/manatacsi apichicorcancho/panas paria cacaca yllaparca tamyarcan/manatacsi huañorcancho*: the parallel structure of this passage (marked here with supplied /) suggests it may be a fragment or an altered rendering of a versified telling, hence the verse presentation in translation.

416. In chapter 9 (sec. 113) and chap. 12 (secs. 166–167), Choc Payco is named as the most senior and privileged of Paria Caca's offspring. This sentence has witness validation.

417. Caca Sica's eminence as *yanca* priests is mentioned in chapter 9 (sec. 118). In chapter 18 (sec. 224) a Caca Sica priest is credited with being the savior of a great *huaca*'s cult. The tendency to elevate Caca Sica suggests that within Checa this *ayllu* may have had a disproportionate share in the testimonies.

418. The curse on the Quinti and the blessing on the Caca Sica do not have an exact verse form, but they show a similarity of sequence (the accusation, the sentence, and the people's comment) and some syntactic resemblance (*-scayquimanta . . . -sonqui*). They seem to be presented as a contrasted set and are perhaps verses blurred in translation or editing.

419. This sentence has witness validation.

CHAPTER 18

We already mentioned that the Inca revered Paria Caca and acted as *huacsa*.[420]

It's said that[421] he, the Inca himself, decreed, "Let thirty men from the Upper Yauyos and the Lower Yauyos[422] serve Paria Caca according to the full and waning lunar cycles."[423]

In obedience to that command, thirty men

served him in shifts of fifteen days,[424] offering him food and feeding him.

One day they sacrificed one of his llamas, a llama named Yauri Huanaca.

When those thirty people examined the heart and entrails[425] of the llama, one of the thirty, a fellow called Quita Pariasca the Mountain Man,[426] spoke up and said, "Alas, brothers, the world[427] is

---

420. This sentence has witness validation. It refers to chapter 17 (sec. 213).

421. 'It's said that' supplied to indicate reportive validation, which continues through the end of section 223.

422. That is, from the two Inca-style moieties (visible on the Dávila Brizeño map; Rostworowski 1988 insert) of the larger region within which this mythology occurs. The division does not necessarily coincide with any locally defined duality.

423. *purapi quillapi* 'full and waning lunar cycles': Urioste (1983: 147) and Arguedas and Duviols (1966: 105) take *pura* to be the name of a month following a weakly attested datum from Juan de Betanzos and Diego Fernández de Palencia.

A better clue is Gonçález Holguín's ([1608] 1952: 296) "*pura quilla* the full moon and the waning," which Taylor (1987b: 277) follows. The 'full moon' meaning of *pura quilla* comes clearer from Urton's ethnographic account of lunar phases in modern Quechua culture (1981: 82–85). There are said to be two moons, a bright one called *pura* and a dark one called *huañu*. They rotate around each other, successively obscuring and revealing the bright (*pura*) one.

Mejía Xesspe (Szemiński 1989: 16) seized on another attested sense of *pura*, 'amongst themselves one with the other', to produce a different reading: "He, the Inka, ordered the Indians of Anan Yauya [*sic*] and Rurin Yauyo to take turns monthly among themselves thirty by thirty in order to serve Pariakaka." This reading harmonizes with the next sentence, but its persuasiveness is vitiated by the case of *pura ñiscapi quilla ñiscapi* in chapter 19 (sec. 234), which clearly puts *pura* in opposition to *quilla* 'moon'.

424. *chunca pihccayoc punchaumantacama* 'shifts of fifteen days': the marking of *punchau*, 'day', with suffixes -*manta* and -*cama*, meaning 'from' and 'up to', respectively, occurs nowhere else in the manuscript and 'shift' is a guess at its sense. Taylor (1987b: 277) reads "from the fifteenth day [of the month]."

425. "Idolatry" trials of the period succeeding the manuscript give information on the reading of llama entrails. In one technique a ritualist would inflate the lungs of the sacrificial llama and read the sentiments of the dead, as well as presages for the future, from the air pockets in the lungs.

426. *llacuas quita pariasca sutioc* 'called Quita Pariasca the Mountain Man': *llacuas* in both colonial and modern Quechua means a herdsman dwelling on the cold heights; it carries connotations of primitivism and coarseness. The antithesis between *llacuas* herders and purportedly more sophisticated valley agriculturalists was richly elaborated in many Lima-region cultures (Duviols 1973).

Llacuas here is likely to be an epithet, not part of the man's name, because, first, in section 222 he is called by name, without the word *llacuas*; and, second, in section 223, he is called *llacuas* without his name, as an insult. *Llacuas* has no English equivalent; 'mountain man' in a usage from the western United States is chosen to convey the idea of a rustic figure from the heights.

Quita, which does seem to be part of the name, means "wild (as of runaway livestock), skittish" (Gonçález Holguín [1608] 1952: 310; cf. the epithet *quita yauyo* in chap. 24, sec. 306), translated 'Yauyo wildmen'.

427. As in most instances, *pacha* leaves room for in-

not good! In coming times our father Paria Caca will be abandoned."

222 "No," the others retorted, "you're talking nonsense!"

"It's a good augury!"

"What do you know?"

One of them called out, "Hey, Quita Pariasca![428] What makes you think that? In these llama innards our father Paria Caca is foretelling something wonderful!"

But at the time he said that, the mountaineer hadn't even approached the llama to inspect its innards. He had prophesied so just by watching from afar.[429]

223 The mountaineer[430] spoke out and rebuked them: "It's Paria Caca himself who says it, brothers."

Then they derided Quita Pariasca with spiteful words:

"That smelly mountain man, what could he know?"

"Our father Paria Caca has subjects as far away as the limits of the land called Chinchay Suyo.[431] Could such a power ever fall desolate?"

"What does a guy like that know?"

They talked in great anger.

But just a very few days after the day when he'd said these things, they heard someone say, "Vira Cochas[432] have appeared in Caxa Marca!"

224 A certain man who was also from Checa, named

Tama Lliuya Casa Lliuya, a member of the Caca Sica *ayllu*, is known to have[433] dwelt as one of Paria Caca's retainers.

At that time, they say,[434] there were thirty priests at Paria Caca and this Casa Lliuya Tama Lliuya was the eldest of them all.

225 When the Vira Cochas, the Spaniards,[435] arrived there, they kept asking insistently, "What about this *huaca*'s silver and garments?"[436]

But the thirty refused to reveal anything.

Because they did, the Spanish Vira Cochas got furious, and, ordering some straw piled up, they burned Casa Lliuya.

When half the straw had burned, the wind began to blow it away.[437]

And so although this man suffered horribly, he did survive.

But by that time the others had handed the clothing and the rest of the things over to the Spaniards.

226 It was then that all the men said, "Very truly indeed were we warned by this mountain man Quita Pariasca!"

"Brothers, let's go away, let's disband."

"The world is no longer good," they said. And so they dispersed, each going back to his own village.

227 When the burned man from Checa healed up, he arrived at a village called Limca[438] in the territory

---

terpretation; alternatives would be 'earth', 'place', 'time', 'situation'.

428. *say quita pariasca*: Trimborn (1939: 48) took this to be a person's name, Sayquita, but in the absence of *sutioc* or any other name-indicating formula, and given the likelihood that *Quita* is part of the man's name, 'Hey, Quita!' seems likelier.

429. This seems to suggest that the augurers in their pedantry had failed to see what a humble man's broad commonsense could see. Perhaps this is how peasants c. 1600 felt about their wise men's failure to foresee the disastrous consequences of the Spanish invasion.

430. 'The mountaineer' supplied.

431. *chinchay suyo*: the northern and most prestigious quarter of the Inca state included most of highland Peru, all of highland Ecuador, and a fringe of southernmost Colombia.

432. That is, the Spanish. *Vira cocha* is left unglossed in the translation to conserve the sense of mystery that the original seems to convey.

433. 'Is known to have' supplied to indicate witness validation of this sentence only.

434. 'They say' supplied to indicate return to reportive validation, which continues through the first sentence of section 227.

435. *vira cocha chayman chayaspaca*: we supply 'the Spaniards' because at this point they are coming into focus as humans.

436. *cay huacap collquin pachan* 'this *huaca*'s silver and garments': a sentence fragment forming a direct quote, perhaps to suggest brusque formless speech (of strangers who do not know Quechua properly?).

437. *pucorimorcan*: translocative *-mo-*, 'began to blow [burning straw] away'. Taylor (1980: 127) thought the wind blew the straw fire out, but this seems unlikely because straw burns violently in wind.

438. The location of Limca is not known, but (by analogy with alternations like *Ñamca/Ñamuc*), Limca/[Limca] might be the pre-*reducción* village of "Lima" (not to be confused with the city of Lima), which Dávila Brizeño ([1586] 1965: 161) mentions as a former Yunca outpost in the highlands.

of the Quinti,[439] carrying along a child of Paria Caca named Maca Uisa.

<**margin**:> [Maca Uisa]
We'll describe these things in the next chapter.[440]

---

439. *quintip llantanpi limca sutioc llactapi: llanta* is problematic; it is treated here as a variant of *llacta* 'vil-

lage' as in Gonçález Holguín ([1608] 1952: 208). *Llanta* recurs in chapter 19 (sec. 235).

440. This sentence has witness validation.

CHAPTER 19

When the former Inca[441] lived, they say,[442] this Maca Uisa, a child of Paria Caca, was taken along to help him in warfare.[443] The provinces of Amaya and Xiuaya had not yet yielded to conquest.

Because of their resistance, the Inca asked Paria Caca for one of his children, to subdue[444] those Amaya and Xiuaya people.

229 Paria Caca gave him the one named Maca Uisa.

Carrying him along, the Inca defeated them in no time at all.

From then on, the Incas revered Paria Caca even more. They bestowed gold and ample amounts of their clothing on him, and every year they made people give maize, coca, and other goods from their villages to provide for Paria Caca's thirty retainers.

230 While it was so, the Spanish Vira Cochas came over, as we said, and took everything Maca Uisa[445] had away from him.

(Subsequently, the late Don Sebastián[446] had all that was left of his things burned.)

231 And so, as we just said, Casa Lliuya resided for many years in the village of Limca, highly honored because he was the upholder of Maca Uisa.

After many years, when the Checa heard how the Quinti had done so well, the late Don Juan Puypu Tacma, who was then *curaca*, sent for Casa Lliuya, saying, "Let him bring Maca Uisa over here."[447]

Then Casa Lliuya, the old man who'd been burned, father of six children, came here with his children.[448]

232 When they arrived here (I mean at Llacsa Tambo)[449] they asked, "Father Maca Uisa, will you not keep careful guard over the Checa in this village?" Casa Lliuya revealed the answer by sacrific-

---

441. *ñaupa ynga* 'former Inca' could be read as 'first' or 'early Incas' but this appears less likely since the manuscript generally treats late Incas (naming only Tupay Ynga Yupanqui and Huayna Capac, the last two who ruled before the period of dynastic war and Spanish invasion).

442. 'They say' supplied to indicate reportive validation. This chapter lacks introductory material and may be a continuation of the testimony interrupted by the last sentence of section 227, namely, the story of Maca Uisa.

443. Avila wrote that he met a young woman, disabled in her legs, married to a blue stone that stood for Maca Uisa in the absence of an original golden image that the Inca had taken to Cuzco ([1645] 1918: 67, 69, 71).

444. *atipai* 'to subdue': word appears truncated (*atipaipac?*) but no other reading is evident.

445. 'Maca Uisa' supplied.

446. That is, Don Sebastián Quispe Ninavilca, *curaca* of Huarochirí village and province. See chapter 7 (sec. 93).

447. *huañoc* 'the late' is interlineated. On May 9, 1608, a Checa *cacique* signed his name "don juan Puipotacma" to a statement at Father Avila's trial (Archivo Arzobispal, Lima, Capítulos, Leg. 1, Exp. 9, f.91r). If this was the same Don Juan mentioned here, the episode of Maca Uisa's retrieval could refer to times as late as the early seventeenth century. On the same assumption, if this man died before the manuscript's last editing, the last editing must postdate May 9, 1608.

448. *sucta runa choriyoc chay chorincunahuan hamurcancu:* or perhaps as Taylor has it (1987b: 287), "came here with (a group of) six men each accompanied by his respective child(ren)."

449. This is the only point at which the text tells where myths were collected. Llacsa Tambo is almost certainly modern Llaquistambo, an outlying hamlet of San Damián de Checa.

ing a llama; and it was just the same as in Huauya Cancha, where the mountain man Quita Pariasca had observed the augury.

233   When Casa Lliuya Tama Lliuya's children had already perished and he himself was about to die, he spoke and said, "That's how things were when I arrived here." For he had said on arriving, "The world really is very good. There won't ever be temptation[450] or disease[451] anymore."[452]

234   It was from that time onward that they upheld Maca Uisa in this village, and all the Checa served him, *ayllu* by *ayllu*, according to the full and waning cycles of the moon.[453]

On a certain night, all of them, men and women alike, would keep vigil together till dawn.

At daybreak, we know,[454] they offered guinea pigs and other things from each person individually, saying,

"Please help us and this village;
You are the one who guards it.

From each and every illness
You are the one who heals us."

235   After that,[455] dwelling in the village of Limca, Maca Uisa[456] enjoyed ample service. A whole thousand[457] of Quinti people reportedly[458] cultivated the fields of Yamlaca in order to provide Maca Uisa's drinks.

And the people who lived there got very rich[459] indeed, with all kinds of possessions in any quantity.

The Checa envied them[460] all this, and so it was that the late Don Juan Puypu Tacma dispatched some people to Casa Lliuya, who was a member of his *ayllu*, saying, "Let him bring Maca Uisa here. Why should he keep such a fine *huaca* in those people's[461] village?"

From that time onward, he lived here.
This is as much as we know about Maca Uisa.[462]

---

450. *huaticay* 'temptation': Gonçález Holguín ([1608] 1952: 187–188) gives many variants of this term, most of them Christian-influenced and emphasizing diabolical temptation. In this passage it may refer to sorcery, or perhaps to the temptations of conversion against which the saving of Maca Uisa was a bulwark.

451. *oncoypas* 'disease': in the wake of the epidemics that lashed postconquest Indian societies, the teller(s) appear deeply preoccupied with health and illness. See section 234 below.

452. *pachaca ancha allinmi mana ñam ymapas huaticay oncoypas cancacho* 'The world really is very good. There won't ever be temptation or disease anymore': this prophecy answers Quita Pariasca's earlier prophecy saying the world was no longer good (chap. 18, sec. 221) and his discouraged fellow-worshipers' assent to it (chap. 18, sec. 226). 'Really' is added to convey the combined force of *ancha* and eyewitness validator *-mi*. The idea seems to be that on dying he sees in the well-being of his neighbors the vindication of the prophecy he had made on arriving. But the meanings of this and the preceding section are far from certain.

453. See chapter 18 (sec. 220) and note 423.

454. 'We know' supplied to indicate witness validation of this sentence.

455. *chaymantam* 'after that': carries witness validation, but the main clause has *-si* reportive. This anomaly is fairly common and makes validation of some sentences less than clear.

456. 'Maca Uisa' supplied.

457. *tucoy huc huaranca* 'a whole thousand': 'thousand' is an Inca bureaucratic term signaling a major demographic unit; such decimal terms remained in use in colonial Huarochirí (Spalding 1984: 54). Its use in this colonial (i.e., post-Inca) reorganization of Andean religion suggests (as do the events of chap. 20) that Inca manipulation had a substantial effect on local cultic organization.

458. 'Reportedly' supplied to indicate return to reportive validation.

459. *rico* 'rich', using the Spanish expression as in chapter 5 (secs. 37, 46, 60).

460. A resurgence of a pervasive theme, the Checa rivalry with the more senior Quinti (see, for example, chap. 17, secs. 214ff.). This is apparently the same incident mentioned in section 231.

461. *ymapacmi runap llantanpi* presents two translation problems. First, *runap* 'of people' does not specify what group is concerned; to minimize supplied elements, 'those' is furnished. Taylor (1987b: 291) speculates that it is a pejorative colonial usage of *runa*, which, like modern *indio*, implies baseness. Second, *llantan* is taken as a variant for *llactan*; see chapter 18 (sec. 227). Hernández Príncipe ([1613] 1919: 184) notes that villages and *ayllu*s regularly stole each other's *huaca*s.

462. This sentence has witness validation.

CHAPTER 20

Here Begins the Life of Llocllay Huancupa. In What Follows, We Shall Also Write about Its End

They say[463] the *huaca* named Llocllay Huancupa[464] was Pacha Camac's child.

A woman named Lanti Chumpi, from Alay Satpa *ayllu*, found this *huaca*'s visible form[465] while she was cultivating a field.

As she dug it out the first time, she wondered, "What could this be?" and just threw it right back down on the ground.[466]

237 But, while she was digging another time,[467] she found once again the same thing she'd found before.

"This might be some kind of *huaca*!"[468] she

thought. And so, thinking, "I'll show it to my elders and the other people of my *ayllu*," she brought it back.

238 At that time there existed in the village named Llacsa Tampo another *huaca*, called Cati Quillay,[469] an emissary of the Inca.[470]

Cati Quillay was a *yanca*,[471] one who could force any *huaca* that wouldn't talk to speak.

Saying, "Who are you?

"What is your name?

"What have you come for?"

he started to make the *huaca* called Llocllay Huancupa talk.

Llocllay Huancupa answered, saying, "I am a child of Pacha Camac Pacha Cuyuchic, World Maker and World Shaker.

"My name is Llocllay Huancupa.[472]

---

463. 'They say' supplied to indicate reportive validation, which continues through the first sentence of section 240.

464. *llocllay huancupa ñiscanchic* means 'Llocllay Huancupa, whom we mentioned above'. But in fact this is the first mention of Llocllay. Perhaps there were other testimonies that have not been included.

465. *ricurimuscantas . . . tarircan* 'she found [Llocllay's] visible form': this could mean a likeness, perhaps a precolumbian artifact (such objects were and still are sometimes taken as signs of the superhuman), but it might also mean some nonfigurative object.

466. *pachallampitac*: since *pacha* means both a location and a moment, could also mean 'immediately'.

467. *huc pachacta* 'another time': again, since *pacha* signifies both time and space, this might also mean 'at another place'. If so, its sense might be that Lanti Chumpi recognized the find's importance by its ability to move underground. Whether one reads two times or two places, the point seems to be that the *huaca* insists on being found by Lanti Chumpi.

468. A *huaca* that belonged to an extinct *ayllu* and had been lost among "roads and crossroads and wildernesses" was called a *purun huaca*, meaning a 'wild' or 'desolate' one. "When they found these . . . they considered themselves lucky and blessed, and they began to en-

noble their lineages and their descent" (Hernández Príncipe [1613] 1919: 184). Hence Lanti Chumpi's excitement. All of chapter 20 through section 243 is the biography of a rediscovered *purum huaca* and the story of its cultic "ennoblement" up to and including cooptation by the Inca state.

469. Possibly identifiable with Catequilla or Catachillay, the Southern Cross (Gonçález Holguín [1608] 1952: 51) as interpreted by Gary Urton (1981: 130–131).

470. *yngap cachan* 'an emissary of the Inca' employs the Inca term for a plenipotentiary and not a mere messenger.

471. Seems to suggest that one *huaca* (presumably via its priest) could act as *yanca* of another. Taylor (1987b: 295) gives "effortlessly," reading *yanca* as the homonymous adverb.

472. Llocllay Huancupa's name signals his association with rain: Gonçález Holguín ([1608] 1952: 215) tells us *llocclla* meant "river in spate, flood." The Jesuit *carta annua* of 1609 (Taylor 1987a: 85–96) tells that *huancupa*,

"It was my father who sent me here, saying, 'Go and protect that Checa village!' "[473]

239   The people rejoiced exuberantly, exclaiming, "Good news! Let him live in this village and watch over us." And since the enclosed courtyard[474] at the house of the woman who'd discovered the *huaca* was a small one, they enlarged it, and all the Checa, along with the Chauti and Huanri people, adorned her house and courtyard with great reverence.

240   They made arrangements among themselves, saying, "We'll enter in to do his service according to the full and waning moon,[475] *ayllu* by *ayllu*, with the Allauca taking the lead"; and they gave him some of their llamas.

(At the full moon they in fact[476] say,

"It's time for his arrival,"

they say,

"It's he who's arriving!")

At the Arrival festival, in the old times, people used to dance wearing the *chumprucu*[477] and the *huaychao* weavings,[478] just the same way as they wore the *chumprucu* and the *huaychao* weavings during Paria Caca's festival season.

241   They served him for many years in the way we have described.

At one time, maybe because people didn't take good care of him, Llocllay Huancupa went back to his father Pacha Camac and disappeared.

When the people saw this happen, they grieved deeply and searched for him, adorning the place where Lanti Chumpi had first discovered him, and building him a step-pyramid.[479]

242   But when they still couldn't find him, all the elders readied their llamas, guinea pigs, and all kinds of clothing, and went to Pacha Camac.

So by worshiping his father again, they got Llocllay Huancupa to return.

People served him even more, with renewed fervor, endowing him with llama herders.[480]

They pastured these llamas in the place called Sucya Villca,[481] declaring, "These are llamas of Pacha Camac." The Inca also ratified this practice.[482]

243   They arrived to worship one *ayllu* after another,[483] and in this fashion they served the *huaca*

---

whose meaning in this context is unclear, formed part of the name of a specific rain *huaca* Tamiahuancupa in Checa. Llocllay Huancupa is there said to be a child of Pacha Camac, the greatest maritime *huaca*, and to be a nephew of Paria Caca, the great embodiment of the stormy heights. Rivers in spate are the connections from the latter to the former. Thus Llocllay's appearance appears a promise that these violent waters would flow to the Checa's benefit and perhaps refrain from creating the washouts and mudslides that often damage villages like the Checa's.

473. Considering that this oracle was mediated by an Inca-sponsored *huaca*, and that Pacha Camac was also a heavily Inca-subsidized cult, the message suggests state cooptation of the newly discovered Llocllay Huancupa. Perhaps, from the Inca point of view, the adoption of such *purum huacas* afforded a safer course than fostering *huacas* of autochthony like Maca Uisa, who, as chapter 19 shows, retained his value as a symbol of resistance.

474. *cancha* 'courtyard': for description of the enclosed Andean residential compound, see Gasparini and Margolies (1980: 181–193).

475. See note 423.

476. This whole parenthesis has witness validation and differs from the surrounding material in tense; it appears to place a contemporary custom in the remembered context of the narrative.

477. Taylor (1987b: 297) suggests a plausible derivation from words meaning 'belt' and 'headdress', hence 'turban'. Turbans are abundantly visible in coastal ceramic portrait vases and are found in prehistoric burials.

478. *huaychao ahua* 'huaychao weavings' is an uncertain translation because the expected form would be *ahuasca*.

479. *husnocta pircaspa*: literally, 'walling an *usnu*'; the term *usnu* could mean a stone-faced step-pyramid, perhaps like the one still visible at Vilcashuamán. But in R. T. Zuidema's explication (1980) the concept expands to signify any *axis mundi*–like vertical conduit. The early "extirpator" Cristóbal de Albornoz ([1583?] 1984: 202) describes *usnu*-type shrines as 'towers' built around an axis or shaft at which worship was celebrated. Felipe Guaman Poma de Ayala also mentions *usnus* ([1615] 1980: 1:236, 239, 2:357, 413).

480. That is, like many other superhumans, he was assigned an endowment of capital goods whose products would support his cult and be distributed at his feasts.

481. Identified by Rostworowski (1978: 43) as a plateau above San Bartolomé.

482. That is, when they felt forced to increase the endowment of this Inca-endorsed *huaca*, they arranged for the Inca state to bear part of the additional cost by contributing use of Inca herding facilities at Sucya Villca. This was appropriate because Llocllay's cult was an extension of the Inca-sponsored Pacha Camac cult, and Pacha Camac's animals were herded at Sucya Villca (chap. 22, sec. 277).

483. Taylor (1987b: 299) interprets *ayllo ayllo ñiscampi chayarcan* to mean that each *ayllu* celebrated the "Arrival" rite in turn.

for a great many years. If diseases of any kind came upon them, they would tell him and implore him for well-being. Whenever any affliction or sorrow befell, or when enemies came, or there was an earthquake, people would fear him greatly and say, "His father[484] is angry!" As for maize offerings, they gave him maize belonging to the Inca from the common granaries,[485] to provide for his drinks.

244 Later on, at the time when a certain Father Cristóbal de Castilla was in this *reducción* and when Don Gerónimo Cancho Huaman was the *curaca*,[486] people stopped worshiping, because both of them hated such practices.

But when the first great plague of measles[487] came, people began to worship him again in all sorts of ways. As if he were thinking, "Llocllay's sending the plague," the *curaca* ceased scolding those people any longer when they drank in the ruined buildings of Purum Huasi.

At that same time, the *huaca's* house caught fire all by itself,[488] because that was God's will.

245 Now it's a fact that[489] after Don Gerónimo died, Don Juan Sacsa Lliuya succeeded to the office of *curaca*,[490] and, since this chief was at the same time a *huacsa* himself, everybody began to live as they'd lived in earlier times; they'd visit both Llocllay Huancupa and Maca Uisa, and they kept vigil the whole night there drinking until dawn.

246 Nowadays, due to the preachings of Doctor Avila, some people have converted back to God and forbidden all these practices. But if it hadn't been for a certain man who converted to God with a sincere heart and denounced the *huaca*s as demons, people might well have kept on living that way for a long time.[491]

We'll let you hear this story in what follows.

247 There was a man named Don Cristóbal Choque Casa, whose father was the late Don Gerónimo Cancho Huaman whom we mentioned before. This man lived a good life from his childhood onward, because his father bitterly scorned all these *huaca*s.

But when he was about to die, Don Gerónimo was deceived by these evil spirits and fell into this same sin. Beguiled by many ancient evil spirits,[492]

---

484. I.e., Pacha Camac.

485. *yngap çaranta sapçicunamantas* 'maize belonging to the Inca from the common granaries': again emphasizes that Llocllay's cult was Inca-subsidized. The suggestion would be that, where maize is concerned, the Inca enabled them to toast Llocllay at Inca, not local, expense.

486. A 1588–1590 lawsuit over the major *cacicazgo* of the Rímac valley contains testimony by Don Gerónimo Cancho Huaman, *curaca* of the Checa. Fron it we learn that he was four or five years old when the Spanish invaded Peru; he was forty years old when Jesuits taught literacy at Huarochirí missions and never learned to write. From childhood onward he attended meetings of chiefs that the Ninavilca (Huarochirí village) lords convoked at Mama and elsewhere (Murra 1980: xviii–xix). His position as a member of the generation that first managed the transition to colonial religious and political forms helps one to understand his ambivalence toward Christianity (see sec. 247; Archivo General de la Nación, Buenos Aires, ms. 9-45-5-15, ff. 105v–112r; Espinoza Soriano 1983–1984).

487. Cook (1981: 60) says the first measles epidemic was perhaps in 1531–1532, with a question mark, and notes another without a question mark for 1558–1559. It seems likely that the teller means the 1558–1559 epidemic. Perhaps the resurgence of Llocllay's cult following it is a phenomenon resembling the Taki Onqoy nativist movement that arose at that time in the south-central highlands. In order to credit this interpretation one must assume that Gerónimo Cancho Huaman's rule lasted thirty-odd years.

If the date is not 1558 but later, the reference might be to the Moro Onqoy period described by Curatola (1978).

488. *paicama* 'all by itself' could also mean 'according to him' (the chief?). Either reading suggests that the fire was taken as the Spanish deity's attack on the native *huaca*.

489. 'Now it's a fact that' supplied to indicate witness validation, which continues through the end of section 247.

490. Since Don Gerónimo was still *curaca* in 1590 according to the source mentioned in note 486, the events that follow can be dated 1590–1608.

491. A nakedly political passage setting up the witness, Cristóbal Choque Casa, as a hero. Choque Casa was Avila's close political ally. Missionary Quechua predominates in the rhetoric of the pure heart and the verbal renunciation of *huaca*s as *supay* ('demons', in missionary lexicon). 'The *huaca*s' supplied. Original has *caycunacta* 'these'.

492. The passage may have a double meaning, reflecting the double Andean and missionary senses of the word *supay*. An Andean person faced with death could well be concerned with ancient spirits, not in the European understanding of false deities, but in the autochthonous sense of deified ancestors or *huaca*s worshiped by ancestors, whose mobile parts (*supay*) could contact the living. The speaker would not have specified *mana alli* unless he supposed that a *supay* could also be good.

he confessed himself just before dying.[493]

As for that fellow, God only knows where he is now![494]

248   The deceased man's son, that is, the same Don Cristóbal we spoke of, is still alive.

It was he who once saw the demon Llocllay Huancupa with his own eyes, when he was also deceived by the same ancient evil spirits because of his father's death.

The story is like this.

To tell it Don Cristóbal first swore an oath by saying, "This is the cross."[495]

249   Don Cristóbal said that one night[496] he went to Llocllay Huancupa's house while his lover[497] was

---

493. *ahcca mana alli supai machucunap llullaycuscan ña huañoypacri confesacorcanmi* 'Beguiled by many ancient evil spirits he confessed himself just before dying': an ambiguous sentence. It could mean, as we indicate, that although Don Gerónimo relapsed into *huaca* worship in old age, his conscience at the last impelled him to confess in Catholic fashion. Or it could mean that he made his last confession to a *huaca* priest. The latter reading presupposes that the Spanish-derived verb *confesacoy* could denominate a non-Christian rite (much as *saçerdote* could mean *huaca* priest).

494. *chaytaca dios aponchictaccha yachan maypi cascantapas* 'As for that fellow, God only knows where he is now!': perhaps with a shade of satirical intent, or perhaps said in pity; since the old man was so indecisive in religious matters, who can say whether he is now in Hell or Heaven?

495. Cristóbal's testimony begins with not one but two narrative formulas: first, *cay simire cay ynam* 'the story is like this', a common one throughout the manuscript and perhaps an Andean phrase; then, *cayta rimaypacca ñaupacracmi don christobal juramentocta mucharcan caymi + ñispa* 'to tell it Don Cristóbal first swore an oath by saying, "This is the cross," ' an emphatic touch of mission culture.

496. *huc tutas don x(christob)al* 'Don Cristóbal said that one night': more literally, taking reportive validation into account, 'One night Don Cristóbal, it's said'. But the fact that we know it was Don Cristóbal himself who swore before telling the story that begins here justifies 'Don Cristóbal said that'. Since Don Cristóbal would presumably have talked in first person, the passage shows that *-si* reportive passages are likely to be paraphrases of testimony, not transcripts, and therefore unreliable as to exact properties of discourse including, for example, versification. (An alternative hypothesis would be that Don Cristóbal himself wrote the passage, trumping up the oath and third person diction.)

there. Cristóbal had abandoned the worship of this *huaca*, and hardly thought of him anymore.

When he arrived at the dwelling he went into a little shed in the corral[498] to urinate.

250   From inside that place, the spot where they've put a cross, that demon appeared before his eyes like a silver plate that, mirroring[499] the light of the midday sun, dazzles a man's eyesight.

When he saw this he almost fell to the ground.

Reciting the Our Father and the Hail Mary, he fled toward the little lodging, the woman's dwelling.

251   When he'd walked halfway there, the demon flashed three times again. When he arrived at the room it flashed[500] another three times, and the first time it had flashed[501] three times also.

So, all in all, it flashed nine times.

Seeing that demon flash so many times, and becoming thoroughly terrified, Don Cristóbal reached the place where the woman slept and woke her up abruptly.

252   Two children were also asleep there.

He was panting[502] so hard, the children got scared and said, "It's our father who's doing that!"

(These children and the young woman, too, were the offspring of the demon's priest.)[503]

---

497. *sipasnin* 'his lover': the referent of the third person possessive marker *-n* is ambiguous (Cristóbal's lover or Llocllay's?) and the translation reflects this. The former, however, seems likelier; why, otherwise, would Cristóbal, a Christian, go to Llocllay's house? And why at night?

498. *racay huasillaman* 'into a little shed in the corral': Taylor (1987b: 305) has "into a little house in ruins (which had been the *huaca*'s sanctuary[?])." The discrepancy arises from readings of *racay*, which can mean either 'corral' or (in the form *racay racay*) 'depopulated town' (Goncález Holguín [1608] 1952: 311).

499. *tincochisca* 'mirroring': more literally, 'caused to match' (i.e., angled so as to reflect) the mid-day sun. The phrase *runap ñauinta tutayachic* reads more literally 'as what benights a man's eyes' and alludes to the darkening of vision caused by gazing at a too-bright light.

500. 'It flashed' supplied.

501. 'It had flashed' supplied.

502. *siuyaptinsi* 'he was panting': original is ambiguous as to whether Llocllay or (more probably) Don Cristóbal is the subject of this verb.

503. I.e., of Astu Huaman, who appears in chapter 21 (secs. 265, 267).

Then, just as a man entering a doorway at dusk
darkens the room even more,[504] so it was also that
night as the demon went in and out. The demon
wanted to overpower Don Cristóbal, making his
ears ring with a "Chuy!" sound, as if he were about
to demolish the house, too.

253   Cristóbal invoked God, shouting out at the top
of his voice all the prayers he knew, <crossed out:>
[knowing] saying the *doctrina*[505] from beginning to
end over and over again.

As midnight passed, the demon was overpower-
ing him. He thought that nothing could save him,
the demon was making him sweat so. Then he invoked our mother Saint Mary, saying:

254   "Oh mother, you are my only mother.
Shall this evil demon overpower me?

You, who are my mother, please help me
Even though I am a great sinner;

I myself served this very demon;
Now I recognize that he was a demon all along,

That he is not God,
That he could never do anything good.

255   You, my only queen,[506]
You alone will rescue me from this danger!

Please intercede on my behalf with your son Jesus.
Let him rescue me right now

From this sin of mine,
And from the hand of this wicked demon."

Thus weeping and sweating[507] he invoked our
mother the Virgin, our one and only queen.

256   After finishing this, he prayed saying the *Salve
Regina Mater Misericordiæ* in Latin.

While he was reciting it, just as he was in the
middle of reciting it, that shameless wicked demon
shook the house and, calling "Chus!" in a very deep
voice, went out of it in the form of a barn owl.[508]

At that exact moment, the place became like
dawn.[509] There were no longer any terrors, nothing
like a man entering and leaving a room.

257   From then on, Cristóbal worshiped God and
Mary the Holy Virgin even more, so that they
might help him always.

In the morning he addressed all the people:
"Brothers and fathers, that Llocllay Huancupa
whom we feared has turned out to be a demonic
barn owl.

258   "Last night, with the help of the Virgin Saint
Mary our mother, I conquered him for good. From
now on, none of you are to enter that house. If I
ever see anybody enter or approach the house, I'll
tell the *padre*. Consider carefully[510] what I've said
and receive it into your hearts completely!" Thus
he admonished all the people.

259   Some people probably assented, while others
stood mute for fear of that demon.

504. The simile likens the alternating glare and gloom
of Llocllay's presence to the interior of an Andean
house—normally windowless—that is thrown into darkness when a person enters its doorway and brightens
when he steps out.

505. *doctrina*: the elementary religious lessons that
Indian neophytes were required to learn.

506. *coyallaytacmi*, 'my only queen', using the word
for an Inca queen, that is, a sister-wife of the Inca.

507. When Jesuits campaigned in Huarochirí in 1571,
they encouraged people to "pour out tears and sobs"
while renouncing the *huaca*s, and intentionally "drew
the business out so that [converts] would feel greater anguish." The 1571 campaign produced behavior something

like Cristóbal's: the missionaries proudly reported that
one convert "passed three hours weeping bitterly and
conversing with Our Lord" before turning himself in to
become a servitor of Catholic priests (Arguedas and Duviols 1966: 241–244). These precedents suggest that
chapters 20 and 21 render the subjective content of what
had perhaps become by 1600 a fairly standardized cultural performance.

508. *chusic* 'barn owl': this bird's appearance echoes
the image of the flashing disk. "*Barn owl, Tyto alba con-
tempta (Lechuza de los campanarios)*. A large owl, buffy-
white below speckled with black, pearl gray to buff
above, finely spotted. The feathers about the eyes form a
white disk in the shape of a heart. Recognized by its light
color and characteristic hoarse screech. Nocturnal, with-
drawing during the day into caves, holes in trees, towers
of churches, etc. In nearly all parts of our region, but
never common; also in Lima. A species of world-wide
distribution" (Koepcke 1970: 76). The barn owl, a nocturnal predator, seems an appropriate likeness of the nocturnal *huaca* Llocllay (his rites are celebrated at night).

509. *pachaca pacaric yna carcan*: could be read in a
grander sense as meaning 'the world was as if dawning'.

510. *alli yachacoy* 'consider carefully': might also be
read 'good thought'. Taylor (1987b: 311) detects a possible
calque to *evangelio*, which (via a Greek etymology)
means 'good news'.

From that time forward, they definitely did refrain from going there.[511]

---

511. *chayaita samarcancu* might also mean "they desisted from performing the Arrival ritual" (Taylor 1987b: 313).

But that night, while Don Cristóbal was asleep in his house, Llocllay Huancupa appeared to him again in a dream.

Next we'll write about this.[512]

---

512. This sentence has witness validation.

Although a Dream Is Not Valid,[513] We Shall Speak about That Demon's Frightful Deeds and Also about the Way in Which Don Cristóbal Defeated Him

We've already heard that Llocllay Huancupa was an evil demon and that Don Cristóbal defeated him.[514]

But Don Cristóbal said[515] the evil demon also wanted to overpower him in a dream.

And so on the night of the very next day, the demon summoned Don Cristóbal from his house by sending a man. He didn't tell him, "I'm going to Llocllay Huancupa."[516] Only when they were about to enter his house did Don Cristóbal catch on.[517]

He got scared and approached an old lady, a Yunca woman,[518] who lived there in that same patio.

This old lady was a Yunca woman.

"Son," she said to him, "Why is it that you don't honor Llocllay Huancupa, child of Pacha Cuyuchic the Earth Shaker? It's to find out about this that he's summoned you now."[519]

---

513. *mana muscoy yupai captinpas* 'Although a Dream Is Not Valid': the original reads 'although a dream is not *yupai*'. A root sense of *yupay* is 'account'. Derivatives include 'to give account of something received, or to enumerate, to evaluate, to esteem, or to assign a price'; "*yupay* honor or esteem" and "*mana yupay* what is null or invalid or worthless or commanding no price" are further derivatives (Gonçález Holguín [1608] 1952: 371–372).

Why does the writer of the title feel a need to disclaim the value or validity of dreams? Mannheim (1987: 137) points out that the Third Council of Lima, laying down the doctrine that Avila enforced, had explicitly attacked the idea that dreams are *yupai*. Mannheim translates the council's strictures from Quechua:

Don't be keeping [*Ama . . .yupaychanquichicchu*]
   dreams
"I dreamt this or that,
   why did I dream it?"
Don't ask:
dreams are just worthless and
not to be kept [*mana yupaychaypacchu*].

"Extirpators" energetically attacked belief in dreams and dream interpreters (Arriaga [1621] 1968: 35; Hernández Príncipe [1613] 1919: 192, [1622] 1923: 25–49).

514. End of an introductory passage with witness validation.

515. 'Don Cristóbal said' supplied to indicated reportive validation, which continues through the second sentence of section 272. Don Cristóbal may be taken as the speaker because in section 248 he is named as the source.

516. *manas paiman rine nircancho* 'He didn't tell him, "I'm going to Llocllay Huancupa"': Llocllay's name supplied as referent of *pai*. Taylor (1987b: 315) reads this differently: "He didn't say to him if he meant to go or not." The discrepancy arises from two points: first, whether one takes the messenger or Don Cristóbal to be the speaker; Taylor seems to accept the latter. Second, whether one understands the quotation to begin before or after *paiman* 'to him'; Taylor accepts the latter.

517. *ña huasinman yaicusparacsi musyacorcan* 'Only when they were about to enter his house did Don Cristóbal catch on': Don Cristóbal, supplied subject. Taylor (1987b: 315) has: "At the moment when he was about to enter his house, [Don Cristóbal] had a presentiment [of something unlucky]." This reading is justified with an explication of *musyay* suggesting it means 'enter into a trance', with connotations of precognition. Our translation is influenced by another usage of *musyasca* to mean 'in the know, aware'.

518. *huc yunga huarmi chacuas* 'an old lady, a Yunca woman': *chacuas* is a modern Quechua I word meaning 'old lady'. The alternative translation would be to take this as her personal name.

519. Presumably the old lady's speech is a reply to Don Cristóbal's invective against Llocllay on the previous day.

262   When she said that, he replied, "Ma'am, he's an evil demon. Why should I honor him?"

Don Cristóbal was gripping a silver coin of four *reales*[520] in his hand.

He dropped it[521] on the ground.

While he was searching for it, Francisco Trompetero called him from outside: "Hey, what're you doing in there?[522] Your father's really angry! He's calling you and he says, 'He'd better come in a hurry!'"

263   As soon as he said this, Cristóbal replied, "Wait a moment, brother, I'm coming right away" and rummaged for his silver coin in frantic haste.

At the moment when he found it, when he was about to leave, the demon, just as he'd scared Cristóbal before with a silvery flash[523] against his face,

flashed out once again from inside the place where the cross was put.

264   Realizing that he couldn't save himself now, Cristóbal suddenly got frightened. Someone called him from inside the room, saying, "It's our father[524] who calls you!"

Saying, "All right," but deeply angry in his heart, he went inside. On entering he sat down close by the door.

265   Right then, Astu Huaman was offering drinks and feeding the *huaca*, saying,

"Father Llocllay Huancupa, you are Pacha Cuyuchic's child,
It is you who gave force and form to people."

As he spoke he fed him with deep veneration.

The demon, unable to speak, repeated "Hu, hu"[525] over and over again.

And when Astu Huaman offered him some coca, the demon made it crackle "Chac, chac" just as a coca-chewer does.

266   While he was doing that, a long time, Don Cristóbal saw from inside the house something that looked like a painting encircling it completely in two patterned bands. It looked as a Roman-style mural painting might if it went on two levels.[526]

---

520. A four-*real* coin is half a *peso de ocho*, very commonly circulated c. 1600. The coin Don Cristóbal held was almost certainly of a design showing the quartered arms of Castile and León on one side and the arms of the Hapsburgs (probably the version obtaining during the reigns of Felipe II [1556–1598] or Felipe III [1598–1621]) on the other. The arms of Castile and León are contained within the upper left quadrant of the Hapsburg arms. The quartered space—reminiscent of Peruvian ideas of the Inca world as a 'fourfold domain'—may have figured in Don Cristóbal's dream thinking (Dasi 1950: 60, 66; Grünthal and Sellschopp 1978: 49, 60; Rodríguez Lorente 1965: 129, 153).

521. *ormachircan* 'he dropped it': ambiguous as to whether he dropped it by accident or let it fall on purpose, but the former seems more plausible since he at once tries to recover it.

522. Francisco Trompetero's surname or nickname means 'trumpeter' in Spanish and suggests a military or church musician. His question sounds rhetorical; he would have known very well why an Andean person carries a coin when visiting a *huaca*: "In some places silver is offered up in the form of *reales*. In Libia Cancharco fifteen silver *duros* [i.e., whole pesos] were found, together with some small pieces of ordinary silver. In the town of Recuay Dr. Ramírez found two hundred *duros* in a *huaca*. They generally hammer the coins or chew them in such a way that you can hardly see the royal arms. Coins are also found around *huaca*s, looking as if stained with blood or *chicha* [i.e., maize beer]. On other occasions, the priests of the *huaca*s keep the silver that is collected as offerings to be spent for their festivals" (Arriaga [1621] 1968: 43; Keating's translation).

523. *collqui ñiscanchichuan* 'with a silvery flash': Taylor (1987b: 317–318) thinks the silvery object might be a silver disk hung in Llocllay Huancupa's shrine and thinks it unlikely to be the silver coin just mentioned, which he considers "a superfluous detail." In dream imagery however, the two might be conflated.

524. *yayanchic* 'our father': inclusive first person plural, conveying the speaker's assumption that the 'father' in question is also the father of the person he addresses, namely Cristóbal.

525. *chaysi chay supaica mana rimacoytaca husachispa hu hu ñicacharcan*: if one takes *hu hu ñicacharcan* to derive from *huñiy* 'to agree' then the sense is that Llocllay here expresses his approval of the offering. But, since Llocllay appears an inarticulate *huaca*, it seems likelier that *hu hu* represents his inarticulate speech. Or perhaps *hu hu* represents an owl's cry, since Llocllay took an owl's form in chapter 20 (sec. 256).

526. *don christobalca chay huasin hucomanta tucoy yscay pachapi muyoc pintasca ynacta ricorcan ymanam rromano pintasca yscai patarapi rinman chay hynacta*: more literally, 'Don Cristóbal saw from inside that house all on two places [levels, bands, or sides] something like a surrounding [rotating?] painted [object? pattern?], the way a Roman painted [object? pattern?] would go on two bands, like that'.

Translators differ in their efforts to visualize this difficult passage.

The wide divergences all turn on the meaning of the Spanish word *rromano*. Trimborn (1939: 114) and Urioste

On one band of the painting was a tiny demon, very black, his eyes just like silver,[527] who gripped in his hand a wooden stick with a hook. On top of him was a llama head. Above that was again the little demon and above that again the llama head.

In this way it encircled the whole house in a twofold pattern.

267   It really scared Don Cristóbal that he kept seeing all these things, and he tried to recall just what he'd meant to say.

Meanwhile, since the demon had finished eating, Astu Huaman made the fire blaze up again to burn all the things he'd offered.

268   After this was done, and when everything was quiet, Don Cristóbal began to speak:[528]

"Listen, Llocllay Huancupa! They address you[529] as the animator of humanity and as the World Shaker. People say 'He is the very one who makes everything!' and all mankind fears you. So why have you summoned me now?[530] For my part, I say,

'Is not Jesus Christ the son of God?[531]
Shall I not revere this one, the true God?
Shall I not revere his word forever?'[532]

(1983: 169) rendered it as concerning a Roman painting, and Taylor earlier accepted a related gloss, seeing it as a retable or mural in the style of a Roman church, but folded double (*yscay patarapi*). Arguedas and Duviols (1966: 123) judged that *rromano* refers to a scale called *romana*, that is, a steelyard scale, which could be said to 'move on two levels', and Taylor later (1987b: 319) accepted this view (see Hartmann and Holm 1985). Teresa Gisbert, the leading specialist in Andean visual arts for this period, endorses 'Roman-style painting' (personal communication). Ferrell (n.d.) considers relevant to a "banded" appearance the 1737 *Diccionario de autoridades* gloss of *romano* as 'a gray and black striped cat' (1976: 3:635).

527. Taylor (1987b: 321) has *monedas de plata* 'silver coins', which apparently echoes the coin theme starting in section 262.

528. Cristóbal now answers Llocllay's summons in section 261 by explaining why he does not respect him.

529. *ñispa ñisonqui* 'they address you': subject unspecified. The implied subject could be people in general, or Llocllay's priest Astu Huaman.

530. The point apparently being, if Llocllay really has these powers and privileges, why should Don Cristóbal's irreverence bother him?

531. Contrasting Jesus' claim to being the son of *dios* with Llocllay's claim of being the son of Pacha Camac.

532. These sentences repeat the suffix sequence -*tac*-

This is what I say.

269   "Or am I mistaken? Then tell me now! Say,

'He is not the true God;
I am the maker of everything!'

so that from that moment on I may worship you."

So Cristóbal spoke, but the demon stayed mute. He didn't say anything at all.

270   At that moment Don Cristóbal defied him, crying good and loud:

"Look!
Are you not a demon?
Could you defeat my Lord Jesus Christ,
In whom I believe?

Look!
This house of yours!
Yes, you dwell surrounded by demons[533]—
Should I believe in you?"

271   At that moment somebody threw what we call[534] a *llaullaya*[535] at him.

Regarding this thing, Don Cristóbal didn't know whether that demon threw it or whether it was from God's side. For, defending himself with the *llaullaya* alone, he fled from that house all the way to the corner of the count's house,[536] always moving sideways and protecting himself with it.

Then he woke up.

---

cha, which in turn derives from two others that bespeak, respectively, forceful contrast (-*tac*) and a conjectural tone (-*cha*); the overall import is something like, but not quite like, a rhetorical question (Urioste 1973: 40–42, 51).

533. *supaipac yntupayascanmi ari tianqui* 'you dwell surrounded by demons': refers to the apparition of the checkered frieze or mural all around Llocllay's dwelling, covered with images Don Cristóbal thought demonic (sec. 266).

534. *ñiycum* 'what we call': exclusive first person plural form, implying that 'we' tellers, as opposed to the person addressed, call the object *llaullaya*. The source senses a cultural or linguistic difference between himself and the addressee.

535. Untranslated; may be an agricultural implement or a garment.

536. *condep huasincama* 'all the way to . . . the count's house': *conde* could mean a person from the *Kunti* quarter of the empire (*Kuntisuyu* in Inca terms), or a person called count (*conde*) in Spanish.

272   From that exact time on, right up to the present, he defeated various *huaca*s in his dreams the same way. Any number of times he defeated both Paria Caca and Chaupi Ñamca, telling the people all about it over and over again, saying, "They're demons!"

This is all we know about this evil demon's existence and about Don Cristóbal's victory.[537]

273   On this matter: it's said that[538] in performing Llocllay's Arrival festival in the old days, the people who celebrated used to dance first until sundown.[539]

Toward dusk, the *huaca*'s priest would say, "Now our father is drunk; Let him dance!" And he would perform a dance "as if in his stead," as they used to say.

Saying, "It's our father who invites you!" he'd bring maize beer in one small wooden beaker, and put another one inside the shrine in a pot, saying, "It's he who drinks this."[540]

274   Regarding this drinking: the priest, we know,[541] would offer drinks starting from the elders, all the way down to the end of the assembly.[542]

<A **marginal addition** in Quechua begins here:>

When they finished the round of drinking, they say,[543] the priest[544] would bring the gourd from which the demon had drunk outside, to where the guests were, so they could worship that gourd.

<**Marginal addition** ends.>

The following day he'd have them carry the leftovers and edible remains to Sucya Villca.

275   In the old days, the people who'd come to celebrate Llocllay Huancupa's Arrival reportedly[545] brought the food to Sucya Villca himself.

However, we know that[546] later on,[547] after finishing Llocllay Huancupa's feeding, people also fed Sucya Villca right at that spot.

In what follows, we'll write about these food offerings to Sucya Villca, and why they fed him, and also about who Pacha Camac was.

---

537. This sentence has witness validation.

538. 'It's said that' supplied to indicate reportive validation, which continues through the end of section 273.

539. *hura pachacama* 'until sundown': see chapter 8 (sec. 103), where the same locution occurs. Other possible readings are 'at the lowlands' and 'Pacha Camac'. The latter is problematic; if Pacha Camac were intended, one would expect final *c* and a locative suffix.

540. This is a description of drinking with paired vessels, one for the deity and one for the worshiper, a gesture of religious reciprocity pictured by Felipe Guaman Poma ([1615] 1980: 1:80).

541. 'We know' supplied to indicate that this passage, to the end of the chapter, has witness validation. The marginal note has reportive *-si*.

542. 'Of the assembly' supplied.

543. 'They say' supplied to indicate that the marginal note has reportive validation.

544. 'The priest' supplied.

545. 'Reportedly' supplied to indicate reportive validation of this sentence.

546. 'We know that' supplied to indicate that this sentence and the remainder of the chapter have witness validation.

547. Possibly meaning after the Spanish conquest.

CHAPTER 22

276

We don't in fact[548] know much about the Incas' great reverence for Pacha Camac.[549]

But we do know a few things. In the highlands, they say,[550] the Incas worshiped the sun as the object of their adoration from Titi Caca, saying,

"It is he who made us Inca!"
From the lowlands, they worshiped Pacha Camac, saying,

"It is he who made us Inca!"[551]

---

548. 'In fact' supplied to indicate witness validation, which predominates through the end of section 279. Some of the exceptions are conjectural -*cha* validations, translated with 'probably', 'it looks like', 'possibly', and 'no doubt'. It appears as though the source of these comments is giving his/her own understanding of Inca thought rather than relaying an informant's.

549. *yngacunap pacha camacta ancha yupaychascantaca manam allicho yachanchic*: Taylor (1987b: 329) has: "We do not know very well whether the Incas held Pachacamac in high esteem." But this seems the less likely of two possible readings, since the next few sections show that the speaker clearly knows the Incas did esteem him highly; in fact that is the point the chapter seeks to explain.

550. 'They say' supplied to indicate reportive validation of this sentence; however, the next sentence, which complements it, has witness validation.

551. *hanac ticsipi muchanantas ynticta titi cacamanta mucharcan caymi yngacta camahuarca ñispa hura ticsimantam canan pacha camac ñiscacta caymi yngacta camahuarca ñispatac mucharcancu* 'In the highlands, they say, the Incas worshiped the sun as the object of their adoration from Titi Caca, saying, "It is he who made us Inca!" From the lowlands, they worshiped Pacha Camac, saying, "It is he who made us Inca!" ': this passage opposes Titi Caca to Pacha Camac as respectively the world's 'upper' and 'lower foundations' (*hanac/hura ticsi*). While its specific sense is uncertain, it appears to

277 The Incas worshiped these two *huaca*s most, far beyond all others, exalting them supremely and adorning them with their silver and gold, putting many hundreds of retainers at their service, and placing llama herds for their endowments in all the villages.

The llamas of Pacha Camac sent from the Checa people stayed at Sucya Villca.[552]

278 Here's how we interpret this.
The Inca probably thought, "The world ends somewhere in the waters of Ura Cocha that are below Titi Caca, and somewhere past the place they call Pacha Camac.[553] It looks like there is no village

---

report an imperial vision of place-shrines on the highest scale, namely, place-shrines categorizing the whole world as one place. The ritual duality expresses the wholeness of the world in the image of centrifugal imperial expansion: from the world's highland center to its maritime edge.

552. Sucya Villca was a lake; see chapter 21 (secs. 274, 275) and chapter 22 (secs. 281–282, 284). From chapter 21 (sec. 275) we see that in the teller's mind Sucya Villca and Pacha Camac are closely linked. María Rostworowski (1978: 43) says Sucya Villca was a plateau above San Bartolomé, 40 km northwest of Huarochirí, and that Sucya Cancha was there, too.

The complex of Sucya Villca and Sucya Cancha figures in the manuscript as the *coca* place par excellence. In chapter 8 (sec. 109), Sucya Cancha is a place of coca fields; in chapter 9 (sec. 124), it is the place where people went to 'trade' (*rantiy*) coca.

553. *cay ñiscanchic titi caca hura cochañicpiri pacha camac ñiscancunallapich pacha puchocan* 'The world ends somewhere in the waters of Ura Cocha that are below Titi Caca, and somewhere past the place they call Pacha Camac': a difficult passage. The teller perhaps thinks the Inca is reconciling two images of the edge of the

beyond these points, possibly nothing at all."[554]

279   It was no doubt with such thoughts in mind that the Incas worshiped these two *huaca*s more than the other *huaca*s, and even placed the sun next to the lowland *huaca* Pacha Camac.

The place where they set it is called Punchau Cancha,[555] the Sun Court, to this very day.

280   Reportedly they gave Pacha Camac each year[556] what's called a Capac Hucha,[557] namely, human beings[558] both female and male, from Tauantin Suyo, the four quarters of the world.

Arriving at Pacha Camac, and saying to Pacha,[559] "Here they are. We offer them to you, father!" they'd bury the Capac Hucha alive, along with gold and silver. And according to the cycles of the full and waning moon, they fed him llamas and served him drinks without pause.

world: the one associated with their origin myth, in which the ocean is imagined as the deep reservoir from which Titi Caca's high-lying waters are lifted, and a coastal one, which identifies the ocean with the great seaside *huaca* Pacha Camac. The attempt to collate southern highland (especially Inca) understandings of Pacha Camac with more local west Andean ones appears analogous to the attempt to coordinate Cuni Raya of the coastal peoples with Vira Cocha of the highlanders. The phrase 'the place *they* call Pacha Camac' may be a clue; Rostworowski (1977: 198) notes that local usage called the place and its polity Ychma and only the *huaca* proper Pacha Camac.

554. The section has a marked predominance of dubitative validators, imparting a speculative tone.

555. The allusion is probably to the huge Inca temple still visible at Pachacámac.

556. In most other sources about *capac hucha*, the rite is described not as annual but as a crisis rite called on such occasions as plague, royal succession, or defeat (Duviols 1976). 'Reportedly' supplied to indicate reportive validation, which continues through the end of section 280.

557. Capac Hucha 'opulent prestation': an all-empire sacrificial and redistributive cycle, in which offerings from all the empire's peoples were collected at Cuzco and then redistributed outward to all the empire's shrines and borders. It heavily emphasized burial of human sacrifices, which became new Inca-sponsored shrines (Duviols 1976; Zuidema 1973).

558. Hernández Príncipe tells us that they were spotless children ([1622] 1923: 60), and Betanzos ([1551] 1987: 142) that they were "married" and buried in pairs together.

559. *pachaman* 'to Pacha': alternative translations, none certain, are 'to the earth', 'to the world', or 'to Pacha' (i.e., the first part of the *huaca*'s name).

281   At any time when it failed to rain in the Checa villages, the Yunca, giving their yearly offering of gold and silver according to the Inca's orders, would send it to Sucya Villca <crossed out:> [mountain] with their maize beer and *ticti*.[560]

They reportedly[561] offered all this to Sucya Villca, saying,

"Father, it is Pacha Camac who sends us here.
And you are the one who rains on the land.

When no water flows from this lake,
We humans suffer from drought.

Therefore send down rain!
This is what we have come for."[562]

282   In such years, the Yunca, too, used to bury the silver and gold that they brought next to Sucya Villca lake.

Sucya Villca's retainers were from the Yasapa *ayllu* and his llama herder from the Allauca.

(Later on, when the Spaniards were already here, a certain Yasapa man called Payco Casa saw them bury some gold and silver there.)

283   And likewise the Inca would have offerings of his gold and silver given according to his *quipu* account, to all the *huaca*s, to the well-known *huaca*s, to all the *huaca*s. He used to have them give gold *auqui*s and silver *auqui*s (when we say *choqui* we mean gold), and also gold *urpu*s and silver *urpu*s, and gold *tipsi*s and silver *tipsi*s; all this exactly according to *quipu* counts.[563]

560. The validation of this sentence is unclear, both *-mi* and *-si* being present.

561. 'Reportedly' supplied to indicate reportive validation, which continues through the second sentence of section 282.

562. These six utterances are not in semantic couplets, but their briefness and tight logical linkage gives them the aspect of an oral set-piece.

563. *choc auqui collqui auqui choqui ñispaca corictam ñinchic chaymantam choc urpo collc horpo choc tipsi collc tipsi ñiscacunactas cochic carcan quipollamanta*: if one were to reproduce the truncated words as such, it would read: 'gol *auqui* and silver *auqui* (in saying *choqui* we mean gold) and things called gol *urpo* and silv *horpo*, gol *tipsi* and silv *tipsi*, are what they used to have given just according to the *quipu*'.

Choque is the word for gold in the Aymara-related languages; that it needs to be explained suggests a discrepancy of dialect or local culture between the teller and one or more of his audiences: scribe, translator (if there was one), compiler, or expected reader. The reason for

Of these major *huaca*s, not a single one went unattended.

truncation is unknown.

Auqui may be "*auquicuna* the nobles, the *hidalgos*, lords" (Gonçález Holguín [1608] 1952: 38), meaning Inca princes. Ferrell (n.d.: 5–6) offers "gold miners and silver miners," using a gloss of *auqui* from Perroud and Chouvenc's dictionary (1970?: 14).

Urpo might be 'beer vessel' (Gonçález Holguín [1608] 1952: 357).

Tipsi remains unknown. Ferrell (n.d.: 7–8) interprets it as meaning *chaquira*, that is, 'small beads', because of likeness to a Junín-Huanca Quechua I term meaning a pinch or nip of something (Cerrón-Palomino 1976a: 133).

The list clearly forms a sixfold (two-sided, three-leveled) ranking of something. Of what? Despite the syntactical fact that *ñiscacunacta* suggests the six items are the things given (*-cta* is a direct object marker), the next sentence strongly suggests the point of the list is to tell the brackets of *huaca*s to whom the *quipu* dictated they be given.

Zuidema (personal communication) thinks it is a classification of shrines and their respective priesthoods, citing Guaman Poma ([1615] 1980: 1:253). Guaman Poma explains that the Inca state subsidized three levels of *huaca* priests (with Paria Caca being served by the highest). The gold/silver opposition may express moiety or gender

284 Following the same criterion, the Inca, when arriving[564] at the shrine of Llocllay Huancupa, would have them feed Sucya Villca the following morning; for there was fear of his father.[565]

This much we know about Pacha Camac, the World Maker.[566]

Regarding Pacha Cuyuchic, the World Shaker, this is what people said:[567]

"When he gets angry, earth trembles.
When he turns his face sideways it quakes.

Lest that happen he holds his face still.
The world would end if he ever rolled over."

dualism.

A *quipu* is a set of cords knotted to make an abacus-like mnemonic record (Ascher and Ascher 1981).

564. *chayaspapas* 'when arriving': or perhaps 'celebrating the Arrival festival' (see chap. 20, sec. 240).

565. *yayanpa manchascan captin*: that is, fear of Llocllay's father, Pacha Camac. But it might also mean 'for he [Llocllay Huancupa] was feared by his [Inca's] father'; that is, that the Incas accepted his cult as a hereditary obligation.

566. This sentence has witness validation.

567. Narrative returns to reportive validation and chapter ends without closing comment.

CHAPTER 23

We Shall Write Here about the Inca's Summons to All the *Huaca*s. We Shall Also Speak Here of Maca Uisa's Victory

285

When Tupay Ynga Yupanqui was king, they say,[568] he first conquered all the provinces and then happily rested for many years.

But then enemy rebellions arose from some provinces:[569] those called Alancu Marca, Calanco Marca,[570] and Chaque Marca.

These peoples didn't want to be peoples of the Inca.

286 The Inca[571] mobilized many thousands of men and battled them for a period of about twelve years.

They exterminated all the people he sent, and so the Inca, grieving deeply, said, "What'll become of us?" He became very downhearted.

287 One day he thought to himself, "Why do I serve all these *huaca*s with my gold and my silver, with my clothing and my food, with everything I have? Enough! I'll call them to help me against my enemies."

He summoned them: "From every single village, let all those who have received gold and silver come here!"

288 The *huaca*s responded, "Yes!" and went to him.

Even Pacha Camac went, riding in a litter, and so did the local *huaca*s from the whole of Tauantin Suyo all in their own litters.

When all the village *huaca*s had arrived at Aucay Pata,[572] Paria Caca hadn't yet arrived. He was still grumbling, "Should I go or not?"

Finally Paria Caca sent his child Maca Uisa, saying, "Go and find out about it."

289 Maca Uisa arrived and sat at the end of the gathering on his litter called *chicsi rampa*.[573]

Then the Inca began to speak: "Fathers, *huaca*s and *villca*s, you already know how wholeheartedly I serve you with my gold and my silver. Since I do so, being at your service as I am, won't you come to my aid now that I'm losing so many thousands of my people? It's for this reason that I've had you called together."[574]

But after he said this not a single one spoke up. Instead they sat there mute.

290 The Inca then said, "Yao! Speak up! Shall the people you've made and fostered perish in this way, savaging one another? If you refuse to help me, I'll have all of you burned immediately!

291 "Why should I serve you and adorn you with my

---

568. 'They say' supplied to indicate that this chapter lacks the usual introductory passage and starts in reportive *-si* validation. Since the previous chapter lacks concluding comments, this may be the direct continuation of an informant's narrative.

569. *llactacunamanta*: *llacta*, usually translated 'village', can carry such expanded meanings as 'province', 'country'.

570. The lower-valley village seen as the outer limit of Tutay Quiri's conquests. See chapter 9 (sec. 138) and chapter 12 (secs. 170–171).

571. 'The Inca' supplied. The unspecified third person subject might also be the rebel peoples.

572. A plaza in the heart of Incaic Cuzco.

573. Guaman Poma ([1615] 1980: 1:313) shows a "second person" or alter ego of the Inca riding in his *chicchi ranpa* or 'gray litter'. The suggestion in section 289 seems to be that the litter embodies Paria Caca's authority and Maca Uisa is his "second person." The teller of this chapter knew the Inca usage; see section 294.

574. This passage and Inca speeches in the following sections appear to afford examples of the teller's idea of how Inca political rhetoric sounded, alternately exalted and brutally threatening.

gold, with my silver, with basketfuls of my food and drinks, with my llamas and everything else I have? Now that you've heard the greatness of my grief, won't you come to my aid? If you do refuse, you'll burn immediately!"

<**margin**, in Spanish:> [from the hand and pen of Thomás]⁵⁷⁵

292   Then Pacha Camac spoke up: "Inca, Mid-Day Sun! As for me, I didn't reply because I am a power who would shake you and the whole world around you. It wouldn't be those enemies alone whom I would destroy, but you as well. And the entire world would end with you. That's why I've sat silent."

293   As the other *huaca*s sat mute, Maca Uisa then spoke up: "Inca, Mid-Day Sun! I'll go there. You must remain right here, instructing⁵⁷⁶ your people and making plans. I'll go and subdue them for you, right away, once and for all!"
      While Maca Uisa spoke, a bright greenish-blue color blew from his mouth like smoke.

294   At that very moment he put on⁵⁷⁷ his golden panpipe (his flute was likewise of gold) and he wrapped the *chumprucu*⁵⁷⁸ around his head. His *pusuca*⁵⁷⁹ was of gold, too, and as for his tunic, it was black.
      For Maca Uisa's journey the Inca gave him a litter, called the *chicsi rampa*,⁵⁸⁰ made for the travels of an Inca in person.

The people called Calla Uaya⁵⁸¹ were chosen by the Inca because they were all very strong.
      These people could carry him, in a few days, a journey of many days.
      They were the ones who carried Maca Uisa and bore his litter to the battlefront.

295   As soon as they brought him up a hill, Maca Uisa, child of Paria Caca, began to rain upon them, gently at first.
      The natives of that country said, "What could this mean?" and began to ready themselves.

296   When they did so, Maca Uisa reduced all those villages to eroded chasms by flashing lightning and pouring down more rain, and washing them away in a mudslide. Striking with lightning bolts, he exterminated the great *curaca*s and all the other strongmen. Only a few of the common people⁵⁸² were spared. If he had wanted to, he could have exterminated them all. When he had overpowered them completely, he drove some of the people back to Cuzco.

297   From that time onward, the Inca revered Paria Caca even more, and gave him fifty of his retainers.
      The Inca said, "Father Maca Uisa, what shall I give you? Ask me for anything you want. I will not stint."
      "I don't want anything," Maca Uisa replied, "except that you should serve as *huacsa* the way our children⁵⁸³ from the Yauyo do."

298   The Inca was deeply afraid when he said this,

---

575. The identity of the scribe(?) Thomás is not known.

576. *carpacuspa* 'instructing': Szemiński (personal communication) suggests that the modern verb *karpay* 'to instruct, to train in mysticism' (Lira [1941] n.d.: 103), although not attested in colonial dictionaries, is a more plausible gloss than one based on *carpani*, that is, 'making your tent'(Gonçález Holguín [1608] 1952: 50).

577. *antaricorcan* 'he put on': the verb is not attested in any relevant sense in Quechua dictionaries. Urioste (1983: 183) draws on likeness to *anta* 'copper' to translate as 'he forged'. Arguedas and Duviols (1966: 133) have 'he raised'. Taylor (1980: 157) has 'he played' and (1987b) 'he carried'. We draw on the possibility of an Aru borrowing related to Aymara *hanttacutha* 'to put on' (e.g., a frontlet; Bertonio [1612] 1956: 119).

578. *chumprucu*, probably 'turban'. See chapter 20 (sec. 240).

579. *pusucanri*: untranslated. Possibly related to Aymara *phuscanca* 'thigh or rump' (Bertonio [1612] 1956: 281), suggesting a lower-body garment, or to *phuska* (modern Quechua) 'spindle with whorl'.

580. Like the *chicsi rampa* litter already mentioned

(sec. 289), which Paria Caca presumably assigned to Maca Uisa.

581. Guaman Poma ([1615] 1980: 1:305) also pictures the *calla uaya* (Kallawaya) as the Inca's fleet-footed litter-bearers. Today a people of this name is still known for wide travels and enjoys special prestige for healing abilities (Bastien 1987; Girault 1984; Saignes 1983). But Callauaya was also the name of an agricultural satellite village of Huarochirí in 1594, according to a petition preserved in the Archbishopric of Lima (Papeles Importantes 3). Whether the two names are related is unknown. See note 604.

582. *atun runacunallas*: *atun runa* 'common people' is more literally 'big man' (or 'person'). This was the Inca bureaucratic term for an able-bodied tribute-paying adult.

583. *ñocaycup churijcuna* 'our children': exclusive first person plural (i.e., children of Maca Uisa and his kin, and not of the Inca). The plural form may express Maca Uisa's self-concept as part of the plural Paria Caca persona.

and answered, "Very well then, father!" He was willing to offer Maca Uisa anything at all, for he thought to himself, "He could destroy me, too!"

299   The Inca then said, "Father, eat!" and had some food served to him, but Maca Uisa replied with a demand:

"I am not in the habit of eating stuff like this. Bring me some thorny oyster shells!"

As soon as the Inca gave him thorny oyster shells, Maca Uisa ate them all at once, making them crunch with a "Cap cap" sound.

300   Since Maca Uisa didn't want anything else to eat, the Inca ordered some of his Inca ladies of the nobility assigned to him; but he didn't agree to that either.

So Maca Uisa went back home to inform his father Paria Caca.

From then on, and for a long time afterward, the Inca acted as *huacsa* in Xauxa and danced ceremonially, holding Maca Uisa in great honor.

301   They gathered in Cuzco at Aucay Pata square as we mentioned, the *huaca*s, all of them.[584]

Among these *huaca*s seated there, as we said before,[585] it was Siua Caña Villca Coto who was the most beautiful of all. None of the other *huaca*s could match this one in beauty.

This much we know about them.[586]

---

584. This sentence appears to have witness validation, but a slight lack of clarity in sentence boundaries makes it difficult to evaluate.

585. Not in fact mentioned before under the name Siua Caña. This allusion may mean that the lovely *huaca* embodying Villca Coto, the mountain that saved humanity (chap. 3), was represented in the Inca pantheon under a personal name Siua Caña.

586. This sentence has witness validation.

CHAPTER 24

Next We Shall Write about the Customs of the Checa, the Machua Yunca Festival and Its Dances, and, Finally, about the Origin of the People

When we talked in a different chapter about the children of Paria Caca, we already said a few things about their birth.

The story of their birth and their origin is like this.

Some people say[587] that there was a wild *quinua*[588] plant in the vicinity of Upper Paria Caca—the same one that's called *quinua* until today—and that humans emerged from its fruit there.

303   Other people say that blood once fell from the high heavens.[589]

It hit the ground at the spot called Vichi Cancha, in the area of that same *quinua*.

304   There the founders[590] established their villages:

Coña Sancha, founder of the Allauca,
Yuri Naya, founder of the Sat Pasca,
Chupa Yacu, founder of the Sulc Pahca,

---

587. Up to this point, including the verb *rimancu* 'say', the passage has witness validation, but it now shifts to -*si* reportive.

588. *quinua*: *Chenopodium quinoa*. "The nutritious seeds of this plant furnish a staple food for a large segment of the native population of Peru, replacing maize in the higher altitudes of the Andes. The red, white, or black seeds are used whole to thicken soup, to make chicha, or to be ground into flour. The ashes of the stalks may be combined with the leaves of coca, a combination that is said to increase the flavor of the latter" (Towle 1961: 36).

589. Chapter 24 owes its complexity to an antiphonal structure. It intertwines two strains of mythology (Yunca and Yauyo) and details a ritual regimen expressing the two groups' coexistence. Section 302 alludes to the origin myth of ancient Yunca *ayllu*-founders seen as the aboriginal precursors of Checa society. In ancient times, when the heights were all under Yunca power, these were born of the high-altitude *quinua* plant. Section 303 alludes to the origin of the blood-born invader groups who would impose themselves by conquest and inmarriage. In the rest of chapter 24 we learn that the blood-born groups from Vichi Cancha, who invaded Checa lands and defined the genealogy of Paria Caca so as to exalt their own mummified heroes (especially Tutay Quiri; chap. 12, sec. 167),

nonetheless retained the mummies of the ancient *quinua*-born Yunca founders (sec. 341; chap. 9, sec. 115) and were concerned to claim linkage with them as a sign of legitimacy. Yunca privileges appear to be a continuing source of anxiety for Tutay Quiri's descendants and Paria Caca is made to chasten the haughty Yunca *ayllu* of Caca Sica for slighting their Yauyo in-laws (secs. 305–314). The invader groups putatively descended from Tutay Quiri claimed to have taken over and preserved the Yunca founders' names, rights, and *huacas* wholesale (sec. 316). *Quinua*-born *ayllu*s like Caca Sica, which were permanently considered Yunca (perhaps because they contained Yunca people or perhaps only because they had obtained the old Yunca titles), enjoyed priestly privileges and danced the role of Yuncas in the Machua Yunca rites (secs. 327–340) as well as taking prominent part in Paria Caca's ceremonies; other rites (secs. 316–326) celebrated the invader-heroes. The unifying theme of this chapter is the ritual arrangement that in Checa joined the Yunca inheritance, symbolizing legitimacy, to the power-oriented ritual of blood-born *huacas* affiliated (perhaps only after the remembered invasions) with Paria Caca.

590. 'The founders' supplied; subject of *llactachacorcan* 'they founded' unspecified. An important fragmentary note by Avila, accidentally included in his trial record and interpreted by Taylor (1987b: 353), clearly identifies three of these (Chupa Yacu, Yuri Naya, and Chauca Chimpita) as founding heroes of San Damián–area *ayllu*s. They were described as "grandfathers" ceremonially fêted and clothed, that is, mummies. They were still extant c. 1608.

Paco Masa, founder of the Yasapa,
Chauca Chimpita, founder of the Muxica,
and, as founders of Caca Sica, those Yunca[591] we have
    called Huar Cancha and Llichic Cancha.

All these, the actual founders of the village, were
Yunca people.
<**margin**, in Spanish:> [Huari Cancha Llichic Can-
cha were Yunca.]

305   The others, the Morales of Caca Sica and also the
forefathers of the Cancha Paycu, were Yauyo.[592]
<**margin**:> [Morales Yauyo]
    Their place of origin is called Maurura,[593] in the
Aya Uire[594] area.
    These people, who used to roam around as
wild[595] nomads, married the sisters of Huar Cancha.
"We and our in-laws will work things out among
ourselves within the community," they said, and
they settled down in this village.

306   When these people went to worship Paria Caca,
their in-laws and all the Checa insulted them, calling them "Yauyo wildmen," so they used to go last,
lagging way behind.
    Since they suffered miserably when these people
insulted them like that, they tagged along in the
rear for a great many years.
    "Father," they told Paria Caca on one occasion,
"here's how it is: these people,[596] they and the
Checa, insult us all the time. And we're your own
creatures, even if we're Yauyo people!" They cried
bitterly as they told this.

307   Then and there Paria Caca gave his command:

---

591. Original has *yañcacuna*; since these groups are
elsewhere said to be *yancas* (chap. 17, sec. 218), the
translation '*yanca*' would be tenable here. But the next
marginal note indicates the meaning here as Yunca.
    592. The point being that the Caca Sica *ayllu* (chap. 9,
sec. 118; chap. 17, sec. 216), although of ancient Yunca
origin, had within it a Yauyo group called Morales. Recently in-married and of foreign stock, they were scorned,
as succeeding sections tell.
    593. Maurura may be Malleuran, a hamlet north of
Ayaviri, 3,346 m above sea level in Yauyos Province (IGM
1970–1971).
    594. A modern town called Ayaviri is 29 km south-
southeast of Huarochirí in Yauyos Province (IGM
1970–1971).
    595. As in the name of Quita Pariasca (chap. 18, sec.
221), the word *quita* 'wild' alludes to the qualities of un-
tamed or skittish animals.
    596. Meaning: the Yauyos' immediate in-laws?

"Children, don't grieve. Take with you this, my
golden headdress. You must dance holding it up in
Llacsa Tambo, at the place called Poco Caya. Then
they'll say, awestruck, 'What people are these?
They're the beloved of Paria Caca!' From that time
on they won't insult you so."

308   And so when the Yauyos arrived in the rear of
the Checa, carrying that golden headdress of Paria
Caca's, jubilant, the other people were seized with
fear.
    The next day, the Yauyos danced and sang hold-
ing up the golden headdress while everybody in
that place stood awestruck.

309   Some others say this:[597] in the old days, people
used to go to consult Paria Caca at night, taking
along llamas or other things.
    They used to go taking turns, *ayllu* by *ayllu*.
    Even though at that time they deeply scorned
the ones called "wild Yauyos," they said, "Let them
carry offerings,[598] too."
    The Yauyos did take them but they arrived at
Paria Caca when the sun was already rising.

310   Because they were grieving bitterly, Paria Caca
said, "Why are you so distressed, O Anta Capsi?"
(Their old name had been Pacuyri.)
    Then and there Paria Caca bestowed on them his
gift, saying, "Take along this golden headdress.
When people see it they'll no longer scorn you."

311   On one occasion they went to worship Paria
Caca, carrying along the golden headdress.
    But while they were crossing the river called Pari
Ayri they dropped it.
    They searched for it like anything, all the way
upstream and downstream. But it didn't turn up, so
they went to Paria Caca without it.

312   When they arrived on the morrow, the golden
headdress stood there right at Paria Caca's side.
    Although they begged for it in tears, he refused.
Rebuking them harshly, Paria Caca said, "You
didn't win it in victorious warfare, that you should
go around showing it off everywhere so boastfully,
and even bringing it here, thinking, 'We'll show it
to the one who gives us power, to our maker.' "

---

597. Witness validation up to the colon, then *-si*
reportive.
    598. 'Offerings' supplied.

313 "Father, are we to be humiliated so?" they cried bitterly. "Please, return it to us or give us something else instead."

"Children," replied Paria Caca, "go back. I'll give you something during my sister Chaupi Ñamca's festival. Wait until then."

And so back they went.

314 And as he'd foretold, on Chaupi Ñamca's festival, in the courtyard called Yauri Callinca, on top of the wall, a very beautifully spotted wildcat appeared.

When they saw it, they exclaimed joyfully, "This is what Paria Caca meant!" and they held up its skin as they danced and sang with it.

(Hernando Cancho Uillca, who used to live in Tumna, was in charge of it.

But by now it's probably gone all rotten.)[599]

315 We've already spoken about the origin of the people.[600]

Those whom we mentioned are said to be Tutay Quiri's children; the others are known to have come forth from the fruit of a tree.[601]

As for Tutay Quiri, they say he was born in Vichi Cancha.[602]

Later on, he came and overpowered all the villages of this area, saying, "My children will live here!"

316 As we said in another chapter, this land was once all full of Yunca. As soon as Tutay Quiri's children[603] had expelled those Yunca, they began to distribute among themselves, according to their own *ayllu*s, the fields, the houses, and the *ayllu* designations.[604] Their names, by *ayllu*, were:

Allauca
Sat Pasca
Pasa Quine
Muxica
Caca Sica
Sulc Pahca
Yasapa.[605]

When we say Yasapa we mean silversmiths. They were silversmiths.

And as they bear that group's name, likewise so do the other *ayllu*s.[606]

317 Then, after sharing the villages out among themselves, they received their *huaca*s, ranking them from Allauca downward:

The Allauca received Maca Calla.

The Sat Pasca, we know,[607] received Quimquilla.

This Quimquilla was considered to be[608] a *curaca* among *huaca*s, and for this reason was esteemed more than any other.

318 Next, the Sulc Pahca and the Yasapa received the *huaca* called Ricra Huanca.

The Muxica received Quira Raya.[609]

The Caca Sica received the *huaca* named Llucma Suni.

The Huanri and the Chauti were in fact[610] the actual natives of the village from early times.

599. The first sentence of the parenthesis has witness validation and the second *-si* reportive.

600. This sentence has witness validation. A different version of how invaders took over the system created by the *quinua*-born founders begins here. This version centers on cults of mummified or preserved heroes of invasion: Tutay Quiri (see note 601), Ñan Sapa (secs. 319–323), and Chuta Cara (secs. 324–326).

601. That is, the above-mentioned Yauyos are Tutay Quiri's children, while those who scorned them were of the *quinua*-born Yunca founding *ayllu* (sec. 302). 'Said to be' supplied to indicate reportive validation, which immediately gives way to witness validation ('are known to have').

602. That is, Tutay Quiri is of the blood-born (sec. 303).'They say' supplied to indicate reportive validation, which continues through the second sentence of section 317.

603. 'Tutay Quiri's children' supplied.

604. That is, the conquerors not only seized the wealth of the vanquished, but even organized themselves according to the pattern and terminology of preexisting autochthonous society. A lawsuit of 1594 explains that *ayllu* Callaguaya of Huarochirí (see chap. 23, sec. 294) took on this name by displacing a Yunca group of the same name (Archivo del Arzobispado de Lima, Papeles Importantes 3, f. 10r). See note 581.

605. This list of captured categories differs in order but not in content from the list associating these groups with their respective ancestral Yuncas in section 304.

606. *chaypac sutintatacsi paicunapas apan ynatac huaquinin ayllocunapas* 'And as they bear that group's name, likewise so do the other *ayllu*': may mean that the other captured names, like Yasapa, imply specializations.

607. This sentence has witness validation.

608. 'Considered to be' supplied to indicate reportive validation of this sentence.

609. This sentence has witness validation.

610. 'In fact' supplied to indicate witness validation in this and the following sentence.

In a different chapter we already told how they worshiped Tutay Quiri.[611]

319   So, as we've said, as soon as Tutay Quiri finished his conquests, his children came here and danced their dance of origin, just as they'd once danced it in Vichi Cancha.[612] They danced and sang, calling the rite Masoma. The one called Ñan Sapa was a human being.[613]

Later on, the Inca took away the *huaca* himself.[614]

But they made another one to be his proxy.

This is the one that we know Señor Doctor Francisco de Avila carried away.[615]

320   They say Ñan Sapa, when he was human, wore the *quisay rinri*[616] in his ears and bore the *canah yauri*[617] scepter in his hands.

In ancient times, these were made of pure gold. The Inca carried off that gold.

His staff was named Engraved Rod.[618]

And the seashell named *cori cacya* came with it.

321   Saying, "He is our origin; it was he who first

came to this village and took charge of it," people flayed his face[619] and made it dance as if in his own persona.

If they captured a man in warfare, they would first flay his face, and then make it dance, saying, "This is our valor!"

And when a man was taken prisoner in war, that man himself would say, "Brother, soon you'll kill me. I was a really powerful man, and now you're about to make a *huayo* out of me. So before I go out onto the plaza, you should feed me well and serve me drinks first."[620]

322   Obeying this, they'd offer food and drinks to the other *huayo*s, saying, "This day you shall dance with me on the plaza."

They actually[621] used to bring out the *huayo*s and carry them in a litter for two days. On the following day, they'd hang them up together with their maize, potatoes, and all the other offerings.

323   About this hanging of *huayo*s, people remarked,[622] "The *huayo*s will return to the place where they were born, the place called Uma Pacha,[623] carrying these things along with them."

611. See chapter 11 (sec. 161). Though not of invader stock and not resident in Checa, these groups take part in many Checa rites (see chap. 20, sec. 239), including those of Tutay Quiri. The next four sentences have reportive validation.

612. Vichi Cancha: where blood fell and invader groups originated (sec. 303).

613. Possibly meaning that this *huaca* consisted of a human mummy, that of a key ancestor. His cult is apparently one component of the "dances of origin" by which invader lineages commemorated their ties to the mummified founders (sec. 304).

614. This may refer to the Inca custom of removing important local *huaca*s for inclusion in the Cuzco pantheon, which is the theme of chapter 23. 'The *huaca*' supplied.

615. The removal of the original *huaca* by the Inca is validated with reportive but the removal of its substitute by Avila is witness-validated ('we know').

616. *rinri* 'ear' indicates this was a specific type of earspool. 'They say' supplied to indicate reportive validation, which continues through the first sentence of section 322.

617. *yauri* (Gonçález Holguín [1608] 1952: 347) means 'scepter' or possibly 'lance'.

618. *quillcas caxo* 'Engraved Rod': a marginal note (supp. II, sec. 480) tells us that *caxo* meant a stick; *quilcas* means 'painted', 'inlaid', or 'engraved'. Avila himself described this object as "a copper spear engraved with various designs" that functioned as a *huaca* in its own right ([1645] 1918: 67).

619. *oyanta cochuspa* 'flayed his face': that is, made a sacred mask that would conserve the persona of the fallen or sacrificially killed hero (and not as torture of the living). *Huayo* in the next passage means, as a 1609 Jesuit report (Arguedas and Duviols 1966: 247) explains, a human face prepared as a mask "with its actual skin and bone." When the preserved face was displayed in a dance, it received offerings of llama fat in return for sharing its vital powers.

620. The point appears to be that when a captive faced sacrifice, he asked that, both immediately before his death and ever afterward when transformed into a facemask, he always be duly fêted before entering into his conquerors' ceremonies.

621. 'Actually' supplied to indicate witness validation in this and the next sentence.

622. This sentence and the next have reportive validation.

623. Uma Pacha, we learn in section 324, was apparently a *huaca* who came from Vichi Cancha, and represented the origin of a group that saw itself as derived from the blood fallen at Vichi Cancha (sec. 303). In chapter 31 (sec. 403), the invaders' union with the Yunca autochthones of Checa is cemented when the surviving Yunca boy Yasali becomes priest of Uma Pacha and serves the blood-born groups derived from Vichi Cancha.

But Uma Pacha is probably a generic category of *sacra* (from the Jaqi word *uma* 'water'), associated with high lakes and seemingly imagined as sources at which bio-

They would speak with a different pronunciation when they addressed one another, twisting their mouths to one side.[624]

During Ñan Sapa's festival, we know they carried on dancing for five days, and the Allauca did the same.[625]

324 In another place, there was said to be someone called Chuta Cara, also known as Uma Pacha.[626]
<margin:> [Masoma Chuta Cara]
He himself had come from Vichi Cancha along with the others.

He existed as a man and congealed into stone.

He still held the sling he'd used as a human being, and his *visa*[627] was decorated with likenesses of birds.

325 And then there was the *huana paya*, a conch trumpet; when he blew it, the local *huacas*[628]
<margin, in Spanish:> [Means 'idol'.]
would divide up the llama herds.

He emerged with that very object.

It was because of the llamas that some people conserved *huana paya* conch trumpets.

We know people from Allauca used to perform these rites at the festival of Chuta Cara.[629] As llama owners, the Checa and the Concha and whatever other people also display those conch trumpets.

326 And it's known that[630] they danced these same rites for two years, just one time per year.

Therefore, since the ritual cycle lasted two years, they performed the dance only twice in all.

After that, they danced the dance named Machua for two years.[631]

327 The people who, as we said before, had Yunca names[632] were the ones who danced for two years in Machua festival season.

Braiding[633] some straw called *chupa*, as they say,[634] and tying together a lot of wooden slats,

---

logical vitality is renewed. The mostly Yunca-oriented Machua rite also addresses it (sec. 335). The ethnographers Valderrama and Escalante (1988: 187–189) suggest that the shrine today called Umahala in the Colca valley belongs to the same class as ancient *oma pacha*.

624. In modern Quechua folk ritual, people performing as mythic personages often speak in unnatural ways (especially falsetto). But another reading is possible. Since Gonçález Holguín ([1608] 1952: 304) gives "*simicta qquencuchini* to twist one's words toward another matter, or not to say plainly and truthfully what one has heard," *chaysi rimacospapas huc rimaytatac simintaca hucman quincochispa rimac carcan* might be read 'when speaking of this, they used to give a different version, distorting their testimony'. The point would then be that, prior to Avila's research, natives dissembled about the tradition of rites involving human trophies. Or, less probably, the sentence might simply mean that other people recount other versions.

625. This sentence has witness validation ('we know' supplied).

626. The narrative now turns to a third formerly human *huaca* who led the invaders from Vichi Cancha. 'Was said to be' supplied to indicate return to reportive validation.

627. *visa* untranslated. 'Shield'?

628. *llactacuna* in original appears to mean 'villages' or 'settlements'. But, as the marginal note clarifies, it is used here to designate the local deities who were understood as the patrons of human settlements.

629. Could also mean the rites were performed in order from Allauca downward (sec. 317). 'We know' supplied to indicate witness validation in this and the next sentence.

630. 'It's known that' supplied to indicate witness validation in this and the following three sentences, which form a passage about the calendric organization of dances.

631. The succession described appears to be an alternation of two-year cycles:

	year 1 First *mita* of Chuta Cara
CYCLE A	
	year 2 Second *mita* of Chuta Cara
	year 3 First *mita* of Machua
CYCLE B	
	year 4 Second *mita* of Machua
	year 5 First *mita* of Chuta Cara
CYCLE A	
	(and so forth).

632. That is, the groups that in section 316 were said to have received the names of pre-existing Yunca groups and taken over their *huacas*. The overall sense is that the Checa community, which was formed by conquest and intermarriage between blood-born invaders from Vichi Cancha and *quinua*-born Yunca aborigines, alternated between two-year periods in which it celebrated Vichi Cancha origins (e.g., in the Masoma rites honoring Ñan Sapa and Chuta Cara as just described) and two-year periods for the rites now to be described, which are rich in Yunca symbolism.

633. *pirtaspas* 'braiding': Taylor (1987b: 381) originated this reading, still conjectural but warranted by *piltay* 'to braid' in modern Tarma and Ancash Quechua.

634. 'As they say' supplied to indicate return to reportive validation, which continues through the second sentence of section 328.

they'd bind[635] two effigy bundles around with the straw.

The height of these bundles was seven and a half armlengths.

Their girth was about what we could hold in a two-armed embrace. On these effigies' heads they'd put some wild straw named *casira*.[636] It has bright red roots. "It's their hair," they'd say.

328   Once they'd prepared everything, they named one of the effigy bundles Yomca and set it as a target symbolizing males.

The other, the one called Huasca, they set as a target symbolizing females.[637]

After they set them up, the men would put on their best clothing and feather ruffs called *tamta*,[638] and they'd begin to let fly at the targets.[639] Their spear was called *vihco*.[640]

329   We know that on the day before this spear-throwing everybody used to go to the *caullamas*.[641] They brought their llamas along adorned with bells and earrings, just as they did on their way to Paria Caca.

All the people would reportedly[642] go to Chaucalla and to the mountain of Tambo Sica, named Curri, each going to his respective *caullama*.[643]

As they traveled to their *caullama*s, they'd go along blowing the conch trumpet, making it resound again and again.

It was in fact[644] for this purpose that each of these people and some who just chanced on them[645] would carry and display these conch shells.

330   <**margin**:> [*chuta*]

As soon as they'd erected the two *chuta*s they began to throw the spears.

They say that[646] while the people threw spears, while they entered into competition hurling spears *ayllu* by *ayllu*, the women would dance without drums and chant these words:

"Receive your poor forlorn children!"
And to the Huasca effigy, they'd likewise say,
    "Receive, too, your poor forlorn children!"[647]

331   If these spear throwers hit the *chuta*'s hair, then whichever person was in charge[648] advanced them into the top rank ahead of all the other *ayllu* members.

Then he'd[649] bring a macaw wing or any such thing and give it to the *yanca*.

332   (The *yanca* of the Checa afterward is known to

---

635. *pilluic carcan* 'they'd bind': on the assumption that *pilluic* is an agentive form, erroneously or irregularly written, of *pilluy* 'to bind', and not related to *pilluini* 'to swim' (Gonçález Holguín [1608] 1952: 285).

636. Unidentified.

637. Taylor (1980: 171) has observed that the terms *yomca* and *huasca* may be interpretable in the light of "Aymara-type transformations which characterize the text." If affected by the same metathesis that causes *ñamca* to appear at times as *ñamoc, yomca* might be *yumac* 'inseminator' (i.e., patrilineal progenitor). Adducing an additional southern Quechua shift, Taylor suggests *Huasca* might be interpreted *huachac* 'one who gives birth' (perhaps implying 'matrilineal ancestress').

638. *tamta* 'feather ruff': same word occurring in chapter 5 in the name of the opulent Tamta Ñamca (see Arriaga [1621] 1968: 50; Keating's translation).

639. 'At the targets' supplied. The sentence has witness validation.

640. *vihco*: an otherwise unattested word, perhaps related to modern *wikch'uy* 'to throw'. 'Their spear' supplied.

641. *caullama*: Arriaga ([1621] 1968: 29; Keating's translation) says a *caullama* was a household deity guaranteeing fertility of livestock. This sentence and the next have witness validation ('We know that' supplied).

642. 'Reportedly' supplied to indicate reportive validation of this and the next sentence.

643. Hernández Príncipe ([1613] 1919: 184) says rights

in each *caullama* were inherited as a *mayorazgo* (i.e., a privilege descending in primogeniture).

644. 'In fact' supplied to indicate witness validation of this and the next sentence.

645. *taricnincunaca* 'who just chanced on them': more literally, 'their finders'; it is not clear whether this means finders of conch shells or those who happened to meet people on the procession.

646. 'They say that' supplied to indicate reportive validation, which continues through the end of section 331.

647. In the invocations to both the male-engendering and the female-bearing effigies, the word for 'child' is *churi*, 'child of a male'. In ordinary speech the child of a female is called *huahua* and not *churi*. It sounds as though both effigies are being addressed as fathers. One possible explanation of the anomaly would be to take *churi* as the "unmarked" term, including all forms of parentage not specified as uterine mother-child tie and therefore including figurative or symbolic motherhood. Alternatively, one might take the two effigies as being in fact both male, one the father of males and the other of females.

648. 'Was in charge' supplied.

649. Or 'she'd'. Whether an officiant or the successful lancer brought it is not explicit. The implication may be that the macaw wing was given to a *yanca* representing the victorious *ayllu*.

have been[650] Martín Misa Yauri, and the late Juan Chumpi Yauri was that of the Allauca.)

333 After one *ayllu* finished throwing, the *yanca* would reportedly[651] shin up the *chuta* effigy carrying the macaw wing called *puypu*.

He'd pull out the *vihco* spear and stick the macaw wing in where it had hit, to mark the spot.[652]

Then another *ayllu* would compete, and then still another, and so forth.

334 Then they threw spears at the Huasca effigy for females, saying,

"She'll give me daughters and all kinds of food!" and then at the Yomca effigy, saying,

"He'll give me sons, agave fiber goods,[653] and all kinds of animals!"

335 When they'd finished throwing spears at both *chuta* effigies, the contestants who'd hit the hair or the part called the "eye" would present one of their llamas to the *yanca* and say, "With this offering, speak on my behalf to Uma Pacha."

Regarding this small llama, the llama-owner wouldn't take away much of it.[654] No matter how many llamas there might be, it was only those who'd been ordained *yanca* who could take them away and eat them.

336 Very early the next morning, we know,[655] all the people would go to Quimquilla.

They say[656] this *huaca* called Quimquilla owned a whole lot of llamas and all sorts of other possessions.

"He'll favor me with some of that wealth!" thought all the people, including the Allauca, as they went along. "I'll ask for some llamas for myself there."

337 On their way there, they used to carry a small amount of their *ticti*, maize beer, and coca leaf, and they made the *huana paya* conch trumpet resound over and over.

On the first day, those of the *vichoc* moiety[657]— that is, all the Sat Pasca, the Sulc Pahca, and Yasapa— would dance at Quimquilla shrine itself, chanting, "We flourish!" as they slaughtered their llamas.

338 Then, as we know,[658] they went down to the flat land that lies above the place where Quira Raya was located.[659]

(This plateau is called Huara Caya.)

Then, just as they'd erected Yomca and Huasca effigies in Llacsa Tambo, so also they set up *chuta* effigies the same way here, this time for llamas.

---

655. 'We know' supplied to indicate witness validation of this sentence.

656. Return to reportive validation, which continues through the end of section 337.

657. *vichuc maricuna* 'those of the *vichoc* moiety': *ichoc* is the usual term complementary to *allauca*. Chapter 11 (sec. 157) has *allaucam ari vichocam ari*, which we translate as 'both the *allauca* moiety and the *vichoc* moiety'. If this is emended to *allaucamari . . . vichocamari* (as in Taylor 1980: 94), *vichuc maricuna* here becomes clearly intelligible in moiety terms. Referring back to sections 304 and 316 would yield a system under which *vichoc* Checa includes the three *ayllu*s named here, and *allauca* Checa includes Allauca, Muxica, and Caca Sica.

There are other possibilities: *vichuc mari* might be the name of an otherwise unattested group comparable with Sat Pasca and the others. Or *vichuc* might be an agentive form of a verb derived from *vihco*, the ceremonial spear (sec. 328). None of these account for the otherwise unknown word or morpheme *mari* (which seems also to occur in the name of Paria Caca's last or next to last "son" Sasin Mari; see chap. 9, sec. 113; chap. 12, sec. 166).

658. 'As we know' supplied to indicate witness validation, which continues through the first sentence of section 340.

659. Quira Raya may be the name of a settlement destroyed by *reducción*, the forced resettlement of the 1580s, or of a *huaca*.

---

650. 'Is known to have been' supplied to indicate witness validation of this sentence.

651. 'Reportedly' supplied to indicate reportive validation, which continues through the end of section 335.

652. The figure of Tamta Ñamca, whom Huatya Curi cured in chapter 5 when all the land was Yunca, shares some of the symbolism of this section and its motif of Yunca-derived ceremony. His name Tamta alludes to the ceremonial garment *tamta* (sec. 328), and his roof decorated with macaw wings resembles the straw effigy similarly decorated here. Contests played for ceremonial rank form the climax of his story as of this rite. A 1609 Jesuit report describes a different ritual game of skill employing feather decorations and Yunca costumes (Arguedas and Duviols 1966: 247).

653. *chauaracta* 'agave fiber goods': based on "*chhahuar cabuya*" (Gonçález Holguín [1608] 1952: 92). *Cabuya* or agave fiber is widely used to make rope, coarse sandals, harnesses, and so forth. Taylor (1987b: 386) explains the discrepancy between -*racta* and the expected -*rta* as an "Aru [i.e., Jaqi] influence."

654. *anchantaca* 'much of it': given the information in the next sentence, it is tempting to read *anchantaca* as an error for *aychantaca*, 'its meat'.

They threw their spears for llamas, both males and females.

339   At the end of the spear throwing, they used to give their llamas to the *yanca* just as they had in Llacsa Tambo, saying, "Worship on my behalf and I shall be well."

On their way back here, they'd travel all in a group, just as when they went away to Quimquilla; they came back hauling their llamas adorned with bells.

340   They call this journey the Carco Caya.

About the way they traveled, with a slow and undulating motion,[660] people said, "We're rounding the Huaroca."[661]

As they rounded the Huaroca, they'd go along blowing the *huana paya* conch trumpet over and over again.

This is all we know, all we know about the Machua festival.[662]

341   About these Yunca populations in Llacsa Tambo, some people say, "They were reputedly Muta Caya people."

"They were Colli," others say.[663] Just so. But the ones we referred to as Colli resided in Yaru Tini.[664]

In what follows we'll write about this group's life.

---

660. *coyoi coyoilla* 'with a slow and undulating motion': might also be read 'just barely moving'.

661. Untranslated; the verb *tumani* denotes circular motion so it may be the name of a round monolith or hill. Or if Huaroca is not a proper noun but a variant of the similar word meaning 'sling', the phrase might be a metaphor for a swinging motion like that of a sling.

662. This sentence and the remainder of the chapter have witness validation.

663. The issue is whether the Yunca people resident in Checa lands were members of the Yunca polity of Collique (near Lima) or of the (otherwise unknown) Muta Caya. Both contrasting opinions are expressed with reportive validation ('reputedly'); that is, the people cited contrary traditions.

664. Yaru Tini may be modern Yelutina, 15 km northwest of San Damián (IGM 1954), a high location far from the coast.

CHAPTER 25

Here We Shall Write How the Wind Blew the Colli People from Yaru Tini Down to the Lower Yunca[665]

The native people whom we call Colli are said to have[666] resided in Yaru Tini.

One day Paria Caca arrived in Yaru Tini, their village, while the Colli were drinking.

Taking a seat at the far end of the banquet, Paria Caca sat there like a poor miserable stranger.

343 Not a single person was willing to offer him a drink.

Only one man finally invited him to drink.

"Give me some more, brother," said Paria Caca to the one who'd offered him the drink.

The man gave him more.

Paria Caca then asked, "Please give me a quid of your coca leaf."

The man[667] gave it to him.

344 Paria Caca said to him, "Brother, when I come back here, you'd better hold on tight to this tree. Don't tell these people anything. Let them have their fun." Then he went away.

345 Five days later, a violent wind rose up.

This wind whirled every single person of the Colli head over heels two or three times and whisked them off into the far distance.

When it swept them off, some of them wandered around disoriented and died.

Others the wind brought alive to a mountain in the vicinity of Carhuayllo.

This mountain is called Colli mountain up to today. The people of the mountain, however, have perished. Not one of them is left.

346 But that one man who'd given Paria Caca a drink in Yaru Tini hung onto the tree as he'd been told, and was spared.

When Paria Caca was finished sweeping everything away, he said to him, "Brother, now you're alone by yourself. You must stay here forever. Later, when my children come to worship me from this spot, a quartet of guest *huacsas*[668] (that means four)[669] will provide coca leaf for you to chew in perpetuity.

"As for your name," he added, "you shall be

---

665. This myth appears related to chapter 11 (sec. 155), which alludes to the expulsion of some Colli Yunca to lands bordering Carhuayllo.

666. 'Said to have' supplied to indicate reportive validation, which continues through the end of section 346.

667. 'The man' supplied.

668. *corpaya huacçacuna* 'guest *huacsas*': the sense is uncertain; *corpaya* may be derived from "*ccorpa* guest" or (less probably) "*ccorppa* clod or clump of turf" (González Holguín [1608] 1952: 69); -*ya* remains unexplained. That they number four is also odd. This myth does not seem relevant to Incaic fourfold (*tahuantin*) organization, while five and its multiples usually signify plenitude in Paria Caca's mythology.

669. *chusco quiere dezir cuatro* 'a quartet . . . (that means four)': this Spanish explanatory parenthesis indicates that someone—teller, translator, scribe, or editor—expected the audience to be unfamiliar with *chusco* 'four', a word common in the Andean north but different from the usual south Andean word *tahua*. The translation uses the Latinate word 'quartet' to contrast with more familiar 'four' and thereby suggest the feeling of lexical discrepancy.

called Capac Huanca."[670] And he froze the man[671] into stone.

When Señor Doctor Avila came to the very spot

---

670. *Huanca*s were and are *huaca*s in the shape of monoliths; *capac*, the opposite of *huaccha* 'poor and friendless', means 'rich and influential'. Like chapter 24, this story explains in mythic terms how the conquest of the Yunca who once occupied the heights resulted in retention of Yunca *huaca*s.

671. 'The man' supplied.

where Capac Huanca dwelled, he in fact[672] broke the *huaca*[673] with some other people's help.

After he broke it, he heaved it downhill.

This much we know about the people called Colli.

And so, exactly according to Paria Caca's command, the *huacsa*s yearly provided that *huaca* with coca to chew forever.

---

672. 'In fact' supplied to indicate witness validation of this sentence and the remainder of the chapter.

673. 'The *huaca*' supplied.

CHAPTER 26

How Paria Caca Defeated Maca Calla. How He Established His Children after His Victory[674]

We know[675] that Maca Calla lived on a mountain overlooking the village of San Damián.

It was on this Maca Calla mountain that the aboriginal people of that village reputedly[676] lived, the ones called Pihcca Marca.

The ones called the Sutica are known to have[677] lived there, too.

One day while these villagers were drinking, they say,[678] Paria Caca arrived in the village.

Arriving, he sat down at the far end of the banquet.

349   As he was sitting there, not a single person offered him a drink.

Paria Caca got angry, and so, five days later, he rose up as red rain and yellow rain and exterminated that village.

350   Some people tell another story.[679]

They say[680] some of the aboriginal villagers in Maca Calla were playing with the hunting *bolas*. Others were drinking.

Meanwhile, a little puff of fog[681] appeared out of the high mountain called Canlli.

And then, little by little, some rain, a red rain, started to fall.

Then lightning began to flash.

351   Everybody got scared when these things happened. "What's this?" they wondered, never having seen anything like it.

Some said, "It's the enemy!" and took a defensive stand.

Others ran away.

352   One was a man called Armicu.

He had lots of children, and rousing them, he cried, "Come on, let's go, let's go and die on our own field!" They ran away to their field.

When they arrived at their field, he[682] froze them and turned them into stone.

That man who turned to stone stands there still, like a man with his children. Even today people call them the Armicu.

353   Some people tried to escape, but wherever they fled the red rain caught up with them. Right on the spot they turned to stone.

The rest of the people back in Maca Calla also froze into stone the same way.

354   Weeping bitterly, one man of the Sutica *ayllu*

---

674. This chapter expands on how the Allauca 'received' Maca Calla (chap. 24, sec. 317).

675. San Damián de Checa is a *reducción* village on the Lurín headwaters at 3,235 m above sea level 22 km west-northwest of Huarochirí (IGM 1970–1971). This sentence has witness validation.

676. 'Reputedly' supplied to indicate reportive validation.

677. 'Are known to have' supplied to indicate witness validation of this sentence. The remainder of sections 348 and 349 have reportive validation ('they say').

678. 'They say' supplied to indicate reportive validation, which continues through the end of section 349.

679. This sentence has witness validation.

680. 'They say' supplied to indicate reportive validation, which continues through the fourth sentence of section 357.

681. *aslla pucutay* 'a little puff of fog': 'fog' supplied; *-tay* unexplained.

682. Reference unclear; could be Paria Caca or Armicu.

said, "Maca Calla, my only father, will it be my lot to up and leave you, just like that? I have to get away right now. There's no more force left in me to overcome this miracle."[683] While he wept, Maca Calla's head fell down right before him.

He picked the head up where it fell, and made it fly away instantly transformed into a falcon.

This man was imbued with a mighty shamanic power!

355   Maca Calla was just like a man, with a head, feet, and hands.

So, after he made the head escape, the man settled again on five mountains in Llantapa[684] and multiplied.

We call the mountains where he settled, where he built the villages, Pihcca Marca.[685]

356   Maca Calla's head exists in Pihcca Marca until today.

The people there say, "Here, we have Maca Calla's protection," and they call their firstborn children Canricha. Likewise the Allauca, who are also members of a community affiliated with Maca Calla, call them Canricha just as the Pihcca Marca do.[686]

357   Later, Tutay Quiri went and conquered them.

During that time, the *ayllu*s called Sutica returned to this area. "We'll go and settle amid our fields and our land, amid our villages. We'll fear and revere Paria Caca and Tutay Quiri," they said, and they came back.

In the village of San Damián the Sutica are now completely extinct.[687] Their survivors are in Sucsa Cancha, in Tumna.

---

683. *milagrocta* 'miracle': usage of the Spanish term 'miracle' to signify a disastrous supernatural retribution is characteristic of Andean writing in this period. Felipe Guaman Poma de Ayala ([1615] 1980) consistently assimilated it to the Andean idea *pachacuti* 'world-changing disaster'.

684. Perhaps the suggestion is that the five members just mentioned—head, feet, and hands—reconstituted themselves as the five parts of Pihcca Marca. Llantapa mountain was one end of the mythic bridge over the Lurín valley (chap. 5, sec. 73).

685. Pihcca Marca means 'Five Settlements'. This may refer to a five-peaked mountain called Cerro Cinco

Cerros ('Five Hills Hill'), visible from San Damián and identified locally as the site of an extinct community.

686. See chapter 24 (sec. 317).

687. Like the genealogical part of chapter 31 (secs. 443–446) this passage apparently alludes to the extinction of whole named corporate groups in the course of the European-introduced epidemics. This sentence has witness validation.

CHAPTER 27

How in Former Times, on the Fifth Day after Their Death, People Said, "I'm Back!" [688] We Shall Write about These Things

In very ancient times, they say,[689] when a person died, people laid the body out until five days had gone by.

The dead person's spirit, which is the size of a fly, would fly away, saying, "Sio!"[690]

When it flew away, people said, "Now he's going away to see Paria Caca, our maker and our sustainer."

359   Some people say, "At that time Paria Caca didn't exist yet, so the souls flew up high to Yauri Llancha."

<**margin,** in Quechua:> [Before Paria Caca or Ca-ruincho appeared, people emerged at Yauri Llancha and at the place called Vichi Cancha.][691]

---

688. This myth evidently belongs to the body of belief about primordial times, because section 359 says major *huaca*s had yet to appear and because the content is pre-figured in chapter 1 (sec. 4).

689. Except for the title, this chapter is entirely in re-portive validation and contains no evidently editorial insertions.

690. *animanri huc chuspi chicallan sio ñispa pahuac carcan* 'The dead person's spirit, which is the size of a fly, would fly away, saying, "Sio!" ': the Spanish and Latin term *anima* may be an attempt to render the sense of terms like *upani* (Duviols 1978), referring to a light, dry, volatile being that contains the vital essence of a person. A fly, which is a light, dry, flying form of life that emerges from the dead body, may be a metaphor for, or the actual body of, this Andean 'anima' (see chap. 28, sec. 367).

691. Yauri Llancha is the place from which the con-querors of Concha (chap. 31, secs. 389, 394, 446) are said to have originated. Vichi Cancha is the place from which the conquerors of Checa originated (chap. 24, secs. 303, 315, 319, 324; chap. 31, sec. 389). The selection of Yauri Llancha as the *pacarina* or origin shrine to which the dead return suggests that this chapter has a Concha source.

360   The dead used to come back[692] after five days.

When they were about to return, people waited for them with prepared food and drinks.

When the dead arrived, they'd just say, "I'm back!" and rejoice immensely in the company of their elders and their brothers.

They'd say, "Now I'll never die again forever!"

361   And so, at that time, people swiftly increased in number. They lived in great suffering, miserably gathering their food, terracing both cliffs and ledges for their fields.

362   When things were like that, a certain man died. After his death his elders, his brothers, and his wife waited for him on the fifth day, when he was due to arrive back.

But the man didn't arrive. It was on the next day, that is, on the sixth day, that he arrived.

So his elders, brothers, and wife were feeling furi-ous as they waited for him.

When he arrived, his wife was enraged, and she gave him a terrible bawling out: "Why are you so damn lazy? Other people never let us down by fail-ing to come. But you, yesterday you made us wait for you, and all for nothing!"

363   In her spite the dead man's wife hurled a maize cob at his arriving spirit.

The moment she threw it, he made a "Sio!" noise and went back where he'd come from.

Since that time, not a single dead person has ever come back.

---

692. That is, presumably, came back as flies and then recovered their full human bodies. Otherwise the next passage would not make sense.

CHAPTER 28

How People Used to Feed the Spirits of the Dead⁶⁹³ during Paria Caca's Festival and How They Thought about All Saints' Day in Former Times⁶⁹⁴

In another chapter⁶⁹⁵ we have already told how, when people traveled to worship Paria Caca, they used to cry for their dead and feed them.

Remembering those meals for the dead, people who hadn't yet sincerely converted to Christianity are known to have⁶⁹⁶ said, "The Spaniards also give food to their dead,⁶⁹⁷ to their bones, on All Saints' Day,⁶⁹⁸ they do feed them. So let's go to church. Let's feed our own dead."⁶⁹⁹

---

693. *animacunacta* 'spirits': the same word is used in chapter 27 (sec. 358) to signify the escaping remnant of the deceased. In the body of this chapter, however, the dead who are fed are not called *animas* but *huañoc*, 'die-ers' (that is, existing though not living persons; see Urioste 1981). The Andean dead were felt to have personal existence as long as any part of their bodies, or even clothing or an effigy, was conserved.

694. *ñaupa pacha* 'former times': this instance of the common phrase is important because it tells us that the makers of the manuscript thought of earlier parts of the colonial era within the category *ñaupa pacha*.

695. That is, chapter 9 (secs. 127–128), the explanation of Auquisna and its rites for the dead.

696. 'Are known to have' added to indicate witness validation, which continues through the first sentence of section 366.

697. *ayanta* 'their dead': *aya* seems to mean a person already established as a deceased member of society (formerly through mummification) as opposed to a person in transition to this status (*huañoc*). *Aya*, not *huañoc*, lived in the 'house of the dead' (chap. 11, sec. 155). The term *mallki* 'mummy' does not appear in the manuscript although at least one *huaca* (Nan Sapa, chap. 24, secs. 319, 320, 323) seems to have been a mummy.

698. That is, on November 1. Olivia Harris (1982: 56–57) has suggested that the modern Laymi Aymara ritual for this day, which resembles the one described here, achieves "the socialization of the graveyard" and

365 In former times people took along all sorts of foods cooked to perfection.

And when a person died, remembering how things used to be long ago, people used to wait, saying, "Our dead will return in five days. Let's wait for him."

They used to keep nightly vigil until the dawn of the fifth day after his death.

366 On the fifth day, a <crossed out:> [person] woman would put on her fine clothing⁷⁰⁰ and go to Yaru Tini, saying, "I'll bring him back from there," or "I'll wait for him and then come back."

Then, they say,⁷⁰¹ that woman would go there carrying different foods and maize beer.

367 At Yaru Tini, as the sun was rising, the dead spirit would arrive.

In the old times, two or three big flies—people

---

the initiation of a wet-season regimen bringing the living and dead close together. It ends at Carnival.

699. Andean tradition required careful conservation of the dead in caves or 'houses of the dead' (chap. 11, sec. 155) where they were regularly visited and fêted. Andean people considered Christian burial, which Spanish clerics forced upon them, an affliction because it precluded feeding and clothing one's departed kin. Ancestors buried in Christian graveyards were imagined as starving and suffering while they decayed. Many natives were punished for rescuing their kin from graves. The ritual described here seems to be an attempt to mitigate anguish about burial.

700. *pachanta* 'her . . . clothing': third person possession marker -n- ambiguous in reference; can also be read as clothing of the deceased.

701. 'They say' supplied to indicate reportive validation, which continues through the end of section 369.

call them *llacsa anapalla*[702]—would light on the garment she brought.

368 She'd sit there for a long while. As soon as those maggots called *huancoy*[703] worms left the corpse, the woman would say, "Come on, let's go to the village." And as if to say, "This is him," she'd pick up a small pebble and come back.

When the woman arrived, and when the dead person's home had been hurriedly swept clean, they started feeding him.

After the food, they offered the deceased drinks. Once the deceased had eaten, they also ate.

369 At <crossed out:> [deep] dusk, all his *ayllu* kinspeople danced five times, wailing.

When they'd finished dancing and wailing five times, they threw the pebble the woman had brought out into the street, saying, "You go back now. It's not time for us to die yet."[704]

370 On that day we know[705] they divined with a spider,[706] asking, "Why did this man go and die on us?"

The diviner[707] would reply, saying of the *huacas*, "Because this one was angry" or "Because that one was angry"; if he mentioned Paria Caca or any such *huaca*, people fulfilled the command by sacrificing a guinea pig or any other thing they had.

This is as much as we know about those who've died.

371 In Huaro Cheri and also in Quinti, people say on All Saints' Day, "Let's leave some nice warm food for the dead alongside the church" and they cook up some potatoes and pieces of jerky[708] well seasoned with red pepper, and put it out, just as if it were food for people to eat, and also toasted maize and boiled meat, as well as a small pitcher of maize beer for each of the dead.

They lay out all the things we've mentioned, because they think, "It's likely that the dead do eat." Maybe this is what they have in mind when they offer them plentiful hot dishes of all sorts.

---

702. Unidentified. *Llacsa* 'blue-green ritual powder' suggests the brilliant color of a bluebottle fly. *Anapalla* may be related to *ayapaura*, the name of "a big fly that dirties the flesh," mentioned in a trial of "idolators" in Otuco in 1656 (Duviols 1986: 64–65). The mourners waited for this fly to appear on the deceased's clothes because they thought it was the returning soul. This idea is also explicit in chapter 27 (sec. 358).

703. Taylor (1987b: 419–420) shows that the word *huancoy curo* used here may be an error conflating *huancuyro* 'bee' with *curu* 'worm' (specifically glossed by González Holguín as a kind that infests "bodies"; [1608] 1952: 56). Taylor gives 'bee' in his translation with the caveat that it appears really to refer to the above-mentioned flies. But perhaps *huancoy curo* is used in the correct sense of *curu* 'worm', meaning a larva or maggot infesting the dead body, and not the sense 'bee'. The point would then be that the cadaver must be left long enough to breed worms so its *anima* can emerge and escape in the form of flies.

704. In the later "idolatry" trials, which often prosecuted Andean mortuary ritual, rites of this sort are de-

scribed as taking place one year after the death. At that time the lingering 'person' here symbolized by the stone was dispatched from his household. The final farewell to the dead, called *kacharpariy* or 'sendoff', has survived into modern Quechua culture.

705. 'We know' supplied to indicate witness validation, which continues to the end of the chapter.

706. The spider is here called by the Spanish-derived word *arañu* (also in supp. I, sec. 450). Spider divining is described by Polo de Ondegardo ([1554] 1916: 32) and in various "idolatry" documents. Spiders were subjected to torture and then inspected to see which feet were injured or missing. A 1613 Jesuit report says killing the appropriate type of spiders other than sacrificially was prohibited by *huaca* priests (Hernández Príncipe [1613] 1919: 188, 194).

707. 'The diviner' supplied.

708. *charquincunactari* 'pieces of jerky': the English term is derived from the Quechua name (*charqui*) of this Andean invention.

CHAPTER 29

How Something Called the Yacana Comes Down from the Sky to Drink Water. We Shall Also Speak about the Other Stars and Their Names

They say[709] the Yacana, which is the animator[710] of llamas, moves through the middle of the sky. We native people[711] can see it standing out as a black spot.[712]

709. 'They say' supplied to indicate that this chapter begins with reportive validation.

710. *camaquin* 'animator': Juan Polo de Ondegardo ([1554] 1916: 3–5) said, "in general [the Incas] believed that all the animals and birds on the earth had their likeness in the sky, in whose responsibility was their procreation and augmentation" and went on to describe a celestial herd prototype much like this one. Bernabé Cobo's *Historia* ([1653] 1964: 2:159) has more details on this astrologylike complex.

Polo seems to be referring to the concept *camay*, of which this sentence is a *locus classicus*. Taylor (1974–1976: 234) suggests imagining *camac* as an entity that (1) is above and outside terrestrial reality; (2) is a prototype of earthly instantiations; and (3) functions to vitalize earthly instantiations by charging them with their specific essence and energy. *Camaquin* employs an agentive suffix and is probably a near synonym to *camac*.

A similar example is *chuchucollor*, two stars considered as creators of twins (Huertas Vallejos 1981: 88).

711. *ñocanchic runacunapas* 'We native people': some Andean constellations are reckoned negatively (consisting of dark spots within the Milky Way) and thus are not easy for non-natives to see. Garcilaso ([1609] 1966: 1:119; Livermore's translation) mentions the Yacana as one that native people tried unsuccessfully to make him see. But *ñocanchic* is inclusive first person plural, indicating that the person speaking included his audience among those who see constellations this way, namely, *runa*. This suggests that the testimony was gathered in a dialogue among *runa* people and not with any Spanish person.

712. The *yacana* is one of the 'dark cloud constellations' discussed by Gary Urton (1981: 169–170, 185–188).

The Yacana moves inside the Milky Way.[713] It's big, really big. It becomes blacker as it approaches through the sky, with two eyes and a very large neck.

This, we know,[714] is what native people call the Yacana.

373 They say[715] if a man was in luck and fortunate, the Yacana would fall right on top of him while it drank water from some spring.

As its woolly bulk pressed down upon him, someone else would pluck out some of its wool.

374 That apparition would occur at night.

In the morning, at daybreak, the man would look at the wool he'd plucked out. Examining it he'd see the wool to be blue, white, black, and brown, of every hue, thickly matted together.

If he had no llamas, he'd worship at the place where he had seen the apparition and plucked the wool, and trade for some llamas right away. After worshiping he'd trade for a female and a male llama.

Just from the two he'd bought, two or three thousand llamas would soon come.

In old times the Yacana[716] revealed itself this way to a whole lot of people all over this province.

713. *mayo* 'Milky Way', literally, 'river': the Milky Way was interpreted as a cosmic river through which water, having run down to the sea, circulates back up into the atmosphere. Urton (1981: 54–69) discusses related modern ideas.

714. 'We know' supplied to indicate witness validation in this sentence only.

715. 'They say' supplied to indicate resumption of reportive validation, which continues through the end of section 375.

716. 'The Yacana' supplied.

375   In the middle of the night, when nobody is aware of it, the Yacana drinks all the water out of the ocean.[717] If the Yacana failed to drink it, the waters would quickly drown the whole world.[718]

376   A small dark spot goes before the Yacana, and, as we know, people call it the Tinamou.[719]

    This Yacana, they say, has a calf. It looks just as if the calf were suckling.[720]

    Also, we know[721] there are three stars in a straight line.[722]

    They call these the Condor, the Vulture,[723] and the Falcon.

377   Next are the ones we call the Pleiades;[724] if they come out <crossed out:> [very] at their biggest people say, "This year we'll have plenty." But if they come out at their smallest people say, "We're in for a very hard time."[725]

    They call another constellation, which stands out as a perfect ring,[726] the Pihca Conqui.[727]

378   Certain other stars always appear very large.

    People give them the names Poco Huarac, Villca Huarac, and Cancho Huarac.

    In the old times, people, or at least some few of them, reportedly[728] used to worship them, saying, "These are the animators, the makers." The rest still worshiped these stars as they were rising,[729] spending the appropriate nights in sleepless vigil, but said, "We'll hold the other *huaca*s in higher honor."[730]

    This is all we know.[731]

717. That is, the Yacana, descending from the center of the sky, sucks up water from the waters surrounding earth. (This may refer to the period during the dry season when the llama and other dark cloud constellations remain below the horizon.) The cosmological metaphor links the way llamas descend from the high slopes to drink at lower-lying waterholes with the way the atmosphere "drinks" water from the ocean.

718. That is, if the Yacana failed to suck water up from the ocean into the atmosphere, the ocean would rise and drown humanity. Compare with chapter 3 (secs. 29–34), where a llama warned a man that the world was about to flood; perhaps the llama knew that Yacana, the master llama, was going to omit drinking.

719. The bird commonly and misleadingly called "partridge" in the Andes; see chapter 6 (sec. 87); see also Urton (1981: 171, 181–185). 'As we know' supplied to indicate witness validation of this sentence only.

720. Taylor (1987b: 429) has: "When it suckles, the Yacana wakes up." This reading rests on the double sense of *rihcan* 'appears'/'awakens'. 'They say' added to indicate reportive validation.

721. 'We know' supplied to indicate witness validation, which continues through the second sentence of section 378.

722. Perhaps Orion's belt.

723. *suyuntuytapas* 'Vulture': black vulture, *Coragyps atratus*, or turkey vulture, *Cathartus aura jota* (Koepcke 1970: 38).

724. Here the Pleiades are called by their Spanish name, *cabrillas*. A common Andean name for the Pleiades is *onqoy*. The Pleiades cult was the astronomical part of the Corpus-tide (summer solstice and preharvest or harvest-time) peak of the ceremonial year. "Confessions are made during the solemn festivals, of which there are three each year. The most important of these is close to Corpus Christi. It is called Oncoy Mitta, which is when the constellation called Oncoy appears. They do homage to this constellation to keep their corn from drying up" (Arriaga [1621] 1968: 49; Keating's translation).

725. Urton (1981: 118–120) discusses their salience in agricultural forecasting; today they are often called *collca* 'the storehouse'.

726. *muyo muyolla hamucta* 'stands out as a perfect ring': could mean either that they move in a circular path or that they are arranged in a ring.

727. Urton (1981: 100–101) identifies a constellation *pisqa coyllur* 'the five stars', probably the Hyades, which might be the same as *pihca conqui*. Alternatively, *pihca conqui* might be the curved tail of Scorpio, which Urton identifies as one of the two *collca*s or constellations of crop augury.

728. 'Reportedly' supplied to indicate reportive validation.

729. *sicamuptin* 'rising': probably heliacal rise, not nightly rise. Heliacal rise is the first day on which the star is visible in the east before dawn.

730. The meaning of the sentence varies slightly depending whether one takes *yallichisac* to mean 'set in higher position' or 'advance one's fortunes'. Taylor (1987b: 431) has: "The other people used to say, concerning these *huaca*s, that according to tradition the fact of worshiping them would make them prosper. And so they worshipped these stars staying awake without sleeping during the night they appeared." Either reading squares with Cobo's understanding of star cults as devotions through which a person might win the *camay* force proper to his or her status or identity ([1653] 1964: 2:160).

731. This sentence has witness validation.

CHAPTER 30

How Two *Huaca*s, a Male and a Female, Dwell in the Lake of the Allauca in Purui. We Shall Write about Their Lives

In very ancient times, so they tell,[732] there was a man called Anchi Cara.

This Anchi Cara came to dwell[733] by the water at a spring named Purui, to ensure that water would come to the fields of the Allauca.

While he was there, a woman from the Surco[734] area, a Picoy[735] woman, came over to him.

The woman's name was Huayllama.[736]

380 "Brother," this Huayllama said as soon as she arrived at Purui Spring, "very little water comes to my field. Are you the only one who draws water here? What are the rest of us supposed to live on?" And she sat down right inside the spring.

381 Since she was a fine and beautiful woman Anchi Cara fell suddenly in love[737] with her, and he greeted her with gentle words.

Then the woman refused to let the water flow in this direction.

When she did that he addressed her in polite language, saying, "Sister, please don't do this. What'll my children live on?"

382 At this point, Anchi Cara's children came over and sloshed[738] the water out toward Lliuya lake.

(Just below that spring there are two small ponds, which we already mentioned, called Lliuya and Tuta lakes.)[739]

Three or four small elongated rocks stand inside Lliuya lake.

These are said to be Anchi Cara's children.

383 If his kids hadn't come and sloshed that water out all the time, very little indeed would flow down here.

(Even so, we know, only a small amount flows down.)[740]

384 Once they'd finished arguing about the water, the two of them, Anchi Cara and his woman Huayllama, sinned together.[741]

"I'll stay here forever!" each one said after they'd sinned together, and they froze into stone.

These stones are there until today. His children likewise dwell in Lliuya lake.

This is all we know about them.[742]

---

732. 'So they tell' supplied to indicate that this chapter begins in -*si* reportive validation, which continues through the first sentence of section 382.

733. *tiamun* 'came to dwell': not in the unambiguously past -*rca*- tense, as the subsequent sentences are.

734. San Gerónimo de Surco (see chap. 3, sec. 31), in warm valley lands of the lower Rímac. The story seemingly allegorizes a rivalry over a high lake coveted by the Allauca of Checa and by Surco.

735. Picoy is mentioned by Dávila Brizeño ([1586] 1965: 163), as San Jerónimo de Picoi, a forced resettlement village close to Surco.

736. This sentence has witness validation.

737. *enamoraspa* 'fell in love': using a Spanish-derived expression.

738. *vischomorcan* 'sloshed . . . out': more literally, 'threw', this word might be a technical term meaning 'diverted'. But, given the sometimes comic tone of sex/irrigation myths, the image here might rather be that of children playfully sloshing the water out of the spring.

739. This sentence has witness validation. These lakes have not been mentioned previously in the manuscript; presumably the phrase refers to material edited out.

740. This sentence has witness validation ('we know' supplied). A crossed-out Spanish phrase meaning 'even so' is replaced with the equivalent Quechua.

741. *huchallicorcancu* 'sinned together': using a shame-oriented colonial term.

742. This sentence has witness validation.

385   Later on, at the time when they were settling into this area, the *huacsa*s of the Allauca *ayllu* used to go to Purui in order to clean the canal at the end of the rainy season.

   As they arrived, the *huacsa*s, however many there were, would walk around Lliuya lake[743] blowing on their panpipes.

386   After walking around the lake, the *huacsa*s would go to greet Anchi Cara, who stood over the water.

---

743. Compare with the Concha *huacsa*s' circuit at Yansa lake (chap. 31, secs. 437, 440). Honorific ritual visits to water sources are still common elements of rural Andean religion today.

With just a few words, they'd throw in a little of their coca, and then return to the lakeshore.

   On the lakeshore they worshiped Anchi Cara first, then his children, and finally Lliuya and Tuta lakes themselves.

387   In the old days they performed worship with a llama, but now that they don't have llamas anymore, they worship with just a guinea pig, some *ticti*, or whatever else they have.

   After finishing this worship, all the people began to dredge out the canal.

   This is as far as the story goes.[744] The account of their existence ends here.

---

744. This sentence has witness validation.

CHAPTER 31

As in the Previous Chapter We Spoke about the Existence of a Certain Lake, Likewise We Shall Now Tell about the Lake of the Concha Ayllu, the One Called Yansa. The Story Is Like This

388

<margin:> [Concha]

We've already explained in other chapters how things were in early times, how these villages were full of Yunca people, and other such things.[745]

So, too, they say, the Yunca resided in Concha village.[746]

389 About the people living there, as we indicated in other chapters, some say they're from Yauri Llancha or from Vichi Cancha, while others say they came from the *quinua* plant. Likewise the Concha people were born from out of the earth's interior, at Yauri Llancha, as five persons.[747]

390 Their names we know;[748] starting from the first one, they were

---

745. This sentence has witness validation.

746. Concha village probably corresponds to Concha Sica, today an outlying hamlet of San Damián de Checa (IGM 1970–1971). It was first Christianized as San Cristóbal de Concha and then, like Llacsa Tambo, "reduced" into nearby San Damián (Biblioteca Nacional, Lima, ms. B-1483, f. 63r). This chapter forms a rough counterpart in scale, argument, and level of detail to chapter 24, which focuses on the other component of San Damián, namely, Llacsa Tambo and the Checa. Both may be examples or reworkings of a common genre, a long "charter" running from origins through mythic genealogy to entitlements and rites that express them. This sentence has reportive validation, which continues to the end of section 389.

747. The remainder of the chapter is concerned with myths and laws relevant to the five local lineages named here. Material about a privileged lineage, the Llacsa Misa lineage specialized in water priesthood, makes up the bulk of it, but sections 443–446 return to the other four.

748. 'We know' supplied to indicate witness validation throughout section 390.

Llacsa Misa and his sister Cuno Cuyo who came along with him.

Then there was Pauquir Buxi.

Then Llama Tanya.

These three men together were the first ones to conquer this village.

<margin:>

[Llacsa Misa
Pauquir Buxi
Llama Tanya
Hualla
Calla]

There were also two other men who were their brothers, one called Hualla, and the other Calla.

391 They say that[749] as their other brothers went on ahead, these two fell somewhat behind.

So, lagging behind, they missed the trail and headed instead toward the Yauyo country,[750] thinking, "Maybe our brothers went over there."

A long time afterward, only after the other three brothers had finished dividing up the fields and other goods among themselves, they did come back.

392 (The descendants of Hualla are the Lázaro Puypu Rocçi lineage.)[751]

---

749. 'They say that' supplied to indicate return to reportive validation.

750. Yauyos Province adjoins Huarochirí to the south and is another mountainous region.

751. 'Lineage' supplied. The grounds are that section 444 uses Lázaro Puypu Rocçi's name as the name of a corporate group and not an individual and that in section 445 three groups belonging to the same set that contains

When Llacsa Misa, the oldest child, was about to die, he addressed Casa Chauca, Lázaro's grandfather, who was also Llacsa Misa's nephew, and said to him regarding the lake called Yansa:[752] "This will enter into my legacy.[753] As for me, I'm already near death." And he left it to him.

From then on Yansa lake was his domain. Here we leave Hualla.[754]

393   Now we will tell about those three men's approach and arrival.

As we explained earlier, people say[755] the natives were Yunca.

At that time, people there lived quite happily, drawing water from Yansa lake, for there was plenty of water and even an excess such that their water[756] reached all the way to the base of Llantapa[757] mountain.

394   While people lived in this manner, the three men we mentioned before—the oldest being named Llacsa Misa—were born from the earth in the locality called Yauri Llancha.

When they were born, they were born with a stone helmet.[758]

(The helmet was called the *llacsa yacolla*.)[759]
These three people came here carrying the *llacsa yacolla.*

395   They arrived in the area above Yansa lake at a place called Yana Pucyo.

There they sat down and drank.

The Yunca people heard somebody say, "Three fearsome-looking men are sitting over there!" and some went to see them.

396   When they were looking him over like that, Llacsa Misa showed those people his helmet, the one called the *llacsa yacolla*.

The moment they saw it, they all died instantly.

When the remaining Yunca saw that anyone who approached died, they panicked. "Come on!" they said. "Let's get out of here! If those three men find us they'll destroy us all!" And they abandoned their village and their fields just like that, and fled.[760]

397   At the time of their flight, there was a Yunca man there—we don't know his name—and while this man was escaping by night, he left one of his children behind at Concha Sica, the one named Yasali.

398   Yasali's father fled, carrying only an orphan boy whom he'd raised.

When he got across to Capari Caya,[761] almost to Yana Siri[762] up on the heights, dawn was breaking and the man recognized the boy.

There he was: just his adopted orphan son.

The man wept bitterly, but, knowing there was no way back, he finally left just as he was.

399   Meanwhile, the abandoned boy Yasali was scared to death, being just a child, and he hid inside the place where a cross now stands in Concha Sica.

---

the Llacsa Misa, and of which the Hualla are another subset, are called *yumay* 'patrilineages'. In this sentence witness validation was crossed out and replaced with reportive.

752. Modern Yanascocha is probably the same as Yansa; it is a small spring-fed lake on the high *puna* 5 km east of San Damián (IGM 1970–1971) and feeds the irrigation system of modern Conchasica.

753. *cay coscajman yaiconca* 'This will enter into my legacy': Taylor's transcription (1987b: 442–443) reads *cascayman*, which means 'into what I was' rather than 'into what I gave'. Accordingly he translates: "This [i.e., Cassa Chauca] is who will inherit my role."

754. This sentence and the next have witness validation.

755. 'People say' supplied to indicate reportive validation, which continues through the second sentence of section 394.

756. I.e., their irrigation canal.

757. Where the great mythic bridge Pullao once stood (chap. 5, sec. 73) and where Maca Calla's people, expelled by those of Tutay Quiri, resettled (chap. 26, sec. 355).

758. *chucuyoc*: 'with a . . . helmet': Gonçález Holguín ([1608] 1952: 118) has "*chucu* bonnet or ancient-style hat." But the same page clearly indicates that *chucu*, if made of hard material (leather, metal), means a helmet and not a hat. The passage can also be read to mean that a stone with a helmet was born along with, but separately from, the men.

759. This sentence has witness validation.

760. These Yunca-expelling heroes from Yauri Llancha play a role in Concha myth parallel to the role of the Yunca-expelling heroes from Vichi Cancha in Checa myth (chap. 24, secs. 315–326).

761. Probably not the same Unca Tupi also called Capari Caya in chapter 12 (secs. 167–168), because that reference is to a locale near the Pacific shore while modern Yanacirí is on the high puna across the Lurín valley from Conchasica.

762. Modern Yanacirí (IGM 1970–1971) is 4 km west-northwest of San Damián, a high plateau on the far side of a deep river ravine, from which one can look back toward San Damián and Conchasica.

At the same time those three men arrived at the village.

As they arrived they shared out the houses and all the rest among themselves, and it was then that Llacsa Misa found the boy.

400   "Son, don't worry," Llacsa Misa told him. "You'll stay with me. If my other brothers say to me, 'Let's kill him,' I'll defend you. But in return, you'll herd my llamas."

When the other brothers saw the child, they bitterly scorned him, and they did say, "This kid should die, because sooner or later he'll tell us, 'These fields are mine; this land belongs to me!'"

401   "No, why should we kill him?" Llacsa Misa replied. "Better to let him live. He'll show us all their customs, their fields, and everything."[763]

402   But the others still refused, saying, "Let him die anyway."

Llacsa Misa got angry and said, "My brothers, I've told you plenty of times. Watch out or your bones might wind up in the lake.[764] I say, let him live!"

Only then did the others finally fall silent.

403   So Llacsa Misa let the boy live, and made him herd his llamas.
<margin:> [Cuno Cuyo]
While Yasali was tending the llamas, he married Llacsa Misa's sister Cuno Cuyo, who'd come with him from Yauri Llancha.

Later, when he'd become a mature man, he even became the *yanca* for Uma Pacha, who had come from Yauri Llancha.

(This boy named Yasali was Cristóbal Chauca Huaman's grandfather.)[765]

404   And where the Uma Pacha festival we mentioned[766] is concerned, just as the Checa put on

huayo masks made of trophy heads and danced for a period of five days, so the Concha,[767] too, danced the same way. They, too, threw spears at the *chuta* target effigies erected for the sake of sons and daughters, and then did the same for llamas.[768]

405   There were likewise *huacsa*s in Concha Sica. They drank to both Paria Caca and Chaupi Ñamca in their respective seasons, and on one certain day they drank together with the Checas as peers.[769]

This is as much as we know about their customs.[770]

406   Now we'll tell about Yansa lake.

When Llacsa Misa arrived at Concha in the company of his other brothers, it's said that[771] they acquired all sorts of subsistence resources, and from among them Llacsa Misa got Yansa lake.

Pauquir Buxi received Huaycho Coto.

Llama Tanya received the house called Uyu Sana.

407   After they received all these properties, we know,[772] each one of them began to provide for his own living.

So Llacsa Misa for his part started to propitiate[773] Yansa lake.

In Yansa lake, they say,[774] there was a *huaca* named Collquiri.
<margin:> [Collquiri]
Since Llacsa Misa propitiated these *huaca*s for many years, all the Concha worked hard growing maize for him to eat.

---

763. As in chapter 24 (sec. 316), the invaders intentionally take on the organizational scheme and attributes of the vanquished Yunca natives, but (as in sec. 306) feel anxious about their resulting position of indebtedness.

764. *cochañicman* 'in the lake': or 'ocean'?

765. 'Grandfather': the kinship term used is a Spanish one, *aguelo* (i.e., *abuelo*). If taken literally, it puts a surprisingly short generational distance between the hero and his descendant who lived to be baptized. But the speaker may have used *aguelo* to mean one's direct patrilineal ancestor at any generational remove.

766. See chapter 24 (secs. 324ff).

767. 'The Concha' supplied.

768. That is, they performed the same rites already described in detail in chapter 24 (secs. 321–339). Conchasica and Checa today still regard their respective rituals as in some senses mirroring and rivaling each other.

769. *pactalla* 'as peers': normally the Checa despised the Concha as juniors in descent from Paria Caca (sec. 441). But in this one context the solidarity of common birth (*yuric*; see chap. 9, sec. 116) was made to override. The exact occasion is unspecified.

770. This and the next sentence have witness validation.

771. 'It's said that' supplied to indicate reportive validation, which continues through the next-to-last sentence of section 406.

772. 'We know' supplied to indicate witness validation.

773. *siruiita callarircan* '[he] started to propitiate': the Spanish-derived root *sirui-* means 'to serve'.

774. 'They say' supplied to indicate reportive validation, which continues through the first sentence of section 432.

408 At that time the *huaca* Collquiri wanted a woman[775] really badly.

He wanted one so much he searched all over the place, even as far as the Yauyo country and Chaclla.

As hard as he searched, he just couldn't find one.

409 One day, Cuni Raya said to him, "Hey, she's right here, right nearby, your woman!"[776]

So he set out, full of joy.

From the mountain that overlooks Yampilla,[777] he gazed out toward Yampilla itself.

As he gazed, he saw a woman dancing very majestically.

That woman's name was Capyama.

410 As soon as he saw how lovely she was, he immediately felt in his heart, "This is the one who'll be my wife."

He sent one of his serving boys, saying, "Go son, go tell that lady, 'Your llama has given birth to a <crossed out:> [female] male calf.' That's all. She'll come right away."

411 As soon as he sent him, the youth went off.

When he arrived, he told the woman, "Ma'am, one of your llamas has given birth just up there on the mountain." She was thoroughly delighted, and rushed straight to her house.

There she hung her golden drum at her midriff,[778] hid two small coca bags in her bosom,[779] took a long-necked jar of her maize beer, and came in a big hurry.

(The Concha call this jar *lataca*.)

412 When he saw her coming the *huaca* Collquiri was overjoyed and sped right back to Yansa.

Meanwhile, his servant boy led the woman along, and as he guided her, he lied to her, saying, "We're almost there now. It's right around here."

413 Then Collquiri turned himself into a *callcallo*[780] and waited for her on the mountain overlooking <crossed out:> [Yansa] Yampilla.

"I think I'll catch that *callcallo*," the woman said as she arrived there.

Each time she thought she'd grab it, the *callcallo* darted hither and yon and wouldn't let itself be caught.

414 Finally she did catch it. The moment she grabbed it, she stuck it inside her dress.

As she was grabbing it, she spilled her maize beer from the *rataca*[781] jar.

Even as she spilled it, the spot where she spilled it immediately turned into a spring.

This spring is called Ratac Tupi[782] until today.

415 The *callcallo* she had put inside her dress grew large inside her belly and made it ache terribly.

"What could this be?" she said when it hurt her. She looked, and there, on the ground where he'd fallen,[783] appeared a man, a fine handsome youth.

He immediately greeted her in his sweetest way, saying, "Sister, I'm the one you stuck in your dress. What can we do about it now? It was I who sent for you."

416 The woman for her part immediately fell in love[784] with him.

Since she felt that way, they slept together.

After they slept together, he took her to his home, Yansa lake.

Meanwhile, her father, her mother, her brothers, and all her relatives went searching for her all in tears. "But where did she go?" they said.

---

775. All the irrigation myths (chap. 6, secs. 81–90; chaps. 7, 30, 31) link maize-bearing land to female *huaca*s and water to male ones, with a sexual episode representing the origin of irrigation and consequent fertility. Dumézil and Duviols explore this motif in "Sumaq T'ika" (1974–1976).

776. Although Cuni Raya is less salient here than in chapters 2 or 14, the Collquiri myth bears resemblances to these major Cuni Raya myths. As in the story of the bride in the box (chap. 14, secs. 192–197), where Cuni inveigles the Inca by offering a woman, Cuni here brings about a male's downfall by manipulating his sexual desire. In the story of Caui Llaca (chap. 2, secs. 9–26), Cuni Raya caused a woman to give birth by tricking her into taking hidden sperm into her body, and here his dupe Collquiri does something similar (secs. 414–415).

777. Modern Llambía, a hamlet 3 km north of Huarochirí (IGM 1970–1971).

778. *chaopipi* 'at her midriff': Taylor (1987b: 459) has "center of [the house]."

779. *hucllayninman* 'in her bosom': Ricardo [1586] 1951: 65.

780. Unidentified; possibly a grasshopper.

781. *rataca* thus in original, discrepant from *lataca* in section 411; *r/l* is a common Quechua variation.

782. Perhaps a wordplay on *lataca*, the name of her beer jar in local language.

783. *hurmascampica*: the third person marker *-m-* could also mean 'where she'd fallen'.

784. *enamorarcan* 'fell in love': a Spanish-derived word.

417   When they'd been searching for a long, long time, a man from Yampilla called Llucaua told them, "Your daughter has turned into a high priestess.[785] She has a husband with all kinds and amounts of possessions." And so they came at once.

"Why did you come to steal our daughter, our sister from us?" they said to Collquiri when they found her. "Are you the one who forced us to search for her through all these villages until we were exhausted?" In high dudgeon they said, "Now we'll make her go back home!"

418   "Fathers, brothers, you have every reason to rebuke me, because I did fail to tell you ahead of time," Collquiri replied. And he inveigled them by saying, "What may I give you as restitution? A house, a field, llamas, people, agave fiber goods,[786] gold or silver? What about it, what do you want?"

419   Despite his enticements they agreed to nothing.
"I'll take their sister back," Capyama's father[787] said, repudiating the offer.
"All the same," Capyama[788] replied when he said this, "I wouldn't go back. It was with all my heart that I took him for my husband!"

420   "Father, please, I hope you won't take my wife away from me," said the man called Collquiri. "I've already told you that I'll give you anything, whatever you like, as much as you want. Or maybe I should give you the Goesunder?"[789]
A man who'd come in and sat down last in the gathering of that woman's brothers spoke up when Collquiri said this: "Father, say yes."
And the brothers[790] deliberated in low voices: "What could it be, that Goesunder?"

421   Their old man came and said, "It's a deal, son.

Marry my daughter. And make good on what you promised." So he said, and they returned home.
"We'll see each other in five days, father, in your village!" said Collquiri.

422   Five days later Collquiri, as good as his word, did go under. Underground he headed[791] toward Yampilla.
After he'd traveled a long stretch, he thought to himself, "I wonder how far I've come?" for he wanted to come out on the opposite side of the Apar Huayqui river.
Right where he got his head out, water squirted upward like a fountain.

423   He plugged the hole with some copper and went back underground.
He went on traveling underground until finally he emerged up above the high side of Yampilla.
The spring where he surfaced bears that woman's name, Capyama,[792] until today.

424   An enormous amount of water surged from Capyama spring and threatened to wash away all the fields of the Yampilla.
It actually did carry away all their *oca*[793] that was drying and all their *quinua* that was spread out in the sunshine, and lots of other things.
The Yampilla people got good and mad. "Why did you ever go and say yes to Collquiri?"
"Send him back immediately!"
"We were already used to getting along with just a little water!" they all said.

425   As they were complaining, Capyama's elders shouted at Collquiri from their <crossed out:> [spring] village:

---

785. *ancham villcayam* 'has turned into a high priestess': more literally, 'has greatly become *villca*'. This passage suggests that the senses of *villca* can include a person wedded to a *huaca*.
786. *chauaractacho* 'agave fiber goods': as in chapter 24 (sec. 334) and problematic for the same reasons.
787. 'Capyama's father' supplied.
788. 'Capyama' supplied.
789. The literal sense of *huco ric* 'the Goesunder' is clear enough; it means 'what goes under or inside'. But its sense in context is enigmatic, and Capyama's kinsmen let their curiosity about the *huco ric* get the better of them in the unmistakably comic episode that follows.
790. 'The brothers' supplied.

791. *hucota cama rircan* '[he] did go under': at this moment we understand the answer to the *huco ric* puzzle. Collquiri himself was the *huco ric*—the thing that goes under or inside—in the double sense of going under or inside Capyama's dress and of burrowing through the earth.
792. Modern Llambía draws its irrigation water still from Capyama spring. The love of Capyama and Collquiri (now renamed Pedro Batán, and imagined as a romantic lover rather than a clownish suitor) is prominent in modern folklore.
793. *oca*: *Oxalis tuberosa*, a potatolike plant with slender edible roots, widely cultivated through the Andes "on terraces in the *quebradas* of the cold sierras and in the altiplano zone to an altitude of 3,800 to 4,000 meters." Because they contain calcium oxalate crystals, *oca* tubers must be cured in the sun before cooking (Towle 1961: 56–57).

"Son-in-law, everybody's mad at us! Don't send us so much water!"

"Shut it off!"

"Hey, Collquiri! Hold back on the water!" they yelled.

426 With them shouting like that, Collquiri plugged the hole with a blanket[794] and other stuff.

But the more he plugged it the more the barrier crumbled and the more the water kept bursting through over and over again.

Meanwhile, the people from down below kept yelling at him nonstop:

"PLUG IT UP!!"

Finally Collquiri jumped in himself, put in his cloak, and sat down in the middle of the water.

427 When he sat down there, the water at last dried up somewhat.

Nowadays, water flows out of that spring passing through Collquiri's cloak as if through a sieve.

Whenever he plugged this waterhole, water flowed from many other springs here and there all over the district. Before, there weren't any.

428 Since their water supply was dried up as a result of all this, the inhabitants of Concha village started to get mad, too:[795] "Why has he given our water away?"

"What about us, what are we supposed to live on?" they said.

All the Concha together spoke to Llacsa Misa, who was in charge of the water: "Listen, Llacsa Misa, why did you go and let that water dry up?"

"What are people supposed to live on?" they said, and threw him into the lake.

429 When the *huaca* Collquiri saw what had happened he thought, "They're right. How are they going to live?" So at once he gave orders to one of his servants, a youngster called Rapacha:

"Dump some dirt and rocks from the shores down into the lake. There we'll measure out what's for the sustenance of the Concha people."[796]

430 So that boy Rapacha breached the lake's bank a little. As soon as it was opened, Collquiri instantly dammed the water up from below by building a great wall there.[797]

This wall, built without mortar, stands as the lake's mouth[798] until today.

431 Collquiri had the man called Llacsa Misa mark this wall carefully in five different places.[799] He said, "When the waters reach this point, you must close the mouth of the lake. After that, at the correct times you will direct the waters to the lower fields. At sunrise, you will release the water. They will water the *añay*[800] maize five times only. It is for this that I ordain you." Carefully he familiarized Llacsa Misa[801] with the marking stones.

432 From the time he made this known up to today, all of Llacsa Misa's descendants followed each other in the exact same custom and continue it even now.

People in fact[802] refer to these markers as "lake measures" and call the stick Turca Caya.

It[803] is said to be[804] accurately aligned over the stoneworks to serve its function; if we went there we might see it[805] by taking a careful look.[806]

---

797. That is, once Rapacha had forced water to breach the lake's bank, Collquiri built a dam in the resulting channel and thereby turned the lake into a controllable reservoir.

798. *cochap simin* 'lake's mouth': a literal translation; the phrase apparently (from context) means the lake's outlet. The stone dam still existed much as described in section 431 as of 1990.

799. That is, the dam was to have five separate sluice gates (now seven). They were to be opened in sequence, from shallowest to deepest, as the lake level fell. When asked why a single sluice gate at the lowest level would not suffice, modern San Damián residents say high water pressure when the lake is full is the reason: using the ancient stone-and-sod technology (with which they are still familiar), a single gate at the lowest level would, at the beginning of the irrigation period, release water with too much force for human musclepower to control.

800. Untranslated. *Añi* is the modern local name of a multicolored maize that needs relatively little irrigation.

801. 'Llacsa Misa' supplied.

802. 'In fact' supplied to indicate witness validation of this sentence.

803. 'It': perhaps the measuring stick *turca caya*. A tentative translation.

804. 'Said to be' supplied to indicate reportive validation. The clauses following the semicolon have *-cha* conjectural validation.

805. 'It': the object of *ricohhuan* 'we might see' is unstated in original.

806. *chayasparaccha alli ñauinchichuan ricohhuan*

---

794. *titahuanpas* 'with a blanket': in supplement II (sec. 478), *huc fresadacta o titactapas* 'a blanket or cover' clarifies this otherwise unattested word. But *tita* might be an error for *titi* 'lead', as other translators suppose.

795. They got mad, that is, because their *huaca* Collquiri had diverted their water to Capyama Spring and Yampilla village just to satisfy his yen for Capyama.

796. Apparently this means Collquiri had the boy Rapacha dump earth and rocks in the lake so as to reduce its capacity and breach its banks, thereby making water spill out; he then apportioned this water to the Concha.

433   During the month of March the Concha go out to close the lake's mouth,[807] all of them, both men and women.

  As for the water measurement mentioned above, Llacsa Misa would decide, "It'll be at so and so a time" or determined some other thing. All the Concha went along, following his exact words.

434   Because he was the *yanca* for this purpose, all the arrangements of the season were made in compliance with his commands.[808]

  When it came to irrigation he'd be the only one to give orders about it, saying, "It'll take place now" or "It'll be so many days." And all the Concha obeyed him to the last word.

435   If the lake ever spilled out in the middle of the night, people dragged Llacsa Misa's descendants to the scene from wherever they happened to be, saying, "Go, it's your responsibility!"[809]

  Because this was their special care both by day and by night, because they thought only of minding the lake, other people worked hard on their maize fields for them and revered them, saying, "It's because they're numerous that we stay alive."

436   Llacsa Misa, and his descendants, watched over the lake very carefully, saying, "Beware the water doesn't spill out of this lake."

  If the lake ever spilled out and the waters of Yansa rushed into the river, a breach would immediately open in the dam. Whenever it did flow into the river, it cracked the dam.

  For this reason they watched it with great care.[810]

437   As we said before, the *huacsa*s went to Yansa lake both to impound and to release the waters.

  To impound the water all the people went out, too. As soon as they arrived, the women deposited their coca, each one in her own right, and likewise their maize beer each in her own right.[811]

438   These offerings were for Yansa lake, but it was in fact[812] the *yanca* who received them all.

  They'd also take one llama, they say.[813] They likewise took guinea pigs, *ticti*, and all the other sacrificial offerings.

  Once they finished collecting things, they took a *quipu* account of all the people who were absent and began to worship Yansa lake.

439   They worshiped, saying,

    "Father Collquiri, the lake is yours and yours are the
      waters;
    This year, give plentiful water to us."

After they finished worshiping, they drank their maize beer and chewed their coca.

  After that the men and women together began to impound the lake.[814]

'if we went there we might see it by taking a careful look': an uncertain translation. *Alli ñauinchichuan*, more literally, 'with our good eye', could perhaps mean 'with our practiced eyes', or 'clearly see with our eyes'; *ñauinchichuan* has inclusive first person plural marking, indicating that the speaker regards the addressee as also having the native's 'good eye' for such matters.

807. The modern lake-closing ritual, called the lake's "anniversary," is practiced on February 3.

808. The position of this priest as irrigation authority affords an important clue to the economic component of priestly power. Chapter 24 (sec. 335) comments on another example of priests' economic privilege. While the Llacsa Misa water priests enjoy a subsidy in agricultural form, the priest sacrificers mentioned in chapter 24 are privileged in consuming animals.

809. *suyoiquim* 'your responsibility': more literally, 'your domain'.

810. The water priests' concern was practical, not magical. Testimony in a 1648 lawsuit between the Con-

cha and their Suni Cancha neighbors (chap. 9, sec. 135) over control of Yansa's waters tells us that the hydraulic system sometimes did in fact suffer damage from overflows: "Last year in a great flash flood that came from the lake of Yanascocha and its streambed, the canal inlet was swept away leaving it [turned] into a washed-out gully, beyond repair" (Biblioteca Nacional, Lima, B-1483, f. 174r).

811. *sapampitac* 'each in her own right': seemingly, asserting a household-level right of access to water. The female ritual role as receiver of water rights parallels the female role of earth as water-receiving *huaca*s in the myths.

812. 'In fact' supplied to indicate witness validation of this sentence.

813. 'They say' supplied to indicate reportive validation, which continues through the end of section 440.

814. In 1990 the *comuneros* of Conchasica conducted "anniversary" rituals for Yanascocha Lake in a fashion closely recalling sections 438–439. The *alcaldes*, holders of rotating magistracies that ritually govern irrigation, officiated in place of the *yanca*s. The officiants first collected and announced offerings of coca, tobacco, and liquor at lakeside, then dedicated them to the lake's "owners" while loading them in a small raft or "boat" made of dry sod. The sail of the raft was a modern analogue of the *quipu*, a legalized list of irrigators handwritten on paper. While launching the raft, officiants made speeches similar to those recorded c. 1608 but using the

440 When it was time to release the water, people always went five times accompanied by two or three *huacsas*.

Just before this, a man and a woman would enter a fairly large field and bring maize beer there in a big jug, and guinea pigs, two or three of them, and coca leaf.

Having worshiped with these offerings, they'd release the water.

These are as many stories as we know about Yansa lake.

441 Now, we know[815] that the Concha were the very last of Paria Caca's and Tutay Quiri's offspring to be born, and the least prestigious of them.

For this reason, Paria Caca and Tutay Quiri[816] gave them only a very little of their territories and very few of their fields.

442 The *huacsas* we mentioned dance the Chanco during the festival seasons of Paria Caca and Chaupi Ñamca just as the Checa dance them.

We already talked about all that in other chapters.

443 Now we'll learn about the children of the three men we mentioned.

They say[817] all the offspring of Llacsa Misa became extinct. When Llacsa Misa was about to die, his nephews, namely, Cuno Cuyo's and Yasali's children, married Hualla's descendants, who'd returned after a long time from the Yauyo region.[818]

These descendants of Hualla are in fact the Lázaro Puypu Rocçi kindred.

444 <**margin**, in Quechua:>
[Hualla's descendants are of the Lázaro Puypu Rocçi kindred. They entered into the Llacsa Misas' position, so the people called Huallas don't exist any more. Only one woman is still living, and this one is childless; she's Anya Ruri's wife.][819]

445 Pauquir Buxi's descendants are in fact[820] still alive today and they're the Ñau Paico, those people.

The descendants of Llama Tanya are now the Ruri Cancha, the Casin Chauca, and the Tacya Cancha.

These three patrilineages are the reported[821] descendants of Llama Tanya.

446 As for the Hualla, we already mentioned the Lázaro Puypu Rocçi.

---

modern names of the "owners": María Capyama and Pedro Batán. The climactic event was the sailing of the boat and tense observation of its course as lake water gradually saturated it. When it sank, the officiants said the "owners" had expressed their approval by pulling the boat down through the center of the lake.

Yanascocha now has a modern dam with a steel sluice gate, so men and women carry out the closing of Collquiri's dam only in what they call "simulacrum" (a ritualized token of the whole job). The traditional technique of closing the dam is called *champería*, that is, sod-laying. *Champeros* were designated by the officiant to cut fresh sod blocks from a nearby marsh, carry them to the dam, and stack them against the ancient dam so as to prevent lake water from passing through it.

815. *yachanchic* 'we know': introduces a passage with witness validation, continuing through the first sentence of section 443.

816. 'Paria Caca and Tutay Quiri' supplied.

817. 'They say' supplied to indicate resumption of reportive validation, which continues to the end of section 444.

818. In Taylor's reading (1987b: 485) it is Hualla's chil-

dren who are called nephews of Llacsa Misa. Since both Cuno Cuyo and Hualla are siblings of Llacsa Misa, the offspring of either could be called his nephews. (The term in question is the Spanish *sobrino*, which, at least in Spanish context, does not distinguish between relationships through male and female siblings.) Therefore, the translation discrepancy does not imply any discrepancy about local principles of genealogical reckoning.

819. Secs. 443–444 are difficult. Assuming that all the named corporate descent groups are *yumay* 'patrilineages' like the three groups so described in section 445, one reading might be as follows:

Llacsa Misa's direct lineage became extinct at an unspecified time. When some collateral descendants through his brother Hualla took over the role to which the direct descendants would have been entitled (see sec. 446), namely, primacy in the water priesthood, they ceased to function in the lineage bearing Hualla's name. This transferred group or sublineage was called the Lázaro Puyo Rocçi. At the time of writing only one member of an untransferred Hualla sublineage remained. Since this was a woman (Anya Ruri's wife) and childless besides, the Hualla patrilineage as such no longer existed.

Descent groups throughout this passage are named after their apical ancestors. The fact that in this case the corporate name includes a baptismal name suggests that the transfer of the Lázaro Puypo Rocçi sublineage to the Llacsa Misa role was recent (an effect of post-invasion epidemics?).

820. 'In fact' supplied to indicate witness validation, which continues with one interruption to the end of the chapter.

821. 'Reported' supplied to indicate reportive validation of this sentence. *yumay* 'patrilineages': more literally, 'sperm'.

Calla's descendants are today the Gonzalo[822] Paucar Casa and the Lazaca Canya, those people.

All these people have multiplied from the five men who came from Yauri Llancha.

Only Llacsa Misa's descendants are now completely extinct.

---

822. Reading the abbreviated baptismal name as *jº* rather than *gº*, Taylor (1987b: 487) gives "Juan."

The Lázaro, Hualla's children, have inherited their office because they're Llacsa Misa's kin, and they say, "We're the Llacsa Misa."

This much is all we know about the life of the Concha.

The end.[823]

---

823. *fin* 'the end': in Spanish.

[Supplement I]⁸²⁴

In what follows, we shall explain case by case what we know[825] happened in all these villages in the old days, and still does up to now, when a person gives birth to two babies in just one birth, whether they are a boy and a girl, or both boys, or both girls.

We call[826] those who are born this way *curi*.[827]

448 When babies were born like this, even if they were born unexpectedly in some other village, people would bring them to their home village that very night.

For example, in the old days, if twins were born in Sucya Cancha or Tumna, people would bring them right away to the Checa village called Llacsa Tambo.[828]

449 When carrying them they would by no means carry them during the daytime, for they used to say, "Be careful, <crossed out, in Spanish:> [it freezes] the earth might freeze!"

Maybe those who are privy to such practice follow it all over the region.

When *curi* were born, as soon as it got completely dark the man and woman—that is, the twins' father and mother—would start living fenced in inside a house, and both man and wife would lie there motionless
<**margin**, in Quechua with partly Spanish gloss:> [lying, that is, on one side][829]
until the fifth day.

450 On the fifth day, they'd turn over onto their other side.

On that same day, all the father's male in-laws[830] would gather in the *curi*'s house and dance while beating their drum themselves.

(At that time, contrary to modern practice, it was the men who beat the drum and not the women.)

---

824. A cross-shaped symbol (*crismón*) appears at the top of the page.

825. 'We know' supplied to indicate witness validation, which predominates throughout the two supplements except where otherwise indicated.

826. *ñinchin* 'we call': an unusual form, perhaps a slip of the tongue or pen due to indecision between *ñinchic* (inclusive first person plural) and *ñin* (third person).

827. The persecutors of "idolatry" from Avila onward attacked twin cults. Arriaga ([1621] 1968: 20–21, 53; Keating's translation) mentions that "bodies of *chuchus*" were commonly venerated and kept in houses. *Chuchu* means a body of a twin or also a double or multiple fruit. He notes: "Human twins are called *curi*, which means two born of one womb, and if they die young, they keep them in jars in the house as a sacred object. One of them, they say, is the son of the lightning. They have many superstitions regarding the birth of twins, . . . each of which implies some form of penance, since they must expiate the sin of having been born together. . . . they do not baptize either *chuchus* or *chacpas* [breech birth babies]" ([1621] 1968: 31; Keating's translation).

828. The example of Sucya Cancha suggests that the teller is thinking of trips downslope to trade or produce coca at the Checa's outposts in the lower Rímac valley.

829. The couple would be required to lie on a bean or grain, and only allowed to turn over when their body warmth and humidity had germinated it. It is as if their bodies themselves were to counteract the danger of earth's freezing (Arriaga [1621] 1968: 53; Keating's translation).

830. *tucoy masancuna* 'all [his (or their)] male in-laws': the wide extension of this term is made clear by Diego Gonçález Holguín: "*massani* brother-in-law of a male; the married man calls his wife's brothers and her male cousins *massaniy*" ([1607] 1842: 215; see also [1608] 1952: 221). *Massani* and *massaniy* are the root *massa* with "empty morph" *-ni-* and first person singular possessive marker *-y* (i.e., 'my *massa*'). Earlier dictionaries include some of the husband's own male consanguineals ("*massa* brother-in-law, brother of the husband"; Santo Tomás [1560] 1951: 319).

Before beginning to dance these rites, they used to consult the demon,[831] using a spider[832] and the object called *pana charapi*,[833] concerning which of his in-laws should lead them by dancing first.

451   Following the demon's word, they'd choose and appoint five of the in-laws who were sitting there.

And these people, from the very moment they got the word, would search for coca day and night, never resting, bartering whatever they had for it.

The other in-laws, thinking only to outdo each other, all joined together no matter how many there were.

452   We mentioned above how the parents turned over on their other side.[834]

From that time on, the dancers[835] never rested from dancing every single night until the fifth day had arrived.

On the day before it did arrive, the in-laws used to show one another a leather bag as if to say, "To-morrow I'll bring coca in this bag." They'd dance shaking the leather bags[836] still empty of coca.

Meanwhile, another five days would have elapsed since the time the parents had turned over on their other side.

So it was ten days in all.

453   On that occasion, beforehand, the five in-laws would catch and bring back a brocket deer, or a *ta-ruca* deer,[837] or any other animals that live on the wild upper slopes. As the leader of those men carried it, the *curi* would emerge onto the open plaza.[838]

454   And some people would go around blowing the conch trumpet called *paya*.

And some would go around carrying a *pupuna*, <**margin**, in Spanish:> [It is the staff with the thong for catching parrots but not with such a long thong.][839]

And some others went around carrying *sacaya*. (This material called *sacaya* was a little maize ground up with some *ticti*.)

Different people carried this stuff.

As for the people who carried these items, it wasn't the *curi*'s in-laws who carried them. It was rather their close blood relatives who carried them.

The brocket deer was the only thing the leader of the in-laws carried.

455   As soon as people had seized the brocket deer, they would force it to step around with its hooves, starting from the dwelling place where the *curi* were fenced in, saying,

"This is the one who has confused you,
Who has outraged you!"[840]

<**margin**, in Spanish:> [And then they took it out and killed it.]

And all the people would eat its meat immediately, leaving absolutely nothing over as remnants.

---

831. *supayta* 'the demon': while to Christian ears *su-pay* meant a devil, this sentence may reflect the word's older sense 'a spirit' or volatile *ánima*. Since the twin ritual is concerned with the propagation of families, its divinations may have called on ancestral shades.

832. See chapter 28 (sec. 370).

833. Untranslated.

834. To begin germinating the second seed of their penance. 'Parents' supplied.

835. 'Dancers' supplied.

836. *hina mana cocayocta huayacallactas taquichic carcanccu*: could also mean 'thus they made [the in-laws] who had no coca bags dance'. 'Shake' is an attempt to render the effect of *huayacallactas taquichic*, more literally, 'making the bags [without coca] dance'. *Taquichiy* is the verb used in all instances where celebrants dance displaying animal skins or human trophies. In chapter 9 (sec. 128) a skin bag full of coca is taken as a sacrifice in lieu of an animal. These data suggest a close symmetry between the coca hunt and the deer hunt in section 453.

837. *tarucactapas* 'taruca deer': *Hippocamelus antisiensis*, a deer larger than the brocket deer, found at altitudes over 3,000 m in the southern Andes and at higher ones in the north (Renard-Casevitz 1979: 21–22; see also Cabrera and Yepes 1940: 271–272).

838. *pampa* 'open plaza': *pampa* means any flat place, but since the context is the *curi* parents' return to their home ceremonial center, the scene is likely to be a plaza.

839. The *pupuna* is also the reed with which Cuni Raya opened the waterways in chapter 2 (sec. 9).

840. *tacurisonqui apllasonqui* 'has confused you, [who] has outraged you': tentative translation of a difficult passage. *Tacuri-* is thought to be from the verb "*ttakuini o ttacuni o chacruni* to mix or interpose one thing with another" (Gonçález Holguín [1608] 1952: 335). The derivatives concern confusion, such as turning a house upside down looking for something. *Aplla-* is likely to be *haplla* (Gonçález Holguín [1608] 1952: 150) as, for example, in *haplla sonco* ('*haplla*-hearted') meaning 'the person who is in the habit of wrath and quarreling and who is overly rude'. Its derivatives concern words of anger or losing one's temper. Perhaps the point is that the deer is taken as a scapegoat for what has confused the parents' reproductive process. But alternatively the parents themselves could also be subjects of these verbs.

456 Then, as we just said, on the tenth day, they went out onto the open plaza. Afterward, the *curi* went wrapped in a large piece of cloth, shrouded from view, while some people, namely, the in-laws in groups of two or three,[841] would pull them along wailing and dancing.

Those who pulled them would also pull the *curi*'s *ayllu* relatives. They used to pull them along, and as they pulled they said, "We'll give you a field or something like that, we'll give you a llama."

457 When arriving at the open plaza, the in-laws used to carry the brocket deer's skin
<margin, in Spanish:> [That is, the pelt and the head stuffed with straw, because the flesh had already been eaten as was mentioned.]
with great ostentation, just as we do today when we carry the base of the cross at the head of a procession.[842]
<margin, in Spanish:> [the base of the cross]
Those who carried *pupuna*s went brandishing them like spears as if to say, "I'll throw!" and striking combative poses over and over again. The one who came first among them struck threatening poses at the *curi* who came along in the rear.

458 When the people who were carrying the brocket deer's skin arrived at the plaza, a man and a woman who were *ayllu* kin to the *curi* offered them a llama or a field. As they did, they would say, "Rest with these gifts"[843] and put them at their ease. Then the *curi* went to their ordained[844] seats and the couple would sit there richly honored, both the husband and the wife together.

459 On that day, all the in-laws would compete in giving away their coca, and they'd dance and drink all day long.

In the evening they'd go back home and return to the same place where they'd dwelt before.

They remained there for another five days.

When those five days were complete, people used

to accompany[845] them back to the[846] <crossed out:> [seat] sealed lodging.[847]

460 Right after this, their in-laws brought firewood and built a big bonfire,[848] as at the beginning, right on the next day after the *curi* were born—we forgot to tell this in our earlier account
<margin, in Spanish:> [What has to go with this is at the beginning.<?>]
—when they collected firewood every night, and, saying, "It will burn until dawn, lest some temptation befall," they lingered there[849] all night.[850]

So that fire never died until after the rituals,[851] not even for a single night.

461 Afterward, once they finished all these rituals, they led the *curi*
<margin, in Quechua:> [and also their parents]
to a certain demon of theirs and asked, "Where shall we wash them clean of their fault?" They'd take them to Yansa lake,
<margin, in Spanish:> [that is, where the Conchas' water comes from]
in due order,[852] following the demon's command.

---

841. *masacunapas yscay quimça* 'the in-laws in groups of two or three': could also be read 'their in-laws, two or three of them', but this makes it difficult to see how they could pull the many people mentioned in the next sentence.

842. Arriaga ([1621] 1968: 53; Keating's translation) mentions that the deer was made into a canopy under which the penitent parents passed.

843. 'Gifts' supplied.

844. *unanchascaman* 'to ... ordained': may mean the place had been chosen by a priestly divination.

845. *asuchic* 'accompany': not attested in old sources; Lira's modern Cuzco dictionary ([1941] n.d.: 22) has an apparently related verb *assuy* meaning 'to approach, to come close, to make one thing closer to another'.

846. Or 'to another'.

847. *aposentoman* 'to the sealed lodging': the following excerpt from a 1656 "idolatry" trial shows that this Spanish word served to designate the specially enclosed house in which (sec. 449) parents of twins were sequestered: "When two are born from one belly, which they call *chuchus*, the wizards [i.e., *huaca* priests] require their parents to fast five days, during each one of which they eat only one row of grains from one maize cob, and during these five days no one may see them, and when they bring food to the said fasting person, who is enclosed in an *aposento*, they cover their eyes so as not to see them ..." (Duviols 1986: 164). The Huarochirí manuscript original has a crossed-out word *tiana*, which *aposento* replaces. *Tiana* means a dwelling, and sometimes a ceremonial stool or seat.

848. *collo camacta* 'bonfire': conjectural translation.

849. *cayta (ca)corcan* 'they lingered there': from *cay* 'to be' with reflexive -*cu*-; *cayta* 'around here or toward here' (Gonçález Holguín [1608] 1952: 53).

850. The sense seems to be that, warming themselves by the fire, they stayed near the ritual house all night so the *curi* parents would not be tempted to lapse from their special discipline.

851. 'The rituals' supplied here and in the next sentence.

852. 'In due order': problematic translation. The origi-

462   There a man with the title of Con Churi,[853] who was that demon's priest, used to ask the earth about them.

They say[854] he would ask,

"Why were they born as *curi*?
For what faults of theirs, and how many?"

About those born *curi* people reportedly said, "They're born so in exchange for someone's death."[855] <**margin**, in Spanish:> [This is the opinion of the common people and not the answer.]

463   Then, saying,
"It's for this offense,"
or
"It's for that offense,"
people would wash both parents. They also bathed the two babies, washing them over and over again, even to the point where they were almost dying

from cold, until at last it was said, "That's enough for the seriousness of their fault."

464   Once they'd finished all this, they used to cut the male's hair. They clipped just a little of the female's hair, but, as for the male,[856] they sheared his off as we do[857] with sinners.[858]
Then, it's said,[859] they returned with the *huachay ruco*.[860]
People put on them a necklace with black and white intertwined strands, which was the sign of a *curi*.
<**margin**, in Spanish:> [somewhat like a golden chain]

465   Then they admonished them,

"You must fast for one whole year.
Neither you nor you may sin sexually[861] with anyone.

<**margin**, in Spanish:> [not with each other either]

If you do, you'll be doing a very bad thing.
You'll have fatigued our in-laws[862] in vain."

So they advised them.

466   When half the year was over, the priest and a lot
<**margin**, in Quechua:> [a lot]

---

nal text is an abbreviation, *hord^a m^de*, for which we suggest the expansion *hordenadamende* 'in due order' or alternatively *hordinariamende* 'normally', 'usually'. Other translations provide the reading 'heretically' (*heretica-mente*). Our reading is partly suggested by the fact that *hordenamy^o* meaning *hordenamyento* 'ordinance' and *hordin^o* meaning *hordinario* 'ordinary' are common abbreviations of the period (Cavallini de Araúz 1986: 59; Rostworowski 1988: 294). The various derivatives of *herejia* 'heresy' are rarely if ever abbreviated. Moreover, *hereticamente* in this context would be surprising since the manuscript does not concern heresies (which at that time typically meant Protestant teachings) but "idolatries" or "gentile" practices. Nor does the visit to Yansa lake seem any more "heretical" than the rest of the ritual.

853. See chapter 13 (sec. 185). The fact that a *con churi* priest, who is specifically a lineage authority, officiated in this ceremony suggests once more that *supay* in the context of twin ritual denotes an ancestral shade.

854. 'They say' supplied to indicate that this sentence has reportive validation, as do several others up to the end of section 467. The validation shifts do not mark transitions as sharp as those in the numbered chapters and are hard to interpret, but the first sentence of section 468 seems to suggest that this part is an interpolated portion of testimony after which the author returns to writing with witness validation.

855. *huañuynin* 'someone's death': attempts to render the ambiguity of the third person possessive -*n*. Whose death is not clear in this passage. But Hernández Príncipe ([1613] 1919: 188) explains that the birth of an extra baby via twinning was understood as restitution given by the deity of lightning to a family one of whose ancestors had been struck or killed by lightning.

856. *huarmictaca . . . carictaca* 'the female . . . the male': the terms denote gender alone. *Huarmi* can mean 'wife', but *cari* is not a synonym of *cosa* 'husband'. So this sentence leaves doubt about whether the parents or the twins are shorn.

857. *rutunchic* 'as we [inclusive, i.e., addressee as well as speaker] do': this implies the speaker identifies with this common practice of "extirpators of idolatry." Taylor (1987b: 502–503) reads *rutunqui* 'you cut', in which case 'you' could mean Avila or another cleric or church officer.

858. 'As we do with sinners' is witness-validated.

859. 'It's said' supplied to indicate reportive validation, which continues to predominate through the end of section 467.

860. *huachay ruco* may mean 'birth headdress' (González Holguín [1608] 1952: 168; Taylor 1987b: 503).

861. *hochalliconqui* 'sin sexually': using the word with which the church translated 'to sin'. But since in this case sex would violate an Andean, not Catholic, norm the usage may not be colonial: that is, the sin inheres not in sex, but in having sex at the wrong moment.

862. *masanchiccunacta* 'our in-laws' with inclusive first person plural possessive marker: implying that the persons in question are in-laws of both addressee and speaker.

of other people would ask their demon, "Have the twins' parents[863] lived right?"

If it turned out all right, they'd be delighted. But <crossed out:> [If it wasn't good,] if he said, "They did sleep together,"
<margin, in Spanish:> [that they had sexual intercourse]
then people would give them a good tongue-lashing.

467   The in-laws would get really mad and berate them: "How dare you wear us out with this burden all for nothing?"

They used to go after them like that until the end of the year.

Only then would they cut their necklace.
In this way, they say,[864] they finished the thing.

468   Now we'll complete[865] what we have just said.
If the twins were born both males or both females, people would say, "Times aren't going to be good."

"There'll be times of terrible hardship."

But if they were born male and female, people interpreted it as a good sign.

469   And as for today's in-laws, on one hand, they're pleased that they don't have to spend as much as they did in the old times.

On the other hand, they may regret it, too, when they think, "We don't do it like that anymore." In some villages, because of the demon's deceptions, they may not have forgotten these practices.

470   At night, or at any other time, when twin llamas are born, they used to ask the demon for their names one by one, inquiring,

"What twin person will he be?"

The names that the demon bestowed were Curi Ñaupa, Curi Yauri, Curi Huaman, Ticlla Curi,[866] or any other name that says *curi*.

It was done[867] that way for each one, whether male or female.

471   Any number of people who are now wealthy in silver used to put all their effort into trading away everything they had for coca during Paria Caca's feast or any other festival, because they didn't yet understand the word of the good God. It was the only thing they'd raise money for, even if they'd had only three or four years to recover from the last festival.

As for the poor, every year they worried, wondering,

"Where'll I find coca?"

"Will I be humiliated this way?"

They searched for it, bartering away their fields and clothing for coca, wandering hither and yon, going up to the guanaco pastures and searching for brocket deer while they themselves went hungry.

472   For the sake of this duty, those who were mindful of such practices used to go to enormous trouble and, fasting rigorously, asked their demon first of all,

"Where'll I find coca?"[868]

"Trading a guanaco for it?"

"Or should I trade off[869] one of my fields, or my clothing?"

"What'll happen to me?"

473   Nowadays, because they have another attitude and don't think so much about this custom,[870] and also because they no longer have to trade off any of their things on account of it, people feel well contented.

On the other hand, they also do cry about it a lot, saying, "Why is it that we don't do these things now?"

474   The time for this rite was at night or at any other

---

863. 'The twins' parents' supplied.

864. 'They say' supplied to indicate the end of a passage in which reportive validation predominates.

865. *tincuchison* 'we'll complete': the verb implies symmetry and suggests that what follows will not just add to, but will complement or match what went before. The phrase may mean that the teller will now make good on a promise to deal 'case by case' with mixed-sex, two-boy, and two-girl births (sec. 447). Or it may mean that in the next passage, which returns to witness validation, he or she will complement the data given by the source whose words are reported in sections 462–467.

866. The meanings of these names are: Curi Ñaupa

'Twin Leader', Curi Yauri 'Twin Scepter' (Gonçález Holguín [1608] 1952: 347), Curi Huaman 'Twin Falcon', and Ticlla Curi 'Two-colored Twin'.

867. 'It was done' supplied.

868. 'Coca' supplied.

869. *huacllichisac* 'should I trade off': this verb means "to damage one's capital or leave it just barely begun or a small amount already spent, or to damage in departing, or to go away damaging something" (Gonçález Holguín [1608] 1952: 170). The concept seems to be that of spending off productive assets and thereby damaging one's own livelihood.

870. 'Custom' supplied.

time that Macoy Llenco designated by declaring, "It'll be on so-and-so a date." At such times people used to cheer up and become merry; the old men and lots of old ladies would go carrying their *ticti* and their other things, for there'd be drinks at the old house[871] or maybe even right here.

---

871. *ñaupa huasipi* 'at the old house': *ñaupa* is more

475   Right in this village people probably abstain from this practice, more or less, even though they may do it at night. We think that in other villages outside of here people do practice it, and we hear as much, too.

---

strictly 'former'. The phrase may refer to dwellings from before the forced resettlements (c. 1580 onward in this area) or to prehispanic buildings.

[Supplement II]⁸⁷²
JHS⁸⁷³

When we speak of an *ata*, we mean a child born with a reverse whorl[874] in its hair.

<**margin**, in Spanish:> [their hair<?> goes backward][875]

About a person who's born like this:

When the baby turns three years old, its elders get together in the house or in the courtyard. Starting at broad daylight,[876] they first inform the father's[877] brothers-in-law or his fathers-in-law,[878] saying, "On that day we'll cut the hair of this *ata* and *illa*[879] of Paria Caca."[880] (When we speak of an *illa*, we mean just the same thing as an *ata*.)

---

872. A cross appears at the top of the page. In combination with the monogram JHS that appears below it, this forms the conventional symbol called *lábaro*.

873. The abbreviation *JHS* is a latinization of the Greek monogram *IHΣ* 'Jesus'. *JHS* and its equivalent *IHS* were popularly interpreted *Jesus Hominum Salvator* 'Jesus, savior of men' or *In Hoc Signo* 'in this sign' (i.e., *In Hoc Signo Vinces* 'in this sign shall you conquer'). But its characteristically Jesuit interpretation may be more relevant, given the early Jesuit penetration of the region and given Father Avila's own Jesuit education. This reading is *Jesum Habemus Socium* 'we have Jesus as a companion' (Cross 1957: 678). *Socium* might also resonate with the Andean ideal of social obligation between humans and sacred beings.

874. *parca* 'reverse whorl': a tentative translation. *Parca* can mean a plural whorl (Albornoz [1583?] 1984: 196) or a six-fingered birth (Gonçález Holguín [1608] 1952: 279). Perhaps its sense was generic, 'a bodily anomaly'. 'Reverse' derives from Urioste's transcription of the barely legible marginal note. Taylor's reading also seems to refer to hair but does not mention reversal.

875. Taylor (1987b: 512) reads the obscure marginal note as "on some it tangles and others not" (*a alg(un)os se les /maraña y a otros/no*).

876. *pacsac punchaomanta* 'Starting at broad daylight': based on Gonçález Holguín ([1608] 1952: 271) "*pacsa* 'resplendent'." Taylor (1987b: 512) reads *pusac* 'eight', that is, eight days ahead of time.

877. 'The father's' supplied, on basis that *massa* (see note 830) and *caca* are terms explicated with reference to a male ego in the colonial Quechua dictionaries and grammars.

878. *cacancunacta* 'fathers-in-law': an inadequate translation, because no English term corresponds to the same set of relatives as *caca*. Quechuists contemporary with the manuscript said *caca* could mean maternal uncle: "*caca* the uncle who is the mother's brother" (Gonçález Holguín [1608] 1952: 42). But the same author's grammar treatise gives additional senses:

Caca, the son-in-law's father-in-law, namely his wife's father; both the son-in-law and his first cousins call both the father-in-law and his father "my *caca*."

The married man and his brothers as well also address those of their male in-laws who are brothers of his (the married man's) mother-in-law as "my *caca*." (Gonçález Holguín [1607] 1842: 214–215)

Ricardo ([1586] 1951: 98) gives usages of *caca* including father and brother of male ego's wife. Zuidema (1977: 20) suggests that the term groups together those male consanguines of male ego's son who do not partake of the patrilineal bond between ego and son. It is to the *massa* (see notes 830, 877) and *caca* (Santo Tomás [1560] 1951: 240, 319) categories that parents of *parca* owe restitution for the disturbance of procreation that irregular births represent.

879. "*ylla* the large bezoar stone, a notable one as big as an egg or bigger, which they carry with them as a charm to become rich and lucky" (Gonçález Holguín [1608] 1952: 366), and more broadly, any sort of amulet stone or effigy (see chap. 9, sec. 134); the term is associated with the cult of lightning. Irregular births, too, were attributed to lightning (see note 827).

880. An infant's first haircutting is still a common *rite de passage* in the Andes (Zamalloa González 1972: 28–29) and follows approximately the same pattern described here. The parents place the baby on a blanket

477 So they let everyone know about it, and begin to brew maize beer. When people hear someone say, "They're brewing half a *fanega*[881] of maize, maybe a whole one!" they ask one another, "What could that maize beer be for?"

Once they find out what day the fiesta will take place, all the people gather together on that day.

478 The *ata*'s father[882] sits with his brothers-in-law and all the men who rank as his fathers-in-law,[883] but down by the low end, and he begins to dance and serve them drinks.

When they get good and drunk, they spread out a blanket or a cover[884] and make the baby go to its center and sit there, and they make this speech:

"Fathers and brothers,
Today we'll cut the hair of this *ata*, this *illa*;

For he's Paria Caca's and Tutay Quiri's *ata* and *illa*,
And it's they who have sent him to me to be born so."

479 On that occasion, the baby's nearest maternal uncle[885] if he was a boy, or her nearest paternal aunt if she was a girl, or alternatively the baby's grandfather or grandmother,[886] would stand up and put on the blanket a token representing a llama or a field, and approach the *ata* with a pair of scissors.[887]

(The llama's token is an object called *cot huato*, one with which they had led a llama to Paria Caca.)
<margin, in Spanish:> [*cot huato* is llama harness]

480 They would also put a token for a field there, called *caxo*.

(This *caxo* was just a stick, a digging tool for women.)

Then the *ata*'s close blood relatives would stand up, one at a time, and make offerings of cloaks and tunics, of sheep[888] or wool, according to their relationship.[889]

481 Once the close blood relatives had finished, the *curaca* or the *alcalde* would get up, starting from the leading positions, and put in one or two *reales* of money.

Thinking, "These people will get even drunker by the time they finish, and the drunker they get the surer it is that they won't hold back on anything," the parents[890] would make them drink hard until nightfall.[891]

482 Once they all finished clipping the hair, it was[892] the *ata*'s father who'd shear it all off the child, for the others would barely have snipped at it. As soon as he finished, he'd immediately start the dancing, calling out his ancestors' names:

"Father Anchi Puma!"
or
"Carhua Chachapa!"
or any other name. They danced and took their ease, saying,

---

with kin and guests around it. The guests, in return for each snip of the baby's hair, give or promise gifts for its future welfare. They bind themselves to the child by accepting drinks from the hosts. The rite is generally called a form of godparentage (*compadrazgo*) today.

881. 'half a *fanega*': Spanish bulk measure; about 0.8 bushel or 29 liters.

882. *atayuc runaca* 'the *ata*'s father': could also mean 'the person(s) who has (have) the *ata*', that is, both parents. We choose 'father' because this person is said to have *caca* and *massa*, terms used relative to a male ego.

883. *cacancunahuampas* 'the men who rank as his fathers-in-law': for reasons given in note 878 to section 476.

884. *titacta* 'cover': see note 794 to chapter 31 (sec. 426).

885. *cacan* '[*ata*'s] maternal uncle': "*caca* the uncle who is the mother's brother" (Gonçález Holguín [1608] 1952: 42) seems the more applicable sense of *caca* when referring to a child ego since the other usages apply to married males; *ypan* 'paternal aunt' (Gonçález Holguín [1608] 1952: 369; Santo Tomás [1560] 1951: 301)

886. Assuming the immediately preceding glosses of *cacan* and *ypan* are right, these words probably imply maternal grandfather and paternal grandmother, respectively.

887. Scissors are a European tool, suggesting that the narrative concerns post-1532 times.

888. *ouejahuanpas* 'of a sheep': using the Spanish word for the Old World animal. Throughout the manuscript sacrificial goods are consistently of Andean provenience, and it is true that c. 1600 *oveja de la tierra* 'native sheep' could still mean 'llama'. But this gift, offered to the child's estate and not for sacrifice, might really be a Spanish sheep. Spanish sheep were herded through many parts of the Andes well before 1600.

889. *cascancama* 'according to their relationship': or 'according to what they had'.

890. Subject is an unspecified third person: the parents? the *alcalde*? The former makes sense since it was in their interest to maximize the gifts.

891. *pacha huraycuscancama*: more literally, 'until *pacha* descends'; translation uses an unattested but plausible meaning for *pacha*.

892. Or 'is'; many of the verbs in this supplement are ambiguous between agentive present and habitual past tenses because auxiliary verbs (forms of *cay* 'to be') are omitted.

"This is your *ata*, your *illa*,
And now we have finished his rites.

Henceforth may Paria Caca send us no other;
We will do right and be well."[893]

483   When people mention an *ata* or *illa*, they reportedly[894] comment, "This is Paria Caca's messenger."
    On the evening of the day before the haircutting
ritual,
<**margin**, in Spanish:> [That is, the night before
the said day.]
people used to worship Paria Caca and Tutay Quiri
with guinea pigs, *ticti*, and other things of theirs,
showing deep respect, and saying,

"Put us truly at peace with this *ata*,
Tomorrow we'll truly be happy."

484   "This is the sign of a *curi*," people say. "He has
sent this *ata* to foretell the coming of a *curi*. People
haven't minded their debts to Paria Caca properly,
and for this, *curi* will be born in exchange for someone's death."[895]

---

893. These two formulas and the one following do not
appear to be strict couplets, but they do have a common
form consisting of a pairing between a sentence of which
the addressed deity is subject and one in which the sup-
plicant speaks of his own conduct.
   894. 'Reportedly' supplied to indicate beginning of a
passage in which *-si* reportive predominates, continuing
up to the fourth sentence of section 484.
   895. *huañonan* 'someone's death': whose death, as in
supplement I (sec. 462), remains unclear.

"They're born in exchange for their death," they
say about those born *curi*.
   This is what we know about the people known
as the San Damián Checa.[896]

485   Who knows what people say in other villages?
   However, when an *ata* is born, everything is the
same. Everybody reveres them all over this whole
corregimiento and in the whole region: the Huanca,
the Yauyo, the Huaman Tanca, all the kinds of
people called Indians.[897]

486   And it's the same in Limac; when someone's
child is an *ata* lots of people gather, from the most
distinguished to the servants.
   And we also know such things about the ones
who are mestizos, some of them.
   When they saw these rituals, certain people fell
into the same sin, thinking, "Maybe this is a good
custom!"
   We said the same thing: "They should be shorn
after they're three years old."
   People perform this rite earlier or later, according
to their customs.
   All of this is a true testimony.

---

896. This sentence and the remainder of the supplement have witness validation.
   897. *runapas yn(di)o ñiscaca* 'people called Indians': a
reprise of the phrase that begins the manuscript (preface,
sec. 1). The effect is as though "zooming out" back to the
wider colonial context by naming three farflung ethnic
groups whose territories reach far beyond that of the
manuscript.

Transcription of the Huarochirí Manuscript
George L. Urioste

F 64 R

[1] runa yn(di)o ñiscap machoncuna ñaupa
pacha quillcacta yachanman carca chayca
hinantin causascancunapas manam cananca
mapas chincaycuc hinacho canman himanam
vira cochappas sinchi cascanpas canancama ricurin
hinatacmi canman [2] chay hina captinpas canan
cama mana quillcasca captinpas caypim churani
cay huc yayayuc guaro cheri ñiscap machoncu
nap causascanta yma ffeenioccha carcan y
ma yñah canancamapas causan chay chay
cunacta chayri sapa llactanpim quillcasca canca
hima hina causascampas pacariscanmanta
[3] CAPITULO 1 COMO FUE ANTEGUAM(EN)TE LOS YDOLOS Y COMO GUERREO EN
TRE ELLOS Y COMO AUIA EN AQUEL TIEMPO LOS NATURALES
ancha ñaupa pachaca huc huaca ñiscas yana ñamca tuta
ñamca sutioc carcan cay huacacunactas quipanpi huc huaca
tac huallallo caruincho sutioc<carcan>atircan ña atispas canan
runacta yscayllacta huachacunampac camarcan huctas quiquin
micorcan huctas mayquintapas cuyascanta causachicorcan yayan
maman [4] chaymantas chay pachaca huañuspapas pihcca punchao
llapitac causarimpuc carcan ynaspa micuyninri tarpuscanmanta
pihcca punchaollapitacsi pocorcan cay llactacunari tucoy hinantin
llactas yuncasapa carcan [5] chaysi ancha ahca runacuna huntaspas   yuncaçapa
ancha millayta causarca chacranpacpas cacactapas patactapas yanca
aspispa allallaspa chay chacracunas canancamapas tucoy hinantin
cacacunapi huchoyllapas atunpas ricurin hinaspari chay pacha pis
cocunaca ancha çumaccamas carcan huritupas caquipas tucoy quellosapa
pucasapa [6] chaycunas quipanpi ña may pacham huc huacatac paria
caca sutioc ricurimurcan chay pachas ynantin rurascanhuan antiman
carcoy tucorcan chay atiscancunacta cay quipampim paria cacap pa
carimuscantauan rimason [7] chaymantam canan huc huacatac cuni   saber si dize q(ue) no se
raya sutioc carca<n> caytam mana allicho yachanchic paria cacaman   sabe si fue antes
tapas hichapas ñaupacnin carcan o quipanpas ychaca cay cunirayap   o despues de carvin
                                                                          cho o de paria caca

F 64 V

cascanracmi ñahca vira cochap cascanman tincon porque caytam
runacuna ña muchaspapas coni raya vira cocha runa camac pacha camac
yma aycayuc cammi canqui campam chacraiqui campac runayqui
ñispa muchac carcan [8] yma ayca saça ruranacta callarijpacpas pai
taracmi machocuna cocanta pachaman vischuspa cayta yuyachiuai
amutachiuai cuni raya vira cocha ñispa mana vira cuchactaca ricus
patac ancha ñaupa rimac muchac carcanco yallin astauanrac
compi camayucri compinampac sasa captin muchac cayac carcan chay
raycom caytarac ñaupacninpi causascanta quillcasson chaysauam
paria cacacta
[9] CAPITULO 2 COMO SUÇEDIO CUNI RAYA VIRA COCHA EN
SU TIEMPO cuni raya vira cochap causascan Y COMO CAUI LLA
CA PARIO SU HIJO Y LO QUE PASSO

notase q(ue) no se sabe   cay cuni raya vira cochas ancha ñaupa huc runa ancha huaccha tucospalla
si fue este antes   purircan yacollanpas cosmanpas lliqui lliquesapa runacunapas huaquin
o despues de carvincho   mana ricsicnincunaca huaccha huçasapa ñispas cayar<>can cay runas
canan tucoy llactacunacta camarcan chacractapas rimaspallas pata
patactapas allin pircascacta tucochircan rarcactas canan llocsimu
nanmanta huc pupuna sutioc cañavelarpa sisayninhuan chucas
pallas yachacuchirca chaymantari yma aycactapas ruraspas purir
can huaquinin llacta huacacunactapas yachascanhuan allcuchaspa [10] chay
si huc mitaca huc huarmi<tac> huacatac caui llaca sutioc carcan cay
caui llacas canan viñay donzella carcan panas ancha sumac cap
tin pi maycan huaca villcacunapas puñosac ñispa munapayar
can chaysi manatac hu ñircancho [11] chaymantas canan quepanpi chay
huarmica chayhina mana pi caritapas chancaycochicuspa huc yura
rucmap siquinpi ahuacorcan chaysi chay cuni rayaca amauta
cayninpi huc pisco tucospa chay yura rucmaman vichayrirca chay
si chaypi huc rucma chayasca captin chayman yumayninta chu
raspa hormachimurca chay huarmi cayllaman [12] chaysi chay huarmica
ancha cusicuspa millpuycorcan chaysi hinalla chichu tucorcan ma
na carip chayascan escon quellanpi himanam huarmicunapas hua
chacon hina huachamurcan yna donzellatac chaysi quiquillantac
huc huata chica ñoñonhuan causachircan pip churinh cayca ñispa
[13] chaysi ña huc huataman huntaptinca taua chaqui ña chay huamra
puriptinca tucoy hinanin huaca villcacunacta cayachircan

F 65 R

yayanta ricsiconcampac chaysi cay simicta huacacuna huyarispa
ancha cusicuspa tucoynin alli pachanta cama pachallispa ñocactapas
ñocactapas munahuanca ñispa hamurcancu [14] chaysi cay tantanacoy
ri anchi cuchapi carcan maypim chay huarmi tiarcan chayman hinaspas   la congreçion fue en
ña tucoynin hinantin huacacuna villcacuna tiaycuptinsi chay huar   anchi cocha
mica ñispa nircan ri<>coy caricuna apucona ricsicoy cay huahuac
ta mayquenniquechicme yumahuarcanquichic camcho camcho ñispas
sapanpi taporcan chaysi manatac pillapas ñocapmi nircancho [15] chaysi
chay ñiscanchic cuni raya vira cochaca manyallapi tiacuspas ancha
huacchalla yna tiacuptinsi chay huacchap churincho canman ñispas
paytaca millaspa mana tapurcancho chica sumac cama caricunaca
tiaptin chaysi mana pillapas ñocap churimi ñispa ñiptinsi chay
huamracta ñispa nircan ri cam quiquique yayaiquicta ricsicoy
ñispa ñircan huacacunactapas churique caspaca camsahuam lluca
musonque ñispa ñaupactac villaspa [16] chaysi chay huamraca man
yanmanta callarimuspas tahua chaquilla purispa hasta<>chay huc
manyan yayan tiascanman chayascancama mana pillamanpas
llocarcancho chaysi ña chayaspaca tuyllapuni ancha cusicuspa yayanpa
chancanman llocaycorca chaysi mamanca chayta ricuspas ancha
piñacuspa hatatay chay hina huacchap churintachum ñocaca hua
chayman ñispas chay huahuallanta aparicuspa cochaman chi
cacharcan [17] chaysi chay cuni raya vira cochaca tuylla munahuanca ñispa
cori pachanta pachallispa tucoy llacta huacacunapas manchariptin
catita ña callarircan ñispa pana caue llaca cayman cahuaycumu
ay ancha sumac ñam cani ñispas pachactapas hillarichispa sayar
can [18] chaysi chay caue llacaca mana huyantapas payman ticrari
chispa cochaman hinallam chincasac chica millay runap cachcaçapap
churinta huachascaymanta ñispa chicacharcan maypim cananpas chay
pacha camac huco cochapi cananpas sutilla escay rumi runa hina
tiacon chayman chaysi chay canan tiascanpis chayaspalla rumi tu
corcan [19] chaymantas cay cuni raya vira cochaca pana ricurimunca
cahuaycumuanca ñispa caparispa cayapayaspa carollapi catircan
chaysi ñaupac huc condorhuan tincorcan chaysi huauqui maypim
chay huarmihuan tinconqui ñiptinsi cayllapim ñahcam tarinque ñip
tinsi ñispa ñircan camca vinaymi causanque tucoy hinantin sall
cacunamanta huañuptinca huanacuctapas viconactapas yma ayca

F 65 V

cactapas camllam micunque chaymanta camta pillapas huañochi
sonque chayca paipas huañuncatacmi ñispas ñircan
[20] chaymantas chaysaua añashuan tincorcan chaysi pana may
pim chay huarmihuan tinconqui ñispa tapuptinsi payca ñispa
ñircan mana ñam tarinquecho ancha caructam rin ñiptinssi
camca chay villahuascayquimanta manam punchaopas purinque
cho tutallam runapas chicniptin ancha millayta asnaspa purin
que ñispa ancha millaypi ñacarcan
[21] chaysauam pumahuan tincorcan chaymi payca cayllactaracmi rin
caylla ñam sihcpayconque ñiptinmi paytaca camca ancha cuyas
cam canqui llamactapas huchayucpa llamantaracmi micopunque
camta huaño<chi>chispapas aton fiestapiracmi homansaua<chu>
churaspa taquechisonque chaymanta huatanpi camta llocsi
chispare huc llamanta nacasparac(mi) taquechisonque ñispa ñircan
[22] chaymantam ñatac huc atochuan tincorcan chaymi chay atoc
ca ancha caructa ñam rin mana ñam tarinquicho ñispa ñiptin
mi camtaca carupi puricuptiquitacmi runacunapas chay hatoc a
coylla ñispa ancha chicnisonque huañochispari yancam camtaca
carayquictapas husuchisonque ñispa ñircan

[23] hinatacsi huc huaman
huan tincorcan chaysi chay
guamanca cayllata
racmi rin ñah cam tarinq(ui)
ñiptinsi camca ancha
cusiocmi canqui micuspa
pas ñaupacracmi quin
ticta armuçaconque chay
mantari piscocunacta
huañuchispari camta
huañuchic runam huc
llamanhuan huacachi
sonqui ynaspari taquis
papas homampim chura
sonqui chaypi sumaspa tian
cayquipac
[24] chaysahuam cay horitocu
nahuan tincorcan chaysi
chay horituca ancha caructa
ñam rin mana ñam tarin
quicho ñiptinsi camca an
cha caparispam porinq(ui)
micoyniquicta husuchisac
ñiptiquipas chay caparij
niquita huyarispa ancha
vtcalla carcosonqui chay
mi ancha ñacarispa cau
sanq(ui) runapas chicniptin

[24cont.] chaymantari pi maycan alli villacochuan tincospaca allicta çapa
camaycospas rircan mana allicta villacnintare millaypi cama
ñacaspas rircan [25] chaysi cocha pa(tapi chayaspaca)<hinalla cochaman yaycuspa
chicacharcan chaytam canan runacunaca castillamanmi chicachar
ca ñispa ñincu ñaupa pachapas huc pachamansi rin ñispaca ñircan>
pacha camacñicman cutimurcan chaysi chaypica pacha camacpac
iscay sipas churin machachuaypa huacaychascan tiacman chaya
murcan chaysi cay yscay sipaspa mamanca ñaupacllantac co
cha hucoman chay caue llaca ñiscacta visitac yaycurcan sutin
pas hurpay huacha<y>c sutioc cay hillaptinsi chay cuni raya vira co
chaca chay sipasta yuyacninta puñochircan chaysi huquen ñañan
tauan puñoyta munaptinsi chayca huc urpai tucospa pauarirca
chaymantas mamanpas hurpai huachac (sutioc) carca [26] chaysi chay pachaca
cochapi manas huc challuallapas carcancho chay hurpai huachac
niscallas huasinpi huc huchuylla cochallapi huyhuacuc carca
chaytas chay cuni rayaca piñaspa ymapacmi chay caue llaca ñis
ca huarmicta cocha ocumanta visitac rin ñispalla tucoyninta <cocha>

F 66 R

haton cochaman vischorapurcan chaymantaracsi cananca chall
huacunapas cochapi huntan [27] chaymantas chay cuniraya vira co
cha ñiscaca miticamurca cocha patañicta chaysi chay hurpai
huachac ñisca huarmica huahuancuna ynam <yuma>(puñu)huan ñispa
villaptinsi ancha piñaspa catimurcan chaysi cayapayaspa catip
tinsi ho ñispa suyarcan chaysi husallayquicta husascayque
cuni ñispas husarcan [28] chaysi ña husaspa pay cayllapi huc aton
cacacta viñarichircan chayta cuni rayacta hurmachisac ñispa
chaysi payca hamauta cayninpi musyacuspa aslla ysmayco
cumusac pana ñispalla cay llactacunaman ñatac miticamur
can chaysi cay quitipi ancha hunay puricorcan ancha ahca llac
tacunacta runactapas llollachispa   <el fin q(ue) tuuo esta huaca se dira abajo ojo>
[29] CAPIT(UL)O 3 COMO PASSO ANTEGUAMENTE LOS Y(NDI)OS QUANDO REUENTO LA MAR
CAYPIM ÑATAC ANCHA ÑAUPA RUNA
CONAP RIMACUSCANMAN ÑATAC
CUTISON
chay simire caymi ñaupa pachas cay pacha puchocayta munarcan
chaysi mama cochap pahcyamunanta yachaspas huc orco llamaca
ancha allin queuayucpi <yayan>(chay llamayoc) çamachiptintac mana micuspa
ancha llaquecuc yna carca yn yn ñispa huacaspa [30] chaysi<yayan>(chay llamayuc)
ca ancha piñaspa sarap curumtayninhuan chucllo micuscampi
chucarca micoy allco chica quehuapim çamachijque ñispa chay
si chay llamaca runa yna rimarimuspa ñispa ñircan hutic ymac
tam cam yuyanquiman cananmi pihcca punchaumanta cocha
pahyamunca chaymi hinantin pacha pochocanca ñispa rima
rirca [31] chaysi chay runaca ancha mancharispa himanam cason
mayman rispam quispison ñispa ñiptinsi haco villca coto   este es un cerro q(ue) esta
hurcoman chaypim quispison pihcca punchaupac micuynij   entre huanri y surco
quicta apacoy ñispa ñircan chaysi chaymantaca chay orco
llamantapas vinaynintapas quequen apaspa ancha hutcaspa
rircan [32] chaysi ña villca coto hurcoman chayaptinca tucoy ani
malcuna ña huntasca pomapas hatucpas huanacopas con
dorpas yma ayca animalcunapas chaysi chay runa chayap
tin pachalla cochaca pahcyamurca chaysi chaypi ancha
quihcquinacuspa tiarca [33] tucoy hinantin hor(co)cunactapas tu
coy pampaptinsi chay villca coto hurcolla aslla puntallan

F 66 V

mana yacup chayascan carca chaysi hatucpac chupantaca
yaco hucocharcan chaysi chay yanamanpas tucorcan chay
si pihcca punchaomantaca ñatac yacuca huraycurcan
chaquerirca [34] chay chaquerispas cochactapas asta hurayman
anchurichircan runacunactari tucoy hinantin runacta collo
chispa chaymantas chay runaca ñatac mirarimurca chay
cacsi canancama runacuna tian cay simictam canan
xp.^(christia)nocuna hunanchanchic chay tiempo dellobioctah paycuna
ca hina villca cutucta quispiscanta hunanchacon

[35] CAPIT(UL)O 4 COMO EL SOL SE   CHAYMANTAM HUC SIMICTATAC
DESPARECIO CINCO DIAS   VILLASON PUNCHAO HUAÑUSCANTA

ñaupa pachas <punchao> (ynte) huañorcan chaysi chay huañuscan
(manta) pihca punchao tutayarcan chayssi rumicunaca paypura
huactanacurcan chaymantas cay mortero muhcacunari
chaymanta cay maraycunapas runacta micuyta callarir
can llama horcocunare ynatac runacta ña catirircan
caytam canan ñocanchic xp.^ono(christiano)cuna hunanchanchic
jesuxp.^to(jesuchristo) apunchicpac huañuscanpi tutayascantah caycuna
ca riman ñispa hunanchanchic ychach ari chay

[36] CAPIT(UL)O 5 COMO ANTEGUA   CAYMANTAM ÑATAC PARIA CACAP
M(ENT)E PARECIO PARIA CACA   PACARIMUSCAN CALLARINCA
EN VN CERRO LLAMADO
CONDOR COTO CIN   ñam hari cay ñaupac tahua capitulopi ñaupa pacha causas
CO HUEUOS Y LO   cancunacta villanchic hichaca cay runacunap <> chay pacha
QUE SUCEDIO   pacarimuscancunactam mana yachanchiccho maymantah
pacarimurcan [37] chaymanta cay runacuna chay pacha causaccuna
ca paypura aucanacuspa atinacuspalla<s>m causac carcan(cu) cura
canpacpas sinchicunallacta rricocunallacta<s> ricsicorcan cay
cunactam purom runa ñispa ñihchic [38] cay pachapim chay
paria caca ñisca condor cotopi pihcca runto yurimurcan cay yu
riscantam huc runa huacchallatac huatya cori sutioc
paria cacap churin ñiscatac ñaupaclla ricumorca yachamurca
cay yachascantari ahca misterio rurascantahuanmi rimason

F 67 R

[39] chay pacha cay huatya curi ñisca huacchalla micuspapas huatya
cuspalla causaptinsi sutiachircan huatya curim ñispa
chay pachas huc runa tamta ñam(ca) sutioc ancha capac atun apo   ojo tamta ñamca
carcan huasimpas tucoy hinantin huassim cassa cancho ñisca
ricchaccuna piscocunap ricranhuan catascas carcan llamanpas
quillo llama puca asol llama yma ayca ricchaccama llama
yocsi carcan [40] chaysi cay runacta chica alli causascanta ricuspas
tucoy hinantin llactacunamanta hamuspa yupaicharcan mu
charcan chaysi payri ancha yachac tucospa pissi yachascanhuan
ancha ahca runa<cta>conacta llollaspa causarcan chay pachas yna
amauta tucoc dios tucoc caspatac chay runa tamta ñam(ca) sutioc ancha mi   tamta ñamca
llay huncoyta tarircan [41] chaysi ancha ahca huata honcoptinsi hima
hinam chica yachac camac caspatac honcon ñispa runacunapas
chay pacha rimarcancu chaysi chay runaca alliyasac ñispa y
manam vira cochacunapas amautacunacta doctorcunacta caya
chin chay hina tucoy yachaccunacta sauiocunacta cayachircan   juntaronse los sauios
chaysi manatac pillapas yacharcancho chay honcoscanta [42] chay
si cay hatya curica chay pacha ura cochañicmanta hamuspa
may pacham sieneguellaman huraycomunchic chay horcucta chay
pis poñomusca chay horcom canan latab zaco sutioc chaypi poñop
tinsi huc hatocca vramanta amusca hocri hanacmanta amusca
tac chaysi chaypi pactalla tincuspas huauque hima ynallam
hanac villcapi ñispa tapurcan [43] chaysi allica allem ychaca
huc apom anchi cochapi villca checa yachac tucoc dios tococmi
ancha huncon chaymi tucoy amautacuna taripan pachacta
ymamantam chica huncon ñispa chaymi manatac pillapas
yachancho honcoscanta chaymi chay honcoscanca huarminpa
pincayninmanmi camchacuptin huc muro sara callanamanta
pahyamuspa chayaicurcan [44] chaytam ñatac pallaspa huc ru
naman caracurca chay carascanmantam chay runa micoc
huan hochallicoc ña tucon chaytam canan pachaca huachuc
ta ña yupan chaymantam cay hochamanta huc machac
huay chay chica sumac huasinsaua pay(cuna)cta micoc tian huc
ampaturi yscay vmayoc maraynin hocopi tian(tac) cay<cuna>
micucnintam (cana) mana pillapas musyancho ñispas villarcan
chay hatoc horamanta amucta [45] chaysi ñatac paytari

F 67 V

huauqui chayca hura villcapi hima hinallam runacuna ñis
pa tapurcan chaysi payri hinatac villarcan huc huarmim
aton apo villcap churinmi hullomanta ñahca huañun ñispa
(cay simin canan ancha ahca chay huarmi alliyascancama
chaytaca quepampiracmi quillcason cananri ñaupacman
cutison)[46]cay caycunacta villanacuptinsi chay huatya curi ñisca huyarcan
chay chica aton apo dios tucospa huncos<canta> cay runas
yscay churiyoc carcan chaysi huc yuyacnintaca huc

casarachircan   ayllonhuantac ancha rricohuan tinquichircan chaysi cay
huaccha huatya curi ñiscaca chay pacha honcoptin chay apoman
chayarcan [47] chaysi chayaspas<huaqui> huaticayllapi tapuyca
charcan manacho cay llactapi pillapas honcon ñispa chaysi
chay quipan sipas chorinca yayaimi honcon ñispa villar

ychaca caytas que   can chaysi ñocahuan cason camrayco yayaiquicta alliya
pampi chaupi ñamcacta   chisac ñispa villarcan (cay huarmip sutintam mana yachanchiccho)
ña sutiachircan   chaysi chay huarmica mana tuy
llaca hu ñircancho [48] chaysi yayantaca yaya caypim huc huac
cha yayaiquicta alliyachisac ñimuan ñispa villarcan chay
si cay simicta hoyarispas chay sauiocuna tiacca asicor
can ñocacunapas alliyachipticho chay huaccharac alliya
chinman ñispa chaysi chay apoca alliyaininta ancha mu
naspas hamuchontac yma yna runallapas ñispa cayachircan
[49] chaysi cayachiptin cay huatya curi ñiscaca yaicuspa ñispa ñirca
yaya alliyaita munaptiquica alliyachiscayqui hechaca chu
riquictam co<uay>anqui ñiptinsi paica ancha cusicuspa alli
tacmi ñispa ñircan chaysi chay ñaupac churinpa cosanca
cay simicta huyarispas ancha piñarcan himapacmi chay huc
huacchahuan tinquichisac ñispa ñin ñoca chica capacpac co
ñaday<ni>ta ñispa [50] cay runa piñacucpa huatya curihuan
aucanacuscantam caysa(ua) villason cananca chay huaccha
huatya curi ñiscap ampiscanman ñatac cotison
chaysi cay huatya curica ampijta ña callarircan yaya huarmiquim
huachuc ñispa chay hina huachoc hochayoc captinmi camta
honcochisonqui camta micucri cay chica collanan huasique
sahuam yscay machachuay tian chaymantam ampatori
yscay homayoctac maray hucopi tian [51] caycunactam canan
tucoyninta huañoshison chaymi alliyanqui chayman

F 68 R

tam ña alliyaspam tucoy hima aycacta yallispa ñocap yayai
ta muchanqui caya minchallam yurimunca camca manam
ari camac runacho canqui camac runa caspaca manam
ari honconquimancho ñispa ñiptinsi ancha mancharirca
[52] chaysi ña chay huasinta chica sumacta pascasac ñiptinsi
ancha llaquicorcan huarminsi hinatac yancam cay huac
cha acoylla ñihuan manam huachuccho cani ñispa capa
rircan [53] chaysi chay runa honcucca alliyaininta ancha
munaspas huasinta pascachircantac chaymantas yscay
machachuayta surcorcan ynaspa huañochircan huarmintari
hinatac suti villarcan ymanam chay huc muro sara pah
yamuspa pincayninman chayaicorcan ynaspa ñatac pallas
pa runacta cararcan chaycunacta chaysi chay huarmi
pas quipampica ancha chicanmi ñispa tucoyta villacorcan
[54] chaymantas ñatac marayninta atarichircan chaysi chay
hucomantaca huc ampato yscay homayoc llocsimuspa
chay anchi cucha huaycomanh pahuarircan chaypis
canancama tiacon huc pucyupi chay pucyus canan chay
pi runacuna chayaptinca ña ñispa chincachin ña ñis
pa locotapas ruran [55] cay tucoy ñiscanchiccunacta ña
puchocaptinsi <yayanca> chay huncuc runaca alliyarcan
ña alliyapuptinsi chay huatya curi ñiscaca ponchao
ninpi huc mita condor cotoman rircan chaypis chay pari
a caca ñisca huacaca pihca runto tiacorcan chay cayllampis
canan huayrapas pucorircan chaysi ñaupa pachaca manas
huayra ricurircancho [56] chayman rinan captinca punchao
ninpis chay alliyac runaca sipas churinta corcan chay
si yscaynillan chay horco quiticta porispa hochallicorcan
[57] cay hochallicoscanta ña chay huc ñaupac masan hoya
rispa<m>s ancha pincayta rurasac chay huacchacta ñispa
yallinacoyta ña callarirca chaysi huc ponchao chay ru
naca huauqui camhuan yallinacuson ymahuanpas cam
huacchcaraccho chica capacpa coñada<ni>yta huarmiyan
quiman ñispas ñircan chaysi chay huacchaca alli
tacmi ñispas yaianman + cayhinam ñihuan ñispa villa
coc rircan chaysi payca allitacmi ymata ñiptin

preguntar como se dize
este pucyu y en q(ue) p(ar)te esta

+ esto es uno de los hu(eu)os
dichos a quien este tenia
por p(adr)e

F 68 V

pas<tu> tuyllam ñocaman hamuanque ñispa ñircan [58] cay ya
llinacoysi cay hina carcan
huc ponchaosi vpyaihuan ynaspa taquihuan yallinacuson
ñispa ñircan chaysi cay huaccha huatya curi ñiscaca ya
yanman villacoc rircan chaysi ri chay huc horcoman
chaypim huanaco tucospa huañusca siriconqui chaymi tu
tallamantam ñocacta ricoque huc atoc añas huarminhuan
hamunca [59] chaymi huc huchoylla porongollapi ashuanta apa
munca ynaspa tinyantapas apamuncatac chaytam canan
camta huañusca huanacucta ricuspam chaycunantapas
pachapi churaspa atucri antaranta churaspatac micoyta
ña callarisonqui chaymi camca runa tucospa ancha na
nacta caparispa pauarimunqui chaymi paicunaca chay
nintapas mana yuyaspa miticaptinmi chayta apaspa
yallinacoypac rinqui ñispas yaian paria caca villarcan
[60] chaysi cay huacchaca ñiscancama rurarcan
chaysi ña yallinacospaca ñaupacñinsi chay runa rrico ñisca
taquircan chaysi huarmicunapas ñahca yscay pachac chica
taquipuptinsi ña pai pochocaptin chay huacchaca
yaycorcan sapallan huarmillanhuan yscaynillan chay
si ponconta yaicospatacsi chay añaspa huancarninta
apamus(can)<chay>huan taquiptin<si> tucoy chay pachapas cuyurcan
ynaspas chayhuanpas tucoyta yallircan [61] chaysi ñatac vpyai
ta callarircan chaysi ymanam canampas corpacuna anac
manta tiamun chay hinas çapallam huarmillanhuan tia
murcan chaysi chay runacunaca tucoy hinantin tiaccuna
ancosamurcan mana samachispa chaysi paica tucoyta
vpyaspapas mana llaquispa tiacorcan [62] chaysi ñatac pairi
chay huchoylla poroncollapi ashuan apamuscanhuan ancusay
ta ña callarircan runacunapas chica ochuyllapicho chica
runacta sacsachinman ñispa<s> asipayaptin chaysi paica
manyanmanta ancosamuspa sapampi tuylla tuylla hur
machircan [63] chaysi cayantin ñatac huc yallinacoyta atipap
tin munarcan cay yallinacoysi huallparicoy carcan an
cha allin cassa ñiscanhuan cancho ñiscanhuan chaysi cay
huatya curi ñiscaca ñatac yayanman rirca chaysi huc

F 69 R

razo pachacta yayanca cumurcan chayhuansi tucoy runacunac   o riti
tapas ñauinta rupachispa atiparcan [64] chaymantas ñatac
pomacta aparispa yallinacoson ñispa ñircan chaysi cay
runaca pomancunacta aparispa yallita munarcan chaysi
chay huacchaca yayan villaptin tutallamanta huc pucyo
manta puca pomacta apamurcan chay puca pomahuansi ca
nan taquiptin ymanam canan huc arco sieloñicpi llocsin
chay hina llocsiptin taquircan [65] chaymantas canan ñatac hua
si pircacoyhuan yallinacoyta munarcan chaysi chay runaca an
cha ahca runayoc caspa huc poncha(u)lla atun huasicta ñahca
tucochircan chaysi <pay> cay huacchaca ticsillanta churaspa
tucoy punchao huarmillanhuan poricorcan chay tutas canan
tucoy piscocuna chaymanta machachuaycuna yma ayca
pachapi caccunas pircarcan chaysi cayaca ña tucoscacta
ricuspa ancha mancharircan [66] chaymanta catanampipas
hinatacsi yallircan ocsantapas tucoy huanacocuna
vicoñaconas astamurcan chay runaptari llamanhuan
chacnacumuptinsi oscullocta mincaspa huc cacallapi
suyaspa mancharichispa tucoyta destruyrca hurmachir
can chayhuanpas hinatac yallircan [67] cay tucoyta yallina
cuspas quipampica cay huaccha ñiscaca ñispa ñircan
yayanpa simincama huauqui ñam chica ahca mita
campa simiquicta ho ñispa yallinaconchic cananca ño
cap simijtapas ho ñihuaytac ñispa ñiptinsi allitacmi
ñispa ho ñircan chaysi ñispa ñircan cananca ancas cusma
yoc chaymanta huaranchicri yurac hutco cachon hina
lla taquison ñispas ñiptinsi allitacmi ñircan [68] chaysi chay
runaca ñaupacmantapas payrac <taquic> ñaupac taquic
caspas taquircan ña taquiptinsi chay hatya curi ñis
caca hahuamanta caparispa callparimuptinsi chay runa
ca mancharispa huc lloycho tucospa miticarcan chay
si huarminpas cosallayhuantac huañosac ñispa catirir
can [69] chaysi chay huaccha ñiscaca ancha piñaspa ri hutic
cammi chica huatuycahuarcanquichic ñispa camtaca
huañochiscayquim ñispas catirircantac chaysi catispa
huarmintaca anchi cocha ñanpi apispas caypim ynantin

F 69 V

runa hanacmanta huramanta hamuc pincaynijque
ta ricupayasonqui ñispas huray çinca humanmanta sa
yachircan chaysi tuylla pachampitac rumi tucorcan [70] chay
rumis canancamapas himanam runap chancan hina

nota
preguntar para q(ue)
se pone esta coca

chancayoc racayoc tian chaytas ymancampach ari
cocacta chaysaua churapon (canancamapas) chaymantas chay lloycho
tucoc runaca hinallatac chay hurcucta sicaspa chin
carcan [71] chay lloychos canan ñaupa pachaca runa micoc
carcan quipampis canan ña ahca lloycho caspas yma
ynam runacta micosonchic ñispa cahchuacorcan chay
si huc huahuallanca hima ynam runa micohuason
ñispa pantarcan chayta hoyarispas lloychoconaca
chiquirircan chaymantas lloychopas runap miconan
carcan [72] cay ñisca<y>(nchic)cunacta ña puchocaptinsi paria caca

paria cacap yuri
muscan

ñiscaca pihca runtomanta pihca huaman pahyamur
can chay pihca huamansi ñatac runaman tucuspa
purirircan chay pachas ancha chaycunap rurascancunac
ta vyarispa ymanam chay runapas   sutioc dios
me cani ñispa muchachicorcan chay chay huchancuna
mantas piñaspa tamya hatarispa mama cochaman<>
tucoy hinantin huasintahuan llamantahuan aparcan
mana hucllactapas quispichispa [73] chaymanta chay pa
chatacsi cay llantapa hurcomanta huc pullao sutioc
chay huc urco vichoca ñiscahuan apinacorca arcohina
chay pullao ñiscas ancha aton sacha carca chaysauas cusi
llupas caquipas yma ayca ricchaccuna piscocunapas
tiacoc carcan chaycunactahuansi tucoy hinantinta cocha
man aparcan caycunactas ña pochocaspa ñatac pari
a caca hanac canan paria caca ñinchic chayman vichay
corca chay vichaycoscantam canan quipan capitulo
pi rimason
[74] CAPIT(UL)O 6 COMO PARIA CACA NAÇIO ÇINCO ALCONES
Y DESPUES TORNO EN PER(SON)AS Y COMO ESTANDO YA
VENÇIDOR DE TODOS LOS YUNGAS DE ANCHI COCHA
EMPEÇO A CAMINAR AL D(ICH)O PARIA CACA Y LO QUE
SUÇEDIO POR LOS CAMINOS

F 70 R

ña paria caca runaman tucuspas aton ña caspa enemigon
ta mascayta ña callarircan chaysi chay enemigonpa sutinri
<ri>huallallo carvincho carcan runacta micoc hupyac cay<mi>
tam cay quipampi churason atinacuscantahuan ñam hari chay
huallallo carvinchup causascantaca runa micuscanta(huan)pas yma
ayca rurascantauanpas ñaupac capitulopi rimarcanchic
[75] canami rimason huaro cheripi chay chay quitipi rurascancunac
ta chay simire caymi ña paria caca haton runa caspas hanac
paria caca ñiscaman huallallo caruinchup tiascanman rir
can [76] chaysi huaro cheri chay hura huaycupica huc llacta huau
qui husa sutioc yuncap llactan carca chaysi chay llactayoc ru
nacunaca chay pacha haton fiestacta rucraspa haton vpiayta
vpyarcancu chay hina vpyacuptinsi paria caca ñiscaca
chay llactapi chayarcan chayaspas payca runacunap manyallan
manta tiaicorcan huaccha ynalla [77] chay hina tiaptinsi chay llac
tayoc runacunaca mana hucllapas ancosarcancho tucoy punchao
chay yna captinsi huc huarmica chay llactayuctac añañi yma
ynam chay huacchallactaca mana ancosayconcho ñispas huc
haton yurac potohuan ashuacta apamuspa corcan [78] chaysi
payca pani ancha cosiocmi canqui cay ashuacta comuaspa
canan punchaomanta pihccantin punchaoninpi himactahc
cay llactapi riconqui chayrayco chay ponchaoca amatac cay
lla(c)tapi tianquicho carollamantac anchorinque pactah cam
tauan huahuayquictauan pantaspa huañochiquiman an
cham cay runacuna ñocacta piñachihuan ñispas chay huar
micta ñircan chaymantari cay runacunactari amatac
huc simillactapas hoyarichicho oyarichiptiquica camtahuan
rni huañochiquiman ñispas ñircan [79] chaysi chay huar
mica huahuancunahuan turancunahuan chay pihca pon
chaomanta chay llactamanta anchoricorcan chaysi chay
llactayoc runacunaca mana llaquispa vpiacorcancu
chay pachas paria caca ñiscaca guaro cheri hanacnin
horcuman vichaycorcan chay horcom canan matao
coto sutioc chay huraynin huc horcom puypu huana
sutioc maytam caymanta rispa huaro cheriman hu
rayconchic chaycunam cay hina sutioc [80] chay orcopis

el capit(ul)o primero

F 70 V

paria caca chimparcan
cuparap llactanman

canan chay paria cacaca haton tamyayta ña callarircan
chaysi quillo runto puca runto hatarispas chay runacu
nactaca tucoyninta mama cochaman aparcan mana
hucllactapas perdonaspa chay pacha chica yaco lloclla
purispas chay huaro cheri anacnincuna huaycucunac
tapas rurarcan chaymantas canan ña chay(cuna)cta pucho
caspas chay llactayoc huaquinin yuncacunactaca mana
rimapayaspa paycunari<ancha alli> chayta ricuspapas
mana musyaptin yachaptinsi chay chimpañic cuparap
chacrancunaman ripurcan [81] chaypis canan chay llactayoc
cupara runacuna ancha yaconmanta ñacarispa pucyo
llamanta chacranmanpas posaspa causarcan <> cay puc
yum canan s(a)n lorenço hanacnin aton orcomanta llocsir
can chay orcum canan suna caca sutioc chaypis canan ha
ton cochalla carcan chaymanta huray pusamuspas ña
tac huchuilla cochacunaman hontachispa chacrancunac
ta parco(cuc) carcan [82] chay pachas chay llactayoc huc huarmi
chuqui suso sutioc carcan ancha sumac huarmi chaysi cay
huarmica sarancuna ancha chaquiptin huacacospa
parcocorcan yacon ancha pisi captin chaysi chay paria caca
ca chayta ricuspa chay huchoylla cochanta yacollanhuan
chay cochap siminta quirpaicoporcan [83] chaysi chay huarmica
ñatac ancha nanacta huacacorcan chay hinacta ricuspa
chaysi chay paria cacaca pani ymac(tam) <> chica huacanque
ñispa taporcan chaysi payca cay sara(llay)mi yacumanta cha
quipuan yaya<ñiptinsi> ñispa ñircan chaysi paria cacaca
ama llaquicho ñocam yacuctaca cay cochayquimanta
ancha ahca yacucta llocsichimusac hichaca camhuan
<> ñaupac(rac) puñuson ñispa ñircan [84] ñiptinsi canan pay
ca ñirca ñaupacrac cay yacocta llocsichemuy <> chac
ray parcusca captinca allitacmi puñoson ñispas ñircan chay
si allitacmi ñispa yacoctaca ancha ahcacta llocsichimurcan
chaysi chay huarmipas ancha cusicospa tucoy chacrancunac
ta parcocorcan chaysi ña parcoyta puchoca<spari>ptinca puño
son ñispa ñircan chaysi manam <cay> cananca caya mincharac
poñoson ñiptinsi paria cacaca ancha chay huarmicta munaspa

F 71 R

puñoymanrac ñispas yma aycactapas chay huarmiman pro
metircan cay chacraiquicta mayomanta yacuyuctam rura
puscayque ñispa [85] chaysi chay huarmica chaytarac ñaupac ruray
chayrac puñuson ñispa ñircan chaysi paria cacaca allitacmi ñispas
coco challa sutioc huaycumantas s(a)n lorenço anacnin huchuilla
hurco chay camaca ñaupamantapas yuncacunap rarcansi ha
murcan ancha huchuylla rarcalla chaytas canan paria cacaca
astauanri hatonyachispa chay hura cuparap chacrancama
rarcacta chayachircan [86] chay rarcactas canan pumacuna
hatuccuna machachuaycuna yma ayca piscocuna picharcan
allicharcan cayta ña allichaypacmi cay pumacuna oturungo
pas yma aycapas pim ñaupac siqueson ñispa camachinacor
can chaysi hucpas hucpas ñocarac ñocarac ñispa ñircancu
chaysi hatoctac atiparcan ñocam curaca cane ñocarac
ñaupasac ñispa chaysi pay atoc ñaupamurcan [87] yna ña
upamuspa ña chaupicta s(a)n lorenço hanacnin hurcucta seque   ñaupamuspa ña
mup<>tinsi concayllapi huc yutuca pisc pisc ñispa pahua
rimurcan chaysi chay hatocca huac ñispa muspaspa hura
man hurmamurcan chaysi chaymanta chaycunaca ñatac
ancha piñaspa machachuayta sequechimurcan chaysi ma
na chay hurmamuptinca astahuan hanacnintas chay rarca
nin rinman carca chaysi cunanca as huranta rin cay atoc
pa hormamuscanmi canancamapas sutilla ricurin yacu
pas huraycumuntac (chay atocpa vrmascanta) [88] cay tucoyta puchocaspam ñatac paria
cacaca puñoson ñispa ñircan chaysi <> ñatac haco anac cacaman
chaypirac poñoson ñispa <llollachircan> (ñircan) chay cacam canan
yana caca sutioc chaypis huaque puñorcan ña puñospas canan
chay huarmica haco yscayninchictac maytapas rison ñiptinsi pai
ca aco ñispa chay coco challa ñisca rarcap llocsimuscanman pu
sarcan [89] chaysi chaypi chayaspaca chay huarmi chuqui suso ñis
ca sutiocca cay <ray>rarcaypitac tiasac ñispas chaypi rumi tu
cuspa chira<hua>yarca chaysi chay paria cacaca chaymanta sa
quispa hanacman vichaycorcan chaytaca cay quipanpin villason
[90] cay coco challa ñisca rarcap siminpim canan rumi chirahuas   cunirayap tiascan
ca tian chay chuqui suso ñisca huarmi ynaspam chay hanac   chuqui susop cayllan
nin huc rarcapi<m>tacmi chay pachapas vincompa sutiocpim   pi

F 71 V

canan ñatac cuni ra(ya) chirahuasca(tac) tian chaypim canan cuni
raya pochocarcan ychaca yma ayca rurascantaca cay
huaquin quepanpi capitulocunapim villason
[91] CAPITULO 7 YMANAM CHAY CUPARACUNA
CHAY CHUQUI SUSO ÑISCACTA CANANCAMAPAS
YUYPAYCHAN
cay cuparacunam huc ayllo cupara ñisca ayllo sutioc cay
cunam canan s(a)n lorençopi reduzisca canancamapas causan
cay ayllomantam canan huc yumay chauincho sutioc cay
chauincho <huarmin>(ayllom) carcan chay chuqui suso ñisca chaymi
caycunaca ñaupa pacha ña may pacham rarca pichana carca
mayo quielapi canancamapas chay pacham tucoy hinantin ru
nacuna chay chuqui suso ñisca huarmip tiascan<huan>man rircancu
<>ashuanhuan tictinhuan cuynhuan llamanhuan [92] chaypi
chay supay huarmicta muchaypac chaymi ña chayta muchaspari
pihca ponchaosi chaypi quishuaruan quenchaspa runacunacta
pas mana purichispa chaypi tiapayarcan chaysi ña chayta pu
chucaspa rarca pichaynintahuanpas tucoyta ña puchocaspas chay
manta taquispa runacuna hamurcan huc huarmictare cay
mi chuqui suso ñispa payta yna alli manchaspa chaopipe
pusamurcancu [93] chaymi ña llactanpi chay huarmi chayaptinri
caymi chuqui suso ñispa huaquin ashuahuan ymauan churapus
pa suyarcan chaypi tucoy huinantin tuta taquispa vpiaspa
runacuna ancha aton fiestacta rurarcancu chaymantam
ñaupa don sebastian apo causaptinpas corpus xp.^(christi)pi aton
pascuacunapipas huc huarmi chuqui susom cani ñispa haton
aquellahuan aton potohuanpas ashuacta manyanmanta
cumuc carcan caymi mamanchicpac ashuan ñispa chay
mantari saractapas camchascacta aton matihuantac cu
muc carcan [94] ña cay rarcacta pichayta puchocamuspari ru
nacunacta anchapunis combidac carcan saracta purotucta
yma aycacta(pas) cuspa cay yna vinaycoc captinsi runa
cunapas ñam chuqui susup rarcanta pichan haco ricumu
son ñispa huaro cherimantapas tucoy llactacunamantapas ric

F 72 R

carcan [95] chaytam canan ña rarcacta pichaspaca musiasca yna
tac ruran muchan runacunari yma yna ruracuptinpas
alcaldepas yma ayca runacunapas manam ymaraycom
chay hina ruranque ñispa amachanmancho canancamapas
porque yallinracmi payhuan taquen vpyan machas
cancama p(adr)ectari rarcactam pichamuni p(adr)e taquecusac v
piacusac ñispam llollachen caytaca tucoy hinantin
runacunam ruraytaca ruran ychaca huaquinca ma
na ñam rurancho alli p(adre)oc caspa huaquenri pacallapica
ynatac canancamapas causanco
[96] CAPIT(UL)O 8 YMANAM PARIA CA
CA VICHAYCORCAN YMANAM
HUC RUNA CHURINUAN PARIA CACAP
SIMENCAMA CUTIMURCAN CHAYMAN
TARI YMANAM ATINACORCAN
HUALLALLO CARUINCHOUAN
ñam ari huallallo caruinchop causascantaca villarcanchic
ychaca caypa tiascantam llactachacuscantam mana ri
marcanchiccho chaysi cayca<huallallo caruincho> ñaupa pacha
hanac pariacañicpi tiarcan chay tiascampas sutintam ma
na allicho yachanchic cananca mullo cocha sutioc ña captin
porque paria cacam payta atispa chay huallalloca nina rupap
tin chayta huañochipac cochaman ña tucochircan [97] chay
mullo cocha ñiscanchic pachapis chay huallallop tiascan car
ca chay pachas canan tucoy hinantin pacha yuncasapa car
can aton <> (ma)chachuaypas caquepas yma ayca animal
cunapas hontaptinsi tiarcan ymanam ñaupac capi(tul)o   1 capi(tul)o
pi runa micuscanta villanchic chay hina [98] chaymantas

ocsa pata   paria cacaca cay huallallo caruinchocta atipac rispas <hucsa>ocsa
es junto a   patapi pihcantin riuicorcan chay hina riuicoptinsi chay   pihca
paria caca   pachapas ancha chirircan runtopas hormamurcantac paypac
                   pucllascanpi [99] chaysi chay pacha huc runaca huaca

F 72 V

DEZIR LO DE LA CULEBRA

cuspa hamurcan huc churinta apaspa chaymanta mullon
tapas cocantapas tictincunactapas huallallocta vpiachi
musac ñispa apaspa chaysi chay paria cacap cap huc

saber los n(ombr)es de estos
5 her(man)os

nin(ca) churi maymanmi yna huacacuspa rinque ñis
pa taporcan chaysi payca yaya cay cuyascay churi
llaytam canan apani huallallocta caramuc ñiptinsi

los n(ombr)es de estos cinco
her(man)os son paria caca
churapa, puncho, pari
a carcu no sauemos
el n(ombr)e de vno de estos
çinco

churi ama apa<y>nquicho llactayquiman cutichicoy chay
mantam chay mulloyquitaca cocayquitaca tictiquita
ca ñocacta coay chaymanta churiquitaca cutichicoy
ñispa ñircan [100] chaymantari pihcantin ponchaopim cay
man cotimunqui ñocacta atinacocta ricoypac ancha ya
cuhuan atipaptica yayanchicmi atipan ñispan ñihuan

#azul claro era

qui ynaspa anchatac ninahuan atipahuanca chay
ca atipay tucontacmi ñispatac ñihuanqui ñiptinsi
chay runaca mancharispa yaya manacho chayca hua

    hijos
curaca o ancacha el 1°
chauca el 2°
lluncu el 3°
sullca el 4°
llata el 5°
ami el 6° -ys-
    hijas
paltacha o cochucha la 1ª
coba pacha la 2ª
ampuche la 3ª
sullcacha la 4ª
ecancha la 5ª
anacha anasi

paria cacap atiscan

llallo caruincho ñocapac pinaconca ñi<ptinsi>spa ñirca
[101] ñiptinsi piña(co)chonpas manam yma nasonquecho yallin
racmi ñocaca runacta camasac amiyocta llatayoc
ta huarmictari añasiyocta hucta cari hucta huar
micta ynam camasac ñispa rimaptinsi siminman
ta samaynin huc humo <asol> (ancas) # yna llocsimorcan chaysi
chay runaca chayta ricuspa mancharispa tucoy apamuscan
ta co<po>rcan chaysi chay pihca runaca chay mullocta
cap cap ñichispa micorcan tucoy hinantin coscantahuan
chaymantas chay runaca cutimorcan churinta apacospa
[102] ynaspas ñatac pihcantin ponchaomanta ñatac chay pa
ria cacap simincama cotircan ricu<>musac ñispa
chaymantas ña paria caca pihca ponchao ñiscanmanta
chay huallallo caruinchocta atita ña callarircan chay simi
ri cay hinam paria caca pihca runa caspas pihca pacha
manta tamyaita ña callarirca chay tamyas canan
quello puca tamya carcan chaymantas yllapaspa
ri pihca pachamantatac yllaparcan [103] chaysi tuta
llamanta ña hora pachacama chay huallallo caruin
choca <nina> ancha aton nina ñahca sieloñicmanpas
chayaspa ruparca mana huañochichicospa chaysi

F 73 R

chay yacocu<paria cacap huquinca>naca paria cacap tamyascancunaca hura
cochañicman tucoy hinantin yacucona rircan chaysi chay yna <ma>
manatac yaycuptin<si> huquenca (llacsa churapa sutioc) hurañicmanta yacucta huc hor
cucta ormachispa arcamorcan [104] ña arcaycomuptinsi chay yacuca
cocha ña tucomurca cay cocham cananca mullo cocha sutioc chay
yna chay cochapi ña yaco hontamup(tinsi)<> chay nina rupacta(ca) ñah

ca pamparca chaysi chay paria cacari chaymanta yllapapayarca   sauer si estos son her(man)os
mana samachispa ynallas chay huallallo caruinchoca anti   pues se dize q(ue) salieron de
ñicman miticarcan [105] chaysi huquenca paria cacap churin catir   los hu(eu)os o si son hijos
can chaysi chay antip yaicunampi pactah cutimunman   del paria caca<>
ñispa canancamapas chaypi tian caypac sutinmi <sullca ylla>   her(man)os eran
<pa> (paria carco) [106] chaymantas ña atisptin<> mana ñamca sutioc huc huar
mi carcan cay huallallo caruinchohuan cac supay cay huarmis
canan mama oraynin chay chaypi tiarcan cayta atipacsi ña
tac payman amorcan chaysi chay mana ñamca<ca> ñiscaca nina
tac ruparcan chaysi cay tumna huranta yaycuspa paria ca
caca <ati> aucanacorca chaysi huc paria cacap churinta chu
qui huampo sutiocta chaquinpi huramanta chucamuspa   sauer como esta este
chayachimurcan chaysi yna captin(pas) paria cacatac atiparcan
cochañicman carcospa [107] ña caycunacta atipaspas
chay churin chuqui huampo sutioc anca chaquen paquisca tia
cucman cotimurcan chaysi chayca amatac cotisaccho cay
llamanta chay huarmi mana ñamcacta huacaychasac pac
tah cutimunman ñispa ñiptinsi allitacmi ñispa yayanca
tucoy miconampac camachiporcan [108] chaysi ñispa ñircan cay escay
huaycocunamantam tucoy runacuna camtarac ñaupac cocacta
comusonque manarac pillapas acuspa ña cam acoptiiqueracmi
chaymanta runacunapas acoconca cocanta mallquiscanmanta
chaymantam llamactari viñay<> (vrua mana huachacoc) cactaracmi naca
pusonque ynaspa rinrin chillpiscacta cay caycunactaracmi
camca viñaypas miconque ñispas camachirca [109] chaysi   este lugar donde
runacunaca chay camachiscan simicta yupaychaspa chay   esta<sullca yllapa>chuqui huampo esta
cama saci cayamanta chontaymanta chichimamanta mama   abajo de tumna entre sici
manta huayo callamanta sucya canchamanta tucoy coca   caya y sucya he de uerlo
yoccuna ñaupacnintaca paymanrac apamoc carcan   sauer como se llama
canancamapas pacallapica ynatacsi causancu

F 73 V

[110] CAPITULO 9 YMANAM PARIA CACA ÑA
TUCOYTA POCHOCASPA PAYTA MUCHACHI
COYPAC HONANCHARCA CALLARIRCAN

ñam hari tucoy hinantin atiscancunacta pochocan
chic ychaca cay huallallo caruinchop quepanpi paria ca
cap sentenciascancama causascantam mana rimanchiccho

suer como esta ahora
este caruincho en
los andes

ña atispas huallallo caruincho antiman ñan miticoptin
chay huallallocta runa micoscanmanta cunanca all
cucta micochon chaytari huancacuna muchachon ñis
pa sentenciarcan [111] chaysi canan huancacunaca payta
muchaspa allcucunahuan muchac carcan payri dios
nin allcocta micuptin allcuctatac micorcancu canan
camapas huanca allco micuc ñispa ñinchic

capit(ul)o 1°

[112] chaymantas canan ymanam ñaupac capitulopi quepan
pipas tucoy llactacunam yuncaçapa carcan ñispa ñinchic
chay hinam cay tucoy hinantin llactacunapi guaro cheri pro
uinciapi chaclla mama prouinciapipas tucoy hinantin
llactacunapipas yuncaçapas carcan cay yuncacunactam
tucoy hinantin yuncacunacta hurañicman anchurichir

paria cacap churin
cuna

can churijcuna cay q(ui)tipi tianca ñispa honanchaspa [113] caycu
nacta aticcunapas sapampi paria cacap churincuna sutioc
sapam hucmi churin ñin huaquenmni manas paycamas sachap
ruruyninmanta yurimurcan ñispa rimanco caycunap su
tinri caymi mayorninmanta chuc paico chancha runa
huari runa vtco chuco tutay quiri huauquinri sasen male cay
chicam chay yuncacunacta atircancu [114] chaymantam huc
paria cacap churinsi pachamanta paycama llocsimurcan cay

quepanpi churason
pacha chuyrop atiscan
ta

pac sutinmi pacha chuyru sutioc (carcan) caypac huc atiscantapas
hanac tucoynin capitulocunapipas concanchicmi chaytaca
cay quipanpiracmi churason cay ñiscanchiccunam tucoy
hinantin yuncacunacta atircan anchorichircan [115] chaymi
cay yuncacunapas ñaupa diosnintaca ña concaspa pari
a cacacta ña muchayta callarirca tucoy yuncacuna chay yun

F 74 R

cacunari caymi cay checap llactanpica colli ñiscam tiar
can tucoy llactampi tiascancunacta<m> ruraspaca ancha
sasam canman chayraicom huaquenintaca hunanchan
canchicpac cay quepampi rurason tucoy causascantahuan
porque yuncacunaca huc causayniocllam tucoynin(pas) carcan
[116] chaymantam cay paria caca ñiscanchicca hanac <pay> maypim
atircan chay pachallanpi tiayta ña callarircan muchachicon
campacri hunancharcan cay hunanchascanmi tucoy hinan
tin llactacunapipas huc vnanchayllam cay honanchay ñis

canchicri cay ynam tucoy hinantin huc yuric canchic [117] chay   esto se entiende de
cunamantas sapampi huquenta camachircan cammi huatam   vna familia
pi ñocap causascayta catispa pascuacunacta ruranque
ñispa caycunap sutinmi huacasa (o huacsa) sutioc canca cay hua
casmi canan huatampi quimça mita taquenca ancha hatun cara
huayacapi cocacta apamuspa [118] caytam ña ñaupac cay huacasa

man tucoypac<ri> huc vnanchaytatac runacuna rurancu chay   el maestro se llama
ri cay ynam huc runam caca sica ayllo(manta) cay causaycuna   yañca
pac maestron ancha ñaupamanta caycunam huquen o yscaypas   esto es la s(om)bra q(ue)
maestron caspa sutinri yañca sutioc cay sutillatacmi ynan   ua haziendo la pared
tin llactacunapipas cay runas huc pircamanta allin ya   con el sol
chacochisca pircascamanta ricon <punchaupa> (yntip) poriscanta chaysi
may pachach chay hunanchasca pircanman chayan chayca ca
nanmi(mana ñispari)cayam ñispapas(risun ñin) runacunacta <villarca>[119] chayta catis
pas runacunapas paria cacaman muchaypac rincu ñaupa
pachaca quequinmansi ric carcan cananca cay checamantaca

huc orco ynca caya sutiocmansi rinco chaymanta muchancan   este cerro se parece
pac chay <pacham> orcom canan ñaupa purom huasimanta ha   la nieue de paria caca
nacnin horco hoc orco huallqueri sutiochuan quellinacon
cay orco ñiscapim canan runacuna tucoy ynantin runa
cuna cari huarmi rispa(muchancu) [120] ña chay orcoman sichpaypac(ri) chay
yañcap simincamas ñocaracpas ñaupac(umanman)chayaiman ñispa ya   q(ue) es de donde se parece
llinacon llama orcontapas catispa ancha sinche runacuna
huchoylla llamanhuanpas (ancha otcaspas) [121] cay ñaupac chay orcoman chayac
llamas paria cacap ancha munascan cay orcoctas ñaupa pacha   nombres diferentes cada
quequen paria cacaca yma sutillactapas suti(a)chec carcan   vez de vna man(er)a y otra
cay sutiocmi canca ñispa huchoylla llama chayactari   de otra como yauri o y
                                         llaca

F 74 V

chay yañca ñisca cay llamayocmi ancha cusioc paria ca
cam coyaijcun ñispa allin sutinchac ñavinchac carcan

auquisna
para n(uest)ro padre o criador
chaycasna
para n(uest)ra m(adr)e

[122] cay muchacuy pacham auquisna sutioc ynatacmi chavpi ñam
ca muchacoypas chaycasna sutioc caytan cay quepanpim villason
cay avquisna sutioc pacham canan junio quella chay chay
pachapi <ormamun> (chayamun) ña ñispa ñahca<corpus xptimanpas>
          (aton pascuapipas tincon)
<tincon> ña ñispari tinconpas cay pachapim cay huacasa

saber este genero
de canto y ponermelo
en vn papel en lengua
de chechhua de
lo q(ue) dizen

ñiscanchic chunca caspapas yscay chunca caspapas taquinco
cay taquicoytas manatac yayancunap chapascan [123] huacsa
caytaca manapuni ancochaspas taquinco cayta ancochac
taca huañuptinpas chay hochanmantam huañon ñispas
ñincu chayraycos ochuillac(ta)pas yma yna runallac
tapas taquichin yallinrac surco runacunaca huay
llascunactapas chay ranti taquichen [124] chay llactayoc
huarmihuan casarasca captinca caycunacta rurap
tinsi manatac chay llactayocpas chacranta yman
tapas quechoncho forastero captinpas yallinrac yupai
chan yanapan chay huayllascunam(canan) mayquin runa
caspapas surcopi tiaccunaca suquia canchaman cocacta
rantic hamuspapas huacasmi cani mama yapahuay
ñispa rantinco[125]cay pascuactam canan yma aton xp.^(christia)nop
pascuancunaman chayachispa taquinco yallin tucoy
llactacunactapas yallispa surcopi runacunaca cay ta
quiscanmantam llactampi padrenpas aguelandocta
mañan huallpacta saracta yma aycactapas caytam
runacunari ancha cusicospa concu

chaupi ñamcap cas
cantaca huc quipan
pi capit(ul)opim churason

[126] ynatacmi chavpi ñamcap pascuanpipas cay huacsacuna
ñisca taquencu cay pascuam canan ñahcca corpus xpi^(chris)ti
man tincon ña ñispari tincompas caypac cascantaca may
pi tiascantapas runacunap muchascantahuanpas quipan
pim huc capitulopi churason
ñatac paria cacap cascanman cutison yma ymactach ru
nacuna chay pacha pascuanpi rurar<n>can [127] chay chaycunacta
villaypac chay simire cay ymam ña caya paria caca
man <chayaypacsi> muchaypac chayaipacsi chay huata
huañocnioc runacuna caripas huarmipas captin tucoy

F 75 R

chay tuta huacac carcan cayam paria cacap cayllanpi
huañocninchicta ricomuson ñispa [128] chay huata huañoc
nincunactari cayallatacmi chaypi chasquechimu
son ñispa chay tuta caraspa micochispa yma ayca rura
nancunactapas chaypi churapuspa cananmi viñaypac
paria cacaman pusani <ñispa> mana ñam cutimunca
cho viñaypas ñispam huchoylla llamanhuan mana
llama captinri haton cara huayacapi cocacta huallquis
pa mucharcanco [129] cay llamactam canan sonconmanta
ricorcan alli captinpas allim ñispa mana alli captin
ri manam allicho ochayocmi canqui paria cacactam
huañocnique(pas) piñachircan cay ochacta perdonta ma
ñay(tac) pacta camman chay ocha anchorimunman ñis
pa chay yamca ñisca ñircanco [130] chaymanta ña chay
chaycunacta puchocaspari chay llamap vmanta hua
santauansi chay yañcacuna ayca huaranga captin
pas apacuc carcan cayca ñocap chanimi ñispa
[131] chaymantam canan cay huacasa ñiscanchic huc huatapi
quimca mita taquispam cay hina ponchaopitac puchocarcan
huc musoc yaicoypacri quepa ña taquicoyta poncho
caypac captinmi tucoynin llacsa tampopi ynatac
conchacunapas pampampi <> chaupiman yaicoc
carcan huc huayta<> huacamaypac ricranta o ymanta
pas puypu ñiscacta apaspa chaytam canan chaupi
pi llacsa tambo ñisca rumipi churac carcancu chayta
ña churaspam tucoynin maypim canan cruz churas
ca chaypi tucoy tuta tiarcancu allicho casac canan hua
ta ñispa [132] chaymantam cayantinri tucoy llactacu
naman rispa macacho orcomanpas chaucallaman
pas quemquellamanpas asta pihcca ponchao on
tascancama ña pihca ponchao ontaptinmi tucoy
huacasacuna cocacta huallquispa taquic carcan
chay ponchaotacmi ancha tutamanta llacsa tambo
pi supayta muchac carcancu llamanhuan yman
huan [133] ynatacmi musiasca tucoy ynantin llac
tacunapipas rurancu ychaca cananca ña concan

F 75 V

cay pisi huatallarac cay doctor fran(cis)co de auila alli cunaqui
yoc yachachiquiyoc caspa chaypas manataccha soncocama
ca y ñinmancho ñatac hoc padreyoc caspaca ynamantac
cha cutinman [134] huaquin runacunaca christiano tucos
papas manchaspallam pactach padrepas pipas yacha
huanman mana alli cascayta ñispallam xp.^(christia)no tucon
rrosariocta resaspapas sumac hillantam apaycachan
mana quequen cay muchanacunacta muchaspapas

<ojo> huaquen machocunacta mincaspa paypac rantin mu
chachispa achica runam yna causanco

[135] cay ñiscanchic ynalla<m>tacmi conchaconapas cay pa
ria cacap mitampi chay hoc vrco huaycho sutiocmanta
muchancu huacasa ñiscanri quequin checacunapas

ojo ruran ynallatacsi ruran taquen
chaymanta suni canchari chay huc vrco   sutioc
manta ynallatac muchancu paria cacap mitanpi
[136] chaymanta santa anacuna s(a)n ju(a)npi cacpas tucoynin chauca
ricma ñiscari chay apar huayqui mayoman hurayconchic
acu sica sutioc vrcocta chaymantatacsi muchanco pari
a cacap mitanpi caycunacta ruraypacca manam ancochan
mancho huaquen aton pascuapi huaquenri ñachca esperi
tu santoman tincochen<corpusmanpas> cayta ruraypacri
ancham cusiconman cay llactapi p(adr)e yllaptin limac
manpas riptin cayca ancha checan simin
[137] cay tucoy ñiscanchic<cuna> vrcocunapi paria caca
muchanacunactaca cay quepanpi vira cochacuna pa
carimurcan ricurimurcan chaymantaracmi yacha
cochircan [138] ychaca ñaupa pachaca quiquin pariacaman
si tucoy ynantin runacuna ric carcan tucoy yunca
cunapas colli ñiscamanta caruayllomanta ruri can
chomanta latimmanta huancho huaillamanta pa
riachamanta yañacmanta chichimamanta mama
manta tucoy ynantin yuncacuna chay huc mayo ñis
camanta chaymantari ynatac caçi cayacuna
pas tucoy ynantin huc mayo ñisca pacha camac
cunapas chaymanta caringa chilcacunapas

F 76 R

chaymanta huaro cheri huray mayopi cac runacunari
tucoy carancocuna yma ayca yuncacunapas tucoy
ynantin chay mayo ñisca yuncacunas tectinhuan
cocanhuan yma ayca muchanancunahuan a
muspas quequin paria cacapi chayac carcanco [139] cay
hamuccuna ña paria cacamanta cutiptinsi llactam
pi runacunapas chayananta yachaspa tocoy runacu
na hoñolla suyac carcan tapucoypac ymanam yayan
chic paria caca alliraccho manacho piñacon ñispa
chaymantas ancha cosicospa taquic carcan asta pocho
cascancama pichca ponchaopas ayca ponchaocha causa
nan carca yna [140] cay muchaycoytaca yuncacuna
ca mana ñach rurancho tucoy yuncacunapas ycha
ca pachallanmantaca ruran cayta mana ruraptin
si chay hochanmantam yuncacuna collon ñispa
rimancu paycona yuncacunari rimacuspa sall
cacunaca allim causan ñaupa causananchicta
chay yna causaspam runapas miran ñincu
[141] CAPITULLO 10 YMANAM CHA
UPI ÑAMCA CARCAN MAYPIM
TIAN YMANAM MUCHACHICORCAN
ñam ari paria cacap causascantaca villacoyta pu
chucarcanchic ychaca chay churincunap cay iscon
nin capitulopi vnanchasca cactaca cay quepampi
racmi sapampi rurascantahuan villason yunca
cuna ñiscanchic cay llactacunamanta atiscancu
nactauanpas chaymantam canan quillcason chaupi ñam
cap cascanta [142] cay chaupi ñamca sutiocsi huc runa anchi
cochapi apo tamta ñamca sutiocpac churin carcan chay huc huac
cha huatya curi ñiscap huarmin cay simictam ari pichcan
tin capitulopipas rimarcanchic [143] cay huarmis pichca ñaña
yoc carcan chaysi cay ñaupac huarmi chaupi ñamucaca

paria cacap churin
cunap atiscancunac
tam cay quepanpi chu
rason

F 76 V

llamase chavpi nanca
o mama nanca

paria cacap simincama hura mama ñiscapi tiaypac rir
can cay mana ñamca ñisca huarmis ñocam runacu
nacta camac cani ñispa purircan huaquem runacunam
canan chaupi ñamcacta paria cacap paninsi carca ñispa
ñinco pay quiquin rimacuspapas paria cacam tu
ray ñispas ñircan [144] cay chaupi ñamcas canan pichca
ricra rumi carcan chirayasca payta muchaypacri yma
nam paria cacaman yallinacuspa rircan ynallatacsi
ña chayaipac yallinacuc carcan llamanta ymantapas
catispa chay llama paria cacaman ric quiquillan(ta)tacsi
chaymanpas pusac carcan (ynaspa) cay chaupi ñamca pichca ric
ra rumictas canan quepanpi vira cochacuna ricurimup
tin chay mamapi padrep huasen cauallo huasi chay chaypi
pacha vcupi pacaycorcan chaypis canancamapas tian pa
cha vcupi [145] cay chaupi ñamcactas canan tucoy ynantin runa
cuna mama ñispa ñircancu chaymantam canan s(a)n pedro
pas mama ñisca cay huarmis canan ñaupa pacha
runa purispa ynantin huacacunahuan vchallicuc
carcan chaysi manatac pi carillactapas cayca allim
ñispa yupaychaccho carcan [146] chaysi huc carica canan
mama hanacnin vrcopi huacatac rucana cuto sutioc
cay rucana coto sutioctas runacunapas vchoylla ollo
yoc caspaca aton canca ñispa mañac carcancu cayssi
huc mita chaupi ñamcacta ancha allinta aton ollo
caspa sacsachircan chayraycos cay carillam alli cari
tucoy huacacunamantapas cayhuantac viñay ti
asac ñispa chay mama ñiscapi tiaycorcan rumi
man tucospa
[147] chaymantam canan cay chaupi ñamcap ñañancuna<c>
<ta> ñiscanchicta villason cay chaupi ñamcas tucoynin
manta mayornin carcan chaysaua ñañansi llacsa hua
to carcan chaysaua yoricsi mira uato carcan chaysauas
vrpay huachac sutioc carcan cay hoquentam mana yachan
chiccho tucoyninca pichcas carcan chaysi ymallata
runacuna yuyachicuptinpas ña ñispaca ñañay
cunahuanrac villanacomusac ñispa ñic carcan

F 77 R

[148] cay chaupi ñamca muchacoytam runacuna junio quella
pi ñahca corpus xp.^(chris)timan chayaicochin chay yañca   yañca
ñiscanchic ynte ricunanmanta ricuptintacmi runacu
napas chay chica ponchaupim canca ñispa ñircancu
[149] chaymantari ñam ari yscoynin capitulopi huc huatanpi
huacsacunap taquiscanta rimarcanchic ychaca chay taquiscantam
mana sutinchanchiccho yma ymactach quimça mita huatan
pi taquin chaycunacta caymi ñaupac auquisna ñis
ca ponchaupi paria cacap pascuanta rurac cancu chayman
tam ñatac chaupi ñamcap mitampi ynatac taquircan
chaymantam ñatac nobiembre quillapi ñachca san andres
pa fiestanman tincuchispa huc taquitatac taquic carcan
chanco ñisca taquicta cay taquictam canan cay quipan
pi allinta villason [150] cananca ñatac chaupi ñamcap
pascuanman cutison chaypac pascuanpim canan chay
huacsa ñiscanchiccuna cocacta huallquispa pichca pon
chao taquircancu huaquin runacuna llaman captin
pumacta aparispa taquircan mana llamayocri ynalla
chaymantam cay puma apariccunactam canan pay
mi pocon ñispa ñircancu chay taquim canan huantay
cocha sutioc huaquin taquictam canan ayño ñiscacta
pas taquircantac [151] huctam canan casa yaco sutiocta
taquic carcanco cay cassa yacocta taquiptinsi chaupi ñam
ca ancha cusicoc carcan porque cayta taquispaca
llatansi huaquillan huallparicunanta churaspallas
taquic carcan pincaynintari huc huara vtco pachalla
huan pacaycospa chaymantaca llatanlla caytam
runacuna taquispa chaupi ñamca <ollon>(pincaynin)<chicta>chicta ricus
pam ancha cusicon ñic carcan cayta taquiptintac
si ancha pucoy pachapas carcan caycunactam
canan chay pascuanpi rurarcancu
[152] CAPITULO 11 YMANAM CHANCO
ÑISCA TAQUICTA TAQUIRCANCU
CAYTA RIMASPACA TUTAY QUIREP

F 77 V

PARIA CACAP CHURINPA CASCANHUAN
MI VILLASON CAY SIMIRE
CAY YNAM

ñam ari ysconnin capitulopi paria cacap churin
cunacta sutinpi rimarcanchic ychaca sapampi ca
usascantam manarac rimarcanchiccho caypim
hoquin tutay quirip atiscancunactauan cay quipam
pi villason caypac mitampi taquiscactam chanco
ñispa ñinchic [153] cay tutay quirim paria cacap chu
rin carcan chaymi ñaupa pachaca cay checaconapas
quintes carcan quintecunap sullca huauquen chay
si chay quintecunaca anchatac cay checacunacta
chicnircan quipam yuric captin [154] chaysi hoc punchaoca
tutay quireca ñispa ñircan ama llaquicho churi yma ñip
tinpas chicnicochonpas yallenmi quepanpica checa
villca sutioc canquichic cay chicnicniquitari quinticha
huanhuacha ñispam runacunapas menospreciaspa
ñinca ñispas ñircan [155] chaysi cay tutay quirica chay pisi
ponchaomantatac huaquinin huauquincunahuan
villanacospa cay llacsa tambomanta yuncacunacta
atimuyta callarimurcan chaysi cay yuncacuna ñis
canchicca cay simicta vyarispa ancha mancharispa

colli sin pronuncia
cion q(u)e haga fuer
ça ayquijta ña callarircan vra colli ñisca llactaman
cay colli ñiscam canan carhuayllocunahuan quellina
con caycunap ayancunam canancamapas anac
ñaupa llactapi yna churarayan aya vasipe [156] cay tutay
quiris cay sici caya huaycucta mama huaycoctauan
vraycospa<n>s quello tamya puca tamya purispa
chaysi runacunaca huaquenca pachan llactanpi su
yarcan muchancampac chae muchaccunactas canan
manatac paipas allcocharcancho yallinrac tiacoy
ychaca yayaitam ricsinquitac chaymanta cay
checacunactam canan huauque ñispatac causanq(ui)

F 106 R

paycunap sullca huauquinmi cani ñispa [157] cay ñis
can simicamam chay sant p(edr)o mamapi cac runacu
napas amichayq(ui) llatachayquin cani ñispa canan
camapas ñincu (ña> cay checacunapri allaucam
ari vichocam ari ñisca huauquiyoctac causar
cancu [158] caytam canan cay checacunaca cay tutay
quirip puriscanta paypac callpanta purini ñispa hua
tancunapi cay llactamanta tucoy ynantin caricuna
chacocta ruraypac llocsic carca cay nobiembre quellapim
[159] chay pachatacmi tamyata mañac carcancu runacunapas
canan chancop mitampim pacha tamyanca ñispa ñircancu
cay tutay quirip callpan ñiscanchictam chacocta ruraspa cay
manta tucoy huacsacuna mana huacsapas llocsispa tupi
cocha hanacnin mayani ñiscapi puñoypac ric carcancu
[160] chay ponchaori huanacucta apispa lloychuctapas yma
aycactapas apispa chay apicmi canan ayllonpi may
quen apispapas ayllon huacsa captinca payman<rac> coc
carcan chaypac chupanta huaytallispa ayño ñisca
taquicta ayñoncampac mana apicri ynatacmi
chancollacta chancuspa taquircan [161] cayantinmi na
tac chay mayani ñiscamanta llocsic carcan tumna
man chaypim canan ynantin runacuna caripas huar
mipas huasuc tambo ñiscapi tucoy hoñolla suyac
carcan tutay quirim ña samon ñispa chay hua
suc tambo ñiscanchicri chay quiquen tumna la
plaçap chaupimpim aslla rumicuna churarayan
chaypis canan ñaupa pachaca ña chaypi chayaspa
muchac carcancu chaypitacsi chauti huanricuna
pas muchaypac asvancunauan chayamuc carcan
[162] ynaspam ñatac cayantinri yma chicacta apis
papas chay apiccuna huacsa ñiscanchic ancha cusi
cuspa cananca macayocmi canchic ñispa cusicus
pa cotimurcancu ñatac pacotapi puñomuypac
[163] cayantinmi ñatac llacsa tamboman chayamuc
carcan chaypi chayamunan captinmi tucoy chay
llactapi quiparic runacuna machopa payapas

F 106 V

yma yna runacunapas tucoynillan asvanuan
suyac carcan chaymi ña chayman chayamuptinca
ancha saycoscam amun ñispa asvavan yanca
ychaspa runasauapas pachapipas chay llacsa tam
boman yaicumuna poncollapi yna ychac carcan
[164] paicuna vramanta amuccunam aslla aychata
paicunap puyñonpa siminsaua churapuc carcan
cayta ña puchocaspam ñatac tucoy ynantin
runacuna pampapi tiaycospa ayño ñisca taquicta
ña callarircan caycunam canan chanco sutioc
chaymantam ña chancuptinca pachapas ña ñispa
tamyamuc [165] cay chancup mitampis ysqui caya ñisca
chay yañcap huasinpi huc sachachos o ymach chay
pis canan chay sacha ñiscanchic(manta) yacosapa vrma
raya<n>c chaycunactas canan paycona<can> chay y
nacta ricuspa canan huataca allin pucoymi canca
ñispa ñircancu mana tamyanampacsi chaquisca
cac chaysi ancha muchoymi canca ñispa ñic carcan<cu>
[166] CAPITULO 12 YMANAM CAY
PARIA CACAP CHURINCUNA TUCOY
YUNCACUNACTA ATIJTA ÑA
CALLARIRCAN
ñam ari cay chuncampi capit(ul)opi rimarcanchic
cay paria cacap churincunap atiscan<cunacta> simicta
y<nas>naspa villarcanchictacmi ari ymanam tu
coy ynantin llactacuna yunca sapa carcan chay
cunacta cananmi cay chuc paico chancha runa
huari ruma vtco chuco tutay quire sasin mari pa
cha chuyro ñiscanchiccunacta rimason ymanam
paicuna puric carcanco chay chaycunacta [167] cay
cuna ñiscanchiccunas ñaupa pacha tucoynin

F 107 R

huauquiyoc sapa caspa ña atijpac tucoynillantac pu
ric carcan chaysi cay chuc paico ñiscaca tucoynin
manta mayornin caspa huc huandopi ancha yupai
chasca puric carcan chaymantas tutay quirire tucoy
nintapas yallispa ancha sinche carcan cay yna sinche
cayninpis cay yscay mayo ñiscanchictapas paitac
ñaupac atircan chay vnca tupi ñisca pariachap fronte
rumpi huc yana vrco chaypi huc curi taunanta
pas churamuspa [168] cay taunactas canan <ña> yunca
cunacta ñacac yna cayta pampachaspam ma
na yupaichac ynam cay quitita yuncacuna yalli
munca ñispas chaypi churarcan chay churascam
hurcom canan vnca tupi capari caya sutioc
[169] chaysi cay huaquennin huauquincunaca rispa
pas chay tupi cochamanta vichaycuspa ñaupa ñanta
rinchic chaymi quisqui tambo sutioc hucmi <tam>tumnacha
sutioc maymantam limacñictapas riconchic chay
mantas ñan tutay quirica tucoyta atita ña puchocan
nicta oyarispa cotimurcancu chaysi tutay quiri
ta anchapuni mancharcanco paicunapas ancha sin
che captin [170] ynatacsi chay huaro cherinictapas <>vra
carancoñicman vraycorcancu chayta vraycus
pari paytacsi ñaupac rircan chaysi chay chu
qui suso ñiscanchicpac huc ñañanca chay
chacranpi suyarcan paita llollachipac <racanta> (pincayninta)
pas ñoñontapas ricorichispa yaya aslla sa
mayrac cay ashuallacta tictillacta vpiay
coyrac ñispa [171] chay pachas paica ynalla ña quipa
rircan chaysi huaquinnin huauquincunapas chay
ynacta ricuspa ynallatac quiparircan chay
hura alloca pacha marca ñiscacamalla atispa
si mana chay<cama> huarmi llollachinman carca
chayca canancamapas hora carangocama chil
cacamas huaro cherip quintippas chacran canman   sapampi ruras
carcan caycunap sapampi rurascantaca cay   cantaca cay qui
quipanpim quillcason yma ayca rurascantahuan   pampim quellcason

F 78 R

[172] MAMA CAPI(TUL)O 13
mama runa<cta>cunacta tapuscam canan chay huaca chau
pi ñamuca huacapac huctatac rimancu chay rimascan
siminri cay hinam ancha ñaupa pachas huc huaca hanan
maclla sutiyoc carcan caypac cosansi ynti carcan caycunap
churinsi paria caca chaupi ñamuca cay chaupi ñamucas ancha
runa camac carcan huarmipac caripacri paria caca [173] yna
captinsi pay mama runacunaca chaypac fiestanta ruray
pac corpus christip vispirampi chay chaupi ñamcacta aslla
asuahuan armachic carcan chaymantari huaquinincuna
yma ayca sacreficioncunacta churapuspa coynhuan yman
huanpas muchaspas tucoy hinantin runacuna huñonacuc caripas
huarmipas curacanpas y alcaldenpas [174] chaysi <caya punchao>
chay tuta pacarispa upiaspa machaspa tucoy tuta tiaccu <cayan
tin corpus punchaopis ynatac mamanchicpa fiestanmi ñispas
curacan callañayoc tucoy ynantin runacuna> aylliua ñisca<>
taquicta taquiypac anchapuni cusicuspa hupyaspa machaspa
chay tuta hasta pacariscancamas taquicuc chaymantas
ña pampaman llocsispas chayca mana ña ymactapas rurac
cho vpiaylla machaylla machac mamanchicpa fiestanmi
ñispatac [175] chaymantam manarac vira cocha ricurimuptinca
yma ynam mucharcanqui ñiscaca ñincum pihcca punchao
si alli huallparicuspa junio quillapitac hupyac carcancu chay
mantaca vira cochacunacta manchaspas corpuspa visperanpi mu
chancu chaymantari chaupi ñamcap ñañansi <prima y segunda>
<ñisca>pay mayornin captin huctas segunda ñañan<si> cassa llacsa
sutioc carcan caytas chay vispirapitac armachic carcan ynatac huc
ñañancunactapas vrpay huachac vichi maclla ñiscactapas
[176] checacunam ñincu chaupi ñamcacta pihcas car
can ñispa caycunap mayorninmi cotacha o pal
ta(cha) sutioc chaupi ñamuca huc segunda ñañan
mi copacha <sutioc> ñiscanchic llacsa huato sutioc cay
llasa huatus chillacopi tian caypac fiestantas canin
pa don diego chauca guaman çaçi caya curaca causaptinpas
chellaco runacuna huaquinin runacunahuampas
rurac carcancu hasta q(ue) don m(art)yn chayascancama
cay fiestactaca manam allicho yachanchic yma

F 78 V

yma quellapih carcan
[177] chaymantam ampuche o ampuxi ñiscanchicri
mira huato sutioc carcan cay mira huato ñiscac
taca manam allichu yachanchic maypi tiascan
tapas ychaca ñispam ñincu llacsa huato ña
ñanhuantacsi tian ñispa [178] caycunactas runa
cuna cay quitimanta o guaro cherimantapas
o mayquen runacunapas churinta o huau
quinta o yayanta o ymantaps huncochecus
pa chayman ric carcancu tapucuypac chay
huacacunap saçerdotinsi canan sucta chunca
huatamanta yuyariscaca chumpi ticlla sutioc(si) car
can ancha chaillas caninpa don diego ñiscanchic
captinsi luzia sutioc carcan (ña tacyasca huarmi) <ychaca chayca cau
san chay> [179] cay huacacunactas ña muchaspa a llac
sa huato mira uato cammi runa camac canque camtac
mi huchayta chaupi namucactapas yallispa ya
chanqui villallahuay ymamantam hun
cuchicuni yma huchaymantam ñacarispa cau
sani ñispas muchac carcancu [180] chay yna captin
ssi yscaynin ñañantinhuantaccha tian ñis
pa hunanchancu chaymantari cay huaca
cunactatac<mi>(ssi) astauan runacuna yupaychac
carcancu porque chaupi ñamucaca manas chica
chu ymactapas runacunacta villac carcan ya
llinpas llullactacssi carcan chayssi haco llac
sa huato mira huato mamanchicta huyarimu
son yma ñincah vchanchicpac chaycama
tac puchucason ñispas runacuna ric carcan
cu [181] ychaca yna muchaspapas manam chau
pi ñamcap fiestanta huatancunapi ymanam
ruran ynachu rurarcancu chaytaca muchaspa
pas musiachicuyllapacmi ric carcancu risac ñis
papas o ama ñispapas munascancama
[182] chaymantam canan sullcacha o xullca paya ñis
canchicta lluncho huachaca sutioc huacacta rimason

F 79 R

caymi ari 4 ñañan cay huacaca cantañicpis
manam yachanchicchu ychapas cantacuna
yupaychan cantamantapas as carullanpiracsi
[183] chaymantas <> añassi o aña paya ñiscanchic<si>
cocha hucopi tian huaquininmi chaymi caue llaca
carca ñispa ñincu huaquininmi huctacmi cocha
patapim tian ñispa ñincu cayssi caca huco
pi tian chaysi manatac saçerdotin canchu
cay hurpay huachac huacacta rimachijpac ris
pas alli hunanchacusparac ric carcancu por
que cayhuan rimaspaca cara a caras rima
nacuc carcan mana huasscayuc captin chay
si chaymanta cutimuspapas payhuanmi rima
muni ñispas <mana> huc huata saçic carcan
mana huarminhuan huchallicuspa
[184] cay ñiscanchiccunas sapampipas ñam
ca sutioc sapa carcan ynaspa ñañayoc
cama hucninta mayquinnintapas chayai
cuspaca a pichca ñamca ñispas villacuc
carcan ymallacta llaquispapas [185] cay chica
llactam cay chaupi ñamca llacsa huatu mira
huatu lluncu huachac hurpay huachac ñis
cap cascanta yachanchic chaymantas cay
ñiscanchiccuna ñau pachaca chayman ric
runacunacta con churiquip yayaiquip ma
chuyquip simincamachu hamunqui ñispas
ñic carcan chaysi manam ñictaca ri cuti
con choriiquictarac huyarichimuy ñiptin
cotimuc carcan [186] chayracsi ymallactapas
chaytam piñachinqui caytam piñachin
que o huachucmi canqui o paria cacap
fiestanpim huarmihuan huchallicurcan
qui ñispa yma aycactapas rimaspa cunac
carcan tincuc mayopim armanqui llamay
quictam nacapunqui ñispapas caycuna ñis
cantas runacunaca ancha cusicuspa puchucapuc car
can huaquininsi canan alliyatamuc huaquinri huañuctac
yma yna puchucaptinpas

F 79 V

ojo

[187] ñam ari chaupi ñamcap huaquinin ñañan
cunap cascancunactapas huyarinchic
ychaca runacuna llactancunapipas ayllo
ayllonpi hucta camatacmi rimancu sutin
tapas ymanam mama runacunapas huc
tatac rimancu checari huctatac [188] huquinmi
chaupi ñamcacta paria cacap paninsi ñincu
hucmi tamta ñamcap churinsi carca ñincu
cay tamta ñamca ñiscanchictam ari ñau
pacnin pichcantin capitulopi rimarcanchic
huaquinmi canan yntip churinsi ñincu chay
ynam mana hunanchaypaccho
[189] CAPI(TUL)O 14
ÑAUPACNIN CAPITULOPIM ARI HU
NANCHARCANCHIC CUNI RAYAP CASCANTA
PARIA CACAMANTA ÑAUPACNINCHUS
O QUEPANCHUS CARCAN CHAYTA
cuni raya vira cocha ñiscanchicca ancha ñaupa
mantatacsi carcan paria cacapas yma ayca
huacacunapas paytaca astahuantacsi yupai
chac carcan huaquinincunaca paria cacapas
cuni rayap churinsi nispam ñincu chayman
tam canan cuni raya vira cochap puchucas
canta rimason [190] cuni rayas ñahca vira co
chacuna ricurimuncampac cuzcoñicman
rircan chaysi chaypi huayna capac yngahuan
rimanacorcan ñispa haco churi titi cacaman
chaypi ñocap cascayta villascayqui ñispa [191] chay
pis ñispa ñircan ynga runayquicta camachi
bruxocunacta yma ayca yachaccunactapas
hura ticsiman canchancanchicpac ñiptinsi
yngaca tuylla camachircan chaysi huaqui
nin runacuna ñocam condorpac camasca canim

F 80 R

ñispa ñircancu huaquinsi ñocam guamanpa
camasca cani ñircan huaquinmi canan ño
cam huayanay piscu pahuac cani ñispa ñircan
[192] chaysi cay ñiscanchiccunacta richic hura ticsi
man chayman(tam) ñocap yayaita churiquim ca
chamuan huc panantas apachihuanqui ñispa
villanqui ñispas conarcan chaysi chay runa
huayanaypac camasca runaca huaquinin ca
mascacunahuan pihca punchaullapi cutimuy
pac rircancu [193] chaysi huayanaypac camasca ru
natac ñaupac chayarcan yna chayaptinsi cu
nascanta villaptin huc huchuylla pitaquillapi
aman caytaca quecharinquichu quiquin huay
na capac apuracmi quicharinca ñispas cuna
murcan chaysi chay runaca ña apamuspa
ñahca cuzcoman chayachispa ma ricuycu
sac ymahc cayca ñispa quicharircan [194] chaysi
chay hucopica huc señora ancha collan sumac
ricurircan chucchanpas crispo cori yna chica
collanan pachayuc ricchayninri ancha huchuy
llas carcan chay ynacta ricuptin pachallas chay
s(eño)raca chincaripurcan [195] chaysi ancha llaquicuspa
cuzcopi titi caca ñiscampi chayarcan chaysi mana
chay yna huayanaypa camasca canquiman chayca
canallanmi huanochichiquiman ri quiquillay
quitac cutij ñispas cacharcan chaysi cutispa
ñatac apamurcan apamuspas ñanpi micuyman
ta<> vpyaymanta huañuptinpas rimaptin
pachallas mesapas mantasca carcan puñonam
pacri ynatac [196] chaysi pihca punchaollapitac
chayachircan ña chayachiptinsi cuni rayaca ynga
huan ancha cusicuspa chasquircan chaysi manarac
quicharispatac cuni raya<>ca ñispa ñirca ynga cay
 pachacta sequison ñocari cay huc pachacta yaicusac
camri cay huc pachactatac panayhuan yaicoy ama ñam

F 80 V

campas ñocapas ricunacosoncho ñispas pachacta
sequispa cayarcan ynaspas chay cofrectaca
quecharircan quechariptin pachallas chaycan
pachapas yllarircan [197] chayssi chay ynga huay
na capac ñiscaca mana ñam caymanta cuti
saccho cayllapitacmi cay ñustayhuan coyayhuan
tiasac ñispas huc runacta aylluntatac cam rij
ñocap rantij huayna capacmi cane ñispa cuzco
man cuti ñispas ñircan chay pachallatacsi chay
señoranhuan chincatamurcan cuni rayari yna
llatac chaymantas ña chay huayna capac ñiscan
chic huañuptin hucpas hucpas ñocarac ñinacospa
apu cayninpac tacuirircan ynaptintacsi vira co
chacunapas caxa marcapi ricurimurcan [198] canancama
pas checa simillactam yachanchic cuni raya vira co
chap cascanta huaquinin cay quitipi purispa rurascan
cunactaca manaracmi quillcacuyta puchucanchiccho
chay chaycunactaca cay quipampim rurason

ojo [199] CAP(ITUL)0 15
CAYMANTAM YSCAYNIN CAPI(TUL)OPI (RIMASCANCHICTA) CUNI RA
YAP CARUINCHUMANTA ÑAUPAC CAS
CANTAPAS O QUIPAN CASCANTAPAS
QUILLCASON
cuni raya vira cochaca ancha ñaupacmanta
tacsi carcan manarac pay captinca manas
cay pachapi ymallapas carcanchu payracssi or
cocunactapas sachactapas mayoctapas yma ay
ca animalconactapas camarcan chacracunac
tapas runap causancampac chayraycutacmi
cay cuni rayacta paria cacap yayansi ñincu
paytacsi paria cacactapas camarca ñispa [200] mana
paypa churin captinca allcochanmancha carca

F 81 R

nispam tucoy runacunapas ñincu huaquinin
llactacunactaca anchas amauta cayninpi allco
charcan yma aycactapas ruraspa caycunactaca
quipampim rurason
[201] CAPI(TUL)O 16
CAYPIM QUILLCASON PARIACA PICHCA RUNTO
MANTA YURIC HUAUQUIYOCCHUS CARCAN
CAYRI PARIA CACACHO PAYCU
NAP YAYAN
CHAY CHAYTA
ñam ari pusacnin capitulopi hunancharcanchic
paria caca pihca runtamanta yurimuspa huauqui
yuc camachos carcan cayri huaquinincunaca pari
a cacap churinchus carcan chaycunacta chayman
tari paycunap sapampi sutintari quillcasontacmi
[202] cay pihcca runtomanta yuric paria caca ñiscanchic
ca ymanam 14 capi(tul)opipas rimarcanchic cuni rayap
churinsi ñispa ynatacsi paycunaca huauquiyoc ca
ma carcan caycunap sutinmi ñaupacninman
ta paria caca chaymantam churapa chaymantam
puncho chaymantam paria carco huquintam
mana yachanchiccho caypi quiparin blancopi ya
chaspam churancanchicpac /sullca yllapa/ [203] chaymanta   ojo sullca yllapa
cay paria ca<rco> ñiscanchicsi canan antiman yaicu   sutiocsi carcan
napi huallallo caruinchoh cutimunman ñispas ca
nancamapas tian chaytahuanpas hunancharcan
chicmi ari cay huallallo caruinchuri manatacsi
tuyllaca miticarcancho may pacham chay mullo
cocha ñiscanchicta churapa paria cacap huquin
yaicuspa cochaman tucochircan chay pachas chay
manta huallalloca pisco yna pahuamurca [204] chaysi

F 81 V

huc orco caqui yoca sutioc orcoman yaicorcan cay <cacas>
orcos ancha atun caca cay cacaman yaicuspas hua
llallo caruincho pacacorcan chaymantas canan paria
cacaca yllapapayaspa huaquinnin pihcca huauquin
cunahuan ancha nanacta yllapaspa ñahcca cacacta
pas tunichispa ñatac chaymanta miticachirca [205] chay
ssi chay huallallo caruinchoca huc atun machachuay a
maru sutiocta paria cacacta tapianca ñispa yscay homayoc
amarocta llocsichimurcan chayssi paria cacaca chay
ta ricospa huc cori taunanhuan ancha piñaspa cha
upi huasampi tucsircan chay pachallatacsi chay
amaroca chirayarca rumiman ña tucorcan
[206] chay chirayasca amaros canancamapas anac caqui
yuca sutioc ñanpi·sutilla ricurin chay amaroc
tas cuzco runacuna mayquin runacunapas yachac
ninca ampipac rumihuan tacaspa hurmacninta
apacon mana oncoyman chayasac ñispa
[207] chaymantas chay huallallo caruincho ña caqui yo
ca cacamanta miticuspa huc huayco caqui yoca
huayqui ñisca huaycoman yaicorcan chaysi hoc
orco puma rauca sutiocta chay huallallo sicaspa
caymanta cay paria cacacta quinchasac mana cay
ta pasamuncanpac ñispas huc orito caque
ñiscacta ricrantapas chuquiri<spa>chispa saya
chircan chaysi chaytapas paria cacaca huc ricran
ta yanca paquerispa chay caquectari rumiman
na cherayachispa yallircantac ña yalliptinsi
huallallo caruinchoca mana ña yma callpallan
pas captinsi antiñicman miticarcan [208] chaysi
paria cacaca huaquinin huauquincunahuan
tucoynin catircan ña antiman yaicuptinsi

paria carco   huc huauquintaca paria carco sutiocta chay
antip punconpi saquimurcan pahtahc cotimun
man ñispa [209] chay paria carcos canan huc orcotac
ancha rra<ç>zosapa tian cayta pihc muchan chaytaca

F 82 R

manam yachanchiccho ychaca ñam ari ysconnin
capitulopi rimarcanchic allcocta cananca micochon
runa micuscanrayco caytari huancacuna carachon
ñiscanta<>
[210] CAPI(TUL)O 17
cananmi rimason ña huauquinta paria carco su
tiocta saquimuspa antip ponconpi ymanam ña
tac paria caca cotimurcan chayta cay simire cay
ynam ñam ari huaquinin simi rimascanta
ca muchachicuypac callariscanta<pas>huanpas ri
marcanchic ychacaca huc simictatacmi concar
canchic [211] ña aticuyta puchocamuspas huaquinin huau
quincunahuan cutimurca cay paria caca ñiscanchic
orcoman chaypis huc horcotac razosapa mana
llocaypac huama yaco sutioc orco cay orcoctam
huaquinin runacunaca chaymi paria caca ñincu
ñispatacmi quipampi vira cochacuna ricurimuptin
pas cay ynca caya ñiscanchicmantapas chay or
co razocta ricuspa chaymi paria caca ñispa ñir
cancu [212] quiquin paria caca ñiscaca huranic huc
cacapitacsi tian chaypitacsi huaquinin huauquincu
napas chay caca ñiscanchicman yascuspas caypim
tiasac caymantam muchahuanqui ñispa chay caca
pi llactachacorcan chaymantam ñircanchic huc
orco<> huama yaco sutioc orcocta razosapas
ñispa chaysauas ña antimanta cutimuspa
samamurcan [213] chaymantas canan tucoy tauan
tin suyo runacunacta cayachirca manarac yn
gapas yurimuptin ancha ñaupatac chay yna
ña runacuna tucoynin huñonacomuptinsi
payta muchancanpac huacsata camachircan
cayta oyarispas ña ynga ricurimuspapas paipas
huacsa tiarcan ancha yupaichaspa chay pacha yma
nam huñonacorcan ninchic tauantin suyocta
[214] chay pachas huallallo caruinchuca mana traycionninta

F 82 V

concaspa huc animalta hugi sutiocta chay qui
quin horco tiascanpi ricorichircan cay pari
a cacacta tapianca ñispa chaysi chay hugi ñis
canchicca tuylla ricurispa pachaman miti
camurcan [215] chaysi chay hugi causaspaca ymac
tapas paria cacap causayninta quichunman
tacsi carcan chayraycos tauantin suyo runa
cunacta chay hugi ñiscacta apimuy ñispa ca
machircan yna camachiptinsi tucoy ynan
tin runacona catirircan manatacsi api
chicorcancho panas paria cacaca yllaparca
tamyarcan manatacsi huañorcancho [216] chay
si ancha caropirac huc runa cay checamanta
caca sica ayllo apircan chaysi huc quinti runa
ca huauqui ñam apinqui ancha cusiocmi can
qui camca cay chupallanta huaytallispa
ri cay aychantaca ñoca apasac ñiptinsi allim
ñircan [217] ñispatacsi chay quinti runaca huc
ñanta rispa ñocam yaya apimoni ñispa
villarcan chaysi ancha cusicuspa yupaichar
can cay quinti runap sutinmi chuc paico sutioc
carcan chaysi quipanpi ña chupanta chaya
chiptinca chuc paicocta camca chay llollahuascay
quimanta quintihuanca macanacoy asnayoc
ñisonquim churiquicunactapas ñispa mi
llaypi anyarcan [218] chay pachas cay caca sica ay
llomanta huar cancha llichic canchaman
ta quiquin paria caca cammi chay apiscay
quimanta yancamusca canqui camllactam
yma villahuascayquictapas vyariscayq(ui)
huaquinin runacunapas camtaracmi ñocacta
villaypacpas huyarichisonqui ñispas sutinta
pas ñamca canca ñamca parya ñispa sutiya
chimurcan [219] chaymantas paycunapas yanca car
can conchacunari ynatac yañcampa sutin
quiquin paria cacap sutichascan huatusi sutioc carcan

F 83 R

ynatacsi tucoy llactancunapi yañcacunaca
paria cacap sutichascan cay chicactam concas
canchicta yuyarinchic paria cacap cascanta
[220] CAPI(TUL)O 18
ñam ari yngap paria cacacta yupaychascanta
huacsa tiascantauanpas rimarcanchic pay yn
gatacsi camachircan anan yauyo rurin ya
uyomanta quinça chunca paria cacacta pura
pi quillapi siruichon ñispa chaysi chaycama
quimsa chunca runa siruircan<cu> chunca pihc
cayoc punchaumantacama caraspa micochispa
[221] chaysi huc punchaoca huc llamanhuan yauri hua
naca sutioc llamahuan mucharcancu chayssi
chay quimca chuncamanta oquen llacuas
quita<par yasca> pariasca sutioc runaca may pa
cham chay quinça chunca runacuna ñatinta
sunconta llamapmanta ricorcan chay pacha ñis
pa ñircan a atac manam allicho pacha
huauqui quipampica cay paria caca yayan
chic puromancatacmi ñispas rimarcan [222] chay
si chay huaquinin runacunaca manam ca
sim<> rimanqui allim ymactam cam yachan
qui ñispas ñircancu chaysi hucninca say
quita pariasca ymamantam cam hunanchan
qui cay sonconpica ancha allictam paria ca
ca yayanchic riman ñispa ñiptinsi payca
manas sonco<>cta ricoypacpas cayllaycorcancho
carollamanta cauaspatacsi yna amutarcan
[223] chaysi rimaspapas quiquin paria cacam ñin
huauqui ñispa chaycunactapas ayñircan
chaysi millaypicama chay quita pariascactaca
ñircan llacuas asnac runa ymactam chay ya
chan yayanchic paria caca chinchay suyo ñisca
maycama runayocmi tiacon chaycho puromanman

F 83 V

ymactam chaycan runaca yachan ñispas
ancha piñaspa cama ñircancu cay ñiscan
manta ancha pisi ponchaomantatacsi ñam
vira cocha caxa marcapi ricorimon ñicta oya
rircancu [224] chaymantam cay checamanta
pas tama lliuya caxa lliuya (sutioc) caca sica ayllotac
chay paria cacap yanan tiasca chay pachas
paria cacapi quimça chunca saçerdotecona
tiaspa cay caxa lliuya tama lliuya sutioc tu
coyninmanta yuyacnin carcan [225] chaysi vi
ra cocha chayman chayaspaca cay huacap
collquin pachan maymi ñispas taporcan
chaysi payconaca manatac villacoyta mu
narcancho yna captinsi vira cochaca piña
rispa hocsacta taucarichispa caxa lliuyac
ta rupachircan chaysi ña patmanta oc
sa rupaptinsi huayraca pucorimurcan chay
si ancha ñacarisparac chay runapas cau
sarircan chay pacharacsi chay pacha nac
nacta yman aycantapas vira cochaman
corcancu [226] chay pachas tucoynin runacuna
ancha chicantatacmi ñihuasca canchic chay
llacuas quita pariasca huauqui aco cheque
risontac mana ñam allicho pacha ñispas
tucoynin llactancama chiquerimurcan
[227] chaysi cay checamanta rupasca runapas ña alli

maca viça

yaspa huc paria cacap churinta maca uisa
sutiocta aparispa quintip llantanpi limca
sutioc llactapi chayamurca caycunactam
cay quipam capi(tul)opi rimason
[228] CAPI(TUL)O 19
cay maca visa paria cacap churinsi ñaupa yn
ga captin aucaman yanapancampac apai
tucorcan amaya xiuaya sutioc llacta
cunas manatac atichicorcancho chaysi

F 84 R

yngaca mana atichicoptin paria cacacta
chorinta mañarcan chay amaya xiuaya
runacunacta atipai [229] chaysi chay maca visa
sutiocta corcan cayta apaspas tuyllapuni
atimurcan chaymantas yngacunaca asta
uanrac paria cacacta yupaicharcan corictapas
yma ayca pachancunactapas cospa huatampi
chay quimça chunca yanancunapacpas sarac
ta cocacta yma aycactapas llactancunaman
ta cochispas causarcan [230] chay yna captinsi
ñaca ñinchic yna vira cochacuna chaya
muspa tucoy yman cactapas tucoy quecho
porcan huaquinin pochocnincunactas
quipampi huañoc don sebastian tucoyta ru
pachichircan [231] chaymantas ymanam ña
ca ñinchic chay sina chay caxa lliuyaca
li<>mca llactapi tiaspa chay maca uisa ñiscac
ta atallispa ancha yupaychasca ahca huata
tiarcan ña ahca huatamantam canan cay che
cacuna chay yna alli causascanta huyarispa
cayman chay maca uisacta apamuchon ñispa
cacharcan don ju(a)n puypu tacma (huañoc) curaca caspa chay
pachas chay caxa lliuya macho rupasca cayman
sucta runa choriyoc chay chorincunahuan hamur
cancu [232] chay pachas caypi digo llacsa tampopi
chayamuspa ñatac yaya maca uisa alli
cho cay llactapi checa runacta huacaychanqui
ñispa huc llamahuan villaptinsi ymanam
huauya cancha ñisca maypim chay llacuas
pas quita pariasca ñisca ricorcan chay ynalla
tacsi carcan [233] chaytapas chay caxa lliuya tama
lliuya ñisca ña chorincunapas colloptinracsi
quiquinpas ña huañuypac caspas chay ynam
chayamuptillay carcan ñispa rimarcan porq(ue)
chayamuspa pachaca ancha allinmi mana ñam
ymapas huaticay oncoypas cancacho ñispas ñircan

F 84 V

[234] chay pachamantaracsi cay maca uisacta cay llacta
pi atallircancu pura ñiscapi quilla ñiscapi
tucoy checacuna ayllompi ayllompi seruispa
huc tutallaca tucoynin cari huarmi hoñolla paca
ricoc carcan ña pacariptinmi canan coynhuan
ymanhuanpas sapa runamanta cococ car
carcan yanapahuay cay llactacta cammi
huacaychanqui yma ayca oncoyconacta
pas cammi alliyachihuanqui ñispa
[235] chaymantam canan limca ñiscanchic llac
tapica anchapuni seruiscas tiarcan yam
laca sutioc chacractas tucoy huc huaran
ca quinti ñisca callpaporcan chay maca
uisa opiancampac chaysi chaypi cac runa
cunari anchaponitac rico tucorcan yman
huanpas aycanhuanpas chayta embidias
pas cay checacuna huañoc don ju(a)n puypu tacma
cassa lliuya ayllon runan captin cayman
apamuchon ymapacmi runap llantanpi
chay chica alli huacacta atallin ñispa cachar
can chay pachamantaracsi caypi tia<n>rcan
checallactam cay maca uisapta yachanchic
[236] CAPI(TUL)0 20
CAYMANTAM LLOCLLAY HUAN
CUPAP CAUSAYNIN CALLARIN
CANAN Q(UE)PAMPI POCHOCASCAN
TAUANMI QUELLCASSON
cay llocllay huancupa ñiscanchic huacas pacha
camacpac churin carcan cay huaca ricurimus
cantas huc huarmi lanti chumpi sutioc alay satpa

F 85 R

ayllo tarircan chacracta oryacospa chaysi huc
mita ñaupac aspispaca ymah cayca ñispas pacha
llampitac vischorcan [237] chaysi ñatac huc pachacta aspis
paca chay quiquin ñaupac tariscantatac tarircan
chaysi cayca ychapas yma huaca ñispas yayaicunac
ta ricuchimusac aylloycunactapas ñispas apamorcan
[238] chaysi chay pacha huc huacatac yngap cachan cati qui
llay sutioc chay llactapi llacsa tampo ñiscapi carcan
cay<ssi> cati quillay ñiscanchicsi yanca yma ayca
huaca mana rimactapas rimachic carcan chaysi
cay llocllay huancupa ñiscanchic huacatata rima
richircan ñispa <pip> pim canqui yman sutique
ymamanmi hamunqui ñispa chaysi ñocaca pacha
cuyochic pacha camacpac churinmi cani sutipas lloc
llay huancupam yayaimi cay checa llactacta<ca>
huacaychamuy ñispa cachamuan ñispas ñircan
[239] chaysi runacunaca ancha cosicuspa allim cay
llactapi tiachon ñocaycocta huacaychahuaspa ñis
pas chay quiquin tarimucpa huasimpi huchoylla can
chan captinpas astahuan atunyachispa tucoy checacuna
huanri chauticunahuanpas tucoynin ancha man
chaspa chaypi huasinta canchanta allicharcancu
[240] payta seruiipacri pura quilla<pi> ñiscapi ayllo ayllo
manta allauca collanamuptin yaicuson ñispas
camachinacorcan llamantapas cospa cay pura que
lla ñiscanchictam paycuna ñam chayana ñincu
paymi chayan ñincu cay chayai ñiscanchicpis ñaupa
pachaca chu(m)p ruco huaychau ahua ñiscacunacta
churacuspa taquic carcancu ymanam paria cacap
mitanpipas churacuc carcan chay chump ruco huay
chao ahua ñiscacta chay yna [241] cay ñiscanchic chay
ynas ahcca huata seruircancu chaysi chay llocllay
huancupaca huc mita mana alli seruiptintaccha
pacha camac yaya<i>nman cutircan chincarispa chay
si chay ynacta ricuspa runacunaca ancha llaquispa
chay may pacham ñaupaclla tarirca lanti chumpi ñiscanchic

F 85 V

chaytapas allichaspa huc husnocta pircaspa mascar
cancu [242] chaysi ñatac mana tarispa pacha camac
man tucoy yuyac runacuna llamantapas coyn
tapas yma ayca vestidontapas camaripuspa
rircancu chaysi yayanta ñatac muchaspa cotichi
morcan chaysi astauanrac rrenouaspa muchar
cancu llama camayocnintapas camachipuspa
cay llamactas sucya villca ñiscapi michircan
cu pacha camacpac llamanmi ñispa ynga
pas cayta camachircantacsi [243] chaymantas yma
nam ayllo ayllo ñiscampi chayarcan chay
yna cay huacacta vinay huata seruircancu
yma ayca honcoycuna amuptinri paita vya
richispa alli cayta mañaspa yma ayca llaqui
cuy puticoy captinpas auca amuptinpas pa
cha cuyomuptinpas yayanmi piñan ñispas
runacuna ancha mancharcan saractari yn
gap çaranta sapçicunamantas corcan
hupyancampac [244] chaymantas ñatac huc
p(adre)e X(christoba)l de castilla captin (cay rreducionpi caspa) curacari don geronimo
cancho guaman caspa ancha chaycunacta chic
ñiptin mana ña mucharcanchu chaysi ña
tac ñaupa haton çarampion hamuptin yma
ayca muchacoytapas callarircancu curaca
ñiscanchicri paymanta cachan ñic yna ma
na ña rimapayarcancho purun huasipi
opyaptin chay pachatacsi cay huacap huasinpas
ruparcan paicama dios munaptin [245] chayman
tam canan don g(eroni)mo huañoptin chay pacha
don ju(a)n sacsa lliuya <yai> curacaman yaicuptin
ca quiquin curacapas huacça captin tucoy runa
cuna ymanam ñaupa pacha causarcan chay
yna causayta<> (ña callarircancu) llocllay huancupacta chayman
ta maca uiçactapas chayaspa chaypi pacarispa
opiaspa [246] cananmi s(eñ)or doctor auila paypac predi
caçionnimpi huaquinin runacuna diosman
                    cuti

F 86 R

cutirispa chaicunacta amacharcancu mana huc
runa diosman checa sonco cutirispa caycunacta su
paimi ñispa ñiptinca ychapas hunayrac chay yna
causanman carca cay simictam cay quipampi
huyarichison [247] huc runam don x(christob)al choque cassa
sutioc yayanri ña ñiscanchic don ge(roni)mo cancho guaman
huañuc cay runam huchuillanmantaca alli cau
sacuc carcan yayanpas chay huacacunacta ancha
chicñiptin ychaca cay mana alli supaipac llullay
cuscan huañonampica cay huchaman hurmar
canmi ahcca mana alli supai machucunap llullay
cuscan ña huañoypacri confesacorcanmi chaytaca dios
aponchictaccha yachan maypi cascantapas [248] cay huañuc
ñiscanchicpac churinmi ari don x(christob)al ñiscanchic canan
causan caymi huc mita cay supay llucllay huancupa
ñiscanchicta ricurcan ñavinuan paipas yayan
huañuscanmantaca ña ñiscanchic mana alli supai
machocunap llollaycuscan caspa cay simire cay y
nam cayta rimaypacca ñaupacracmi don x(christob)al jura
mentocta mucharcan caymi + ñispa [249] huc tutas don
x(christob)al chay llocllay huancupap huasinman rircan chaypi
sipasnin captin chay huacactaca ña haquispa mana ña
asllapas chaytaca yuyaspa chaysi ña chay huassi
pi chayaspa yspacuypac chay huchoylla racay huasilla
man yaicorcan [250] chaysi canan maypim chrusta
churarcan chay hucomantas huc collque plato
ponchao yntiman tincochisca runap ñauinta tuta
yachic ynas ñauinman chay supai ricurichimur
can cayta ricuspas ñahcca pachamanpas hormarcan
chaysi padre nuestro aue mariacta resaspa chay
huchuilla aposentoman huarmip tiascanman
miticamurcan [251] chaysi ñatac quimça mita cha
upicta purimuptin chay ynatac yllarichimurcan
ña aposentoman chayaptinri ñatac quimça mita
ñaupacninri quimça mitatac chaymi tucoyninca
yscon mita (yna) yllarechircan cay chica mita cay

F 86 V

yllarichic supaita ricuspa anchapuni manhharispa
chay huarmip puñoscanman chayarcan paitari
tuylla atarichispa [252] yscay huamrari chaypitac po
ñusca cay huamracunapas ancha siuyaptinsi
yayanchicmi ynan ñispa mancharircancu
cay huamracunari chay sipaspas cay supaipac sa
çerdotinpa churinsi carcan chaysi chay tuta
ymanam tutayacman runa yaicuc astauan tu
tayachispa chay ynas ahuamanpas llocçic
yaicuc ynas carcan rinrintapas chuy ñichispa
chay huasictapas ña tunichic ynas cay don x(christob)al
ta atipaita munarcan [253] chaysi oraçion yachas
cancunacta ancha nanacta huacyarispa dios
aponchicta mucharcan doctrinactari ñatac ña
tac<yachaspa> callarispa pochocascancama
cay yna mana y<lla>mallahuanpas quis
pinanta hunanchaspas ña chaopi tutacta
pas yalliptin suapaica ynatac ompichic captin
<si> mamanchic santa m(ari)acta huacyarcan
ñispa [254] a mamay cammi sapai mamay canqui
ynataccho cay mana alli suapaica atipahuanca
cam mamaytac yanapallahuay pana yna
huchaçapactapas ñocatacmi cay quiquin çu
paita siruircani cananca ñan ricsini supai
cascanta manam cayca dios(cho) manatacmi cay
ca ymactapas allintaca ruranmancho
[255] cam çapai coyallaytacmi cay peligroman
ta quispichihuanq(ui) huahuayq(ui) jesusnita villapu
llahuaytac canallanca cay huchaymanta
quispichihuachuntac cay mana alli supai
pa maquinmanta ñispas huacaspa om
pispa mamanchic virgen sapai coyanchic
ta huacyarcan [256] cay<ña>ta ña pochucaspas
latinpi salue regina mater misericordia
ñispa rresarcan cayta rimaptinsi na chao
pita rimaptin chay hacoy mana alli supaica

F 87 R

chay huasictapas coyorichispa ancha racupi
chuss ñispa chusic llucsircan chay pachalla
tacsi pachaca pacaric yna carcan mana ñas
yma manchachicuypas runa yna llucsic yai
cumucpas carcanchu [257] chaymantas astahuan
rac diosta mucharcan virgen s(an)ta mariactapas
viñay yanapancampac cayantillantacsi tucoy
runacunacta ñispa villarcan huauquicuna yayacuna
chaycan manchascanchic llucllay huancupa ñis
caca chusic supaimi casca [258] cunam tutam
virgin s(an)ta maria mamanchicpac yanapainin
huan atiparcomuni amatac cananmantaca
pillapas chay huasiman yaicunquichiccho yai
cucta chayacta ricuspaca padremanpas villay
manmi porque alli yachay cay ñiscayta tucoy
soncoyquipitac chasquicuychic ñispas tucoy
runacunacta villarcan [259] chaysi huaquin
ca ychapas ya ñispa huaquinri chay supai
ta manchach caspa hupalla tiarcancu chay
pachamantaracsi checanpunica chayaita
samarcancu chaymantas chay tutari ña
tac don x(christob)al huasimpi puñocuptin muscoypi
ricuchicorcan caytam caysaua quillcasson
[260] CAP(ITUL)O 21
CAYMANTAM MANA MUSCOY
YUPAI CAPTINPAS CHAY MA
NA ALLI SUPAYPA MANCHA
CHISCANTA RIMASON YMA
NAM DON X(CHRISTOB)AL ATIPARCAN CHAYTA
HUANPAS

F 87 V

ñam ari llucllay huancupa mana alli supai
cascanta don x(christob)al atipascantauanpas oyarir
canchic ychaca chay mana alli supai muscoy
pipas atipaitatacsi munarcan chaysi cayan
tin tutallatac huasinmanta don x(christob)alta caya
chircan huc runahuan manas paiman rine
nircancho ña huasinman yaicusparacsi
musyacorcan [261] chaysi ancha mancharispa chay
huc yunga huarmi chacuas tiacocman chay qui
quiquin patiopitac cayllaycorcan cay chac
uassi yunga huarmi carcan chaysi huahua
ymapacmi llucllay huancupa pacha cuyo
chicpa churinta mana manchanquicho
cananmi chayta yachaypac cayachimu
sonqui ñispas rimarcan [262] ñiptinsi canan
paica chayca mana alli supaimi mamay
ymapacmi chayta manchayman ñispas
ñircan chaysi maquinpiri taua rreal
collquicta atallircan chaytas don x(christob)al pa
chaman ormachircan chayta mascaptin
si franc(isc)o trompeteroca hahuallamanta yao
yma conquim chaypin yayaiquica ancha piñas
pa hutca amuchon ñispa cayamusonqui ñispas
huacyamurcan [263] ñiptin pachallas suyallahuai
rac huauqui ñam amuni ñispa collquenta
ancha vtcaspa mascarcan chay pacha ña
tarispas rijpac captinsi ñatac ymanam
oyanpi quiquinta chay collqui ñiscanchichuan
manchachircan chay yna ynamurcan chay
cruzpa tiascan ocumanta(tac) [264] chayssi tuylla
mancharispa mana ña quispinampas yacha
cuptin chay hucumantaca cayamurcan
yayanchicmi cayasonqui ñispa chaysi
paica allim ñispas sonconpica ancha piñaspa
yaicorcan yaicuspas poncollampi tiay<coy>
corcan [265] chaysi chay pachaca cay astu guamanca

F 88 R

opiachich carcan carahc carcan chay huacacta
ñispa yaya llucllay huancupa cammi pacha
cuyochicpac churin canqui camtacmi runactapas
camarcanqui ñispas chaypi ancha manchas
pa cararcan chaysi chay supaica mana
rimacoytaca husachispa hu hu ñicacharcan
chaymantari cocacta caraptinri acoc ynas
chac chac ñichircan [266] caycunacta hunayrac
ruraptinsi don x(christob)alca chay huasin hucomanta
tucoy yscay pachapi muyoc pintasca ynacta
ricorcan ymanam rromano pintasca yscai
patarapi rinman chay hynacta chay pin
tasca ñiscanchicsi hucpi huc huchuylla supai
ancha yana ñauinpas collqui yna chaymanta
maquinpiri huc caspi garauato<>yucta atallir
can chaisauas llamap human carcan chay
sauas ñatac chay huchuilla supai carcan chay sa
uari ñatac llamap human chay ynas tu
cuy huasinta yscay patarapi muyorcan [267] cay
cunacta ricuspas don x(christob)alca ancha mancharircan
rimanallanta camarispas   chayssi ña cay su
pai micoyta puchocaptinsi ñatac ninacta
raurarichircan chay astu guaman chayman
yma ayca carascantapas rupachipac [268] cay
ta puchocaptinsi ña casilla ymapas captin
don x(christob)alca rimayta callarircan ñispa yao lluc
llay huancupa camtam ari runa camac pacha
cuyochic ñispa ñisonqui <ñocaca ñinim> pai
tacmi yma ayca rurac ñispam ari tucoy
runacunapas manchasonqui ymapacmi
canan cayachimuarcanqui ñocaca ñinim
jesu xp(christ)o diospac churin caytaccha checan
dios paipac simintataccha viñaypas yupay
chasac ñispam ñine [269] cayri pantanicho cam
canan villahuay   chayca manam dioscho
ñocam yma ayca rurac cani ñispa chay pacha

F 88 V

camta manchancaypac ñispa ñiptinsi chay
supaica hopayarcan mana ña ymactapas
rimarcancho [270] chay pachas don x(christob)alca ricoy ma
nacho supai canqui ñocap y ñiscay jesuxp(christ)o
apuytacho camca atipanquiman ricoy cay
huasiquipas supaipac yntupayascanmi ari
tianqui camtacho ñoca y ñiquiman ñispas an
cha caparispa ayñircan [271] chay pachas huc llau
llaya (ñiycum) chayta vischomurcan caytas ma
na don x(christob)al yacharcancho ycha chay supai ycha
pas diospac partenmanta vischomurca por
qui chay llaullaya ñiscanchicllahuan har
cacuspas chay huasimanta huc ysquina
condep huasincama huacta<manta>ñic
manta chayllahuan arcacuspa mitica
murcan chay pachas riccharircan [272] chayman
ta pachas canan<ca>cama huaquinin huaca
cunactapas atipaspa yna moscoyllapipas
ancha ahcca mitatacsi paria cacactapas chaopi
ñamucactapas atiparcan runacunactari
tucoytapas villapayaspa caycunaca supai
mi ñispa cay chicactam cay mana alli su
paipac cas(can)ta yachanchic don x(christob)alpac atispascantahuanpas
[273] chaymantari ña chayaspa ñaupa pachaca
chayac runacunaracsi taquic carcan ña
hura pachacama chaysi ña chesiñicmanca
yayanchic cananca ñan machan taquichon
ñispas chay saçerdoten paipac rantin yna ñis
ca taquicta taquic carcan yayanchicmi an
cusasonqui ñispatac huc huchoylla quirullapi
apamuc huctas canan ocupi huc manca
mantac churac paimi opian ñispa [274] cay opia
chicoytam yuyacnicmanta callarispa man
yancama opiachicoc carcan ynaspam cayan
tinri ñatac chay puchuscancunacta micoycu

cay ancusayta puchocaspas
chay supaipac upyascan
maticta ahuaman chay
ancusascanman apa
muc carcan chay matic
ta muchancampac

F 89 R

nacta sucya villca ñiscaman apachic carcan
[275] ñaupa pachaca chay chayac runacunas quiquin
sucya villcaman apac carcan cay quipampim
canan pachallampitac sucya villcactapas
llucllay huancupacta caracuyta puchocaspa
carac carcan cay sucya villca caracoytaca
ymaraicum cararcan chaytaca cay quipampim
quillcason pacha camacpac cascantahuan<pas>
[276] CAPI(TUL)O 22
yngacunap pacha camacta ancha yupaychascan
taca manam allichu yachanchic ychaca huaqui
nillantam yachanchic hanac ticsipi muchanan
tas ynticta titi cacamanta mucharcan caymi yngac
ta camahuarca ñispa hura ticsimantam canan
pacha camac ñiscacta caymi yngacta camahuarca
ñispatac mucharcancu [277] cay yscaynin huacacuna
ñiscallanchictas astahuanca tucoy yma aycactapas
yallispa mucharcan collquinhuan corinhuanpas
astauanrac yallichispa allichaspa yanancunactari
ahcca pachac runacta churaspa llamantari tucoy
ynantin llactacunapi churapuspa cay pacha camac
ñiscanchicpac llamancunami ari sucya villca
ñiscanchicpipas cay checa runamanta sayarcan
[278] caytam hunanchanchic yngaca cay ñiscan
chic titi caca hura cochañicpiri pacha camac ñis
cancunalla<>pich pacha puchocan mana ñah chay
mantaca huc llactapas canchu manataccha yma
llapas cancho ñispach ari hunancharcan [279] cay
ta yuyaspataccha yscaynin ñiscanchic hua
cacta astauanrac huaquinin huacacunaman
tapas yallispa mucharcancu hura pacha camac
pa cayllanpiri <ponchao digo> yntictapas sayachispa
chay sayachiscanmi ari canancamapas ponchao

F 89 V

cancha sutioc [280] chaymantas canan tauantin
suyo runacunacta capac hucha ñiscactapas
huarmicta caricta huatanpi corcan cay ca
pac hucha ñiscanchictas ña pacha camacman
chayaptinsi yna causacllacta pachaman cay
mi coyqui yaya ñispa pampac carcan ynatac coric
tapas collquictapas llamacunactari purapi
quillapi mana ancochaspa opiachircan mi
cochircan [281] chaymantam ña may pacham
cay checap llactancunacta mana tam
yarcanchu chay pachas yngap simincama
tac yuncacuna ashuanhuan tictinhuan
cori collqui ñiscactari huatanpi cuspa suc
ya villca ñisca<horcom>man cachamurcan
chaysi sucya villcacta yaya pacha camacmi
cachamuan cammi pachacta tamyachinqui
mana cay cochamanta yaco riptintacmi
runacunapas yacomanta muchuyco tam
yaicuytac caypacmi amuycu ñispas ofre
cicoc carcan [282] yuncacunapas chaymantas coll
qui cori apascantari chay sucya villca cocha
cayllapi huatancunapipas pampac carcan
chaypac yanancu(na)pas yaçapa ayllomantas<>
carcan llama michicninri allaucamanta
cay yaçapa ñiscanchicsi huc runa paico casa sutioc
quipampi ña vira cochacuna captinpas coricta
collquicta pampacta ricorcan [283] ynatacsi ynga
cunari tucoy ynantin huacacunaman alli
ricsisca huacamanca corinta collquinta qui
pollamanta tucoy ynantin huacacta cochic
carcan choc auqui collqui auqui choqui ñispaca
corictam ñinchic chaymantam choc vrpo collc<>
horpo choc tipsi collc tip<>si ñiscacunactas
cochic carcan quipollamanta cay hatunin hua
cacunaca manatacsi huquillanpas pasuccho
[284] cayta hunanchaspatacsi llocllai huancupa

F 90 R

ñiscanchicman chayaspapas cayantin sucya
villcacta carachic carcan yayanpa man
chascan captin cay chicactam yachanchic cay
pacha camacmanta pacha coyochi ñiscanta
ri pai piñaptinsi yna coyon ña ñispari
hucman hoyanta ticrachiptinsi coyomun
manatacsi paica huyanta asllapas coyochincho
tucoy <cuerpon> (cuerpon)ta ticrachiptinca ynallas pacha
puchocanman ñispam runacuna ñircancu
[285] CAPI(TUL)O 23
CAYPIM QUILLCASSON YNGAP
TUCOY YNANTIN HUACACUNAC
TA CAYACHISCANTA CAYPITAC
 MI MACA UISA ÑISCANCHICPA
ATI<N>SCANTAPAS RIMASSON
<ynga>tupay ynga yupanqui ñisca apo caspas
ña tucoy ynantin llactacunacta conquistaspas
ahca huata samarcan ancha cusicuspa chaysi huc
llactacunamanta auca atarircan alancu marca
calanco marca chaque marca ñiscas cay cay
runa(cunas) mana yngap runan cayta munarcancho
[286] chaysi chaycunahuan ahcca huaranga runancunacta
quiuicuspa aucanacorcan doze año chica
cama chaysi tucoy cachascancunactapas collo
chimuptin ancha llaquispa ymanam casson
ñispas yngaca ancha puticorcan [287] chaysi huc
ponchaoca yuyacorcan ymaraycoh cay
huacacunacta siruine corihuan collquihuan

F 90 V

pachayhuan micunayhuan yma aycayhuanpas ma
cayachisac tucoyta cay aucacunata yanapa
huancampac ñispas tucoy ynantin llactacu
namanta cori collqui chasquiccuna amuchon
ñispas cayachircan [288] chaysi ari ñispa rircancu
pacha camacpas rircantac huc huantuhuan
ynatac tucoy llactacunapas huantuhuan
cama tucoy ynantin tauantin suyo ñiscaman
ta chaysi ña aucay patapi tucoy llactacuna
chayaptinsi paria cacaca manarac chayarcan
cho manachos risac risacchos ñic ynas aynicachar
can chay pachas paria cacaca maca uisa churin
ta cacharcan ri cam oyarimuy ñispa [289] chaysi
chayaspa manyallamanta tiaycorcan chicsi
rampa sutioc andasuan chay pachas ynga
ca rimarircan ñispa yayacuna huaca
villcacuna ñam ari yachanqui ymanam
ñoca camcunacta tucoy suncoyhuan
corihuan collquihuan seruiqui chayta ynas
pa camcunaca yna ñoca seruiptica ma
nacho yanapallahuanquimantac checa ahc
ca huaranca runayta perdipti chayraicum
camcunacta cayachimuyquichic ñispa rimap
tinsi manatac hucllapas ay ñircanchu ya
llinrac hupayaspa tiarcancu [290] chay pachas ña
tac yngaca yao rimarichic ynatacchum
campac casmascayqui rurascayqui runacuna
aucanacospa collonca mana yanapahuaita
munaptiquica canallanmi tucoyniquichicta
rupachichiscayqui [291] chayca ymaraicum ñoca
ca corihuan collquiuan huantarcunapi mi
coycunahuanpas opiayhuanpas llamayhuan
pas yma aycayhuanpas seruiqui allichayque
chayca manacho cay checa llaquicoscayta
huyarispa yanapahuanquiman manam
ñiptiquica canallantacmi rupanqui

F 91 R

ñispas ñircan [292] chay pachas pacha camacca ri   D
marimurcan ynga yntiya ñocaca tucoy cam   E
tauanpas ynantin pachacta cuyochic caspatacmi
mana rimarinicho manam ari chay aucallata   L
chu ñocaca collochiman tucoy camtahuampas   A
ynantin pachactahuanpas puchocaymanmi
chayraicutacmi opalla tiacuni ñispas rimarcan   M
[293] chaymantas canan huaquinin huacacunaca   A
opalla tiaptin maca uisa ñiscanchicca rimarir   N
can ynga yntiya ñoca chayman risac ychaca   O
campas cayllapi alli carpacuspa hunanchacuspa
tiay ñocam chaytaca tuy checallapi atipamus   Y
cayqui ñispas ñircan chaysi maca uisa ri
mariptinca seminmantapas llacça llacça pu   P
corimurcan cosni llocsic yna [294] chay pachalla   L
tacsi cori antaranta antaricorcan curitac   U
pincullonpas carcan humanpiri chump rucoc   M
ta pillorispa pusucanri curitac cusmanri   A
yana chay pachas maca uisa rinampac huc qui
quin yngap rinan chicsi rampa sutioc ram   D
pacta corcan chaysi calla uaya runa ñisca   E
ancha sinchi cama yngap acllascan carcan cay ru
nas ahcca ponchao ñantapas pisi ponchaollapis   T
chayachic carcan caycunas maca uisacta aparir   H
can huanturircan chay aucaman [295] chaysi huc or   O
collapi chayachiptinsi chay maca visa paria cacap churin   M
ca allimantarac(si) tamyaita callarircan ynaspas   A
chay llactayoc runacunaca ymah cayca ñispa ca   S
marico<>rcanrac [296] ynaptintacsi yllapaspa asta
uan tamyaitapas yapaspa tucoy llactancunac
ta huaycu huaycucta ruraspa lloclla aparcan
atunnin curaca cactari sinchicunactauanpas
yllapaspas collochircan atun runacu<na>nallas
huaquillan quispircan munaspaca tucoytapas
collochinmansi carcan ynallas huaquinin
runacunactaca tucoyninta atispa cuzcoman

F 91 V

catimurcan [297] chay pachamantaracsi paria cacac
ta astauan yngapas yupaicharcan yanancu
nactapas pihcca chuncacta cuspa ynaspas yaya
maca uisa ymactam coscayqui ymallactapas
munascayquicta mañahuay manam micha
cusaccho ñiptinsi manam ñocaca ymac
tapas munanicho ychaca huacçaca tianqui
tacmi ymanam ñocaycup churijcuna yauyo
ñiscamanta rurancu [298] chaytaca ñiptinsi
allitacmi yaya ñispas ancha mancha
rispa pactah cayca ñocactapas collochihuan
man ñispas yma aycantapas ofrecicoyta mu
narcan [299] chaysi micoy yaya ñispa carachiptin
ca manam ñocaca cay ynacta micoccho cani
mullocta apamuy ñispas mañarcan chay
si mullocta coptinca cap cap ñichispa tui
lla micorcan [300] chaysi mana ymactapas mu
naptintac yñaca ñustancunactaca cama
chiporcan chaytapas mana ho ñiptintac y
naspas ñatac maca uisa paria caca yayanta
villaypac cotimurcan chaymantas canan
yngacunapas ancha quipapipas xauxapi huac
çapas tiarcan y taquircan ancha yapaichaspa
[301] chaymantam canan cay cuzcopi aucay pata
ñiscapi tantanacorcan ñinchic chaypis cay
huacacuna tucoy ynantin ñaca ñircanchic
chay yna tiaspa tucoyninmanta sumacnin
si siua caña villca coto ñisca tiarcan manas
cayhuanca sumacninpica ynantin huaca
cunapas pactar cancho cay chicactam caycu
napta yachanchic
[302] CAPI(TUL)O 24
CAYMANTAM CAY CHECACUNAP
CAUSASCANCUNACTA QUILLCA

F 92 R

SON MACUA YUNCA ÑISCACTA
TAQUISCANCUNACTAPAS CHAY
MANTARI RUNAP PACA
RIMUSCANTAHUANPAS
ñan mari huaquinin capitulopi paria cacap chu
rincunacta rimaspa asllacta yurimuscanta
pas rimarcanchic ychaca cay yurimuscan pacari
muscan simiri cay ynam huaquinmi canan rimancu
hanac paria caca ñiscanchic quitipis huc sacha quiñhua
sutioc canancamapas quinhua sutioctac chaypis çachap
ruruyninmanta runacuna pacarimurcan [303] huaquin
mi runacuna ñincu hanac pachamantas yahuar hor
mamurca chaysi vichi cancha sutioc pachapi chay quiñ
hua ñiscanchic quitipitac<si> chayarcan [304] chaypis canan
llactachacorcan allaocamanta coña sancha cutioc sat
pascamanta yuri naya sullc pahcamanta chupa yacu
yaça(pa)mantam paco masa muxicamantam chauca chim
pita caca sicamantam canan huar cancha llichic cancha
ñiscanchicca yañcacuna cay caycunaca quiquin llactayoc
yuncacunas [305] huaquinin caca sica moralespac chaymanta   huarcancha lli
cancha paicup yayancunas yauyo carcan caycunap paca   chic cancha eran
rimuscansi maurura sutioc aya uireñicpi caycunaca   yungas
quita puricucsi huar canchap paninhuan caçaraspas cacay
hucopitac camachinacusac ñispas paicunaca cay llacta   morales yauyo
pi tiaycorcancu [306] chaysi ña paria cacaman muchaypac ris
pas cacancuna tucoy checacunapas quita yauyo ñispa
chicniptin quipallarac ancha carollapi ric carcan
chaysi anchapuni llaquicuspa caycunaca ynas chicnep
tin ahca huata quipalla cama ric carcancu chaysi
huc mitaca paria cacacta villarcan ñispa yaya cayca
caycunapas checacunapas ancham checnihuan campa
camascayquitacmi pana yauyo runapas caycu ñispas

F 92 V

ancha huacaspa villarcan [307] chay pachas paria caca chu
ri ama llaquicho cay curri chuncullayta apacoy cay
ta atallispa llacça tampopi poco caya ñiscapi ta
quinqui chay pacham yma runam cayca chica pa
ria cacap cuyascan ñispam anchapuni mancha
rinca chaymantaca mana ñam anchacho chicnison
qui ñispas camachimurcan [308] chaymantas cay ya
uyo ñiscanchiccunaca tucoy checacunamantapas
quipampirac chayamuspas chay chuqui chuncullan
ta apaspas ancha cusicuspa runacunapas man
chariptin chayamurcan cayantin ponchaopis pam
papi tucoy ynantin runacunapas mancharip chay
curri chuncullacta atallispa taquircan [309] huaquin
mi canan ñincu tutas ñaupa pacha pariacaman
llamahuan ymahuanpas villac carcancu chaysi ay
llo ayllompi mitanacospa ric cancancu chay pachas
chay quita yauyo ñiscanchicta apachon paipas
ñispa ancha chicñispatac ñircan pay apaspas
canan ña ynti sicamuptin paria cacaman chayarcan
[310] chaysi anchatac llaquicuptin paria cacaca ymapacmi
chica llaquicunqui yao anta capsi ñispas ñircan ñaupa
sutinca pacuyris carcan chay pachas cay cori chuncollac
ta apacoy cayta ricuspam runacuna mana ña chicni
sonquicho ñispas comurcan [311] cay cori chuncullac
tas canan huc mita ñatac paria cacaman muchaypac
rispa chayta apaspa rircan chaysi huc mayo pari ayri
sutioc mayocta chimpaspas chaypi hurmachircan chay
si panatac yma ynapas tucoy hanacman huraman
mascarcan manatac ricuriptinsi ynallatac paria
cacaman rircan [312] chaysi cayantin chayaptinca quiquin
paria cacap cayllampi chay corri chunculla ñiscanchicca
sayacorcan chaysi ñatac huacaspa mañaptin mana ña
ho ñircanchu ñispa manam aucamantacho atispa
apamurcanqui chay yna sumachispa apaycacha<>(n)ayqui
pac caymanri camacnita ruracnita ricuchimusac
ñispa apamuncayquipac ñispam anchapuni anyarca

F 93 R

[313] chaysi yaya ynataccho pincay casac cotichillahuaytac cay
ri ymallactapas chaypac rantinta collahuay ñispa ñip
tinsi ancha huacaptin churi cutij ñocap panay
pac chaupi ñamcap mitampim coscayqui chay pacha
pac suyai ñispas ñimurcan chaysi ynallatac cuti
morcan [314] chaysi ñatac ñiscan yna chaupi ñamcap mi
tampi yauri callinca sutioc canchanpi pircasaua
huc gato montes ancha sumac pintascacama ricurir
can chaysi chayta ricuspa caymi paria cacap ñiscam
ñispas cusicuspa chayta atallircancu taquichispa
tac caytam canan tumnapi cac her(nan)do cancho uillca
huacaycharcan ychaca ñas tucoy ysmurcan
[315] ñam ari runacunap pacarimuscanta rimarcanchic
ychaca caycuna ñiscanchiccunaca tutay quirep churin
si huaquinmi canan çachap ruruyninmanta llocsic
cay tutay quiri ñiscanchictacsi vichi cancha ñiscan
chicpi yurimurcan chaymantam paytac cay llacta
cunactapas atimurcan churijcuna caypi tianca
ñispa [316] chaysi ymanam huaquinin capitulopipas
rimarcanchic yunca çapas carcan ñispa chay ynas
chay yuncacunactaca ña carcospa ayllo ayllompi
cunacoyta callarircancu chacrantapas huasintapas
llactantapas ayllonpi sutintapas paycunap ayllom
pi sutinsi allauca sat pasca passa quine muxica caca
sica sulc pahca yaçapapas carcan yaçapa ñispaca plate
roctam yaçapa ñinchic plateros carcan chaypac su
tintatacsi paicunapas apan ynatac huaquinin
ayllocunapas [317] chaymantas canan llacta ñiscan
chicta conacuspari allaucamanta collanaspa
chasquircan cay allaucas maca callacta<   >
<ta> chasquircan chaymantam sat pasca ñiscanchic
cunam quimqui llacta chasquircan cay quimquillas
curaca huaca ñisca tucoymantapas astauan yupaisi
carcan [318] chaymantas canan chasquircan sulc pahca yaça
pa ñiscanchic ricra huanca ñisca huacacta chayman
tam muxicacuna chasquircan quira rayacta

F 93 V

caca çicacunam llucma suni huacacta chasquircan
huanricuna chauticunam canan paicunaca quiquin
llactayoc ñaupamanta ñam ari ymanam tutay
quiricta mucharcan chaytapas huaquinin capitulo
pipas rimarcanchicmi ari
[319] cay yna ña ñiscanchic yna tutay quiri aticoyta
pochucaptinsi churincunari cayman hamuspas
pacariscan taquicta ymanam vichi cancha
pi taquircan chayta masoma ñispa taquircan
cu <ñam ari> ñam çapa ñiscanchicri runas car
can cay quiquintaca yngas quipampi aparcan chay
pac tenientas ñatac hucta rurarcancu chay
tam s(eñ)or doctor ña aparcan [320] cay ñam cçapa ñiscan
chic<>si runa caspa quisay rinri ñiscacta rinrim
pi churac carcan <cayta> chaymanta maquinpiri
canah yauricta caycunas ñaupa pachaca cori sapa
carcan cay corictaca yngatacsi aparcan chay
mantas cay quillcas caxo ñiscanchicsi tau
nan carca chaymanta chay cori cacya sutioc
caracolsi paihuan amuctas [321] caytas paimi
pacarinchic caymi ñaupac cay llactaman hamuc
chapac ñispas quiquinta oyanta cochuspa ta
quichircan chaymantas aucapi apimuspari hu
yantatac cochuspa caymi sinchi cascay ñispa
taquichircan cay aucapi ña apiptinsi qui
quin chay runa huauqui ñam ari huano
chihuanqui ancha camasca runatacmi
carcani huayotatac rurahuanqui ño
cactari ña pampaman llocçipac capti alli
carahuanqui opiachihuanqui ñispas ñic
carcan [322] cayta oyarispatacsi cay <huc> huaqui
nin huayocunacta carac opiachic carcan
canan ponchaomi pampapi taquinqui ñocahuan
ñispa chaymantam cay huayocta aparispa
tac yscay ponchao huantunacoc carcan
cayantin ponchaomi çarahuanpas papa

F 94 R

huanpas yma ayca cascanhuanpas huarcunacuc
carcan [323] cay huarcunacoytas caycunacta apa
cuspa oma pacha ñisca yurimuscanman cutin
ca ñispa hunancharcancu chaysi rimacospapas
huc rimaytatac simintaca hucman quincochis
pa rimac carcan chaypac fiestanpi cay taqui
cuytam pihca ponchaopi puchocarcan allauca
cunari ynatac [324] hucpi cay chuta caras oma pacha   masoma
ñiscatac cay quiquintacsi vichi canchamanta   chuta cara
huaquinincunahuan hamurcancu chaysi
runa caspatac rumiman chirayarca chay ru
na caspa huaracacuscansi chay huaracampas
chaymanta chay pisco yna ricchaccunas paipac
visan [325] chaymanta chay huana payas canan chay
ta pucoptin llamacunacta llactacuna raquimuc   significa ydolo
cayhuantacsi pacarimurcanpas chay llamarai
cutacsi huaquinin huana payacunactapas
huacaycharcancu cay caytam allaucamanta
chuta carap fiestanta rurac carcancu checa
cunapas conchapas mayquin runapas chay
caracoltaca atallintacmi llamayoccuna
[326] chaymantam canan cay quiquin ñiscanchiccu
nacta yscay huata taquircan huatampi huc
mitalla chaymi yscay huata captinpas yscay
mitallatac taquircan chaymantam canan
yscay huatatac machua sutioc taquicta ta
quircan [327] cay ñaupa ñiscanchicca yunca
sutiocmi cay machua ñiscanchicpac mitam
pim canan yscay huatatac taquircan huc
chupa ñisca ychucta pirtaspas ancha quero
cunacta chacnaspa chayman pilluic carcan
yscayta caymi suninman canchis ricra chic
tayoc chaymantam atunninmanmi yscay
<>braço alli macallanchic yna humampim
canan caçira sutioc hocsatac caypa sapinmi
puca pucalla caytas churac carcan caymi

F 94 V

acchan ñispa [328] chaymantas ña tucoyta allichas
pa hucta yomca ñispa carip hunanchay
ninta churarcan huctari huasca sutiocta
huarmip onanchayninta churarcan ña
churaspam canan tucoy runacuna alli pachan
ta tamta ñiscantapas churacuspa sitayta
ña callarircancu cay si(ta)na<>m vihco suti
oc [329] cayta sitaipac ña<>upacnin ponchaopitac
mi tucoy ynantin caullamacunaman ric car
cancu llamantapas ymanam paria caca
man campanillayocta chaymanta sarçillo
yucta aparcan chay yna chaysi tucoynin
runacuna chaucallamanpas curri ñisca tambo
sica orcomanpas ric carcancu çapampi caulla
mancunamanpas chay pacha cay caullama
cunaman rispas chay caracol ñiscanchic
ta huacachispa pucupayaspa ric carcancu chay
pacmi çapampi runacunapas huaquinin
taricnincunaca cay caracol ñiscanchicta
atallircancu [330] chaymantam canan cay

chuta   chuta ñiscanchicta ña yscayninta sayachis
pa sitayta callarircan cayta sitaptinsi huar
micunaca ayllo ayllo yaicuspa sitaptin ma
na huancarayoc huarmicunapas taquipuc
carcan cay simicta rimaspa huaccha churi
quicta chasquipuy ñispa huasca ñiscanchictari
huaccha churiquicta chasquipuytac ñispatac
[331] chaysi cay sitaccuna chay chutap chucchanpi
chayachiptinca cayri maycancha tucoy huc ayllo
cunamanta hanacnin manyanpi chayachircan
chaysi huc huacamaypac ricranta o ymallanta
pas apaspa yañcacta coc carcan [332] cay yañcan
checamanta quipampas m(art)yn misa yauri carcan
allaucamantam ju(a)n chumpi yauri huañuc [333] cay
yañca ñiscanchicsi ña huc ayllo ñiscan
chic pochocaptin chay chutaman llocarcan

F 95 R

chay puypu ñisca huacamayap ricranta apas
pa <chaysi> chaysi may pihc chayachircan chay
ta sorcuspa chaypi chay puypu ñiscahuan
hunanchamurcan chaysi ñatac hoc ayllo yai
cuspapas ynatac hocri ynatac <n> [334] chaymantas
ñatac huasca ñiscanta huarmipac sitar
ca churita yma ayca micunallaytapas coanca
ñispa chaymanta yomca ñiscanchictari
cari churita chauaracta yma ayca causaycu
nacta coanca ñispa [335] ña may pacham yscay
nin chutacunacta sitayta puchocarcan chay
pachas chay ñaui ñiscapi chucchapi chayachic
cuna yañcaman llamanta cayhuan cay
homa pacha ñiscacta villapuay ñispa coc
carcan chaysi cay huchuylla llamactaca
chay llamayoc manatac anchantaca apacoc
cho yañcamusca ñiscallanchictacsi ayca
llama captinpas apacoc micococ
[336] chaymantam canan ñatac cayantin pon
chao ancha tutamanta quimquillaman tucoy
runacuna ric carcancu chay quimquilla ñis
canchic huacas ancha llamayoc yma ay
cayoc chayta coyaicuanca ñispas tucoy
runacuna allaucapas ric carcan chaypi
llamayta mañamusac ñispa [337] chayman
rijpacsi aslla tictinta ashuanta cocanta
apac carcan chay huana paya ñiscanchic
tari huacachipayaspa chaymantas ñaupac
nin ponchaopitacsi vichuc maricuna cay
mi tucoy sat pasca sulc pahca yaçapacuna
chay quiquin quimquillapitac taquic car
can llamantapas nacaspa poconim ñis
pa [338] chaymantam ñatac huraycumor
can maypim quira raya tiarcan chay anac
nin pampaman cay pampam huara ca
ya sutioc caypim ñatac ymanam llac

F 95 V

sa tampopi yomca huascacta sayachircan
chuta ñiscacta chay ynallatac sayachir
can llamapac cay llamapacmi horcopac
chinapac ynatac sitarcancu [339] cay sitayta
puchucaspam canan ymanam llacsa tam
pupi carcan ynallatac llamanta yañcaman
coc carcan cayhuan muchapuay allitac
casac ñispa chaymantam canan cayman
cutimuspa ymanam quimquillaman
pas hoño hoñolla ric carcan llaman
tapas campanayocta aysaspa ynallatac
cutimorcancu [340] caytam carco caya ñin
cu ymanam allimanta coyoi coyoilla
rihuan yna caycuna puricoytas huaro
cactam tumani ñispa ñircancu cay hua
roca ñiscanchicta tumaspas chay hua
na paya ñiscanchictapas pocopayaspa
ric carcancu cay chicallactam yachanchic
cay machua ñiscacta yachanchic [341] chayman
tam canan cay llacça tampopi yunca ñiscan
chicta huaquinin muta caya runas carcan
ñincu huaquinmi canan collis carcan
nincu ynam ychaca cay colli ñiscanchicca
yaru tinepis tiarcan caypac cascantam can
cay quipampi quillcasson
[342] CAPI(TUL)O 25
CAYPIM QUILLCASSON YMANAM
COLLI RUNACUNACTA YARU TI
NI ÑISCAMANTA HORA YUNGA
MAN HUAYRA APARCAN
CHAYTA

F 96 R

cay colli ñiscanchic llactayocsi yarutini ñis
capi tiarcancu chaysi huc ponchaoca paria caca
chay yaru tini ñiscanchic llactampi collicuna vp
yaptin chayarcan chaysi manyallamanta pa
ria cacaca tiaycuspa ancha huacchalla yna tiar
can [343] chaysi manatac pillapas vpiachita munar
canchu chaysi huc runalla ancusaycorcan cay
acusacnintas yapaicuay huauqui nispa ñircan
chaysi yaparcantac chaymantas cocallayquicta
acuchihuay ñispa ñatac mañarcan chaysi cor
cantac [344] chay pachas huauqui cay sachactam a
piconqui ñoca may pacham cayman amusac
chayca cay runacunactari ama villaycho yna
cusicochon ñispas riporcan [345] chaysi pihca pon
chaomantaca ancha huayra atarimurcan
cay huayratacsi cay colli runacunactaca çapam
pi yscay quimça mita tumaycochispa huayra
ancha caroñicpi aparimurcan chaysi huaqui
ninca yna apariptintac muspaspa huañorcan
huaquintas canan causacllacta caruaylloñic
orcopi chayachircan cay orcom canancamapas
colli ñisca <> orco runacunaca collorcansi mana
tacsi hucllapas canchu [346] chaymantas cay huc ru
na yaru tinipi paria cacacta vpiachicca ñiscan
yna huc çachacta apicuspa yna quispircan ña tu
coyta apaita puchocaspas ñircan huauqui çapallai
quim canqui caypim viñay tianqui caymantam ño
cap churicuna ñocacta muchaypac hamuspa chusco
quiere dezir quatro corpaya huacçacuna cocacta
viñaylla acochisonqui ñispas sutiyquipas capac
huanca ñiscam canqui ñispas rumiman chiraya
chircan [347] caytam s(eñ)or doctor auila chay quiquin <> tias
campi chayaspa huaquin runacunahuan paquir
can ña paquispam hurañicman vischurcan
cay chicactam cay colli ñiscacunamanta
yachanchic yna ñiscancamatacmi huacçacunari acochircancu
viñay huata

F 96 V

[348] CAPI(TUL)O 26 YMANAM
MACA CALLACTA PA(RI)A CACA
ATIRCAN YMANAM
ÑA ATISPA CHURARCAN
CHURINCUNACTA
ñan mari maca calla ñiscanchicta yachan
chic s(a)n damian llactamanta hanacnin
orcupi cascanta cay maca calla ñiscanchic
orcopis chay llactayoc runa carcan pihcca
marca ñisca chaymantam sutca ñiscapas car
cantac caycuna llactayoc huc punchao vp
yacuptinsi paria caca chay llactaman cha
yarcan yna chayaspas manyallamantatac
tiaycorcan [349] yna tiaycuptinsi manatac pilla
pas ancusaycorcanchu chaymanta piñaspas
pihccantin punchaonimpi chay llactacta collo
chircan puca tamya quello tamya atari
muspa [350] huaquim runacunam canan huc
simictatac rimancu ñispa cay maca callapi
llactayuc runacunas huc punchaosi huaquinin
runacuna riuihuan pocllacorcan huaquinin ru
nacunas vpyacorcan chay yna captinsi hanac
orco canlli ñiscamantaca aslla pucutay ricuri
morcan chaymantari tamyari puca tamya orma
murcan as asllarac chaymantas ñatac yllapa
murcan [351] cay yna captinsi runacunaca tucoy
nin mancharircan ymam cayca ñispa mana
cay ynacta ricuc caspa chayssi huaquininca aucam
ñispa sayaicorcan huaquinsi miticarcan [352] huc runas
armicu sutioc carcan cayssi ahcca churicoy caspa
churinta catirespa aco rison chay chacranchic

F 97 R

huauapitac huañomuson ñispas chacranman miti
carcan cay chacra ñiscampi chayaptinsi chaymanta
tucoyninta chirayachircan rumi tucochircan cay
rumi tucucsi canancamapas runa ynalla churin
cunahuan tiancu canancamapas runacunapas ar
micu ñincu [353] chaymantas huaquinin runacuna
ayquispapas mayta ayquictahc puca tamya apircan
pachallampitacsi rumi tucorcan ynatacsi maca
callapi huaquinin runacunapas rumiman cama
chirayarcan [354] huc runas canan cay sutca ñiscanchic
ayllomanta ancha huacaspa ynallataccho saquiscay
qui yayallacta maca calla ñam ripac cani ma
natacmi yma callpallaypas canchu cay milagrocta
atipancaypac ñispa huacaptinsi maca callap
vmanca paycamalla vrmamurcan chay yna vr
mamuptinsi chayta sucarispa tuylla mitica
chircan huaman yna cay runatacsi ancha ca
masca carcan [355] chaymantas cay maca callari y
manam runa ynas vmayoc chaquiyoc maqui
yoc carcan chaysi cay vmanta chay yna mi
ticachispa ñatac runa miramuspa llantapapi
pihcca orcupi tiaycorcan cay orco tiaycuscantam
llactachacuscan captin pihcca marca ñinchic [356] chay
pihcca marca ñiscanchicpis maca callap humanca
canancamapas tian chaysi chaypi caypi maca calla
yocmi canchic ñispa churincunactapas ñaupac
yuricta canricha ñincu allaucacunari maca calla
llactayoc caspas canricha ñintac ynatac pihcca
marcacunapas [357] chaymantas ña tutay quire con
quistamurcan chay pachaca chay sutica ñisca
ayllocunaca cay quitiman cutimurcan chacray
allpai hucopitac llactay vcupitac tiamusac pa
ria caca tutay quiricta manchaspa yupaychaspa
ñispas cutimurcancu chay sutica ñiscanchicmi ca
nan cay llacta s(a)n damianpica tucoy collorcan causac
nincunapas sucsa canchapi tumnapi chayllay

F97 V

[358] CAPI(TUL)O 27 YMANAM RUNACUNA
ÑAUPA PACHA HUAÑUSPA PICHCA PUNCHAO
PIM CUTIMONI ÑISPA RIMARCANCU
CHAY CHAYCUNACTAM QUELLCASON
ancha ñaupa pachaca huc runa huañuptin ayan
taca yna<cta>llas churarayachircan pichca pon
chao cascancama chaysi animanri huc
chuspi chicallan sio ñispa pahuac carcan
cay ña pahuaptinsi ñam rin paria caca
camacnicchic ruracninchicta ricumuypac
ñispas ñircancu [359] huaquinmi canan ma

manarac paria ca   nas chay pachaca paria caca carcancho ynallas
capas caruinchupas   hanacñicman pahuarcan (yauri llanchaman) [360] chaymantas ca
ricuriptintacsi yauri nan pi<c>hca ponchaomanta ñatac cutimuc
llanchapi vichi cancha carcan chay ña cutimuptinsi micuycunacta
ñiscapipas runacuna   vpyaitapas camarispas suyac carcan chaysi
ca pacarimurcan   ña chayamuspaca ñam cutimuni ñispalla
                      yayancunahuanpas huauquincunahuanpas an
                      cha cusicuc carcan mana ñam cananca vi
                      ñaypas huañosaccho ñispa [361] chay pachas canan
                      runacuna ancha mirarcan micunampacpas
                      ñacayta rispa cacactapas patactapas chacran
                      pac allichaspa ancha ñacarispa causarcancu
                      [362] chay yna captinsi chay pacha vc runa hua
                      ñurcan ña huañuptinsi chay runap yayan
                      cuna huauquincunapas huarminpas suyarcan
                      ña chayamunan captin pihcca ponchaonimpi chay
                      si cay runaca manatac chayamurcanchu cayantin
                      ponchaopis soctantin ponchaopi(rac) chayamurcan chay
                      si yayanpas huauquinpas huarminpas ancha piñas
                      pa suyarcancu ña chayamuptinsi huarminca
                      piñaspa ymanam chica quella canqui huaquinin
                      runacunaca mana pisipaspam chayacumon
                      camcho cayna yanca suyachicuhuanqui ñispas
                                                              ancha

F 98 R

ancha piñapayarcan [363] chay hina piñaspas huar
minca huc curumtayhuan chay anima chayamuc
ta chocarcan hina chucaptinsi tuylla sio ñispa
cutircan chaymantas canan mana ña pi runa
huañuptinpas cutimuccho carcan
[364] CAPI(TUL)O 28 YMANAM PARIA CACAP
MITAMPI ANIMACUNACTA CARAC
CARCAN CHAYMANTA TODOS SAN
TOSPACRI YMA YNAM ÑAU
PA PACHA HUNANCHARCAN
ñam ari huaquinin capitulopi paria caca<p fiestan>cta
<ta> muchaypac rispa ymanam runacuna huañoc
nincunacta huacac carcan (caracpas carcan) chay chaycunacta rimar
canchic chay carascancunacta yuyarispam canan
runacuna manarac alli xp(christia)noman tucospa rimar
cancu cay todos santopac ynatacmi vira cochacuna
pas ayanta tullunta caran micochin ñispa <ygle>
aco ygleciaman huañucninchiccunacta caramu
son ñispa [365] ñaupa pachaca yma ayca micoycu
nactapas alli chayascacamata apac carcan
chaymantam canan huc runa huañuptinpas an
cha ñaupac cascanta yuyarispa huañucninchicca
pihcca ponchaomantam cutimunca suyasuntac
ñispa suyac carcancu cay pi<>ch<>(ca) ponchao ñiscanchic
camam huañuscanmanta tutancuna pacaric <car>
carcan [366] ña pihcantin ponchaonimpin yarutiniman
huc<runa> huarmi alli pachanta churaspa ric carcan
chaymanta pusamusac ñispa o suyamusac ñispapas
chaysi chay huarmi ñiscanchicri ashuanhuan micoy
cunactari apaspa ric carcan [367] chaysi yaru tini ñiscan
chicpi ña ynti sicamuptin chay anima chayac carcan
chaysi ñaupa pachaca yscay quimça atun chuspi

F 98 V

runacunaca llacsa anapalla ñispam ñincu chaysi
chay pachan apascansaua tiaycoc carcan [368] chaysi
hunaycama tiaspa ña huaquinin huancoy curo
ñiscanchic ripuptin haco rison llactaman ñispas
huc huchoylla rumillacta cay(mi) pai ñic <h>yna aparis
pa amuc carcan chaysi cay huarmi ña chayamup
tin tuylla huasimpas alli pichasca <> captin caray
ta ña callarircan ña caracoyta puchocaspas ña
tac vpyachircan paycunari ayan micuptin
micorcantac [369] ña <ancha> chisiñicpis pihca mita
taquircan huacaspa tucoy aylloncuna canan
ña may pacham pihca mita taquicoyta huaca
cuytapas puchocarcan chay pachas chay rumi apa
muscanta calliman vischuc carcan cananca
cuti amaña ñocaycoca huañosaccho ñispa [370] chay
ponchaotacmi arañuhuan huaticacoc carcan y
mamantam cay runa huañopuan ñispa chaymi
pay piñaptinmi chay piñaptinmi ñispapas ñip
tin chaycunacta paria cacacta ñiptinpas o may
quintac ñiptinpas chaycama coynhuan yma yman
huanpas puchocac carcan cay chicactam cay hua
ñuc runacunamanta yachanchic
[371] chaymantam canan guaro cheripi o quintipipas
cay todos santos ñiscanchicpi ygleçiapi coñicllac
ta churapuson ñispa papactapas yanospa chayman
ta charquincunactari alli huchoyucta runap mi
concampac yna churapuncu camchacta aycha
yanuscactapas chaymantari çapa runanpi huc
cantarillo ashuantauan caycuna ñiscanchic
ta churaspaca paicuna vnamchaptinca ayan
cunahc micon chayta yuyaspataccha coñic
llata cama ymactapas aycactapas churaponcu
[372] CAPI(TUL)O 29 YMANAM HUC
YACANA SUTIOC HANAC PACHA
MANTA HURAYCUMON YACOCTA
                    HUP

F 99 R

HUPYAIPAC CHAYMANTARI
HUAQUININ COYLLORCUNACTA
HUANMI RIMASON YMA SU
TINTAHUANPAS
cay yacana ñiscanchicsi llamap camaquin çi
eloñicta chaupicta purimon ñocanchic runacuna
pas riconchicmi ari yanalla hamocta chaymanta
chay yacana ñiscanchicsi mayo hucocta purimon
ancha atunmi ari yanayaspa çieloñicta yscay
ñauiyoc concanpas ancha hatun captin hamun
caytam runacuna yacana ñincu [373] cay yacana
ñiscanchicsi ña huc runap cussinpi venturan cap
tin paysaua hurmamuspa mayquin pucyollaman
tapas yacucta vpyac chaysi chay runa ancha mill
huasapa ñitimuptin chay millhuanta huaquinin
runaca tirac [374] cay ricachicuysi tuta cac ynaspas cayan
ti pacha pacarimuptinca chay millhua tirascanta ricuc
ricuptinsi chay millhuaca ancaspas yuracpas yana
pas chumpipas yma ymana ricchaccuna millhuas ta
cu tacu cac caytas canan mana llamayoc caspapas
tuylla ranticuspa pachan ricuscanpi tirascanpi mu
chac carcan ña muchaspas huc china llamacta
horcontauan ranticoc chay rantiscallanmantas
ñahca yscay quimça huaranca llamamanpas chayac
cay ñiscanchictaca ancha ahca runactas ñaupa pa
cha cay tucoy proui(nci)api yna ricachicurcan [375] cay ya
ca ñiscanchictacsi chaupi tuta mana pipas yachaptin
mama cochamanta tucoy yacocta vpyan mana
vpyaptinca hutcallas tucoy ynantin mundocta
pampahuahhuan [376] cay yanaca ñiscanchicpi aslla
yanalla ñaupac rin chaytam yutum ñincu
chaymantari cay yacanatacsi huahuayoc hua
huanpas ñoñocuptinsi rihcan chaymantam
quimça coyllor checalla rin chaytam condormi

F 99 V

ñincu ytatacmi suyuntuytapas guamantapas
[377] chaymantam chay cabrillas ñinchic chaytam
<ancha> atuchac cama hamuptinca canan hua
ta pocoymi cason ñincu huchochac cama amuptin
ri ancha muchoymi cason ñincu huaquinin coy
llor muyo muyolla hamuctam pihca conqui ñispa
ñincu [378] huaquin coyllormi ari ancha atuchac
ca(ma) amon chaytam canan poco huarac villca
huarac cancho huarac ñispa sutiachinco cay
caycunactas ñaupa pacha cayca camacmi
ruracmi ñispa runacuna huaquinillan
muchac carcan huaquininric cay ñiscanchic
huacacunacta caymantas astauan yalli
chisac ñispas cay coyllorcunacta muchac carcan
ña sicamuptin chay<> tutari mana aslla
pas puñospa cay chicallactam yachanchic
[379] CAPI(TUL)O 30 YMANAM ALLAUCAP
COCHAMPI YSCAY HUACA CARI HUAR
MI TIAN PORUIPI CAYCUNAP CAS
CANTAM QUILLCASSON
ancha ñaupa pachas huc runa anchi cara sutioc
carcan cay anchi cara ñiscanchicsi <> huc pucyo
purui sutiocpi yacucta tiamun cay allaucacu
nap chacranman hamuncampac cay hina
tiaptinsi huc huarmica surcoñicmanta picoy
huarmi hamurcan cay huarmip sutinmi
huayllama [380] cay huayllama ñiscanchicsi chay
purui ñiscanchicpi chayaspa <> tura ñocap
chacraymanca ancha pisim yaco hamun cam
llacho caypi yacocta pusanqui ñocaycoca
ymahuanmi causayman ñispas chay

F 100 R

quiquin pucyo hucopi tiaycorcan [381] chaysi chay
anchi cara ñiscanchic<p>ca alli sumac huarmi cap
tin tuylla enamoraspa alli simipitac napai
corcan chaysi chay huarmica manatac chay
yacocta cayman cacharijta munarcancho y
na captinsi panatac ama pani hinaycho yma
huanmi ñocap churicunaca causanca ñispas alli
simipi <huan>tac napaicorcan [382] yna captinsi chay
anchi cara ñiscanchicpa churincunaca hamuspa
chay yacocta cay<cocha> lliuya cocha ñiscaman vischo
morcan chay quiquin pucyo hurayllapitacmi yscay
huchuylla cocha ña ñiscanchic lliuya cocha tuta cocha
ñisca cay lliuya cocha hucupim quimça taua
huchuylla suytucama rumicuna sayancu chaymi
anchi carap churincuna ñisca [383] mana cay churin
cuna yna ñatac ñatac rispa yacocta vischu
munman chayca ancha pisitacsi caymanca lluc
simunman carca <con todo esso> yna captinpas
ancha pisitacmi llucsimun [384] chay pachas cay ñis
canchic anchi cara huarminri huayllama
ña cay yna yacupacri manacoyta pochucaspas
yscaynin huchallicorcancu ña huchallicuspallas
caypitacmi ñocaca viñaypas tiasac ñispas
rumiman chirayarcan cay rumin canancama
pas yna tiancu churin(cuna)pas lliuya cocha vcu
pitac tiancu cay chicallactam caycunamanta
yachanchic [385] ychaca cay quipampi ña cay llacta
pi yachaycuspas huacçacuna allauca ayllomanta
chay purui ñiscanchicman ña tamya mita pucho
captin ric carcancu rarca pichaypac chay pachas
chay huacçacuna ayca runa caspapas ña chayas
pa chay lliuya cocha ñiscanchicta antarintapas
pucuspa chay cocha sauacta tumaycoc [386] ña tumay
cuspas anchi cara yaco tiamucta napaycoc riccu
chaysi simillahuan aslla cocallanta vischupus
pa ñatac cocha sahuaman cutimuc chay cocha

F 100 V

CONCHA

llacxa misa
pauquir buxi
llama tanya
hualla
calla

sauas ñatac anchi caracta chaymanta churincu
nactapas chay quiquin lliuya cocha tuta cocha
ñiscanchictapas muchaccu [387] ñaupa pachaca lla
manhuan canan quipanri mana llamayoc
caspa coyllanhuan tictillanhuan ymallan
huanpas cay muchacoyta puchocamuspas rarca
allayta callarimurcancu tucoy runacuna cay
chica simillam caycunap cascan pochucan
[388] CAPI(TUL)O 31 YMANAM CAY HANACNIN
CAPITULOPI COCHAP CASCANTA RIMAR
CANCHIC CHAY YNALLATACMI CAY
MANTA CAY CONCHA AYLLOMANTA
YANÇA ÑISCA COCHACTA RIMASON
CAY SIMIRE CAY HINAM
ñaupa pacha cascantaca ymanam cay llactacu
napi yunga runa çapa carcan chay chaycunacta
ca ñam ari huaquinin capitulocunapipas ri
marcanchic cay yna yuncatacsi cay conchap llan
tanpipas tiarcancu [389] yna tiaptinsi ymanam hua
quinin capitulocunapipas rimarcanchic yauri llan
chamantas vichi canchamanta huaquinmi canan
quiñhuamantas ñispa rimancu ynatacssi
cay conchacunapas yauri llancha ñiscanchic
manta pihcca runa yurimurcan (pacha vcumanta) [390] caycunap su
tinmi canan ñaupacninmanta llacsa misa panin
ri cuno cuyo sutiocsi paihuan hamurcan chay sauam
pauquir buxi chay sahuam llama tanya cay quim
cantim runam ñaupaclla cay llactacta atimur
can chaymantam yscay runatac huauquincu
na hualla sutioc hucri calla sutioc [391] cay yscayninsi
huaquinin huauquincunaca ñaupamuptin

F 101 R

aslla quiparimurcan yna quiparimuspas ñanta
pantaspa yauyoñicman rircancu chaymancha
huauquicuna rincu ñispa chaysi ña hunaymanta
rac cay quimça huauquincunaca chacractapas y
mactapas ña tucoy raquinacoyta puchocaptinrac
cutimurcancu [392] cay hualla ñiscanchicpac churincu
na<m>s cay lazaro puypu rocçi chaymantas chay ñaupac
churi llacxa misa ñisca ña colloypac caspas cay la
zarop aguelon cassa chauca sutioc pai llacxa misap
sobrinon captin yansa ñisca cochacta caytacmi
cay coscajman yaiconca ñocaca ñam ari collo
ni ñispas haquiporcan chaymantaracsi paipac
yança cochapas suyon carcan caypim cay hua
lla ñiscanchicta saquinchic [393] cananmi chay quim
ca runa hamuscanta chayamuscantauanpas rima
son yma ñam ñaca ñircanchic yuncacunas car
can ñispa chay ynas chay pachaca cay yansa
cochamanta yaconta pusamuspa ancha ya
conpas sobra captin chay llantapa horcup si
quincama yaconpas chayaptinsi ancha cusicus
pa causarcancu [394] yna causaptinsi cay quimça
runa ñiscanchic chay yuyacnin llacxa misa
ñisca ña may pacham yauri llancha ñiscapi
pachamanta yurimurcan chay pachas huc ru
mi chucuyoc yurimurcan caypac sutinmi llacsa
yacolla carcan cay llacça yacolla ñiscanchicta
apacuspas chay quimça runa ñiscanchic hamurcan
[395] chaysi chay yança hanacninpis yana pucyo sitioc
chaypi chayamurcan chaysi paicunaca chayllapi
tiacorcancu vpiacuspa chaysi cay yunca runa
cunaca chaypim quimça runa tiacon ancha man
chaypac ñicta vyarispas huaquinin runacuna
ricoc rircancu [396] yna ricuptinsi chay llacxa misa
ñiscanchicca chay chucon llacxa yacolla ñiscan
ta ricochircan chay runaman chayta ricuspa
llas chaycunaca tucoynin tuylla huañurcan

F 101 V

yna huañocta ricuspas huaquinin runacu
na pi ricpas ynatac huañomuptinsi chay yun
cacuna ñiscanchicca hacochic risontac
caymanta chay 3 runacuna tarihuahchuan
chayca tucoytam collochihuahchuan ñispas
mancharispa llactantapas chacrantapas yna
lla saquispa miticarcancu [397] cay yna miticas
pas huc yunca runaca manam sutintaca yachan
chiccho cay runas huc churinta tuta miticaspa
concha sicapi saquircan yaçali sutiocta [398] huc huac
cha vyhuascallanta aparispas <y>cay yaçali
ñiscanchicpa yayanca miticarcan chaysi
ña chay(chimpa) capari caya ñahca yana siriman vichay
cunapi pacha pacariptin ricsircan chaysi chay
ca chay huaccha vyhuascallan carcan chaysi
ancha huacaspa manatac cutinampas ya
chacuptin ynallatac ripurcan [399] chay pachas
cay saquisca huamra yaçali ñiscanchicca
chay concha sica cruz sayan chay oculla
pi pacacorcan huamra caspa ancha mancha
rispa chay pachas cay quimça runa ñis
canchicca chay llactaman chayarcancu
ña chayaspas huasinta ymantapas cona
cuspas chay pacha llacxa misaca chay huamrata
tarimorcan [400] chaysi churi ama llaquicho ñoca
huanmi tianqui chay huaquinin huauquicuna
huañochison ñispa ñihuaptinpas ñocam
amachascayqui ychaca ñocap llamaytam
michinqui ñispas ñircan chaysi cay huamrac
ta chay huaquinin huauquincunaca ricuspa
huañochontac cay huamraca porqui caymi
caya mincha ñocap chacraymi pachaymi ñis
pa ñihuahhuan ñispas ancha chicnispa ñir
cancu [401] chaysi chay llacxa misa ñiscanchicca
manam ymapacmi hañochison yallin ca
usacochon caymi yma ayca causascantapas
                    chac

F 102 R

chacrantapas ymantaps aycantapas ricuchihua
sson ñispas ñircan [402] chaysi chaycunaca mana
tac munarcancho huañochuntac ñispa chaysi
chay llacxa missa ñiscanchicca piñarispa hua
uqui ñam chica mita ñiqui pactah tulloyquipas
cochañicman rinman ñocam causachon ñini
ñispas ñircan chayracsi huaquinincunapas vpa
llarcan [403] chaysi chay llacxa missa ñiscanchicca chay huam
racta llamanta michichispa causachircan yna michis
pas chay yauri llanchamanta cuno cuyo llaxsa misap   cuno cuyo
panin hamuchuan tinquinacorcan yna captinsi
quipampi ña yuyac tucospaca oma pacha ñisca
yauri llanchamanta hamucpacpas yañca carcan
cay yaçali huamra ñiscanchicsi x(Christob)al chauca guamanpac
aguelon carcan [404] chaymantam canan cay oma
pacha ñiscanchictaca ymanam checacunapas hua
yo ñiscacta churaspa pihcca ponchao taquircan
ynallacsi paicunapas taquircan chaymanta
chuta ñiscacta vihcohuan sitaspapas caripac
huarmipac sayachispa chaymantari llamapac
ri hinatac [405] chaymanta huacçacunari yna
tacsi concha sica ñiscanchicpi tiarcancu mitampi pa
ria cacacta chaupi ñamucacta vpiaspapas huc pon
chaollatacsi checacunahuampas pactalla vpiar
cancu cay chicactam caycunap causascanta ya
chanchic
[406] chaymantam canan yança cocha ñiscanchicta
rimason cay llacxa missa ñiscanchicsi ña may pacham
huaquinin huauquincunahuan conchaman chaya
murcan chay pachas yma ayca causaycunacta chas
quispa yança cochacta chasquircan llacxa misa ñiscan
chic chaymantas pauquir buxi ñiscanchic huaychu coto
ñiscacta chasquircan chaymantam llama tanya
ñiscanchicri huyo sana huasicta chasquircan [407] chay
yna caycunacta chasquispam canan causanampac

F 102 V

collquiri

çapampi callarircancu chaymantam cay llac
xa misa ñiscanchicri yança cocha ñiscacta siruii
ta callarircan chay yança ñiscanchicpis huc hua
ca collquiri sutioc carcan caycunacta siruiptinsi
cay tucoy conchacunaca miconcampac çaracta call
paporcan viñay huata [408] chay pachas chay collquiri
ñiscanchic huacaca <huc> huarmicta ancha munar
can yna munaspas yauyocamapas chacllacama
pas tucoy ynantin pachacta mascarcan chay yna
mascaspas manatac tarircanchu [409] chaysi huc
ponchaoca cuni raya ñiscanchicca yao caylla
pim sispallapi huarmiquica ñispas ñircan chaysi an
cha cosicuspa rircan chaysi yampilla hana<>(c)nin hur
cumanta chay yampilla ñiscanchicman cahuay
corcan yna cauarispas huc huarmicta ancha
collananta taquicocta ricorcan cay huarmip su
tinsi capyama carcan<can> [410] chaysi cay hina chi
ca sumacta ricuspa tuylla soncompi caytacmi
huarmi canca ñispa yuyacorcan ynaspas huc
muchachontaca rij churi chay huarmicta villamuy
llamayquim huc <china> orco llamallacta huachan
ñispa villayconqui chaymi payca tuylla ha
munca ñispas cacharcan [411] yna cachaptinsi chay
runaca rircan ña chayaspas mamay llamay
quim hanac orcullapi huachan ñispa villaptin
si ancha cosicuspa tuylla huasinman chica
cacharcan chaypis <huan> curi huancarantapas
chaopipi churaycuspa yscay huchuylla coca hua
yacallanta hucllayninman choraycucuspa
chaymantari huc purongo ashuallanta aparispa
ancha vtcaspa hamurcan cay purongo ñiscanchictam
conchaconaca lataca ñincu [412] chaysi cay huaca
collquiri ñiscanchicca yna amucta ricuspa an
cha cusicuspa tuylla cay yança ñiscaman cu
timurcan chaysi chay chay muchachon ñiscanchicca

F 103 R

chay huarmicta pusamuspa ñahcam chayanchic
cayllapim ñispas llullaspa pusamurcan [413] chaysi
cay collquiri ñiscanchicca huc callcallo tucuspa chay
<yança> yampilla hanacnin hurcupi suyarcan chay
si ña chayaspa cay huarmica chay callcallucta api
sac ñircan yna apisac ñiptinsi chayman cayman
as aslla pauarispa mana apichicorcancho [414] ynaspas
quipampica apircantac apispas micllaricurcan cayta
apispas chay rataca ñiscanmanta ashuanta sichay
corcan cayta sichaycuptinsi tuylla chay sichascanpi
pu<y>cyo ña tucorcan chay pucyos canancamapas
ratac tupi sutioc [415] chaysi chay callcallo hucllaycus
canca chay huarmip vicsan hucopi hatun tucomur
can ancha vicsantapas nanachispa yna captinsi
cayca ymah ñispa ricuptinsi chay pachaman hur
mascampica huc cari alli sumac huamralla ricurir
can chaysi tuylla pana ñocactam hucllaycoarcanq(ui)
ymanasonmi ñocam cayachimurcayqui ñispas
ancha misqui siminhuan napaicorcan [416] chaysi huarmi
ri ynatac tuylla enamorarcan payhuan yna caspas
puñorcancu ña puñospas canan cay yança cocha llactan
man pusamurcan chaymantas canan yayanca ma
manca turancunapas ayllonpas maymanmi rircan
ñispa huacaspa cama mascarcancu [417] yna mascaspas
ancha hunaymantarac huc yampilla runa llucaua
sutioc churiquica ancham villcayan ymanpas aycan
pas cosayucmi ñispa villaptinsi tuylla hamurcan
chaysi ña tarispa ymapacmi churita panita suhua
muarcanqui camcho tucoy ynantin llactacunacta
saycuspa mascachihuanqui ñispas ancha piñaspa
cananmi cutichisac ñispa ñircan [418] yna ñiptinsi
yaya huauqui ancha chicantatacmi mana cam yayai
ta villascaymanta anyahuanqui ymactam cos
cayqui huasictacho cayri chacractacho llamactacho
runactacho chauaractacho corictacho collquictacho

F 103 V

yma ymactam munanqui ñispas munachircan [419] y
na munachiptinsi manatac ymallactapas vñir
canchu chaymantas mana vñispa<s> panantaca
cotichisactacmi ñispa ñircan ñiptinsi panan
ca manam cutimancho ñocapas tucoy soncoyhuan
mi cosayacorcani ñispa ñiptinsi [420] chay collquiri
ñiscanchic carica yaya manatacmi huarmita
quichohuanquimancho ñam ari tucoy yma ay
cactapas coscayqui ñispa ñircayqui manacho
huco ricta coyquiman ñiptinsi chay huarmip
turancuna tiascanpi huc runa quipalla tiamuc
rimarican yaya hu ñijtac ymahc chay huco
ric ñispas allimanta rimanacorcancu [421] chayssi
yuyacnin rimarimuspa allitacmi churi ynatac chu
rita huarmayai chay ñiscayquicta pochocanquitac
ñispallas cotircan [422] chaysi pihcantin ponchaopim
ñatac riconacoson llactayquipi yaya ñispa ñircan
chaysi chay collquiri ñiscanchicca simincama pihc
cantin ponchaopi hucota cama rircan yampillañic
man chaysi ña carota rispa maytah ña rini
ñispas hahuaman llucsita munarcan apar
huayqui chay chimpapi chaysi ñahcca ahuaman
vman quispictintacsi yacoca hahuañicman
fuente yna pacchamorcan [423] chaysi ñatac aslla
antallahuan llutaycuspa hucoñicmantac
cutircan yna hucotacama rispas yampilla
hanacnin sauapi llucsircan chay llucsiscan
pucyos canancamapas chay huarmip sutin
ta capyama ñiscacta apan [424] chay capyama
ñiscanchicmantas ancha ahca yaco llucsispa
tucoy yampillacunap chacranta apayta mu
narcan yma ayca ocan chaquictapas quinhuan
maçarayactapas ymallantapas tucoysi apapurcan
chaysi chay yampillacunaca ancha piñaspa
ymapacmi chay ynacta hu ñimurcanquiya

F 104 R

tuylla cutichicoy ña yachascam canchic yna pisi
yacoyucpas ñispas tucoy runacuna rimarcancu
[425] yna rimaptinsi chay capyamap yayancuna
ca chay quiquin <pucyo> (llactan)manta cayar(can) maça tu
coy runacunam piñapayahuan amatac chica
yacocta cachamuycho vihcay, yao collquiri
chay yacocta vihcaytac ñispas cayarcancu [426] y
na cayaptinsi collquirica titahuanpas yma
huanpas vihcarcan yna vihcaptinsi ñatac
ñatac tunimurcan yaco atipamuspa yna cap
tinsi chay huramantaca vihcay ñispa caya
payamuptinsi ñatac quiquin collquiri
yaicuspa yacollantapas chuquirispa chaopi
pi tiaycorcan [427] yna tiaycuptinracsi asllapas
chaquirircan chay pucyos canan chay collqui
rip yacollanta passamuspa suysusca yna ya
copas llucsimon cayta quirpaicoptinsi hua
quinin pucyocunamantapas chay chay qui
tipica llucsircan ñaupacca manas carcancho
[428] chaymantas canan cay concha llactayoc runa
cunaca yacon chaquiptin ñatac piñayta ca
llarircancu ymapacmi cay yaconchicta cocon
ñocanchicca ymahuanmi causason ñispa
chaysi chay llacxa misa ñiscanchic yaco camayoc
taca yao llacxa misa ymapacmi cay yacocta
chaquichimunqui runaconaca ymahuanmi
causanca ñispas cochaman vischorcan tucoy
conchacona [429] chay pachas collquiri ñiscanchic
huacaca chay ynacta ricuspa chicantacmi pai
cunaca ymahuanmi causanca ñispas ña
tac huc huamranta rapacha sutiocta cama
chircan ñispa cay cochacta aslla chay man
yanmanta vcupi huraman allpacunacta
rumicunactapas vrmachi chaypi hunancha
son cay concha runacunap causancampac
ñispas ñircan [430] chaysi chay rapacha ñiscanchicca

F 104 V

chay cochacta aslla pascaycorcan ña pascasca
captinsi chay collquiri ñiscanchicca tuylla
pircaycorcan hurañicmanta atun pircacta
ruraspa chay pircas canan mana allpayoc
canancamapas cay cochap siminsi [431] pihca pacha
caytas cay llacxa misa ñisca runacta alli hunan
chachircan cayman yaco chayaptinmi cochap
siminta quirpanqui chaymantari cay chica
pachapim ñatac cay yacocta hura chacraman
pusanqui ña ynti sicamuptinmi cay yacoc
ta cacharinqui canan pihca mitallam par
conca añay saracta caypacmi camta cama
chiqui ñispas chay vnanchan rumicunacta
allin ricsichircan [432] yna ricsichictinsi canan
camapas paypac paypac churincunapas tucoy
nin catinacuspa chay costumbrellatac canan
camapas catincu chay cocha tupunan ñincum
runacuna caspictari turca caya ñincutacmi chay
si chay rumisaua yma yna ruranampacpas alli
yachacochisca chayta chayasparaccha alli ñauinchic
huan ricohhuan [433] chaymantas canan conchaco
na ña março quilla chay chaypi chay cochap
siminta vihcaypac llucsin tucoy cari huarmi
cay tupucoy ñiscampacsi cay llacxa misa ñiscan
chic chica pacham canca ñispa yma ñispapas
hunancharcan paypac simillantas tucoy concha
cunapas y ñispa rircancu [434] caypac yañca cap
tinsi ña mitampica paipac simincamalla
yma ayca camachicoypas carcan ña par
coypacri cananmi canca chica ponchaomi canca
ñispas pailla chayta camachicorcan conchari
simincamallatac tucoypas rurarcancu [435] canan
cocha chaupi tuta pahyamuptinpas ri cam
pac suyoiquim ñispas cay llacxa misa ñiscan
chicpac churincunacta mayquin tiaptinpas
carcoc carcan chaylla oficion captinsi pon

F 105 R

chaopas tutapas paicunapas chayllacta cama yu
yarcancu sarampacpas callpaptin runacuna
pas ancha pai captinmi causanchic ñispa man
chaptin [436] chaymantari cay llacxa misa ñis
canchicsi pana churincunapas pactah cay ya
co cochamanta pahyamunman ñispas an
cha cuydadouan huacaycharcan ña ñispa
pachyamuptinsi yansapi cac yaco mayo
man yaicuptinca tuylla caça ataric
yna yaicuptinca caçarcantacsi cayrai
cus alli cuydadohuan huacaycharcan
[437] chaymantari cay ña ñiscanchic yna chay yança
cochacta quirpaipacpas ña yacocta cachamuypac
pas hua(c)çacunaca rircantacsi ychaca cay ña quir
paipacca tucoy ynantin runas llucsircan huarmi
cunari ña chayaspas cocanta çapampi churac
carcan ashuantari çapampitac [438] caycuna churas
cantam cay yança ñiscanchicpas yañacan tu
coyta chasquircan huc llamactari ynatacsi
apac carcan coyconactari tictictapas yma
ayca muchanancunactapas tucoytas aparcan
chaysi ña tucoyta juntayta pochucaspas yllacnin
cunactari tucoytatac quipuspa, chay yancac
ta muchayta callarircan [439] yaya collquiri cam
pam cochayqui<pacta> campactacmi yacoyqui
canan huata allitac yacocta coay ñispas mu
charcan ña muchayta puchocaspas ashuanta vp
yac cocantapas acoc carcan chaymantas cari huar
mi chay cochacta quirpaita callarircan [440] chaymantam
canan ña yaco cachamuna captinri yscay quim
ca huacçacunahuansi viñaylla pihcca mitapas
ric carcan cay ñaupacllas huc runa huarmipas
as atun chacraman yaicocsi ashuacta aton puyño
uan apac carcan coyntari huc yscayllacta cocan
tauan cayconahuan muchaspas yacocta cacha
muc carcan cay chica simictam cay yança ñiscan

F 105 V

chicmanta yachanchic [441] chaymantam canan
yachanchic cay conchaconaca paria caca tutay qui
rip ancha sullca pisi yupai churillansi chaysi cay
pachancunactapas chacrantapas ancha pisillata
tac corcan [442] huacça ñiscanchic paria cacap
chaupi ñamucap mitampipas chancu ñiscacta
pas ymanam checacuna ruran yna
llatacmi paiconapas rurancu chaytaca ñam
ari tucoytapas huaquinin capitulocunapi ri
marcanchic
[443] chaymantam canan yachason cay quimca runa ñis
canchicpac churincunacta chay llacxa misa ñiscan
chicca tucoysi collorcan ña colluypac captinsi
ñaca ñircanchic hina paipac sobrinoncuna
cuno (co)yo ñiscanchicpac huahuancuna yayanri
yaçali sutiocpa churincunactas huarmayarca hua
lla ñiscap churincuna yaoyoñicmanta cotimuspa
ancha quiparac cay hualla ñiscap churincuna

[444] cay hualla ñiscan
chicpac churincu
na lazaro puypu
roçi chay llacxa mi
ssa ñiscanchicman
yaicuptinca mana
ñas hualla ñisca
ca cancho huc huar
millas chaypas ma
na huachacoc cau
san anya rurip
huarmin

m ari lazaro puypu rocçi- [445] chaymantam ca
nan pauquir buxi ñiscanchicpac churincuna
canan ñau paico chay chaycuna causan, chay
mantam canan llama tanya ñiscanchicpac
churincunam canan <casin chauca> ruri cancha casin
chauca tacya cancha cay quimça yumay ñiscas
cay llama tanya ñiscanchicpac churincuna
[446] chaymantari chay hualla ñiscanchictaca ñam
ari rimarcanchic lazaro puypu rocçicta chayman
tam calla ñiscanchicpac churincunam
canan g(onzal)o paucar cassa lazaca canya chay chay
cuna cay chica runam ari miramun pihca runa
<h>yauri llanchamanta amucpac churincuna
cay llacxa missa ñiscanchicpac churincuna
llam ari tucoy collosca cay llacxa misam cani
ñispam ari cay lazaro huallap churincuna
cay oficiocta heredan sanin cascanrayco
cay chicallactam cay conchap cascancunacta ya
chanchic---- FIN

F 108 R

+

[447] ñaupa pacha canancamapas tucoy hinantin llactacunapi
may pacham huc runa huc yoriillapi yscayta huachachin
pana cari huarmicta mana ñispari cari puracta mana ñispari
huarmi puracta(pas) caytaca sapampi quipampiracmi villason cay
hina ñisca yuriccunactam curi ñinchin [448] cay hina yurip
tin(mi) may llactapi concayllamanta yuriptinpas chay tutalla
tac llactanman chayachimuc carcan ymanam sucya canchapi
tumnapipas yurinman chayca ñaupa pachaca tuyllatacmi
llacxa tambo ñisca checap llactanman apamuc carcan [449] cayta apa
muspari manatacmi ponchaoca apamuccho carcan pactach<hilan>

pacha casanman ñispa ynataccha tucoy quitipipas musyasca rurancu
chaymantari ña may pacham curi ñisca yurircan chay pacha
llatacmi huc huasi ocupi quimchasca ancha tutayacpi tiayta

huc manyanmanta   callarircancu(yayan maman) caripas huarmipas mana cuyurispa asta
esto es de un lado ci   pihcca ponchaocama [450] chay pihcca ponchaopim hucman ña ticrac
rispa   carcan chay ponchaopitacmi tucoy masancuna   chay curip
huasinpi huñonacoc carcan taquispa huancarnintapas
quiquin huactaspa manam canan hinacho huarmicuna
huactac carcan sino caricunam manarac caycunacta
pas taquijta callarispatacmi supayta tapuc carcan(cu)
arañohuampas pana charapi ñiscahuanpas cay masan
cunamanta maycanmi ñaupac taquispa pusarinca [451] < chay>

huaquin chaypi (tiac masan)cunacta chaymi paypac simincama pihcca runacta
hacllaspa señalac carcan(cu) caycunari ña may pacham
huyarircan chay pachallatacmi tutauan punchaohuan
mana samaspa yma aycanta rantichispapas cocacta
mascac carcan<>cu ynatac huaquinin masacunapas
yallinacoyllata yuyaspa ayca runa caspapas tucoynin
huñonacoc carcancu [452] ynaspa ymanam anacpipas hucman
ticrar(can) ñinchic chay punchaomantam tucoy tutancuna ña taquij
ta mana samarcancho asta pihca ponchao chayascancama
manarac chayaptin cayantin ponchaopim masacuna (cara) hua
yacanta ricuchinacuc carcan cayhuanmi caya cocacta apa
risac ñic hina mana cocayocta huayacallactas taquichic
carcan(cu) chaymi ña may pacham chay hucman ticrarcan
chaymanta canan huc pihcca ponchaoman huntaycon chay
mi ari chunca ponchao [453] chay pacham ñaupacnintac huc
lluychucta tarucactapas yma ayca animalcunacta
                           pas

F 108 V

sallcapi cactaca apimuspa chaytam chay pihca runa ñiscanchic
masacuna chaycunap ñaupaquin apaptin pampaman chay cu
ri llocsic carcan [454] hucmi chay caracol (paya) ñiscacta pucospa ric car

es la uara con el la
zo q(ue) coje papaga
yos pero co(n) lazo
ni tan largo

cancu hucmi pupunacta apaspa ric carcan hucmi sacaya
ñiscacta apaspatac rircan cay sacaya ñiscaca aslla sara
cutascam carcan aslla tictihuan caytam huc runatac aparcan cay
cunacta apaccunaca manam masacunacho aparcan sino chay
curip sispa aylloncunam aparcan ychaca chay lloychullactam
masap ña ñisca ñaupaquin aparcan [455] cay lloychucta apimuspa chay
pachallatacmi chay curip qu(e)mchasca huasipi tiascanmanta cha
quinhuan saruchic carcan caymi ña tacurisonqui apllasonq(ui)

y luego lo sacauan
y matauan

ñispa ynaspam aychantaca tuyllatac tucoy hinantin runa
cuna micoc carcancu mana asllactapas puchuspa
[456] chaymantam (canan) ymanam ñacapas ñinchic chay hina ña chon
ca ponchaopi pampaman llocsic carcan quipampi chay curi
cuna huc atun yma pachahuanpas pintusca mana ricurispa
riptinmi runacunaca pana masacunapas yscay quimça aysa
nacuspa huacaspa taquispa ric carcancu cay aysacri chay
curip aylloncunactam aysac carcan aysaspari huc chacrac
ta ymactapas llamactapas cuscayqui ñispam aysanacuc
carcan [457] chaymi pampapi ña chayaspa ymanam canan

la manga de la +

pas mangacta ñaupac proçeçionta rispa apanchic yna
tacmi chay lluychoctapas ancha sumachispa apac carcan

esto es el pellejo
y cabeça embutida
de paja porq(ue) ya
la carne era co
mida como se ha
d(ic)ho

pupunactam canan lansacta yna chayhuan chucasac ñic
yna camaycuspa camaycuspa apac carcan tucoymantapas ñau
pacnin chay camaycuspari curictam quipa amuptin camaycor
can [458] chaymantam canan ña may pacham chay lluycho apac chay
pi pampapi chayarcan chaymi huc runa huarmipas chay curip
aylloncuna huc llamacta pana chacracta cuspapas sama
chic carcan cayhuan samay ñispa ynaspam chay curiri pay
pa tianan vnanchascaman chayaspa yscaynin cosantin
huarmintin tiac carcan ancha alli yupaychasca [459] chay pun
chaupim tucoy hinantin masancuna cocahuan yallinacus
pa taquic opiac carcancu tucoy ponchao chaymi ña chisimanta
ñatac huasinman cutimuspam ñatac chay quiquin tiascanmantac
cutic carcan chaymantam canan ñatac pihca ponchao tiarcan
ña pihcca ponchao huntaycoptinmi ñatac <huc tiana> (aposento)man
asuchic carcan [460] chaymantam ñatac chay quipampi masa
cuna yamtacta ancha atun collo camacta apamuc car
                                                              can

F 109 R

ynatac ñaupacninpas may pacham curi yurircan chay
cayantillan caytam ñaupac simipi concarcanchic cay

las
q(ue) con esto

yamtacunactari tucoy tutancuna cayta masaspa
pacarinca pactach yma huatica ymanpas chayanman

q(ue) ha de estar
al principio

ñispam cayta (ca)corcan hinatac quipancamapas mana
tacmi huc tutallapas nina huañurcancho [461] cay tucoyta
ña puchucaspam quipampi ñatac chay curicunacta

yayancunactapas chay supayninta tapuspa maypim armachimusac
<ñispa> huchanmanta ñispam pusarcan paypac simin

esto es de donde viene
el agua de los conchas

cama yansa cochamantacsi hord(enad)am(en)(de) pusac carcan[462]chay
pis canan chay huc runa con churi sutioc supaypa saçer
dotin pachacta tapuc carcan ymamantam curi
yurircan yma ayca huchanmantan ñispas tapor

esto es la opinion del
vulgo no la respu
esta

can cay curi yuric runactaca huañuynin rantim
yurin ñispas runacuna ñircancu [463] <chaysi> chayssi chayman
tam caymantam ñispa yscayninta armachic car
canco ynatac chay yscay huahuacunactapas
ñatac ñatac armachispa asta qui chicallam
huchan ñiscancama yma yna chiripi huañuna
yaptinpas [464] ña caycunacta puchucaspa carictaca
chucchanta rutuc carcan huarmictaca asllacta
carictaca ymanam huchayoccunacta rutunqui
yna chayssi huachay rucoyuc ña cutimuc carcancu
chaymantari huc huallcacta yana yurachuan cay

a manera de cadena
de oro

chuscactas huallcarichircan curip hunanchaynin
ta [465] cunaspari huc huata enterom sasinque a
matac campas campas pillahuanpas huchallicon
qui huchallicuspaca ancha mana allictam ruran

ni entre ellos

quiman casem masanchiccunacta saycuchinqui
man ñispas conaycuc carcan [466] chaymantas ña
patman huata caspa ñatac allichus tian ñis

achcan

pa chay saçerdote runatac huaquinin a<n>chca runa
cunahuan tapuc carcan supayninta chaysi alli
captinca ancha cosicorcan <mana alli captinsi>ynaspa pu

q(ue) tuieron coito

ñorcantacmi ñiptinsi canan allinta anyac
carcan [467] chay masacunapas anchapuni piñacus
pa ymaraycum ñocanchictaca cassi saycochihuanchic

F 109 V

ñispas anchapuni piñacuc carcancu
chaymantam canan ñatac <huc huata captinca>chay huatap huntascancama yna
tac huaticac carcan chay pacharacsi chay huallcan
taca cuchupuc carcan ynallas puchucarcan
[468] chaymantam ñatac ñaca ñiscanchicta tincuchison
cari pura yuriptinca pana huarmi pura yuriptin
pas manam alli pachacho canca ancha muchoy
pacham canca ñispam ñic carcancu chayman
ta cari huarmi yuriptinmi allipac hunan
charcancu
[469] chaymantari yma chicam canan masacuna
huc pachamantaca cusicon mana ñaupa pa
cha yna chicacta gastaspa huc pachamanta
ri llaquiconcha mana chay hina ruranicho
ñispa supaypac llullayninhuan huaquin llac
tacunapica manataccha concancho [470] tutapas
yma yna pachapas ynatac llama yuriptinpas
sutintari sapamanta yma curim canca ñis
pas supayta tapuc carcan chay supaypa
sutichascanmi curi ñaupapas curi yauripas
curi guamanpas ticlla curipas yma ayca su
ti cacpas curihuan rimaricca yna sapatacssi
caripas huarmipas--[471] chaymantari yma chi
cam runacuna collquiyoc (cananca) ñaupa mana
rac cay alli diospac siminta hunanchaspa
paria cacap mitanpi pana yma aycap
mitanpipas tucoy callpanhuan yma ayca
cascallantapas cocarayco rantichispa collqui
llantari chayraycollatac mascaspa canan
ca pa(na) quimça tahua huata(lla) samaptinpas huac
chacunari tucoy hinantin huatancunapi lla
quicuspa maymantah cocacta tarisac ñispa
ynataccho pincay casac ñispa chacrantapas

F 110 R

pachantapas rantichispa mascarcan chayta
cayta purispa huanacumanpas rispa lloy
chuctapas sasispa mascaspa [472] chayraycu
llatac ynaspa tucoy hinantin yuyascan
tapas supaynintaracmi ñaupac alli sasis
pa maymantam tarisac huanacuancho
cayri chacraytacho pachaytacho huacllichi
sac ymanam casac ñispa tapuspam an
chapuni musyasca trauajopi puric car
canco [473] cananca huc yuyaymanta mana
chicacta yuyaspa manatac ymallanta
pas chayrayco rantichispa anchapunihc
cusicon huc pachamantah chayca ancha
huacan ymaraycohc mana chayta rura
nicho ñispa [474] chaypa mitanpica tutapas y
ma yna pachapas may pachah macoy llen
co chay pacham canca ñispa ñircan chay
pachallatacmi runacuna ancha cusi
cuspa cochocuspa ari machucu(na)pas an
cha chachuaspas tictinta ymantapas apas
pa ric carcancu ñaupa huasipi opianan
captinpas pana caypi cancanpacpas
[475] chaymanta cay llactallapitaccha chaytapas tu
ta ruraspa(pas) aslla huananman hahua llactacuna
pica hinataccha ruran(cu) ñispam yuyanchic
oyarinchicpas

F 112 R

[476] JHS

ata ñispaca huamrap chucchampi parca
yurictam ata ñinchic cay hina yuric
tam canan chay huamrap yayancuna
ña quimça huata captin huñonacoc
huasimpi o canchampi pacsac punchao
manta ñaupac paypac cacancunac
ta o masancunactapas huyarichispa
chay punchaupim cay paria cacap <>
atanta yllanta rutuson ñispa
ylla ñispaca ata ñiscallantatacmi
hunanchanchic [477] chay hina ña tucoy
ta huyarichicuspam ashuacuyta ca
llarincu ashuaconmi media saracta
o huc hanigacta<pas> ñicta huyaris
paca quiquin runacunallatacmi
tapunacuc ymapacmi ashuan ñispa
ña yachaspam canan yma punchao
pich fiesta canca chay punchao tucoy
hinantin runacuna huñonacumuc
[478] ynaspam canan chay <h>atayuc ru
naca masancunahuan tucoy cacan

F 112 V

cunahuampas hu<y>rañicmanta tiaspa
taquicuyta opiachicuyta callaric chay
mi ña may pacham ancha machanco
chay pacham huc fresadacta o titacta
pas mantapuspa chay huamracta cha
upiman yaycuchispa tiachic cay simic
ta rimaspa yayacuna huauquicuna
cay ata yllacta canan punchautac ru
tuson paria cacap chaymanta tutay
quirip atan yllanmi ari paytacmi ari
ñocaman cachamuarca cay hina yu
rincampac ñispam rimaric [479] chay pa
cham chay huamrap<a> sispa cacan cari
captin huarmi captinri paypac ypan
mana ñispari aguelo o aguelanpas sa
yarispa huc llamahuan o chacrahuan
pas huc señalllanta churaspa chay a
tacta tejerahuan camaycuc chay
llama ñiscanchicpac hunanchay

cothuato
es cabresto
de llama

ninmi canan huc cothuato ñisca
ymahuammi llamacta paria cacaman
pusarca chayhuan [480] chacrap huna<y>nchaynin
tam canan huc caxo ñisca<huan>cta chu
rapuc carcan cay caxo ñiscaca huc cas
pillam huarmip allacunallan chay
mantam huaquinin sispa yahuar ma
sincunam yacullahuanpas cusmahuan(pas)

F 113 R

ouejahuanpas o millhuahuanpas
cascancama ofrecicuc sapampi
sayarispa [481] chaymantam ña may
pachah sispa yahuar masin puchu
can chay pacham curaca o alcal
de culla(na)mantapas sayarispa ys
cay<> rreal o huc rrealtapas chu
raspa sayarimuc hasta puchucas
cancama caycuna astahuan ma
chanca machaspari manam ari y
mallantapas michacuncacho ñispam
ancha hupyachic ña pacha huraycus
cancama [482] chay pacham canan ña
tucoy<> rutucoyta puchocaptin ya
yan chay churinta tucoy rutuc porq(ue)
runacunaca llamcayllam llamcac
ña puchocaspari tuyllam taquicuy
ta callaric machoncunap sutinta
rimarispa yaya anchi puma o carhua
chachapa o yma yma ñispapas cam
pa atayquim yllayquim canan
ca ñam puchocarcani cananman
taca ama ñatac paria caca cacha
muchoncho allitac casac ñispam
taquicuc haucacuc

F 113 V

esto es
la noche antes
de el dia d(ic)ho

[483] cay ata ñispaca ylla ñispapas
paria cacap cachanmi ñispas
runacuna hunanchancu cay
ta rutuypacri cayantin chisis an
cha manchaspa coynhuan tictin
huan ymanhuampas pari cacacta
tutay quiricta muchac allichahuay
tac cay atahuan caya puncahuri an
cha cusiyuctac casac ñispa [484] paycuna
hunanchaptinca curip señalninsi
curi hamuypacsi cay atacta cacha
mun mana alli paria cacaman hu
chanta yuyaycuptin huañonan ran
ti curi yurinca ñispa curi yuricta
ca huañonan rantin yurin ñicmi
ari cay checallatam cay san damian
checa ñiscamanta yachanchic
[485] chaymantari huaquinin llactacuna
piri yma ñispah rimancu ycha
ca ata yuriptinca ynallatac
mi tucoypas cay tucoy corregemiento
pica yupaychancu tucoy may quitipi
pas huancapas yauyopas huaman
tancapas yma runapas yn(di)o ñiscaca

F 114 R

chaymantari ahcca runa ancha co
llanan yanacuna cacpas [486] ynatacmi
limacpi pip churin ata captinpas
huñonacuc chaymanta mestiço
cactapas yachanchictacmi huaqui
nincunacta caytaca ychapas chay
yna alli causana ñispatacmi hua
quinin runacunapas huchaman
chayaycurcancu - chaycunacta ricus
pa ynaspari cay quimça huata
mantam rutuna ñispa ñircanchic
chaytaca yachacuscancamam ñau
pacpas o quipampas rurarcancu
cay chicallam checa simica

Glossary of Untranslated Words

The following entries correspond to the non-English words italicized in the translation. Numbers correspond to section numbers in the margin of the translation. Definitions are given where feasible.

alcalde (Spanish): colonial village official (95, 173, 481)

allauca: group name, possibly implying righthand part (moiety?) of a village (157)

añay: a kind of maize (431)

ata: baby with abnormal hair, taken to be a messenger of Paria Caca (476, 478–480, 482–486)

auqui: in this context, untranslated; possibly a ritual ornament or vessel (283)

ayllu: social group, often localized, self-defined as ancestor-focused kindred; scope of term varies (46, 91, 118, 160, 187, 216, 218, 224, 234–237, 240, 243, 282, 309, 316, 330, 331, 333, 354, 357, 369, 385, 388 [title])

bolas (Spanish): hunting weapon made of stones connected by thongs, which entangle prey's legs when thrown (98, 350)

callcallo: untranslated; grasshopper? (413, 415)

canah yauri: lance? belonging to a mummy-*huaca* (320)

cancho: feather-weaving (39, 63)

caqui: toucan? (207)

casira: unidentified type of straw (327)

cassa: feather-weaving (39, 63)

caullama: class of *huaca*s guaranteeing fertility of livestock (329)

caxo: women's digging tool (480)

chicsi rampa: litter belonging to Inca (289, 294)

choqui (Jaqi): gold (283)

chumprucu: turban for ritual wear (240, 294)

chupa: a kind of straw (327)

chuta: large target effigy at which lancers threw spears in the Machua festival rites (330, 331, 333, 335, 338, 404)

cori cacya: seashell-shaped insignia of a mummy-*huaca* (320)

corregimiento (Spanish): administrative district of a *corregidor* or Spanish governor of natives (485)

cot huato: llama harness (479)

curaca: a native political lord or noble (86, 101, 173, 174, 176, 231, 244, 245, 296, 317, 481)

curi: twins, considered messengers from Paria Caca (447, 449, 450, 453–462, 464, 470, 484)

doctrina (Spanish): elementary text of Christian doctrine, to be memorized by Indians; also, a parish of Indians (253)

fanega (Spanish): bulk measure equaling about 1.6 bushels or 58 liters (477)

huaca: a superhuman person; any place, object, image (etc.) embodying a superhuman person (3, 6–8, 9, 10, 13–15, 17, 28, 92, 145, 146, 172, 178–180, 182, 183–185, 189, 225, 235–239, 243, 244, 246, 247, 249, 265, 272, 273, 277, 279, 283, 285 [title], 287–289, 293, 301, 317, 318, 319, 325, 336, 347, 370, 378, 379, 407, 408, 412, 429)

huachay ruco: ceremonial garment probably associated with birth; possible synonym of *huaychao* (464)

huacsa: person appointed to a term of priestly duties that included dancing a reenactment of a *huaca*'s life (117, 118, 122, 123, 124, 126, 131, 132, 135, 149, 150, 159, 160, 162, 183, 213, 220, 245, 297, 300, 346, 347, 385, 386, 405, 437, 440, 442)

huana paya: conch trumpet for use in ceremony; possible synonym of *paya* (325, 337, 340)

huancoy: worm or larva; maggot? (368)

huaychao: a ceremonial garment (240)

huayo: human trophy mask made from flayed face (321, 322, 323, 404)

hugi: untranslated; a dangerous animal that Huallallo Caruincho turned loose to afflict Paria Caca (214, 215)

illa: amulet (or) magical person, such as twins (134, 476, 478, 482, 483)

JHS (Latinized Greek): monogram containing the first three Greek letters of the name Jesus, variously interpreted (476)

lataca: a kind of jar associated with the Concha (411)

llacsa anapalla: fly, perhaps bluebottle (367)

llacsa yacolla: stone helmet (394, 396)

llaullaya: untranslated; agricultural tool? garment? (271)

lúcuma: *Lucuma bifera*, a fruit tree (11)

maca: an edible tuber, probably *Lepidium meyenii* (162)

muro: colored, possibly hard and/or spotted maize (43, 53) *oca*: an edible tuber, *Oxalis tuberosa* (424)

padre (Spanish): father; Catholic priest (95, 258)

pana charapi: untranslated; object used in divining with spiders (450)

paya: conch trumpet used in ceremony; *see also* huana paya (454)

pupuna: a device for catching birds, made of a reed or cane with a loop or thong (9, 454, 457)

pusuca: untranslated; an insignia of Maca Uisa (294)

puypu: macaw-wing ornament (131, 333)

quinua: edible grain, *Chenopodium quinua* (302, 303, 389, 424)

quipu: mnemonic device made of knotted cords (283, 438)

quisay rinri: ornamental earspool(?) worn by a mummy-huaca (320)

quishuar: a tree, *Buddleia*, used to make ritual enclosures (92)

real (Spanish): Spanish coin, one-eighth of a common *peso* (262, 481)

reducción (Spanish): Spanish-style village into which natives were forcibly resettled, especially c. 1570–1590 (244)

riti: snow (63)

sacaya: sacrifice for *huaca*s made of ground maize mixed with *ticti* or thick maize beer (454)

Salve Regina Mater Misericordiæ (Latin): Catholic prayer to Saint Mary (256)

tamta: feather ruff (328)

taruca: a deer, *Hippocamelus antisiensis* (453)

ticti: sacrificial food made of thick maize beer residue (91, 99, 138, 170, 281, 337, 387, 438, 454, 474, 483)

tipsi: ? (283)

urpu: ? (283)

vichoc: left-hand part (moiety?) of a village (157, 337)

vihco: spear(?) used in the rite of spearing *chuta* effigies (328)

villca: high-ranking *huaca* or *huaca* priest (10, 13, 14, 43, 45, 154, 289)

visa: untranslated (shield?); insignia of Chuta Cara (324)

yanca: *huaca* priest by hereditary title (118, 120, 121, 129, 130, 148, 165, 218, 219, 238, 331–333, 335, 339, 403, 434, 438)

Bibliographic References

Acosta, Antonio. 1979. "El pleito de los indios de San Damián (Huarochirí) contra Francisco de Avila, 1607." *Historia y Bibliografía Americanistas* 23: 3–33. Sevilla.

———. 1987a. "La extirpación de idolatrías en el Perú: Origen y desarrollo de las campañas. A propósito de *Cultura andina y represión.*" *Revista Andina* 5(1): 171–195.

———. 1987b. "Francisco de Avila Cusco 1573(?)–Lima 1647." In *Ritos y tradiciones de Huarochirí del siglo XVII,* edited and translated by Gerald Taylor, pp. 551–616. Historia Andina, no. 12. Lima: Instituto de Estudios Peruanos/Instituto Francés de Estudios Andinos.

Adelaar, Willem F. H. (ed. and trans.) 1988. *Het boek van Huarochirí: Mythen en riten van het oude Peru zoals opgetekend in de zestiende eeuw voor Francisco de Avila, bestrijder van afgoderij.* Amsterdam: Meulenhoff.

Albornoz, Cristóbal de. [1583?] "Instrucción para descubrir todas las guacas del Piru." Reprinted in Pierre Duviols. 1984. "Albornoz y el espacio ritual andino prehispánico." *Revista Andina* 2(1): 169–222.

Allen, Catherine. 1982. "Body and Soul in Quechua Thought." *Journal of Latin American Lore* 8(2): 179–196.

Aranguren Paz, Angélica. 1975. "Las creencias y ritos mágicos religiosos de los pastores puneños." *Allpanchis* 8: 103–132.

Arguedas, José María (trans.), and Pierre Duviols (ed.). 1966. *Dioses y hombres de Huarochirí: Narración quechua recogida por Francisco de Avila [¿1598?].* Lima: Instituto Francés de Estudios Andinos/Instituto de Estudios Peruanos.

Arriaga, Pablo José de. [1621] 1968. *The Extirpation of Idolatry in Perú.* Translated by L. Clark Keating. Lexington: University of Kentucky Press.

Ascher, Marcia, and Robert Ascher. 1981. *Code of the Quipu: A Study of Media, Mathematics, and Culture.* Ann Arbor: University of Michigan Press.

Avila, Francisco de. [1608] 1873. "A Narrative of the Errors, False Gods, and Other Superstitions and Diabolical Rites in Which the Indians of the Province of Huarochiri Lived in Ancient Times." In *Narratives of the Rites and Laws of the Yncas,* edited and translated by Clements R. Markham, pp. 121–147. Works Issued by the Hakluyt Society, First Series, no. 48. London: Hakluyt Society.

———. [1608] 1966. *Tratado y relación de los errores, falsos dioses y otras supersticiones y ritos diabolicos en que vivian antiguamente los indios de las provincias de Huaracheri, Mama y Chaclla y hoy también viven engañados con gran perdicion de sus almas.* In Arguedas and Duviols 1966, pp. 198–217.

———. [1645] 1918. "Prefación al libro de los sermones, o homilías en la lengua castellana, y la índica general Quechhua." In *Informaciones acerca de la religión y gobierno de los Incas,* edited by Horacio H. Urteaga and Carlos A. Romero, pp. 57–98. Colección de Libros y Documentos Referentes a la Historia del Perú, vol. 11. Lima: Sanmartí.

Bastien, Joseph W. 1987. *Healers of the Andes: Kallawaya Herbalists and Their Medicinal Plants.* Salt Lake City: University of Utah Press.

Bertonio, Ludovico. [1612] 1956. *Vocabulario de la lengua aymara.* La Paz: Don Bosco.

Betanzos, Juan de. [1551] 1987. *Suma y narración de los Incas.* Edited by María del Carmen Martín Rubio. Madrid: Ediciones Atlas.

Beyersdorff, Margot. 1986. "La tradición oral quechua vista desde la perspectiva de la literatura." *Revista Andina* 4(1): 213–236.

Bonavia, Duccio, Fabiola León Velarde, Carlos Monge C., María Inés Sánchez-Griñán, and José Whittembury. 1984. "Tras las huellas de Acosta 300 años después: Consideraciones sobre su descripción del 'mal de altura'." *Histórica* 8(1): 1–31.

Briggs, Lucy Therina. 1985. "A Critical Survey of Literature on the Aymara Language." In *South American Indian Languages: Retrospect and Prospect,* edited by Harriet E. Manelis Klein and Louisa R. Stark, pp. 546–594. Austin: University of Texas Press.

Cabello Valboa, Miguel. [1586] 1951. *Miscelánea antártica.* Lima: Facultad de Letras, Instituto de Etnología, Universidad Nacional Mayor de San Marcos.

Cabrera, Angel, and José Yepes. 1940. *Mamíferos sudamericanos (vida, costumbres, y descripción).* Buenos Aires: Compañía Argentina de Editores.

Calancha, Antonio de. [1638] 1974–1982. *Crónica mora-*

lizada de Antonio de Calancha. 6 vols. Edited by Ignacio Prado Pastor. Lima: Ignacio Prado Pastor.

Castelli, Amalia, Marcia Koth, and Mariana Mould de Pease (eds.). 1981. *Etnohistoria y antropología andina.* (Symposium entitled) *Ayllu, parcialidad, y etnía.* Lima: n.p., 1981. "Segunda jornada del Museo Nacional de Historia, organizada por el Museo Nacional de Historia y con el auspicio de la Comisión para Intercambio Educativo entre los Estados Unidos y el Perú."

Cavallini de Araúz, Ligia. 1986. *Elementos de paleografía hispanoamericana.* San José: Editorial de la Universidad de Costa Rica.

Cerrón-Palomino, Rodolfo. 1976a. *Diccionario quechua Junín-Huanca.* Lima: Ministerio de Educación/Instituto de Estudios Peruanos.

———. 1976b. "Notas para un estudio científico de la toponimía quechua." *Revista San Marcos* 17: 189–211.

———. 1985. "Panorama de la lingüística andina." *Revista Andina* 3(2): 509–572.

Cobarruvias, Sebastián de. [1611] n.d. *Tesoro de la lengua castellana o española.* Madrid: Ediciones Turner.

Cobo, Bernabé. [1653] 1964. *Historia del nuevo mundo.* Madrid: Ediciones Atlas.

Cook, Noble David. 1981. *Demographic Collapse: Indian Peru, 1520–1620.* New York: Cambridge University Press.

Cotler, Julio. 1958. "Las comunidades de San Lorenzo de Quinte." In *Las actuales comunidades de indígenas: Huarochirí en 1955,* edited by José Matos Mar, pp. 113–166. Lima: Facultad de Letras, Instituto de Etnología, Universidad Nacional Mayor de San Marcos.

Cross, F. L. 1957. *The Oxford Dictionary of the Christian Church.* London: Oxford University Press.

Curatola, Marco. 1978. "El culto de crisis de 'Moro Oncoy'." In *Etnohistoria y antropología andina: Primera jornada del Museo Nacional de Historia,* edited by Martha Koth de Paredes and Amalia Castelli, pp. 179–192. Lima: Museo Nacional de Historia.

Cusihuamán, Antonio. 1976. *Gramática Quechua Cuzco-Collao.* Lima: Ministerio de Educación/Instituto de Estudios Peruanos.

D'Altroy, Terence. 1987. "Transitions in Power: Centralization of Wanka Political Organization under Inka Rule." *Ethnohistory* 34(1): 78–102.

Dammert Bellido, José. 1974. "Procesos por supersticiones en las provincias de Cajamarca en la segunda mitad del siglo XVII." *Allpanchis* 6: 179–200.

———. 1984. "Procesos por supersticiones en la provincia de Cajamarca en la segunda mitad del siglo XVIII." *Allpanchis* 20: 177–184.

Dasi, Tomás. 1950. *Estudio de los reales de a ocho también llamados pesos, dólares, piastras, patacones o duros españoles.* Vol. 2. Valencia: Tipografía Artística.

Dávila Brizeño, Diego. [1586] 1965. "Descripción y relación de la provincia de los yauyos." In *Relaciones geográficas de Indias,* edited by Marcos Jiménez de la Espada, vol. 1, pp. 155–165. Madrid: Ediciones Atlas.

Demarest, Arthur A. 1981. *Viracocha: The Nature and Antiquity of the Andean High God.* Cambridge, Mass.: Peabody Museum of Archaeology and Ethnology, Harvard University, 1981.

Denevan, William M. (ed.). 1976. *The Native Population of the Americas in 1492.* Madison: University of Wisconsin Press.

Diccionario de autoridades: Edición facsímil. [1737] 1976. Madrid: Real Academia Española/Editorial Gredos.

Dumézil, Georges, and Pierre Duviols. 1974–1976. "Sumaq T'ika: La princesse du village sans eau." *Journal de la Société des Américanistes* 63: 15–198.

Duviols, Pierre. 1966. "Estudio biobibliográfico." In Arguedas and Duviols 1966, pp. 218–229.

———. 1972. *La lutte contre les réligions autocthones dans le Pérou colonial.* Lima: Institut Français d'Etudes Andines.

———. 1973. "Huari y Llacuaz: Agricultores y pastores, un dualismo prehispánico de oposición y complementaridad." *Revista del Museo Nacional* (Lima) 39: 153–191.

———. 1976. "La Capacocha: Mecanismo y función del sacrificio humano, su proyección, su papel en la política integracionista, y en la economía redistributiva del Tawantinsuyu." *Allpanchis* 9: 11–57.

———. 1978. " 'Camaquen, Upani': Un concept animiste des anciens Péruviens." In *Amerikanistische Studien: Festschrift für Hermann Trimborn,* edited by Roswith Hartmann and Udo Oberem, vol. 1, pp. 132–144. Collectanea Instituti Anthropos, 20. St. Augustin: Haus Völker und Kulturen, Anthropos-Institut. .

———. 1986. *Cultura andina y represión: Procesos y visitas de idolatrías y hechicerías, Cajatambo, siglo XVII.* Archivos de Historia Andina 5. Cuzco: Centro de Estudios Rurales Andinos "Bartolomé de las Casas."

Earls, John, and Irene Silverblatt. 1978. "La realidad física y social en la cosmología andina." *Actes du XLIIe Congrès International des Américanistes: Paris, 2–9 Septembre 1976,* vol. 4, pp. 299–325. Paris: Musée de l'Homme.

Espinoza Soriano, Waldemar. 1960. "El alcalde mayor indígena en el virreinato del Perú." *Anuario de Estudios Americanos* 17: 183–300.

———. 1971. "Los Huancas, aliados de la conquista." *Anales Científicos de la Universidad del Centro del Perú* 1: 3–407.

———. 1974. "El templo solar de Paramonga y los acuarios de Pachacamac." *Bulletin de l'Institut Français d'Etudes Andines* 3(3): 1–22.

———. 1983–1984. "Los señoríos de Yaucha y Picoy en el abra del medio y alto Rímac (Siglos XV y XVI)." *Revista Histórica* (Lima) 34: 157–279.

Ferrell, Marco Aurelio. n.d. "Aclaraciones sobre dos pasajes del manuscrito quechua de Huarochirí." Unpublished manuscript.

Flores Galindo, Alberto. 1987. *Buscando un Inca: Identidad y utopía en los Andes.* Lima: Instituto de Apoyo Agrario.

Flores Ochoa, Jorge. 1977. "Enqa, enqaychu, illa, y khuya rumi." In *Pastores de puna/Uywamichiq punarunak-*

una, edited by Jorge Flores Ochoa, pp. 211–237. Lima: Instituto de Estudios Peruanos.

Fuenzalida V., Fernando. 1979. "Los gentiles y el origen de la muerte." *Revista de la Universidad Católica* (Lima) 5: 213–222.

Gade, Daniel. 1977. "Llama, alpaca, y vicuña: Ficción y realidad." In *Pastores de puna/Uywamichiq punarunakuna*, edited by Jorge Flores Ochoa, pp. 113–120. Lima: Instituto de Estudios Peruanos.

Gade, Daniel, and Mario Escobar. 1982. "Village Settlement and the Colonial Legacy in Southern Peru." *Geographical Review* 72(4): 430–449.

Galante, Hipólito (ed. and trans.). 1942. *Francisco de Avila de priscorum Huaruchiriensium origine et institutis . . .* Madrid: Instituto Gonzalo Fernández de Oviedo.

Garcilaso Inca de la Vega. [1609] 1966. *Royal Commentaries of the Incas and General History of Peru*. Translated by Harold V. Livermore. Austin: University of Texas Press.

Gasparini, Graziano, and Luise Margolies. 1980. *Inca Architecture*. Bloomington: Indiana University Press.

Gelles, Paul. 1984. "Agua, faenas, y organización comunal en los Andes: El caso de San Pedro de Casta." Tesis de Maestría. Lima: Departamento de Ciencias Sociales, Pontificia Universidad Católica del Perú.

Gentile Lafaille, Margarita E. 1976. "Los Yauyos de Chaclla: Del siglo XV al siglo XVIII." Tesis de Bachillerato. Lima: Departamento de Ciencias Sociales, Pontificia Universidad Católica del Perú.

Girault, Louis. 1984. *Kallawaya: Guérisseurs itinérants des Andes: Recherches sur les pratiques médicinales et magiques*. Collection Memoires, 107. Paris: Editions de l'ORSTOM.

Gonçález Holguín, Diego. [1607] 1842. *Gramática y arte nueva de la lengua general de todo el Perú llamada lengua Qquichua o lengua del Inca* [1607]. Genoa: Pagano.

———. [1608] 1952. *Vocabulario de la lengua general de todo el Peru llamada lengua Qquichua o del Inca*. Lima: Universidad Nacional Mayor de San Marcos, Instituto de Historia.

Grünthal, Henry, and Ernesto A. Sellschopp. 1978. *The Coinage of Peru*. Frankfurt am Main: Numismatischer Verlag P. N. Schulten.

Guaman Poma de Ayala, Felipe. [1615] 1980. *Nueva corónica y buen gobierno*. Edited by John V. Murra and Rolena Adorno with translations by Jorge L. Urioste. 3 vols. Mexico City: Siglo XXI, 1980.

Guillén Araoz, Teresa. 1953. "La comunidad de Huarochirí." *Revista del Museo Nacional* 22: 191–230.

Harris, Olivia. 1982. "The Dead and the Devils among the Bolivian Laymi." In *Death and the Regeneration of Life*, edited by Maurice Bloch and J. H. Parry, pp. 45–73. Cambridge: Cambridge University Press.

Hartmann, Roswith. 1975. "En torno a las ediciones más recientes de los textos quechuas recogidos por Francisco de Avila." In *Atti del XL Congreso Internazion-*

ale degli Americanisti, Roma-Genova, 1972, vol. 3, pp. 31–42. Genoa: Tilgher.

———. 1981. "El texto quechua de Huarochirí: Una evaluación crítica de las ediciones a disposición." *Histórica* (Lima) 5(2): 167–208.

Hartmann, Roswith, and Olaf Holm. 1985. "Zur sogenannten 'romana' im Andengebiet." *Zeitschrift für Ethnologie* 110(2): 239–251.

Hernández Príncipe, Rodrigo. [1613] 1919. "Idolatrías de los indios Huachos y Yauyos." *Revista Histórica* 6: 180–197.

———. [1622] 1923. "Mitología andina: Idolatrías de Recuay, 1622." Nota final de Carlos A. Romero. *Inca* 1: 25–78.

Hocquenghem, Anne Marie. 1987. *Iconografía mochica*. Lima: Pontificia Universidad Católica del Perú, Fondo Editorial.

Huertas Vallejos, Lorenzo. 1981. *La religión en una sociedad rural andina (siglo XVII)*. Ayacucho: Universidad Nacional San Cristóbal de Huamanga.

Husson, Jean-Philippe. 1985. *La poésie quechua dans la chronique de Felipe Waman Puma de Ayala: De l'art lyrique de cour aux chants et danses populaires*. Paris: L'Harmattan.

Hymes, Dell H. [1977] 1981. "Discovering Oral Performance and Measured Verse in American Indian Narrative." In *"In Vain I Tried to Tell You": Essays in Native American Ethnopoetics*, pp. 309–341. Philadelphia : University of Pennsylvania Press.

IGM. 1954. Hojas Topográficas serie 1 : 200,000. Lima: Instituto Geográfico Militar.

———. 1970–1971. Hojas Topográficas serie 1 : 100,000. Lima: Instituto Geográfico Militar.

Itier, César. 1988. "Las oraciones en quechua de la *relación* de Joan de Santa Cruz Pachacuti Yamqui Salcamaygua." *Revista Andina* 6(2): 555–580.

Koepcke, María. 1970. *The Birds of the Department of Lima, Peru*. Translated by Erma J. Fisk. Newtown Square, Penn.: Harrowood Press.

Lambert, Bernd. [1977] 1980. "Bilateralidad en los Andes." In *Parentesco y matrimonio en los andes*, edited by Ralph Bolton and Enrique Mayer, pp. 11–54. Lima: Pontificia Universidad Católica del Perú.

Lavallé, Bernard. 1982. "Las doctrinas de indígenas como núcleos de explotación colonial: Siglos XVI–XVII." *Allpanchis* 19: 151–171.

Lira, Jorge A. [1941] n.d. *Breve diccionario Kkechuwa-Español*. Cusco: n.p.

Lumbreras, Luís. 1974. "The Regional States." In *The Peoples and Cultures of Ancient Peru*, pp. 179–235. Washington, D.C.: Smithsonian Institution.

MacCormack, Sabine. 1985. " 'The Heart Has Its Reasons': Predicaments of Missionary Christianity in Early Colonial Peru." *Hispanic American Historical Review* 65(3): 443–466.

Málaga Medina, Alejandro. 1974. "Las reducciones en el Perú." *Historia y Cultura* 8: 141–172.

Manelis de Klein, Harriet E. 1973. "Los Urus, el extraño pueblo del altiplano." *Estudios Andinos* 7: 129–149.

Mannheim, Bruce. 1985. "Semantic Coupling in Quechua Verse." Unpublished manuscript.
———. 1987. "A Semiotic of Andean Dreams." In
Dreaming: Anthropological and Psychological Inter-
pretations, edited by Barbara Tedlock, pp. 132–153.
New York: Cambridge University Press.
———. 1991. *The Language of the Inka since the Euro-*
pean Invasion. Austin: University of Texas Press.
Marcos, Jorge. 1980. "Intercambio a larga distancia en
América: El caso del *Spondylus." Boletín de Antro-*
pología Americana 1: 124–129.
Millones, Luís. 1967. "Introducción al estudio de las
idolatrías." *Aportes* 4: 47–82. Paris: Instituto Latino-
americano de Relaciones Internacionales.
———(ed.) 1971. *Las informaciones de Cristóbal de Al-*
bornoz: Documentos para el estudio del Taki Onqoy.
Cuernavaca: Centro Intercultural de Documentación.
———. 1984. "Shamanismo y política en el Perú colonial:
Los curacas de Ayacucho." *Histórica* 8(2): 131–149.
Molina, Cristóbal de, "cuzqueño." [1575?] 1959. *Relación*
de las fábulas y ritos de los Incas. Edited by Ernesto
Morales. Buenos Aires: Editorial Futuro.
Murra, John V. [1972] 1975a. "El control vertical de un
máximo de pisos ecológicos en la economía de las sociedades andinas." In *Formaciones económicas y polí-*
ticas del mundo andino, pp. 59–116. Lima: Instituto
de Estudios Peruanos.
———. 1975b. "El tráfico de *mullu* en la costa del Pací-
fico." In *Formaciones económicas y políticas del*
mundo andino, pp. 255–267. Lima: Instituto de Estudios Peruanos.
———. 1980. "Waman Puma, etnógrafo del mundo andino." In *Nueva corónica y buen gobierno* by Felipe
Guaman Poma de Ayala [1615] 1980, vol. 1, pp. xiii–
xix. Mexico City: Siglo XXI.
ONERN. 1976. *Mapa ecológico del Perú.* Lima: Oficina
Nacional de Evaluación de Recursos Naturales.
Ortiz Rescaniere, Alejandro. 1977. *Huarochirí, cuatro-*
cientos años después: Informe preliminar. Lima: Departamento de Ciencias Sociales, Pontificia Universidad Católica del Perú.
———. 1980. "El dualismo religioso en el antiguo Perú."
In *Historia del Perú*, vol. 3, pp. 9–72. Lima: Editorial
Juan Mejía Baca.
Ossio, Juan. 1973. "Guaman Poma: Nueva corónica o
carta al rey." In *Ideología mesiánica del mundo an-*
dino, edited by Juan Ossio, pp. 153–213. Lima: Ignacio
Prado Pastor.
Pachacuti Yamqui Salcamaygua, Joan de Santa Cruz.
[1613] 1968. *Relación de antigüedades deste reyno del*
Perú. In *Crónicas peruanas de interés indígena*, edited
by Francisco Esteve Barba, pp. 279–319. Madrid: Edi-
ciones Atlas.
Patterson, Thomas C. 1984[?]. "Pachacamac—an Andean
oracle under Inca rule." In *Recent Studies in Andean*
Prehistory and Protohistory, edited by D. Peter Kvie-
tok and Daniel H. Sandweiss, pp. 159–174. Ithaca,
N.Y.: Cornell University Latin American Studies
Program.

Paulsen, Alison C. 1974. "The Thorny Oyster and the
Voice of God: *Spondylus* and *Strombus* in Andean Prehistory." *American Antiquity* 39: 597–607.
Pease G.Y., Franklin. 1984. "Nota sobre la *Doctrina cris-*
tiana de 1584." *Boletín de la Biblioteca Nacional*
39(91/92): 3–8.
———. 1986. "Notas sobre Wiraqocha y sus itinerarios."
Historica 10(2): 227–235.
Perroud, Pedro Clemente, and Juan María Chouvenc.
1970[?]. *Diccionario castellano kechwa/kechwa-*
castellano. Santa Clara, Perú: Seminario San Alfonso/
Padres Redentoristas.
Platt, Tristan. [1978] 1986. "Mirrors and Maize: The Concept of *Yanantin* among the Macha of Bolivia." In *An-*
thropological History of Andean Polities, edited by
John V. Murra, Jacques Revel, and Nathan Wachtel,
pp. 228–259. New York: Cambridge University Press.
Polo de Ondegardo, Juan. [1554] 1916. "Los errores y supersticiones de los indios sacados del tratado y averi-
guación que hizo el licenciado Polo." In *Informaciones*
acerca de la religión y gobierno de los Incas, edited by
Horacio H. Urteaga and Carlos Romero, pp. 1–43. Colección de Libros y Documentos Referentes a la Historia del Perú, series 1, vol. 3. Lima: Sanmartí.
———. [1571] 1916. "Relación de los fundamentos acerca
del notable daño que resulta de no guardar a los indios
sus fueros . . . " In *Informaciones acerca de la religión*
y gobierno de los Incas, edited by Horacio H. Urteaga
and Carlos Romero, pp. 45–188. Colección de Libros y
Documentos Referentes a la Historia del Perú, series 1,
vol. 3. Lima: Sanmartí.
Renard-Casevitz, Marie-France. 1979. *Su-Açu: Essai sur*
les cervidés de l'Amazonie et sur leur signification
dans les cultures indiennes actuelles. Travaux de l'Institut Français d'Etudes Andines, vol. 20. Paris/Lima:
Centre Nationale de la Recherche Scientifique.
Ricardo, Antonio. [1586] 1951. *Vocabulario y phrasis en*
la lengua general de los indios del Perú, llamada Qui-
chua. Publicaciones del Cuarto Centenario. Lima: Facultad de Letras, Instituto de Historia, Universidad
Nacional Mayor de San Marcos.
Rodríguez Lorente, Juan José. 1965. *Catálogo de los re-*
ales de a dos españoles. Madrid: Altamira Talleres
Gráficos.
Rostworowski de Diez Canseco, María. 1977. *Etnía y so-*
ciedad: Costa peruana prehispánica. Lima: Instituto
de Estudios Peruanos.
———. 1978. *Señoríos indígenas de Lima y Canta.* Lima:
Instituto de Estudios Peruanos.
———. 1981. *Recursos naturales renovables y pesca, sig-*
los XVI y XVII. Lima: Instituto de Estudios Peruanos.
———. 1988. *Conflicts over Coca Fields in XVIth-Cen-*
tury Perú [sic]. Studies in Latin American Ethnohistory and Archaeology, volume 4. Ann Arbor: Museum
of Anthropology, University of Michigan.
Rowe, John H. 1946. "Inca Culture at the Time of the
Spanish Conquest." In *Handbook of South American*
Indians, edited by Julian Steward, vol. 2, *The Andean*
Civilizations, pp. 183–330. Bureau of American Eth-

nology, Report no. 143. Washington, D.C.: Smithsonian Institution.

—. 1960. "The Origins of Creator Worship among the Incas." In *Culture in History: Essays in Honor of Paul Radin*, edited by Stanley Diamond, pp. 408–429. New York: Columbia University Press.

—. 1981. "Una relación de los adoratorios del antiguo Cuzco." *Histórica* 5(2): 209–261.

—. 1985. "La constitución inca del Cuzco." *Histórica* 9(1): 35–73.

Saignes, Thierry. 1983. "¿Quiénes son los Kallawaya? Nota sobre un enigma etnohistórico." *Revista Andina* 1(2): 357–384.

Salomon, Frank. 1983. "Shamanism and Politics in Late Colonial Ecuador." *American Ethnologist* 10(3): 413–428.

Santo Tomás, Domingo de. [1560] 1951. *Lexicon, o vocabulario de la lengua general del Peru*. Publicaciones del Cuarto Centenario. Lima: Facultad de Letras, Instituto de Historia, Universidad Nacional Mayor de San Marcos.

Silverblatt, Irene M. 1987. *Moon, Sun, and Witches: Gender Ideologies and Class in Inca and Colonial Peru*. Princeton, N.J.: Princeton University Press.

Souffez, Marie-France. 1986. "Los piojos en el mundo prehispánico." *Anthropologica* 4: 155–190.

Soukup, Jaroslav. 1970. *Vocabulario de los nombres vulgares de la flora peruana*. Lima: Colegio Salesiano.

Spalding, Karen. 1984. *Huarochirí: An Andean Society under Inca and Spanish Rule*. Stanford, Cal.: Stanford University Press.

Stern, Steve J. 1982. *Peru's Indian Peoples and the Challenge of Spanish Conquest: Huamanga to 1640*. Madison: University of Wisconsin Press.

Szemiński, Jan (ed. and trans.). 1985a. *Bogowie i ludzie z Huarochirí*. Cracow-Warsaw: Wydawnictwo Literackie.

—. 1985b. "De la imagen de Wiraqucan según las oraciones recogidas por Joan de Santa Cruz Pachacuti Yamqui Salcamaygua." *Histórica* 9(2): 247–265.

—. 1989. "Toribio Mejía Xesspe, autor de una traducción inacabada de *Hombres y dioses de Huarochirí*." Unpublished manuscript.

Taylor, Gerald. 1974–1976. "*Camay, camac*, et *camasca* dans le manuscrit quechua de Huarochirí." *Journal de la Société des Américanistes* 63: 231–243.

— (ed. and trans.). 1980. *Rites et traditions de Huarochirí: Manuscrit quechua du début du 17e siècle*. Série Ethnolinguistique Amérindienne. Paris: Editions l'Harmattan.

—. 1982. "Las ediciones del manuscrito quechua de Huarochirí: Respuesta a Roswith Hartmann." *Histórica* 6(2): 255–278.

—. 1983. "Lengua general y lenguas particulares en la antigua provincia de Yauyos (Perú)." *Revista de Indias* 171: 265–289.

—. 1985. "Un documento quechua de Huarochirí—1607." *Revista Andina* 3(1): 157–185.

—. 1986. "Nota sobre 'Un documento quechua de Huarochirí—1607' [*sic*]." *Revista Andina* 4(1): 211–212.

—. 1987a. "Cultos y fiestas de la comunidad de San Damián (Huarochirí) según la Carta Annua de 1609." *Bulletin de l'Institut Français d'Etudes Andines* 16 (3–4): 85–96.

— (ed. and trans.), with Antonio Acosta. 1987b. *Ritos y tradiciones de Huarochirí del siglo XVII*. Historia Andina, no. 12. Lima: Instituto de Estudios Peruanos/ Instituto Francés de Estudios Andinos.

Tedlock, Dennis. [1971] 1983. "On the Translation of Style in Oral Narrative." In *The Spoken Word and the Work of Interpretation*, pp. 31–61. Philadelphia: University of Pennsylvania Press.

— (ed. and trans.). 1985. *Popol Vuh: The Mayan Book of the Dawn of Life*. New York: Simon and Schuster.

Tello, Julio C. 1923. "Wallallo: Ceremonias gentílicas realizadas en la región cisandina del Perú central." *Inca* 1(2): 475–549.

Tercero catecismo y exposición de la doctrina christiana por sermones. [1585] 1985. In *Doctrina christiana y catecismo para instrucción de indios: Facsímil del texto trilingüe*, pp. 333–777. Madrid: Consejo Superior de Investigaciones Científicas.

Torero, Alfredo. 1974. *El quechua y la historia social andina*. Lima: Universidad Ricardo Palma.

Towle, Margaret A. 1961. *The Ethnobotany of Pre-Columbian Peru*. Viking Fund Publications in Anthropology, 30. New York: Wenner Gren Foundation for Anthropological Research.

Treacy, John. 1984. "A Preliminary Chorography of the Waru Chiri Myths." Unpublished paper. Madison, University of Wisconsin, 1984.

Trimborn, Hermann (ed. and trans.). 1939. *Francisco de Avila: Dämonen und Zauber im Inkareich*. Quellen und Forschungen zur Geschichte der Geographie und Völkerkunde, vol. 4. Leipzig: K. F. Koehler Verlag. [Republished with additional introduction and notes as] Hermann Trimborn and Antje Kelm (eds. and trans.). 1967. *Francisco de Avila*. Quellenwerke zur Alten Geschichte Amerikas Aufgezeichnet in den Sprachen der Eingeborenen, vol. 8. Berlin: Ibero-Amerikanisches Institut/Mann Verlag.

Turner, Terence. 1988. "Ethno-ethnohistory: Myth and History in Native South American Representations of Contact with Western Society." In *Rethinking History and Myth: Indigenous South American Perspectives on the Past*, edited by Jonathan D. Hill, pp. 235–281. Urbana: University of Illinois Press.

Urbano, Henrique. 1981. *Wiracocha y Ayar: Héroes y funciones en las sociedades andinas*. Biblioteca de la Tradición Oral Andina, no. 3. Cuzco: Centro de Estudios Rurales "Bartolomé de las Casas."

Urioste, George. 1973. *Chay Simire Caymi: The Language of the Huarochirí Manuscript*. Dissertation Series, no. 79. Ithaca, N.Y.: Cornell University Latin American Studies Program.

—. 1981. "Sickness and Death in Preconquest An-

dean Cosmology: The Huarochirí Oral Tradition."
In *Health in the Andes*, edited by Joseph W. Bastien
and John M. Donahue, pp. 9–18. Special Publication
no. 12. Washington D.C.: American Anthropological
Association.

———. 1982. "The Editing of Oral Tradition in the Huarochirí Manuscript." In *From Oral to Written Expression*, edited by Rolena Adorno, pp. 101–108. Foreign
and Comparative Studies, Latin American Series, no.
4. Syracuse: Maxwell School of Citizenship and Public
Affairs, Syracuse University.

——— (ed. and trans.). 1983. *Hijos de Pariya Qaqa: La
tradición oral de Waru Chiri (mitología, ritual, y costumbres)*. 2 vols. Foreign and Comparative Studies,
Latin American Series, no. 6. Syracuse: Maxwell
School of Citizenship and Public Affairs, Syracuse
University.

Urton, Gary. 1981. *At the Crossroads of the Earth and
the Sky: An Andean Cosmology*. Austin: University
of Texas Press.

Valcárcel, Luis E. 1980. "La religión incáica." In *Historia
del Perú*, vol. 3, pp. 73–202. Lima: Editorial Juan Mejía Baca.

Valderrama, Ricardo, and Carmen Escalante. 1988. *Del
Tata Mallku a la Mama Pacha: Riego, sociedad, y ritos en los Andes peruanos*. Lima: DESCO.

Vansina, Jan. 1985. *Oral Tradition as History*. Madison:
University of Wisconsin Press.

Wachtel, Nathan. 1971. *La vision des vaincus: Les indiens du Pérou devant la conquête espagnole 1530–
1570*. Paris: Gallimard.

Zamalloa González, Zulma. 1972. "Ciclo vital en Sayllapata." *Allpanchis* 4: 21–32.

Zuidema, R. Tom. 1964. *The Ceque System of Cuzco*.
Leiden: Brill.

———. 1973. "Kinship and Ancestorcult in Three Peruvian Communities: Hernández Príncipe's Account of
1622." *Bulletin de l'Institut Français d'Etudes Andines* 2(1): 16–33.

———. 1977. "Mito e historia en el antiguo Perú." *Allpanchis* 10: 15–52.

———. 1980. "El ushnu." *Revista de la Universidad
Complutense* 28: 317–362.

———. 1981. "Inca Observations of the Solar and Lunar
Passages through Zenith and Anti-zenith at Cuzco." In
Archaeoastronomy in the Americas, edited by Roy A.
Williamson, pp. 319–342. Los Altos: Ballena Press.

———. 1985. "The Lion in the City: Royal Symbols of
Transition in Cuzco." In *Animal Myths and Metaphors in South America*, edited by Gary Urton,
pp. 183–250. Salt Lake City: University of Utah Press.

Index